# Online Resources

With our test prep books, we also provide Online Resources to help you in your test prep journey! With this book, you can access -

**Conquer the GRE: Stress Management and a Perfect Study Plan** - This stress management e-book is specially designed for test-takers to manage the stress experienced when preparing for the GRE. It includes:

- Stress Management Techniques
- A 6-Month Study Plan
- An 8-week Study Plan
- Practical Tips to get a good score on the GRE

**To access the e-book, follow the steps below:**

1. Go to **www.vibrantpublishers.com**
2. Click on the '**Online Resources**' option on the Home Page
3. Login by entering your account details (or Create an Account if you don't have one)
4. Go to the Test Prep section and click on the **'6 Practice Tests for the GRE'** link and get your e-book!

**Have fun learning!**

*This page is intentionally left blank*

# What experts say about this book!

Vibrant Publishers provides you with six dress rehearsals that will inform your exam-day opening night; by applying yourself to the challenges found in the book, you will uncover the areas in which you excel, and the areas on which you might need to focus your studying efforts.

**– Elizabeth Weilbacher, Head of Adult Services and Outreach**
**Goffstown Public Library**

I appreciated the rather short, direct, and helpful instructions and tips at the start of the book. It was short enough that students could engage with it.

**– Edward Palmisano**
**Test Prep Tutor**

The tests in this bundle are realistic in both structure and content.

**– Daniel Hughes, President**
**Spider Web Education**

The overview section, in addition to the answers and explanations for each question, will reassure anyone who needs to prepare for the GRE.

**– Jeremy J. Freeman, Young Adult Librarian**
**North Mankato Taylor Library**

This page is intentionally left blank

TEST PREP SERIES

# 6 PRACTICE TESTS FOR THE GRE®

**6** Full-length tests

**480+** Updated Practice Questions in total

**Elaborate** Explanations

**Tips** and Strategies

Fifth Edition

# 6 Practice Tests for the GRE®

## Fifth Edition



Paperback ISBN 10 : 1-63651-090-6
Paperback ISBN 13 : 978-1-63651-090-3

Library of Congress Control Number: 2015901113



Vibrant Publishers books are available at special quantity discount for sales promotions, or for use in corporate training programs. For more information please write to bulkorders@vibrantpublishers.com

Please email feedback/corrections (technical, grammatical or spelling) to spellerrors@vibrantpublishers.com

To access the complete catalogue of Vibrant Publishers, visit www.vibrantpublishers.com

# Table of Contents

*This page is intentionally left blank*

Dear Student,

Thank you for purchasing **6 Practice Tests for the GRE®**. We are committed to publishing books that are content-rich, concise and approachable enabling more students to read and make the fullest use of them. We hope this book provides the most enriching learning experience as you prepare for your **GRE** exam.

Should you have any questions or suggestions, feel free to email us at
**reachus@vibrantpublishers.com**

Thanks again for your purchase. Good luck for your GRE!

– Vibrant Publishers Team

## ////////////// GRE Books in Test Prep Series //////////////

| TITLE | PAPERBACK ISBN |
|---|---|
| **6 Practice Tests for the GRE** | 978-1-63651-090-3 |
| **GRE Analytical Writing Supreme: Solutions to the Real Essay Topics** | 978-1-63651-143-6 |
| **GRE Analytical Writing: Solutions to the Real Essay Topics - Book 1** | 978-1-63651-135-1 |
| **GRE Analytical Writing: Solutions to the Real Essay Topics - Book 2** | 978-1-63651-137-5 |
| **GRE Master Wordlist: 1535 Words for Verbal Mastery** | 978-1-63651-139-9 |
| **GRE Quantitative Reasoning Supreme: Study Guide with Practice Questions** | 978-1-63651-091-0 |
| **GRE Reading Comprehension: Detailed Solutions to 325 Questions** | 978-1-63651-131-3 |
| **GRE Text Completion and Sentence Equivalence Practice Questions** | 978-1-63651-133-7 |
| **GRE Verbal Reasoning Supreme: Study Guide with Practice Questions** | 978-1-63651-141-2 |
| **GRE Words In Context: The Complete List** | 978-1-63651-129-0 |

# Before you start using this book

The six practice tests in this book are meant to give you a simulated practice of the GRE so that you become confident of appearing and cracking the actual test. But before you dive in to give the tests, there are certain things you should know about solving each section.

## Analytical Writing

### Analyze an Issue (30 mins)

Take time to carefully read the question, which asks for specific information, such as how much you agree with a claim about a familiar topic. You are not judged on a "correct" answer, but rather, how well you address the question and compose your argument. Even if you write a good essay, it will not receive high points if you write off-topic. After reading the prompt, jot down notes, both for and against your view; address ones against your view as potential counterarguments. Organize these points in a logical order to refer to as you write. Taking time to do so allows you to think about and develop the ideas before committing them to paper. Finally, write the essay and make sure to use clear transitions and paragraph breaks.

### Analyze an Argument (30 mins)

You are given a passage and question. You need no specialized knowledge on the topic, but instead must be able to determine if the argument is constructed using solid logic. This section has many different prompts, so carefully read the entire question and address what is being asked. Do NOT write about your opinion of the proposal. Instead, jot down what claims are made, and what information is needed to prove that the claims are true. Ask what assumptions are made or what evidence is missing. Only after analyzing the argument point by point should you create an outline and write your essay.

For both Issue and Argument tasks, practice from the official pool of issue and argument topics given by the ETS to get an idea about the types of essays asked. Before you start writing essays, learn how to approach the task from Vibrant's GRE Analytical Writing Supreme: Solutions to the Real Essay Topics. After writing your essay, compare it with the sample essay given in the book.

## Verbal Reasoning (20 questions/30 mins)

### Reading Comprehension

These questions have a passage followed by one or more questions. Most questions are multiple choice in which you select the best answer from five choices. Each question prompt is different and relates to the content of the text, so you must read the prompts to know what facts are needed. Start by eliminating the answers you know are wrong, then read through the text again to isolate which of the few remaining is the correct answer. Many choices are partially true and appear correct at first reading, so you must be careful when reading each answer.

A few of the questions are multiple choice with three answers. You are asked to select any of the three that are true. Note that one, two, or three may answer the prompt, and you must select all of the correct ones.

You may also find a question that asks you to select one sentence from the text. Read through the text for the best sentence that answers the specific points in the prompt and highlight that one sentence. As with multiple choice questions, eliminate the answers which are obviously wrong and compare the few remaining choices against the prompt to make your final selection.

One question has a hypothetical text and question based on the logical structure of the text rather than its content. The prompt asks what phrase completes the idea, what assumptions the author makes, or what are the weaknesses in the argument. These questions often require time-consuming reasoning, so consider marking them and returning later to ensure sufficient time to complete the section.

## Text Completion

There are also short items with one or more blanks and a following list of words. You are asked to fill in the best word or words to complete the sentence. Read the sentence before choosing the correct word because often the information to solve the problem is subtle, such as a transition word that changes the meaning.

If there is one blank, you will be given five answer choices and you must select one answer. Eliminate the ones that are definitely wrong, then read through the sentence with the possible correct ones to make your decision.

If there are two or three blanks, you will be given two or three columns that have three choices each. You must select one choice from each column. These types of questions can be tricky because several answer choices might be correct for any given blank, but only a combination of all two or three will make a logical sentence. After you make a tentative selection, be sure to read the entire sentence with all the blanks replaced to confirm that the meaning is still sensible.

## Sentence Equivalence

These questions have sentences with blanks, followed by seven answer choices. You must select TWO answer choices that complete the sentence with the same meaning. Usually there is at least one choice that fits the context well, but which is eliminated because it has no synonym among the answer choices. Often there is a pair of close synonyms that do not fit logically; for example, they might give the sentence the opposite meaning. Read the remaining options in the sentence and compare them to each other to find which ones result in the idea that is most identical.

This section, though all about filling blanks, requires practice as you need a decent grasp on your vocabulary. Read books, newspapers, or other materials as much as possible to learn new words. You may also refer to GRE Verbal Reasoning Supreme: Study Guide With Practice Questions for practicing all types of questions asked in the Verbal Reasoning section.

## Quantitative Reasoning (20 questions/ 35 mins)

### Multiple-choice questions – One answer choice

You are given a question related to basic mathematical calculations such as algebra, and five answers. Solve the problem and look for the answer. If your answer is not there, then redo the calculation, as one of the choices must be true.

### Multiple-choice questions – One or more answer choices

You are asked to select all of the correct answers, and sometimes the actual number of correct ones is not specified. Therefore, you must evaluate each answer choice for correctness. To avoid wasting time doing lengthy calculations for each choice, look for patterns (such as the answer must be an odd number) or isolate the highest or lowest possible number that the correct answers could be.

### Numeric Entry

You are given a mathematical question to solve but no answer choices to select from. You must do the calculations to arrive at the answer and write in the value that you decide is correct. Remember that the answers are all real numbers, but that the graphs and figures may not be drawn to scale. Use the information in the problem rather than relying on the visual data for an answer.

### Quantitative Comparison

You are given two equations and asked if one is greater than the other, if the values are equal, or if there is not enough information to decide. The answer choices for these questions are always the same, so memorize the options to save time. The equations are often complicated at first glance, but can be easily simplified. For algebraic equations, substitute a number to solve and compare the relationship between both quantities.

### Data Interpretation

You are given a set of data, such as a short passage and graph. Look over the information, but do not take time to memorize all the details. Then read the question to find what information is needed in the answer. All of the information is provided in the question. Be sure to look at the scale carefully; the measurements may be different than in the question. Note that the answer to data interpretation questions comes in two forms. One is multiple choice, where you must select the best of five answers. The other is numeric entry, where you must do the calculations and write in the answer that you generate.

A diligent and thorough practice of Quant questions will make you confident on cracking this section. Make use of the calculator wherever required but do not use it for simple calculations. A useful and recommended practice book for this section is the GRE Quantitative Reasoning Supreme: Study Guide With Practice Questions. The book has 520 questions of different types so that you can get a complete practice.

*This page is intentionally left blank*

# How to use this book

Before diving in to give the first test, read the Overview of GRE to know the registration process, the types of questions asked, the time limit for each section, the scoring procedure, etc. Even if you have taken the test before, there have been changes to the registration process and locations where the test is offered due to the Covid-19 pandemic, so reading through the information will keep you up-to-date about the test.

After reading through the information, consider taking one of the complete practice tests first. In the first test, give yourself as much time as you need rather than trying to finish within the allotted GRE time frame. However, write down how long each section takes to solve, so you can determine how to budget your time. Then compare your answers with the correct answers given in the 'Answer Key' section of each test. Understand what went wrong by referring to the detailed solutions given in the 'Explanations' section. Look over the categories of questions that you consistently had difficulties with or consistently made errors on. This will help you determine your strengths and weaknesses and which areas you need to focus on.

Identify and practice the question types that you found difficult. Familiarize yourself with their pattern. Refer to the 'Before You Start Using This Book' section for tips on how to solve each section and which resources to use for getting a thorough and focused practice.

After completing your practice, try another complete practice test. This time, have your timer at hand and take breaks only at the intervals given in the real test. This more realistic testing experience will also show you how well you can concentrate for extended periods. After you complete the second practice test, check your answers and compare them with the answers given in the 'Answer Key' section after each test and look for patterns in the questions you missed. Are they the same style as before, or do you have different weaknesses? Try reviewing these weaknesses before taking the next complete practice test.

Create a study schedule with the help of two study plans given in the Conquer the GRE: Stress Management and a Perfect Study Plan ebook that comes along with this book or devise your own plan according to your schedule. Attempt to take a practice test every week for 6 weeks. This will help you become well-versed with the format of the GRE and also increase your confidence.

Continue alternating review of specific question types with complete practice tests throughout your preparation period. Do not worry if you miss a day on your study plan; just revise your schedule as needed so you can complete every practice test in this book. The practice tests isolate areas that need improvement and the specific practice raises those areas to the next level. When the day arrives for your actual GRE test, you will be comfortable with the length of the test and ready to solve any style of question that might be on it, whether it is related to language or mathematics. You can be confident of getting your best possible score!

Good luck on your GRE journey!

*This page is intentionally left blank*

## Chapter 1

# Overview of the GRE General Test

The Graduate Record Examinations (GRE) General Test, while previously required for admission to most graduate programs, is now a part of a larger picture. A strong GRE score can provide evidence of strong scholarship on an application. This book is designed to prepare students for the GRE General Test. The GRE revised General Test was renamed in 2016 and is now known as the GRE General Test, but the content and scoring of the test remain the same. Note that some graduate programs require applicants to take specialized GRE Subject Tests which will not be covered in this book. Before preparing to take the GRE, please review the admissions criteria for the programs that you are interested in applying to so that you know whether you need to take subject tests in addition to the GRE General Test. To learn more about subject tests, visit the Subject Tests section at ets.org.

The GRE General Test is not designed to measure your knowledge of specific fields. It does not measure your ability to be successful in your career or even in school. It does, however, give a reasonably accurate indication of your capabilities in certain key areas for graduate-level work, such as your ability to understand complex written material, your understanding of basic mathematics, your ability to interpret data, and your capacity for reasoning and critical thinking. By using this book to prepare for the GRE General Test, you will not only improve your chances of scoring well on the test, you will also help to prepare yourself for graduate-level study.

## Format of the GRE General Test

The GRE General Test is offered as a computer-delivered test throughout the year. Post-Covid, ETS provides test-takers with the option to take the test from home.

Whether you are taking the GRE General Test at the testing center or at home, the format of the test will essentially be the same. The GRE General Test At Home follows the same format as the computer-delivered version of the GRE General Test. The test consists of three main components: Analytical Writing, Verbal Reasoning, and Quantitative Reasoning. The total time for the test will be about 3 hours 45 minutes.

The first section of the test is always the Analytical Writing component which is broken into two sections. In the first section, you will be asked to write an argumentative essay that takes a position on an issue of general interest. In the second section, you will be asked to analyze an argument for logical validity and soundness. You will be given 30 minutes for each section.

The remainder of the test will be split between sections devoted to Verbal Reasoning and Quantitative Reasoning. There will be two sections devoted to Verbal Reasoning, and another two devoted to Quantitative Reasoning. You will be given 30 minutes to complete each section of Verbal Reasoning and 35 minutes to complete each section of Quantitative Reasoning. Each section will contain 20 questions. At any point during the test, you may be given an unscored section on either Verbal or Quantitative Reasoning; since this section will not be identified, it is important that you try your best at all times. Also, it is possible that you will be asked to complete a research section that will allow ETS to test the efficacy of new questions. If you are given a research section, it will appear at the end of your General Test. Unscored and research sections may vary in the number of questions and time allotted.

## Outline of the GRE General Test

The Verbal Reasoning and Quantitative Reasoning sections of the GRE General Test are section-level adaptive. This means that the computer will adapt the test to your performance. Since there are two sections each for Verbal Reasoning and Quantitative Reasoning, the difficulty of the second section will depend on how well you did in the first section. The overall format of the GRE General Test will be as follows:

| Component | Number of Questions | Time Allowed |
|---|---|---|
| Analytical Writing (2 sections) | 1 Analyze an Issue<br>1 Analyze an Argument | 30 minutes<br>30 minutes |
| Verbal Reasoning (2 sections) | 20 questions per section | 30 minutes per section |
| Quantitative Reasoning (2 sections) | 20 questions per section | 35 minutes per section |
| Unscored Section | Variable | Variable |
| Research Section | Variable | Variable |
| | | **Total Time: 3 hours 45 minutes** |

Note that the GRE General Test At Home follows the same format as the computer-delivered version of the GRE General Test.

While taking the GRE General Test, here are some things to remember:

a) You can review and preview questions within a section, allowing you to budget your time to deal with the questions that you find most difficult.

b) You will be able to mark questions within a section and return to them later. This means that if you find a question especially difficult, you will be able to move on to other questions and return to the one that you had trouble with, provided that you stay within the time limit for the section.

c) You will be able to change or edit your answers within a section. This means that if you realize that you made a mistake, you can go back and correct yourself provided you stay within the time limit for the section.

d) You will have an on-screen calculator during the Quantitative Reasoning portions of the test, allowing you to quickly complete any necessary computations.

The following section will briefly introduce the three main components of the GRE General Test.

## Analytical Writing Assessment

The first section of the GRE General Test is the Analytical Writing Assessment. This component of the GRE is designed to test your ability to use basic logic and critical reasoning to make and assess arguments. The Analytical Writing Assessment is broken into two assignments, each of which must be completed within 30 minutes. In the first assignment, you will be asked to develop a position on an issue of general interest. You will be given an issue and a prompt with some specific instructions on how to approach the assigned issue. You will be expected to take a position on the issue and then write a clear, persuasive, and logically sound essay defending your position in correct English. You will be assessed based on your ability to effectively defend your positions with supporting evidence and valid reasoning, your skill in organizing your thoughts, and your command of English. In the second assignment, you will be presented with a passage in which the author sketches an argument for their position on an issue. Here, you will be expected to write an essay that critically evaluates their argument in terms of the evidence they use and the logical validity of their reasoning. You will be assessed based on your ability to parse the author's argument and effectively point out the strengths and weaknesses of their reasoning using good organization and correct English.

| Task | Time Allowed | Answer Format |
|---|---|---|
| Analyze an Issue | 30 minutes | Short essay on an issue of general interest that clearly and carefully addresses the prompt |
| Analyze an Argument | 30 minutes | Short essay that analyzes another person's argument for validity, soundness, and supporting evidence |

The Analytical Writing assessment tests your ability to:

- Coherently develop complex ideas
- Write in a focused, organized manner
- Identify relevant evidence and use it to support your claims
- Critically evaluate another person's argument for clarity and effectiveness
- Command the elements of standard written English

## Verbal Reasoning

The Verbal Reasoning portion of the GRE assesses your reading comprehension, your ability to draw inferences to fill in missing information, and your vocabulary. You will be given two sections on Verbal Reasoning, each consisting of 20 questions and lasting 30 minutes. Verbal Reasoning questions on the GRE General Test are mostly multiple-choice and will be drawn from the following three types: Reading Comprehension, Text Completion, and Sentence Equivalence. Reading Comprehension questions will ask you to read a short passage several paragraphs long, and then answer questions about the passage. Text Completion questions will have a short passage with 1-3 blanks which you will need to fill in by choosing the best of several multiple-choice options. The Sentence Equivalence section will ask you to fill in the blank in a passage using the two words that will complete the sentence in such a way that the meaning will be as similar as possible.

| Time | Question Type | Answer Format |
|---|---|---|
| You will have 30 minutes to complete the entire section, which will include a mixture of different question types | Reading Comprehension | Multiple choice: select one answer choice<br>Multiple choice: select one or more answer choices<br>Highlight a section of text |
| | Text Completion | Multiple choice: fill in one or more blanks to complete the text |
| | Sentence Equivalence | Multiple choice: select the two options that produce two sentences with the most similar meanings |

The Verbal Reasoning section tests your ability to:

- Comprehend, interpret and analyze complex passages in standard written English
- Apply sophisticated vocabulary in context
- Draw inferences about the meaning and authorial intent based on written material

## Quantitative Reasoning

The Quantitative Reasoning section of the GRE evaluates your ability to use basic mathematics, read and interpret graphs and figures and engage in basic reasoning involving math and numbers. You will be given two sections on Quantitative Reasoning with 20 questions in each section. You will have 35 minutes to complete each section. There are two basic question types, multiple-choice and numerical entry. For multiple-choice questions, you will be asked to choose the best answer or answers from several possibilities; for numerical entry questions, you will be asked to enter a numerical answer from your own calculations. Some questions will be designed to test your knowledge of basic algebra and geometry; others will be designed to test your ability to read and interpret different presentations of data.

| Time | Question Type | Answer Format |
|---|---|---|
| You will have 35 minutes to complete the entire section, which will include a mixture of different question types | Multiple Choice | Select one answer choice<br>Select one or more answer choices |
| | Numeric Entry | Solve the problem through calculation and enter a numeric value |
| | Quantitative Comparison | Evaluate two quantities to decide whether one is greater than the other, whether they are equal, or whether a relationship cannot be determined |
| | Data Interpretation | Multiple choice: choose the best answer or answers<br>Numeric entry: enter a value |

The Quantitative Reasoning section tests your ability to:

- Use mathematical tools such as basic arithmetic, geometry, algebra and statistics
- Understand, interpret and analyze quantitative information
- Apply basic mathematical and data interpretation skills to real-world information and problems

### On-screen Calculator

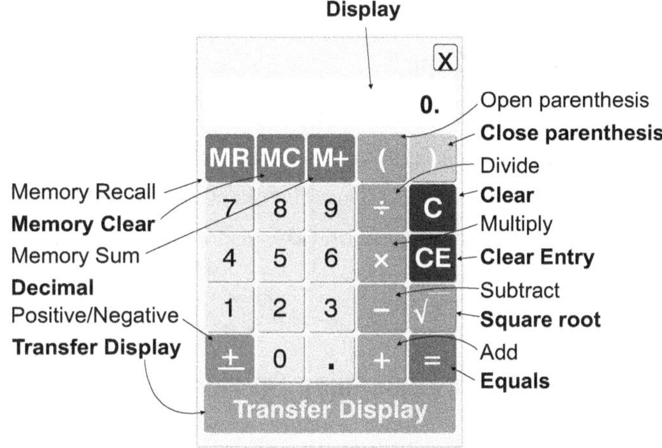


The on-screen calculator in the GRE is a handy tool for you to make computations faster. However, you should only use the calculator for complex equations that will take a longer time to do manually such as square roots, addition, subtraction, and multiplication of numbers with several digits.

Guidelines for using the on-screen calculator

- The on-screen calculator follows the order of operations (PEMDAS). This means that it computes equations in the following order - parentheses, exponentiation (including square roots), multiplication and division (left to right), addition and subtraction (left to right). So, for an equation like 2 + 3 * 6, the on-screen calculator will give the answer 20 but some calculators will give the answer 30 as they first add 2 and 3 and get 5 which is multiplied by 6 to get the final answer 30.
- The Transfer Display button will be useful for Numeric Entry questions. The button will transfer the number on your calculator display to the numeric entry answer box. But remember to check the transferred answer as sometimes you may be required to round up your answer; adjust it accordingly.
- The Memory Recall (MR), Memory Clear (MC), and Memory Sum (M+) buttons work as per normal calculators.

## Registering for the GRE

Before you register to take the GRE, be sure to consider your schedule and any special accommodations that you may need. Be aware that the availability of testing dates may vary according to your location. Be sure to give yourself plenty of time to prepare for the GRE and be sure that you know the deadlines for score reporting and application deadlines for all the schools you are applying to. For general information about deadlines and the GRE, visit the GRE section at ets.org. For more information on how to register for the GRE, visit the Register for the GRE section at ets.org. For information on special accommodations for disabled students, visit the Disabilities or Health-related Needs section on ets.org.

If you are taking the GRE General Test At Home, there are certain equipment, environment, and testing space requirements that you need to fulfill before you can start the registration process. For more information on these requirements, read the At Home Testing section on ets.org.

## How the GRE General Test is Scored

### Scoring for the Analytical Writing Section

In the Analytical Writing section, you will be scored on a scale of 0-6 in increments of 0.5. The Analytical Writing measure emphasizes your ability to engage in reasoning and critical thinking over your facility with the finer points of grammar. The highest scores of 5.5-6.0 are given to work that is generally superior in every respect - sustained analysis of complex issues, coherent argumentation, and excellent command of the English language. The lowest scores of 0.0-0.5 are given to work that is completely off-topic or so poorly composed as to be incoherent.

### Scoring for the Verbal and Quantitative Reasoning Sections

The Verbal and Quantitative Reasoning sections are now scored on a scale of 130-170 in 1-point increments.

## General Strategies for Taking the GRE

There are strategies you can apply that will greatly increase your odds of performing well on the GRE. The following is a list of strategies that will help to improve your chances of performing well on the GRE:

- Review basic concepts in math, logic, and writing.
- Work through the test-taking strategies offered in this book.
- Work through mock GRE tests until you feel thoroughly comfortable with the types of questions you will see.
- As you are studying for the GRE, focus your energy on the types of questions that give you the most difficulty.
- Learn to guess wisely. For many of the questions in the Verbal and Quantitative Reasoning Sections, the correct answer is in front of you - you only need to correctly identify it. Especially for questions that you find difficult, you should hone your ability to dismiss the options that are clearly wrong and make an educated guess about which one is right.
- Answer every question. You won't lose any points for choosing the wrong answer, so even a wild guess that might or might not be right is better than no answer at all.

## Preparing for Test Day and Taking the GRE

How you prepare for the test is completely up to you and will depend on your own test-taking preferences and the amount of time you can devote to studying for the test. At the very least, before you take the test, you should know the basics of what is covered on the test along with the general guidelines for taking the GRE. This book is designed to provide you with the basic information you need and give you the opportunity to prepare thoroughly for the GRE General Test.

Although there is no set way to prepare for the GRE, as a general rule you will want to:

- Learn the basics about the test - what is being tested, the format, and how the test is administered.
- Familiarize yourself with the specific types of questions that you will see on the GRE General Test.
- Review skills such as basic math, reading comprehension, and writing.
- Learn about test-taking strategies.
- Take a mock GRE test to practice applying your test-taking skills to an actual test.

Remember, you don't need to spend an equal amount of time on each of these areas to do well on the GRE - allot your study time to your own needs and preferences. Following are some suggestions to help you make the final preparations for your test, and help you through the test itself.

## Preparing for Test Day

- In the time leading up to your test, practice, then practice some more. Practice until you are confident with the material.
- Know when your test is, and when you need to be at the testing center or in front of your computer at home.
- Make a "practice run" to your testing center, so that you can anticipate how much time you will need to allow to get there. For the At Home test, make sure to sign in at least 15 minutes before the test.
- Understand the timing and guidelines for the test and plan accordingly. Remember that you are not allowed to eat or drink while taking the GRE, although you will be allowed to snack or drink during some of the short breaks during testing. Plan accordingly.
- Know exactly what documentation you will need to bring with you to the testing center. If you are testing at home, you will have to provide a valid government-issued identification document as well.
- Relax, especially on the day or night before your test. If you have studied and practiced wisely, you will be well prepared for the test. You may want to briefly glance over some test preparation materials but cramming the night before will not be productive.
- Eat well and get a good night's sleep. You will want to be well-rested for the test.

## The Test Day

- Wake up early to give yourself plenty of time to eat a healthy breakfast, gather the necessary documentation, pack a snack and a water bottle, and make it to the testing center well before your test is scheduled to start.
- Have confidence: You've prepared well for the test, and there won't be any big surprises. You may not know the answers to some questions, but the format will be exactly like what you've been practicing.
- While you are taking the test, don't panic. The test is timed, and students often worry that they will run out of time and miss too many questions. The sections of the test are designed so that many students will not finish them, so don't worry if you don't think you can finish a section on time. Just try to answer as many questions as you can, as accurately as possible.

- If there's a question you're not sure of, don't panic—the GRE test allows you to skip and return to questions when you are ready, so take advantage of that. Remember, the value of each easy question is the same as the hard questions!

- Remember the strategies and techniques that you learn from this book and apply them wherever possible.

## Frequently Asked Questions

### General Questions

***What changes have been made to the GRE General Test post Covid-19?***

Due to Covid-19 restrictions, test-takers are now able to take the GRE General Test at home. Content and scoring have remained the same. Study materials that reference the GRE General Test are still valid and may be used for test preparation.

***Can I take the GRE test at home?***

Yes. ETS now provides students with the option to take the test from home. If your local test centers are closed or you prefer a familiar testing environment, you can take the GRE from home. You will have to check the equipment, environment, and testing-space requirements for the at-home test and whether it's an option for you. For detailed information on the requirements for the home test, check the At Home Testing section at ets.org.

***Are there any changes in the format and content of the GRE test due to COVID-19?***

No. The format and content of the GRE General Test remains the same.

***How do I get ready to take the GRE General Test?***

To take the GRE General Test, there are several steps you'll need to take:

- Find out what prospective graduate/professional programs require: Does the program you're interested in require additional testing beyond the GRE General Test? What is the deadline for receipt of scores?

- Sign up for a test date. You need to sign up for any GRE testing. Act in a timely manner so that you have plenty of time to prepare and are guaranteed that your scores will be sent and received on time. For the in-center test, testing dates are much more restricted, so if you know that you will need to take the GRE General Test at the center, make arrangements well in advance of the application deadline for your program. There are additional requirements if you're taking the test at home, so make sure to check the requirements well in advance.

- Use resources provided by ETS and Vibrant Publishers to familiarize yourself with the format of the GRE and the types of questions you will face. Even if you are confident about taking the test, it is essential to prepare for the test.

***Does the GRE General Test measure my proficiency in specific subject areas?***

No. The GRE General Test is designed to measure general proficiency in reading, critical reasoning, and working with data, all abilities that are critical to graduate work. However, you won't be tested on your knowledge of any specific field.

***Where can I get additional information on the GRE General Test?***

Educational Testing Service (ETS), the organization that administers the GRE, has an informative website entirely devoted to information about the test at the GRE section at ets.org. There, you can find links that further explain how to sign up for testing, fees, score reporting and much more.

## Preparing for the Test

***How should I start to prepare for the test?***

The first thing you should do is thoroughly familiarize yourself with the format of the GRE General Test. Read about each section of the test, how many questions are there per section, and the required format for answers. You can find general information about the structure of the test earlier in this chapter.

***How do I prepare for the questions I will be asked on the GRE General Test?***

There are plenty of resources by Vibrant Publishers, including this book to help you prepare for the questions you will face on the GRE General Test. A list of books is provided at the beginning of this book. For the most updated list, you may visit the Test Prep Series section on www.vibrantpublishers.com.

***How much should I study/practice for the GRE?***

Study and practice until you feel comfortable with the test. Practice, practice and practice some more until you feel confident about test day!!

***Are there additional materials I can use to get even more practice?***

Yes. ETS offers a free full-length practice test that can be downloaded from the GRE section at ets.org. Also, after you have signed up for testing through ETS, you are eligible for some further test preparation materials free of additional charge.

## Test Content

***How long is the GRE General Test?***

The overall testing time is about 3 hours and 45 minutes.

***What skills does the GRE test?***

In general, the GRE is designed to test your proficiency in certain key skills that you will need for graduate-level study. More specifically:

- **The Analytical Writing section** tests your ability to write about complex ideas in a coherent, focused fashion as well as your ability to command the conventions of standard written English, provide and evaluate relevant evidence, and critique other points of view.

- **The Verbal Reasoning section** is an assessment of your ability to understand, interpret and analyze complex passages, use reasoning to draw inferences about written material, and use sophisticated vocabulary in context.

- **The Quantitative Reasoning section** is an assessment of basic, high school-level mathematical skills and knowledge, as well as your ability to analyze and interpret data

***What level of math is required for the Quantitative Reasoning section?***

You will be expected to know high school level math - arithmetic, and basic concepts in algebra and geometry. You will also be expected to be able to analyze and interpret data presented in tables and graphs.

## Scoring and Score Reporting

***How are the sections of the GRE General Test scored?***

The GRE General Test is scored as follows:

- **The scores of the Verbal Reasoning section** are done in 1-point increments on a scale of 130-170.
- **The scores of the Quantitative Reasoning section** are done in 1-point increments on a scale of 130-170.
- **The scores of the Analytical Writing section** are done in increments of 0.5 on a scale of 0-6.

***Read the GRE scores chapter for a detailed overview of how the GRE is scored.***

***When will my score be reported?***

It depends on which version of the test you are taking, and also when you decide to take the GRE General Test. In general, scores for the computer-based version of the test are reported within two weeks; for the paper-based test, they are reported within six weeks. Check the GRE section at ets.org for updates on score reporting and deadlines.

***When will my score be reported?***

It depends on when you decide to take the GRE General Test. In general, scores for the test are reported in 10-15 days. You can find your scores in your official ETS account. An email notification from ETS is sent when the test scores are made available. ETS will also send an official Institution Score Report to the institutions you've chosen to send the test scores to.

Check the GRE section at ets.org for updates on score reporting and deadlines.

***How long will my scores be valid?***

Your score for the GRE General Test will remain valid for five years.

## Other Questions

***Do business schools accept the GRE instead of the GMAT?***

An increasing number of business schools accept the GRE as a substitute for the more standard test for admission to an MBA program, the GMAT. Before you decide to take the GRE instead of the GMAT, make sure that the programs you are interested in applying to will accept the GRE. You can find a list of business schools that currently accept the GRE in the GRE section at ets.org.

***How is the GRE administered?***

The GRE is administered continuously year-round at designated testing centers, where you can take the test free from distraction in a secure environment that discourages cheating. The GRE Test At Home is also available for those who are more comfortable in a familiar environment. For information on testing centers in your area and important dates, visit the GRE section at ets.org.

***I have a disability that requires me to ask for special accommodation while taking the test - what sort of accommodation is offered?***

ETS does accommodate test-takers with disabilities. For information on procedures, visit the GRE Disabilities and Health-related Needs section at ets.org.

***Will there be breaks during testing?***

Yes. You will be given an optional 10-minute break after the third section of the test and one-minute breaks between the remaining sections.

***Will I be given scratch paper?***

Yes. The test administrator will provide you with scratch paper to use during the test, which has to be returned to the testing center staff without any pages missing.

For the At Home test, you cannot use regular notepaper. You may use either of the following materials:

- One small desktop whiteboard with an erasable marker.
- A sheet of paper placed inside a transparent sheet protector. You can write on this with an erasable marker.

At the end of the test, you will need to show the proctor that all notes you took during the test have been erased.

***Should I bring a calculator to the test?***

No. There will be an on-screen calculator for you to use.

This page is intentionally left blank

Chapter **2**

# Scoring for the GRE

The grading scale for the GRE can be rather confusing, so hopefully, this chapter will help you demystify the calculations involved in tallying your final score. First, let's take a look at how the scores are reported for individual sections.

## The GRE is scored as follows:

- **Analytical Writing:** 0-6, in half-point increments
- **Verbal Reasoning:** 130-170, in 1-point increments
- **Quantitative Reasoning:** 130-170, in 1-point increments

Please note that if you leave an entire section blank, you'll receive the 'NS' (no score) for that particular section.

## Scoring Guide for Analytical Writing section

### Score 6

In addressing the specific task directions, a 6 response presents a cogent, well-articulated analysis of the issue and conveys meaning skillfully.

A typical response in this category:

- articulates a clear and insightful position on the issue in accordance with the assigned task
- develops the position fully with compelling reasons and/or persuasive examples
- sustains a well-focused, well-organized analysis, connecting ideas logically
- conveys ideas fluently and precisely, using effective vocabulary and sentence variety
- demonstrates facility with the conventions of standard written English (i.e., grammar, usage, and mechanics), but may have minor errors

## Score 5

In addressing the specific task directions, a 5 response presents a generally thoughtful, well-developed analysis of the issue and conveys meaning clearly.

A typical response in this category:

- presents a clear and well-considered position on the issue in accordance with the assigned task
- develops the position with logically sound reasons and/or well-chosen examples
- is focused and generally well-organized, connecting ideas appropriately
- conveys ideas clearly and well, using appropriate vocabulary and sentence variety
- demonstrates facility with the conventions of standard written English but may have minor errors

## Score 4

In addressing the specific task directions, a 4 response presents a competent analysis of the issue and conveys meaning with acceptable clarity.

A typical response in this category:

- presents a clear position on the issue in accordance with the assigned task
- develops the position with relevant reasons and/or examples
- is adequately focused and organized
- demonstrates sufficient control of language to express ideas with reasonable clarity
- demonstrates control of the conventions of standard written English but may have some errors

## Score 3

A 3 response demonstrates some competence in addressing the specific task directions, in analyzing the issue, and in conveying meaning, but is obviously flawed.

A typical response in this category exhibits ONE OR MORE of the following characteristics:

- is vague or limited in addressing the specific task directions and/or in presenting or developing a position on the issue
- is weak in the use of relevant reasons or examples or relies largely on unsupported claims
- is poorly focused and/or poorly organized
- has problems in language and sentence structure that result in a lack of clarity
- contains occasional major errors or frequent minor errors in grammar, usage, or mechanics, that can interfere with meaning

### Score 2

A 2 response largely disregards the specific task directions and/or demonstrates serious weaknesses in analytical writing.

A typical response in this category exhibits ONE OR MORE of the following characteristics:

- is unclear or seriously limited in addressing the specific task directions and/or in presenting or developing a position on the issue
- provides few, if any, relevant reasons or examples in support of its claims
- is unfocused and/or disorganized
- has serious problems in language and sentence structure that frequently interfere with meaning
- contains serious errors in grammar, usage, or mechanics, that frequently obscure meaning

### Score 1

A 1 response demonstrates fundamental deficiencies in analytical writing.

A typical response in this category exhibits ONE OR MORE of the following characteristics:

- provides little or no evidence of understanding the issue
- provides little evidence of the ability to develop an organized response (i.e., is extremely disorganized and/or extremely brief)
- has severe problems in language and sentence structure that persistently interfere with meaning
- contains pervasive errors in grammar, usage, or mechanics, that result in incoherence

### Score 0

A typical response in this category is off-topic (i.e., provides no evidence of an attempt to respond to the assigned topic), is in a foreign language, merely copies the topic, consists of only keystroke characters, or is illegible or non-verbal.

## Scoring Guide for Verbal Reasoning and Quantitative Reasoning sections

The Verbal and Quantitative Reasoning sections are 'section-level adaptive.' This means that as the Verbal and Quantitative Reasoning sections are divided into two sections, the difficulty of the second section depends on your performance in the first one.

The number of questions that you get right in these sections is your raw score. This raw score is then scaled between 130-170 but the exact scaling process is not revealed by ETS.

According to your score in each section of the GRE, you'll also be assigned a percentile ranking. The following table illustrates the % associated with each score for two sections of the GRE:

## Verbal Reasoning Concordance Table

| GRE Score | Rank in % |
|---|---|
| 170 | 99 |
| 169 | 99 |
| 168 | 98 |
| 167 | 98 |
| 166 | 97 |
| 165 | 96 |
| 164 | 94 |
| 163 | 92 |
| 162 | 90 |
| 161 | 88 |
| 160 | 85 |
| 159 | 82 |
| 158 | 79 |
| 157 | 75 |
| 156 | 72 |
| 155 | 67 |
| 154 | 63 |
| 153 | 59 |
| 152 | 53 |
| 151 | 49 |
| 150 | 44 |

| GRE Score | Rank in % |
|---|---|
| 149 | 39 |
| 148 | 35 |
| 147 | 31 |
| 146 | 28 |
| 145 | 25 |
| 144 | 22 |
| 143 | 19 |
| 142 | 16 |
| 141 | 14 |
| 140 | 12 |
| 139 | 10 |
| 138 | 8 |
| 137 | 7 |
| 136 | 5 |
| 135 | 4 |
| 134 | 3 |
| 133 | 2 |
| 132 | 2 |
| 131 | 1 |
| 130 | |

### Quantitative Reasoning Concordance Table

| GRE Score | Rank in % |
|---|---|
| 170 | 96 |
| 169 | 94 |
| 168 | 91 |
| 167 | 89 |
| 166 | 86 |
| 164 | 81 |
| 163 | 79 |
| 161 | 74 |
| 160 | 70 |
| 159 | 67 |
| 158 | 64 |
| 157 | 61 |
| 156 | 57 |
| 155 | 54 |
| 154 | 50 |
| 153 | 46 |
| 152 | 43 |
| 151 | 39 |
| 150 | 35 |
| 149 | 32 |

| GRE Score | Rank in % |
|---|---|
| 148 | 28 |
| 147 | 25 |
| 146 | 21 |
| 145 | 18 |
| 144 | 15 |
| 143 | 13 |
| 142 | 11 |
| 141 | 9 |
| 140 | 7 |
| 139 | 6 |
| 138 | 4 |
| 137 | 3 |
| 136 | 2 |
| 135 | 2 |
| 134 | 1 |
| 133 | 1 |
| 132 | 1 |
| 131 | |
| 130 | |

You'll also need to make sure that you check with your university what the required GRE scores are for the program of study you are considering applying for. These can vary greatly from one university to another and even from one program of study to another. You'll also want to ask around to figure out what the preferred GRE score for your program of study is. Of course, you'll need to score what is required, but you are much better off getting a higher score if the department you are applying to is known to prefer a higher range than what is normally required.

This page is intentionally left blank

# Chapter 3

# Practice Test 1

You are about to begin a full length Practice Test. The Test has five sections. The time allotted for each section is marked at the beginning of the section. Work on one section at a time. Use a timer to keep track of the time limits for every section.

Try to take the Practice Test under real test conditions. Find a quiet place to work, and set aside enough time to complete the test without being disturbed. At the end of the test, check your answers by referring to the Answer Key and fill in your raw score in the score card below. Also, note down the time taken by you for completing each section.

Pay particular attention to the questions that were answered incorrectly. Read the answer explanations and understand how to solve them.

## My Score Card (Raw Score)

| | Section 2 | Section 3 | Section 4 | Section 5 |
|---|---|---|---|---|
| **Out of** | 20 | 20 | 20 | 20 |
| **My Score** | ________ | ________ | ________ | ________ |
| **Time Taken** | ________ | ________ | ________ | ________ |

# Section 1 – Analytical Writing

Task 1 – Analyze an Issue | 30 mins

*In order to become well-rounded individuals, all college students should be required to take courses in which they read poetry, novels, mythology, and other types of imaginative literature.*

*Write a response in which you discuss the extent to which you agree or disagree with the recommendation and explain your reasoning for the position you take. In developing and supporting your position, describe specific circumstances in which adopting the recommendation would or would not be advantageous and explain how these examples shape your position.*

You may start writing your response here

## Task 2 – Analyze an Argument Task | 30 mins

*The following appeared in a letter from the owner of the Sunnyside Towers apartment complex to its manager.*

*"One month ago, all the showerheads in the first three buildings of the Sunnyside Towers complex were modified to restrict maximum water flow to one-third of what it used to be. Although actual readings of water usage before and after the adjustment are not yet available, the change will obviously result in a considerable savings for Sunnyside Corporation, since the corporation must pay for water each month. Except for a few complaints about low water pressure, no problems with showers have been reported since the adjustment. Clearly, modifying showerheads to restrict water flow throughout all twelve buildings in the Sunnyside Towers complex will increase our profits further."*

*Write a response in which you discuss what specific evidence is needed to evaluate the argument and explain how the evidence would weaken or strengthen the argument.*

You may start writing your response here

# Section 2 – Verbal Reasoning

20 questions | 30 mins

---

**For Questions 1 to 3, for each blank, select one entry from the corresponding column of choices. Fill all blanks in the way that best completes the text.**

1. Zoology broadens our understanding of the conditions that early humans lived in by explaining the adaptive measures taken by animals that existed ______ to them.

| |
|---|
| coetaneously |
| inventively |
| transcendentally |
| incredulously |
| mysteriously |

2. He (i)______ his teachers. Any complex mathematical problem they put in front of him he solved immediately, but even the simplest of grade school calculations he found hopelessly (ii)______. It was as if his mind was programmed to operate solely on an advanced level, and was incapable of slowing itself down for (iii)______ work. He seemed to function in the exact opposite way as all of their other students.

| Blank (i) | Blank (ii) | Blank (iii) |
|---|---|---|
| conquered | palliative | rudimentary |
| confounded | esoteric | rustic |
| cohabitated | pellucid | invective |

3. There has always been a strong parallel between religious (i)______ and health benefits. Many studies have shown that religious involvement increases life expectancy and decreases depression. These (ii)______, of course, are not always so simple: the benefits of religious participation on health fluctuate depending on the religion, the sex of the individual, and many other factors. Still, there is (iii)______ bond between general health benefits and religious participation.

| Blank (i) |
|---|
| partaking |
| renunciation |
| eloquence |

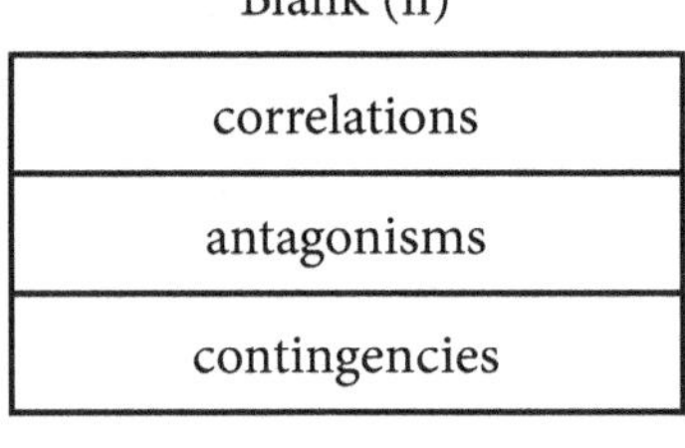

| Blank (ii) |
|---|
| correlations |
| antagonisms |
| contingencies |

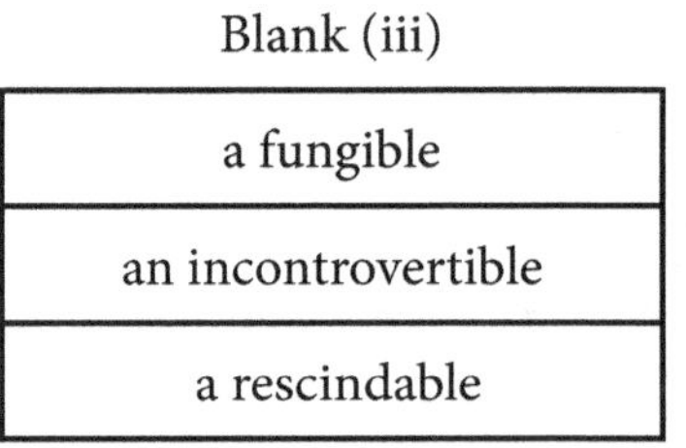

| Blank (iii) |
|---|
| a fungible |
| an incontrovertible |
| a rescindable |

**Question 4 is based on the following passage.**

Complete Cable Company in northern Idaho offers 120 channels. A recent survey determined that the Handyman and Cuisine Galore channels have the most viewers on a daily basis. Local businesses who spend the bulk of their advertising dollars on these two channels will see a significant increase in sales.

**Select only one answer choice.**

4. Which of the following is an assumption on which this argument depends?

   (A) Television advertising is the best way to increase sales.

   (B) Television advertising is less expensive than radio or print ads.

   (C) Complete Cable Company is the only cable television provider in northern Idaho.

   (D) Residents of northern Idaho perform their own home improvements and cook their own meals.

   (E) Local businesses sell products that appeal to the typical viewers of the two popular channels.

**Questions 5 to 7 are based on the following passage.**

A true visionary, Albert Camus changed the way people think about the world. Although he rejected the label himself, Nobel Laureate Camus is most commonly associated with the 20th century existential movement in art, philosophy, and literature. Born in Algeria to French colonists, Camus used his writing to explore the philosophical idea of the absurd. In novels such as *The Stranger* and *The Plague*, Camus underscored his belief that human beings desire meaning and understanding in a world that cannot fulfill this need. This ultimately leads to the erection of civil societies that, if examined more closely, are mired in and permeated by the absurd "at every street corner."

**For Questions 5 and 6, select only one answer choice.**

5. Based on the information given in the passage, which of the following can be inferred about existentialism?

   (A) Existentialism concerns itself mainly with the humanities.

   (B) Existentialism is a method of exploring the absurdity of modern life.

   (C) Existentialism is a school of philosophical thought.

   (D) Existentialism teaches people that life has no inherent meaning.

   (E) Existentialism helps delineate the various structures found in civil society.

**Consider each of the three choices separately and select all that apply.**

6. According to the passage, why are people unable to extract meaning and understanding from the world?

   A Because there is no meaning in the world

   B Because people do not yet possess the knowledge needed to understand the world

   C Because people do not pay close enough attention to the way in which civil societies are structured

7. Select the sentence that best describes the flaw of the search for meaning in the world according to Camus.

**For Questions 8 and 9, select the two answer choices that, when used to complete the sentence, fit the meaning of the sentence as a whole and produce completed sentences that are alike in meaning.**

8. Although financial solvency is a vital component of a healthy enterprise, a business will not survive for long with _______ leader; a strong, sound decision maker who is willing to enforce or even fractious decisions is an imperative component for sustaining an enterprise through difficult times.

   A a craven

   B an impolitic

   C a limpid

   D a ribald

   E a brusque

   F a prosaic

9. The prosecution had grandiose plans to spring a surprise witness and subvert the defense's narrative, but the vehement ________ of the formerly acquiescent witness rendered the plan useless.

   A aimlessness

   B obstinacy

   C simplicity

   D insinuations

   E recalcitrance

   F effervescence

**For Questions 10 and 11, for each blank, select one entry from the corresponding column of choices. Fill all blanks in the way that best completes the text.**

10. Airlines have seen a steady decrease not just in profits, but in (i)______. Gone are the days when picturesque teams of stewardesses roamed plane aisles and when pilots enjoyed some of the highest professional salaries available. However, like any (ii)______ enterprise, the industry has managed to evolve. (iii)______flying experiences have been toned down to functional affairs, promoting good value above all else.

| Blank (i) | Blank (ii) | Blank (iii) |
|---|---|---|
| eminence | sprightly | regal |
| loquaciousness | brusque | immaterial |
| ire | indolent | nominal |

11. Although many do not realize it, historical writing often fits into the category of literature. More specifically, it often falls into the wide category of "creative nonfiction." This category allots for significant (i)______ in the writing. In order to claim the "nonfiction" part of the title, an author must build their story on (ii)______ events. However, the actual story itself that takes place within the (iii)______ of those true events may be completely original.

| Blank (i) | Blank (ii) | Blank (iii) |
|---|---|---|
| ire | contentious | antipathy |
| solemnity | farcical | trepidation |
| latitude | authentic | purview |

**Questions 12 to 15 are based on the following passage.**

Emerson stated in an early letter to his brother Edward: "Do you draw the distinction of Milton, Coleridge, and the Germans between Reason and Understanding? I think it a philosophy itself, and, like all truth, very practical. Reason is the highest faculty of the soul, what we mean often by the soul itself: it never reasons, never proves, it simply perceives, it is vision. The understanding toils all the time, compares, contrives, adds, argues; near-sighted, but strong-sighted, dwelling in the present, the expedient, the customary." And in 1833, after he had left the Unitarian pulpit, Emerson made in his diary this curious attempt to reconcile the scriptural language of his ancestral profession to the new vocabulary of Transcendentalism: "Jesus Christ was a minister of the pure Reason. The beatitudes of the Sermon on the Mount are all utterances of the contemning the phenomenal world. The understanding can make nothing of it. 'Tis all nonsense. The Reason affirms its absolute verity. St. Paul marks the distinction by the terms "natural man" and "spiritual man." When Novalis says, "It is the instinct of the Understanding to contradict the Reason," he only translates into a scientific formula the doctrine of St. Paul, "The Carnal Mind is enmity against God."

It is obvious that this "contemning the phenomenal world," this "revulsion against the intellect as the sole source of truth," is highly dangerous to susceptible minds. If one habitually prints the words Insight, Instinct, Intuition, Consciousness with capitals, and relegates equally useful words like senses, experience, fact, logic to lower-case type, one may do it because he is a Carlyle or an Emerson, but the chances are that he is neither. Transcendentalism, like all idealistic movements, had its "lunatic fringe," its camp–followers of excitable, unstable visionaries. The very name, like the name Methodist, was probably bestowed upon it in mockery, and this whole perturbation of "staid New England" had its humorous side. Witness the career of Bronson Alcott. It is also true that the glorious affirmations of these seers can be neither proved nor disproved. They made no examination and they sought no validation of consciousness. An explorer in search of the North Pole must bring back proofs of his journey, but when a Transcendentalist affirms that he has reached the far heights of human experience and even caught sight of the gods sitting on their thrones, ordinary people are obliged to take his word for it. Sometimes we hear such a man gladly, but it depends upon the man, not upon the trustworthiness of the method. Finally, it should be observed that the Transcendental movement was an exceedingly complex one, being both literary, philosophic, and religious; related also to the subtle thought of the Orient, to mediaeval mysticism, and to the English Platonists; touched throughout by the French Revolutionary theories, by the Romantic spirit, by the new zeal for science and pseudo–science, and by the unrest of a fermenting age.

Our present concern is with the impact of this cosmopolitan current upon the mind and character of a few New England writers. Channing and Theodore Parker, Margaret Fuller and Alcott, Thoreau and Emerson, are all representative of the best thought and the noblest ethical impulses of their generation. Let us choose first the greatest name: a sunward–gazing spirit, and, it may be, one of the very Sun–Gods.

**For Questions 12 and 13, consider each of the three choices separately and select all that apply.**

12. The author of this passage would most likely agree with which of the following statements?

    [A] The philosophy of Transcendentalism arose as a rejection of traditional religious beliefs.

    [B] Periods of stability and contentment are unlikely to give rise to new schools of philosophy.

    [C] Building a case for a philosophical movement resembles the collecting of evidence to support a scientific hypothesis

13. Which of the following support the author's premise that Transcendentalism owes part of its philosophy to religion?

    [A] His suggestion that the vocabulary of Transcendentalism has its roots in spiritual language.

    [B] The mention of Emerson's career as a minister.

    [C] The inclusion of the words of Jesus, specifically the Beatitudes.

**Select only one answer choice.**

14. Why does the author provide definitions of reason and understanding in the highlighted portion of the first paragraph in the text?

    (A) To explain the historical development of reason and understanding.

    (B) To illuminate the similarities of the two concepts.

    (C) To summarize the differences between clerical and secular beliefs.

    (D) To demonstrate the contrast between the two concepts.

    (E) To help the reader better understand Milton and Coleridge.

15. Select the sentence in the second paragraph that best demonstrates that the author's attitude is skeptical about any school of thinking.

**Questions 16 and 17 are based on the following passage.**

Cryptolopha x anthoschista and Hodgson's grey–headed flycatcher–warbler are the names that ornithologists have given to a very small bird. But, diminutive though he be, he is heard, if not seen, more often than any other bird in all parts of the Western Himalayas. It is impossible for a human being to visit any station between Naini Tal and Murree without remarking this warbler. It is no exaggeration to state that the bird's voice is heard in every second tree. Oates writes of the flycatcher–warblers, "they are not known to have any song." This is true or the reverse, according to the interpretation placed on the word "song." If song denotes only sweet melodies such as those of the shama and the nightingale, then indeed flycatcher–warblers are not singers. Nevertheless, they incessantly make a joyful noise. I can vouch for the fact that their lay is heard all day long from March to October.

Before attempting to describe the familiar sound, I deem it prudent to recall to the mind of the reader the notice that once appeared in a third–rate music–hall:—"The audience are respectfully requested not to throw things at the pianist. He is doing his best." To say that this warbler emits incessantly four or five high–pitched, not very musical notes, is to give but a poor rendering of his vocal efforts, but it is, I fear, the best I can do for him. He is small, so that the volume of sound he emits is not great, but it is penetrating. Even as the cheery lay of the Otocompsa bulbuls forms the dominant note of the bird chorus in our southern hill stations, so does the less melodious but not less cheerful call of the flycatcher–warblers run as an undercurrent through the melody of the feathered choir of the Himalayas."

16. Select the sentence in the passage that most closely paraphrases the adage, "Beauty is in the eye of the beholder."

**Select only one answer choice.**

17. Which of the following identifies the author's tone in this passage?

(A) frivolous

(B) fanciful

(C) lugubrious

(D) lighthearted

(E) flippant

**For Questions 18 and 19, select the two answer choices that, when used to complete the sentence, fit the meaning of the sentence as a whole and produce completed sentences that are alike in meaning.**

18. Even authors of tremendous directness and incisiveness will sometimes use the guise of a fictional story, a technique known as a roman à clef, to tell details about themselves in what is ostensibly an attempt to overcome their own ________.

[A] reticence

[B] arrogance

[C] bombast

[D] reserve

[E] structure

[F] cynicism

19. Despite memorizing every detail necessary for an Organic Chemistry test on polyannulated rings, it is still possible for the mind to wander upon hearing an indolent professor's ________ reading of testing center rules.

[A] meandering

[B] wily

[C] craven

[D] cacophonous

[E] rambling

[F] harrowing

**For each blank, select one entry from the corresponding column of choices. Fill all blanks in the way that best completes the text.**

20. He never expected to find any semblance of (i)______ between his two favorite activities. He always viewed basketball and guitar as being totally separate endeavors. But when he stopped playing at full speed and instead focused on establishing a (ii)______, he began to play basketball better. (iii)______, when he viewed guitar as a series of discrete skills that could be developed through repetition, he became a better musician, too.

| Blank (i) | Blank (ii) | Blank (iii) |
|---|---|---|
| delusion | conjecture | Furtively |
| synergy | clout | Analogously |
| deprecation | cadence | Menacingly |

# Section 3 – Quantitative Reasoning

20 questions | 35 mins

---

**For question 1, refer to the figure below:**

Use the table below for the following two problems:

| Site Area | Number of Wells | Number of Wells with Exceedence of Petroleum Limit | Number of Wells with Exceedence of TCE Limit | Number of Wells Deeper than 25’ | Number of Wells Deeper than 50’ | Number of Abandoned Wells |
|---|---|---|---|---|---|---|
| North–1 | 47 | 23 | 13 | 23 | 10 | 5 |
| North-2 | 32 | 21 | 20 | 15 | 4 | 3 |
| East-1A | 11 | 2 | 4 | 5 | 5 | 5 |
| East-1B | 32 | 21 | 6 | 18 | 7 | 8 |
| East-2 | 21 | 3 | 3 | 12 | 8 | 6 |
| South-1 | 6 | 1 | 0 | 6 | 4 | 0 |
| South-2 | 55 | 32 | 27 | 43 | 39 | 2 |
| South-3 | 31 | 18 | 5 | 27 | 7 | 4 |
| West-1 | 17 | 11 | 8 | 13 | 4 | 2 |
| West-2A | 24 | 3 | 0 | 16 | 6 | 4 |
| West-2B | 2 | 0 | 1 | 1 | 0 | 0 |
| West-2C | 13 | 6 | 6 | 3 | 2 | 4 |
| **TOTALS** | **291** | **141** | **93** | **182** | **96** | **43** |

The client would like to know which site areas contain a percentage of wells exceeding the petroleum limit by at least 5% over the total average for the site. The site areas should also contain no greater than 12% abandoned wells and no more than 25% of the wells deeper than 50’.

1. Which of the following meet the clients criteria?:

   A North-1

   B North-2

   C East-1B

   D South-3

   E West-1

**For questions 2-4, refer to the following graphs and answer.**

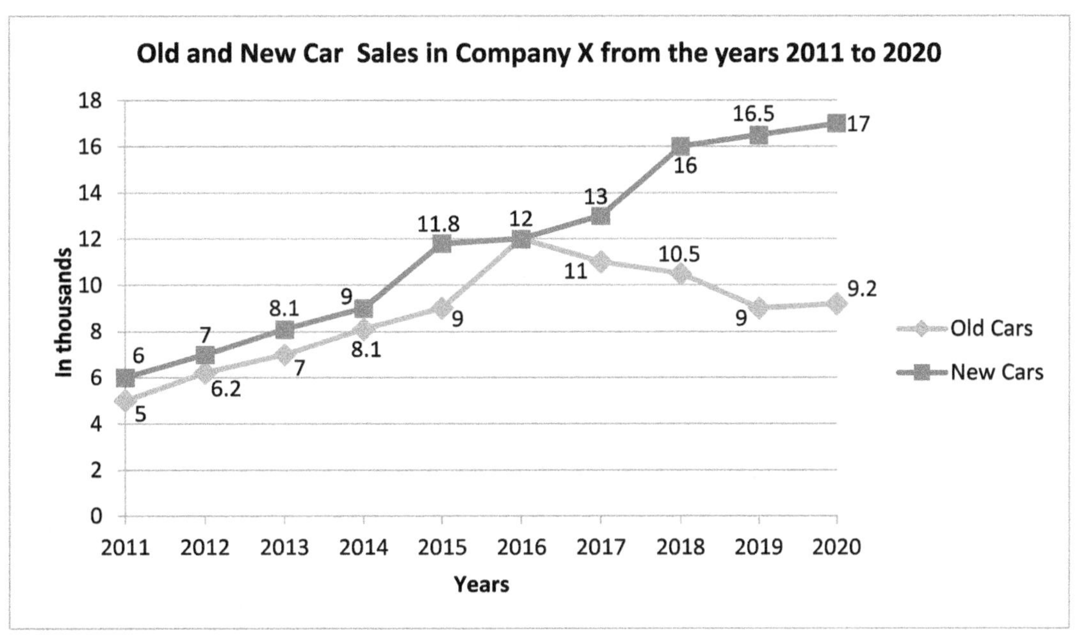


2. In which two years total cars sold are equal?

(A) 2012, 2013

(B) 2018, 2019

(C) 2016, 2017

(D) 2015, 2019

(E) 2019, 2020

3. In how many years the old car sales was less than the previous year but the new car sales were more than the previous year?

(A) 1

(B) 2

(C) 3

(D) 4

(E) 5

4. In which year was the percentage increase in sales of new cars from the previous year, the largest?

Ⓐ 2012

Ⓑ 2014

Ⓒ 2015

Ⓓ 2016

Ⓔ 2017

5.

Daniel has a distance of 279 miles to drive. He drives the first 186 miles in 3 hours. Georgia drives 73.25 miles at 58.6 mph, then drives for 1.5 hour at 58 mph and the last leg of 2.5 hours at 64 mph.

| Quantity A | Quantity B |
|---|---|
| The time it would take Daniel to drive the whole 279 miles at the same speed as the first 186 miles | The time it would take Georgia to drive 244 miles at the same speed as her average speed for her whole journey |

Ⓐ Quantity A is greater.

Ⓑ Quantity B is greater.

Ⓒ The two quantities are equal.

Ⓓ The relationship cannot be determined from the information given.

6.

| Quantity A | Quantity B |
|---|---|
| The probability of picking a perfect cube when choosing any two digit positive integer | The probability that by choosing any positive integer less than 100, that is a perfect square or it is divisible by 25 |

Ⓐ Quantity A is greater.

Ⓑ Quantity B is greater.

Ⓒ The two quantities are equal.

Ⓓ The relationship cannot be determined from the information given.

7. The simplified value of $\dfrac{(125)^{\frac{2}{3}} \times (729)^{\frac{1}{2}}}{(27)^{\frac{2}{3}}}$ is [ ]

8.

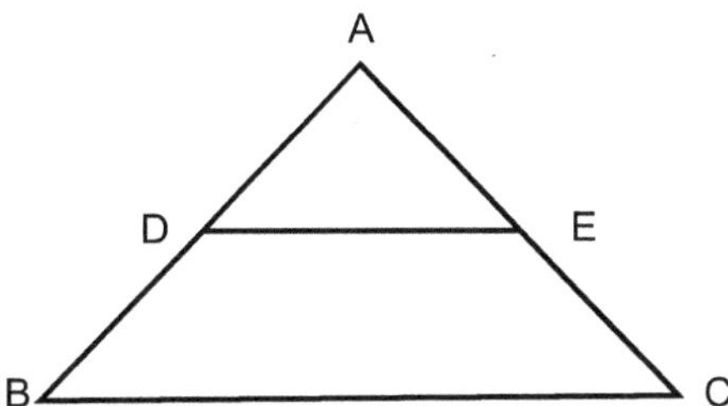


ABC is an isosceles triangle with the perimeter equal to 128 inches. DE is parallel to BC and it is crossing line segments AB and AC through the middle (i.e. AD = DB and AE = EC).If DE = 24 inches, what is the area of ΔABC?

(A) 656 square inches

(B) 693 square inches

(C) 768 square inches

(D) 812 square inches

(E) 848 square inches

9. James weighs 236 lb now and his wife's weight was 210lb a week ago. Since then she lost 2 lb per day. The weight average of their four children is 60 lb. What is the average weight of this family?

(A) 132 lb

(B) 131 lb

(C) 112.5 lb

(D) 112 lb

(E) 110 lb

10.

Albert and Benjamin borrowed \$8000 at 6% per annum simple interest and \$6000 at 10% per annum simple interest respectively. If after N years their total debts are equal what is the value of N?

| **Quantity A** | **Quantity B** |
|---|---|
| N | 16 |

(A) Quantity A is greater.

(B) Quantity B is greater.

(C) The two quantities are equal.

(D) The relationship cannot be determined from the information given.

11. Assume that $m$ is a negative integer and $n$ and $y$ are positive integers, and $x = m$, $y = \sqrt{n}$ and $z = n^2$. Select the correct answers.

[A] $x > y > z$

[B] $y > x > z$

[C] $z > y > x$

[D] $xy > x + y + z$

[E] $xz > x - y + z$

[F] $yz > x - y - z$

12. Three positive numbers are such that the first number is 10% of the third number and second number is 60% of the third number. If the third number is increased by 25% and the first number is reduced by 10%, identify the numbers that are greater than the first but less than the second number, considering the initial value of the third number to be 24.

[A] 14.1

[B] 16.5

[C] 3.2

[D] 1.2

[E] 15.7

[F] 2.1

13. From 100 gallons of milk you can make 22 gallons of cream and from 100 gallons of cream you can make 25 gallons of butter. Also, it takes 4 gallons of milk to make 90 kgs of chocolate. How many kilograms of chocolate can you produce from the milk used to make 88 gallons of butter?

(A) 29,700 *kg*

(B) 34,200 *kg*

(C) 36,000 *kg*

(D) 39,600 *kg*

(E) 45,000 *kg*

14.

Pipes A and B used together can fill a tank in 10 minutes. If they were open separately, pipe B would take 15 minutes more than pipe A to fill the tank on its own. A third pipe C would take 15 minutes more than pipe B to fill the same tank alone.

| **Quantity A** | **Quantity B** |
| --- | --- |
| The time it takes pipe A alone to fill the tank | The time it takes pipes B and C together to fill the tank |

(A) Quantity A is greater.

(B) Quantity B is greater.

(C) The two quantities are equal.

(D) The relationship cannot be determined from the information given.

15.

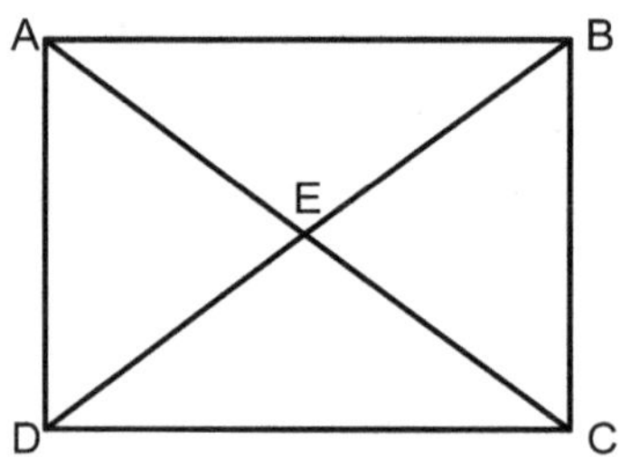


ABCD is a rectangle

| **Quantity A** | **Quantity B** |
| --- | --- |
| The perimeter of ABCD | The sum of the diagonals |

(A) Quantity A is greater.

(B) Quantity B is greater.

(C) The two quantities are equal.

(D) The relationship cannot be determined from the information given.

16. If $\frac{x^2-4}{y^2-9}=m$ and $\frac{(x+2)(x^2-4x+4)}{(y+3)(y^2-6y+9)}=\frac{1}{n}$, which expression is equivalent to $\frac{x-2}{x-3}$ in terms of $m$ and $n$?

(A) $\frac{1}{mn}$

(B) $mn$

(C) $\frac{m}{n}$

(D) $\frac{n}{m}$

(E) $\frac{1}{m^2n^2}$

17.

| Product | Sales Price | Cost | Cases Ordered | Sell-Through Rate |
|---|---|---|---|---|
| Coke | $5.00 | $4.25 | 1,500 | 80% |
| Bubly | $4.75 | $3.50 | 1,000 | 75% |
| Pepsi | $5.50 | $4.75 | 1,250 | 80% |
| Fanta | $6.00 | $4.75 | 600 | 85% |
| Store Brand | $4.00 | $2.00 | 1,500 | 70% |

The above graph shows the breakdown of cases of drinks from the first quarter at a local gas station. What is the profit, in dollars, the store made on Store Brand drinks?

(A) $6,000

(B) $3,000

(C) $4,200

(D) $1,2000

(E) $900

18.

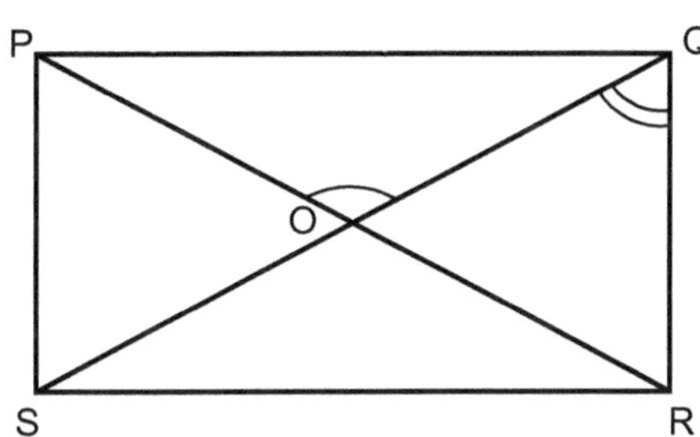


The above figure PQRS is a quadrilateral. What could be the degree measures of the marked angles? Select one or more answer choices

[A] 100°, 40°

[B] 110°, 55°

[C] 120°, 60°

[D] 130°, 60°

[E] 140°, 75°

[F] 150°, 75°

19. John sells very expensive trucks. His last two sales before the accounting books were closed for the year made a profit of $20,000 and a loss of $900 respectively. The average profit per sale for the year is $3,650, but before the last two sales it was only $3,550. How many trucks did John sell in total over the year?

(A) 150

(B) 140

(C) 130

(D) 120

(E) 100

20. If $x - y = 1$ which is the value of $\frac{3^x \times 5^y \times 7^{x+z}}{3^y \times 5^x \times 7^{y+5}}$?

(A) $\frac{21}{5}$

(B) $\frac{15}{7}$

(C) $\frac{35}{3}$

(D) $\frac{28}{5}$

(E) 105

# Section 4 – Verbal Reasoning

20 questions | 30 mins

**Questions 1 to 3 are based on the following passage.**

Analyzing the facts, the habits of thought, the emotions behind competition can help determine where and how it may be applied to the task of increasing manager and employee efficiency.

The experienced horseman knows that a horse is unable to attain his greatest speed apart from a pacemaker.

The horse needs the stimulus of an equal to get under way quickly, to strike his fastest gait and to keep it up. In this particular an athlete in sprinting is like the horse. He is unable by sheer force of will to run a hundred yards in ten seconds. To achieve it he needs a competitor who will push him to his utmost effort.

The struggle for existence, one of the main factors in the evolution of man, has raged most fiercely among equals; without it, development scarcely would have been possible.

So fundamental has been this struggle that the necessity for it has become firmly established within us. We require it to stimulate us to attain our highest ends.

As is made evident by a consideration of imitation we are eminently social creatures. We imitate the acts of those about us. Imitation is, however, only the first stage of our social relationship. We first imitate and then compete. I purchase an automobile in imitation of the acts of my friends, but I compete with them by securing a more powerful or swifter car. By erecting a new building because some other banker has done so, the second individual does more than imitate. He competes with the first by planning to erect a more magnificent structure and on a more commanding site. Or a great retail store, announcing a "February sale" of "white goods" or furniture, invariably tries to surpass the bargains offered by rival establishments.

We do indeed imitate and compete with all our associates, but those whom we recognize as our peers are the ones who stimulate us more to the instinctive acts of imitation and competition.

Our actual equals stimulate us less than those whom we recognize as the peers of our ideal selves—of ourselves as we strive and intend to become. The man on the ladder just above me stirs me irresistibly. The effect of one individual upon others, then, is not confined to imitation. There is a constant tendency to vary from and to excel the model. My devotion to golf is mainly due to the example of some of my friends. My ambition is to outplay these same friends. Imitation and competition, apparently antagonistic, are in reality the two expressions for our social relationships. We first imitate and then attempt to differentiate ourselves from our companions.

The manufacturer or merchant imitates his competitor, but tries also to surpass him. Indeed it is a truism that competition is the life of trade. In the shop and in the office, on the road and behind the counter, in all buying and selling, competition is essential to the greatest success. Competition, the desire to excel, is universal and instinctive. It gives a zest to our work that would otherwise be lacking. In every sphere of human activity competition seems essential for securing the best results.

We assume ordinarily that competition exists only between individuals. As a matter of fact, a slight degree of competition may be aroused between a man's present efforts and his previous records.

While not so tense or so compelling as is competition between individuals, it has the advantage of avoiding the creation of jealousies. In all the more exciting and stimulating games, rivalry between individuals is a prominent feature. In golf the game is frequently played without this factor, the only competition being with previous records or with the mythical Bogy.

1. Select the sentence in the passage that informs the reader that the author's intention is similar to that of a chemist's when he breaks down a compound into its component elements.

**For Questions 2 to 4, for each blank, select one entry from the corresponding column of choices. Fill all blanks in the way that best completes the text.**

2. If there's one good thing that can be said about the (i)______ of the construction industry, it's that it makes it a good (ii)______ for economic health. The construction industry is usually one of the first industries to come to a halt during a recession, and one of the first to regain capital during a recovery. As a result, trends for the overall economy can be (iii)______ from the trends of the construction industry.

| Blank (i) | Blank (ii) | Blank (iii) |
|---|---|---|
| affectability | benchmark | ameliorated |
| frugality | complication | extrapolated |
| insignificance | impediment | enervated |

3. The father of modern psychology is (i)______ Sigmund Freud. His development of psychoanalysis opened the door for systematic investigation of the human mind. More importantly, it also promoted the (ii)______ of previously ignored psychological conditions. Paranoid schizophrenia or manic depression were no longer (iii)______as the results of a defective mind, but rather the manifestations of deep–seated emotional conflict.

| Blank (i) | Blank (ii) | Blank (iii) |
|---|---|---|
| allegedly | appreciation | denigrated |
| incontrovertibly | discounting | alleviated |
| disconcertingly | presumption | conflated |

4. Pediatric heart surgeons are an elite group. They go through more than ten years of training in their field before becoming fully qualified. The stress alone can (i)_______ even the best. They are responsible for correcting defects in hearts that are oftentimes barely a month old. The (ii)______of these surgeons creates a massive demand for their services; oftentimes patients are flown in from great distances, the risk of travel (iii)________ by necessity.

| Blank (i) | Blank (ii) | Blank (iii) |
|---|---|---|
| debilitate | paucity | superseded |
| buttress | opalescence | delineated |
| assuage | ubiquity | critiqued |

**For Questions 5 to 8, select the two answer choices that, when used to complete the sentence, fit the meaning of the sentence as a whole and produce completed sentences that are alike in meaning.**

5. Although its name is synonymous with high science and the consequences of its role in the universe require massive cross-disciplinary studies in order to fully appreciate, the String Theory can still be ________ into simple principles by a good teacher.

A fulminated

B condensed

C inverted

D interpolated

E reduced

F expanded

6. Casual observers of chemistry wouldn't be quick to ________ such an innocuous element like carbon if they knew that it was the foundation of the most complex creations ever seen inside of organic systems.

A question

B vilipend

C denigrate

D corroborate

E endorse

F invigilate

7. Office managers who had long concerned themselves with procedural efficacy were thrilled to witness the global technological revolution in which computers _______ written documents and left them in the wastebasket of history.

A fulminated

B ousted

C integrated

D prioritized

E galvanized

F superseded

8. The "profit at all cost" approach to businesses can, if left unchecked, introduce________ at a fundamental level and undermine any legitimacy the company might have with the public.

A villainy

B velocity

C complaisance

D turpitude

E indolence

F articulacy

**Question 9 is based on the following passage.**

In passing from the drama to sculpture we make a great leap. We pass from the living thing, the dance or the play acted by real people, the thing done, whether as ritual or art, whether dromenon or drama, to the thing made, cast in material rigid form, a thing that can be looked at again and again, but the making of which can never actually be re–lived whether by artist or spectator.

Moreover, we come to a clear threefold distinction and division hitherto neglected. We must at last sharply differentiate the artist, the work of art, and the spectator. The artist may, and usually indeed does, become the spectator of his own work, but the spectator is not the artist. The work of art is, once executed, forever distinct both from artist and spectator. In the primitive choral dance all three—artist, work of art, spectator—were fused, or rather not yet differentiated. Handbooks on art are apt to begin with the discussion of rude decorative patterns, and after leading up through sculpture and painting, something vague is said at the end about the primitiveness of the ritual dance. But historically and also genetically or logically the dance in its inchoateness, its undifferentiatedness, comes first. It has in it a larger element of emotion, and less of presentation. It is this inchoateness, this undifferentiatedness, that, apart from historical fact, makes us feel sure that logically the dance is primitive.

**Select only one answer choice.**

9. In the context of this passage, which of the following statements explains the author's attitude toward art history?

   Ⓐ Art historians have left significant gaps in the discussion of art's progression through time.

   Ⓑ Handbooks about art have omitted any overview of music as art.

   Ⓒ Art historians have made an egregious error in the chronological discussion of art forms.

   Ⓓ Art historians have overlooked primitive artistic expression.

   Ⓔ Art historians have focused too much on the spectator and too little on the artist.

**For Questions 10 to 12, for each blank, select one entry from the corresponding column of choices. Fill all blanks in the way that best completes the text.**

10. The Hundred Schools of Thought was a profoundly (i)______ period in the history of philosophy. From roughly 800 BCE to 200 BCE, philosophers and teachers enjoyed then–unprecedented development and influence in Chinese politics. Unfortunately, many of these influences were (ii)______ from history when the Qin Dynasty launched a campaign of bloody retribution against those it felt promoted dissent. Still, the (iii)______ ideas from the Hundred Schools of Thought have had lasting influences in our modern world.

| Blank (i) | Blank (ii) | Blank (iii) |
|---|---|---|
| inane | liberated | lamented |
| vibrant | expunged | defunct |
| avaricious | inoculated | extant |

11. The United States faces no greater economic (i)______ today than healthcare reform. With roughly fifty million uninsured citizens in the country, medical care costs frequently drag families into bankruptcy. The numbers can(ii)______: more than 60% of Americans filing for bankruptcy cite medical expenses as the cause. The problem is a (iii)______one, as well – bankruptcy problems can poison the economic waters even for the financially solvent.

| Blank (i) | Blank (ii) | Blank (iii) |
|---|---|---|
| windfall | corroborate | reserved |
| calamity | mitigate | counter–intuitive |
| evolution | exonerate | communal |

12. The topic of public sector finance has long been (i)________. Issues such as who to tax, the cost–benefit models of government institutions, and income distribution have polarized political parties and private citizens alike. The sheer size of public finance means that every citizen, regardless of social status, has a tremendous stake in the structure of the economy. (ii)_______, the number of voices participating in public debate often overwhelms any attempt at (iii)_______ engagement.

| Blank (i) | Blank (ii) | Blank (iii) |
|---|---|---|
| acrimonious | Equally | sardonic |
| acquiescent | Ruinously | sagacious |
| frank | Pensively | rancorous |

**Question 13 is based on the following passage.**

Last winter, Mogul Mountain Ski Resort reduced the price of its lift tickets by thirty percent. Despite the price cut and adequate snowfall to attract visitors and keep runs fresh throughout the season, Mogul Mountain's ticket sales were twenty percent less than the previous three years.

**Select only one answer choice.**

13. Which of the following best explains the discrepancy?

(A) A nearby ski resort slashed lift ticket prices by forty percent.

(B) Mogul Mountain hosted Olympic downhill trials during the traditional public school winter break.

(C) One of the mountain's snow-making machines was broken for a month.

(D) The mountain invested in new skis and boots for its rental shop.

(E) The prices of meals at the base lodge increased by twenty percent.

**Questions 14 to 17 are based on the following passage.**

Anthropologists who study the primitive peoples of to–day find that the worship of false gods, bowing "down to wood and stone," bulks larger in the mind of the hymn–writer than in the mind of the savage. We look for temples to heathen idols; we find dancing–places and ritual dances. The savage is a man of action. Instead of asking a god to do what he wants done, he does it or tries to do it himself; instead of prayers he utters spells. In a word, he practises magic, and above all he is strenuously and frequently engaged in dancing magical dances. When a savage wants sun or wind or rain, he does not go to church and prostrate himself before a false god; he summons his tribe and dances a sun dance or a wind dance or a rain dance. When he would hunt and catch a bear, he does not pray to his god for strength to outwit and outmatch the bear, he rehearses his hunt in a bear dance.

Among the Tarahumares of Mexico the word nolávoa means both "to work" and "to dance." An old man will reproach a young man saying, "Why do you not go and work?" (nolávoa). He means "Why do you not dance instead of looking on?" It is strange to us to learn that among savages, as a man passes from childhood to youth, from youth to mature manhood, so the number of his "dances" increase, and the number of these "dances" is the measure paripassu of his social importance. Finally,

**For Questions 14 and 15, select only one answer choice.**

14. Which of the following is the most effective concluding sentence to end the passage?

   (A) Finally, he performs his death dance.

   (B) In extreme old age, he leaves his village to die in the wilderness.

   (C) Because he is no longer able to dance, his social status passes to another, younger man.

   (D) Because he cannot dance, he becomes a slave.

   (E) The younger men ignore the elders.

15. Which of the following is the best definition of "savage" as it is used in the passage?

   (A) A rude, boorish person.

   (B) A member of a preliterate society.

   (C) An uncivilized human being.

   (D) A fierce, brutal, or cruel person.

   (E) A person living in rough circumstances.

**For Questions 16 and 17, consider each of the three choices separately and select all that apply.**

16. Which of the following attitudes toward savages does the author express in this passage?

   [A] Admiration for their self-reliance.

   [B] Concern for the elderly members of the society.

   [C] Acceptance for their performing magical acts.

17. What is the main function of the highlighted sentence?

   [A] It tells the reader that primitive people have torn down their temples to heathen gods and created places for ritual dancing.

   [B] It explains the mistaken concerns of anthropologists who study primitive cultures.

   [C] It prefaces the author's narrative about the important place that ritual dance has in primitive societies.

**Questions 18 to 20 are based on the following passage.**

Analyzing the facts, the habits of thought, the emotions behind competition can help determine where and how it may be applied to the task of increasing manager and employee efficiency.

The experienced horseman knows that a horse is unable to attain his greatest speed apart from a pacemaker.

The horse needs the stimulus of an equal to get under way quickly, to strike his fastest gait and to keep it up. In this particular an athlete in sprinting is like the horse. He is unable by sheer force of will to run a hundred yards in ten seconds. To achieve it he needs a competitor who will push him to his utmost effort.

The struggle for existence, one of the main factors in the evolution of man, has raged most fiercely among equals; without it, development scarcely would have been possible.

So fundamental has been this struggle that the necessity for it has become firmly established within us. We require it to stimulate us to attain our highest ends.

As is made evident by a consideration of imitation we are eminently social creatures. We imitate the acts of those about us. Imitation is, however, only the first stage of our social relationship. We first imitate and then compete. I purchase an automobile in imitation of the acts of my friends, but I compete with them by securing a more powerful or swifter car. By erecting a new building because some other banker has done so, the second individual does more than imitate. He competes with the first by planning to erect a more magnificent structure and on a more commanding site. Or a great retail store, announcing a "February sale" of "white goods" or furniture, invariably tries to surpass the bargains offered by rival establishments.

We do indeed imitate and compete with all our associates, but those whom we recognize as our peers are the ones who stimulate us more to the instinctive acts of imitation and competition.

Our actual equals stimulate us less than those whom we recognize as the peers of our ideal selves—of ourselves as we strive and intend to become. The man on the ladder just above me stirs me irresistibly. The effect of one individual upon others, then, is not confined to imitation. There is a constant tendency to vary from and to excel the model. My devotion to golf is mainly due to the example of some of my friends. My ambition is to outplay these same friends. Imitation and competition, apparently antagonistic, are in reality the two expressions for our social relationships. We first imitate and then attempt to differentiate ourselves from our companions.

The manufacturer or merchant imitates his competitor, but tries also to surpass him. Indeed it is a truism that competition is the life of trade. In the shop and in the office, on the road and behind the counter, in all buying and selling, competition is essential to the greatest success. Competition, the desire to excel, is universal and instinctive. It gives a zest to our work that would otherwise be lacking. In every sphere of human activity competition seems essential for securing the best results.

We assume ordinarily that competition exists only between individuals. As a matter of fact, a slight degree of competition may be aroused between a man's present efforts and his previous records.

While not so tense or so compelling as is competition between individuals, it has the advantage of avoiding the creation of jealousies. In all the more exciting and stimulating games, rivalry between individuals is a prominent feature. In golf the game is frequently played without this factor, the only competition being with previous records or with the mythical Bogy.

18. Select the sentence in the passage that informs the reader that the author's intention is similar to that of a chemist's when he breaks down a compound into its component elements.

**Consider each of the three choices separately and select all that apply.**

19. Which of the following does the passage imply about competition?

[A] A man cannot compete with himself to become more successful.

[B] The only route to true success is through competition with those whose accomplishments are better than our own.

[C] Competition is an essential element of evolution.

**Select only one answer choice.**

20. What is the author's attitude toward his audience?

(A) supportive

(B) antagonistic

(C) patronizing

(D) conventional

(E) didactic

# Section 5 – Quantitative Reasoning

20 questions | 35 mins

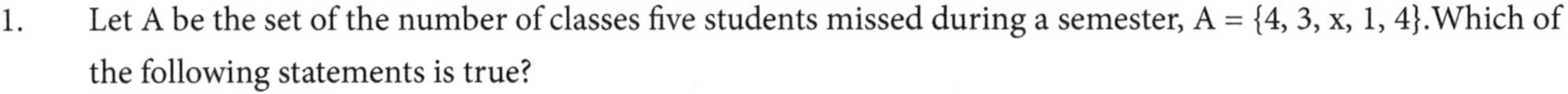

1. Let A be the set of the number of classes five students missed during a semester, A = {4, 3, x, 1, 4}.Which of the following statements is true?

   Ⓐ If the median of the set is 4, $x$ could be 2

   Ⓑ If another student with 5 absences is introduced to the set, the median becomes 5

   Ⓒ The mode is 4

   Ⓓ The range is 3

   Ⓔ If $x$ was 8, the median, the mode and the mean would be the same

2. Find the points which lie inside a circle given by $x^2+y^2+2x-4y+1=0$

   [A] (3, 1)

   [B] (1, 1)

   [C] (2,–3)

   [D] (–2, 1)

   [E] (–3, 3)

   [F] (–1, 3)

3. A chest of drawers is shaped like a rectangular prism. It has a height of 42 *inches*, a length of 38 *inches* and a width of 30 *inches*. There are 5 identical drawers in total inside the chest. The ratio of the drawers height: *length* : *width* is 2:9:7. What are the height, length and width of the drawers if only 7,560 *cubic inches* of the chest's volume are not occupied by drawers?

   Ⓐ Height = 7 *inches*, Length = 37 *inches*, Width = 29 *inches*

   Ⓑ Height = 7 *inches*, Length = 36 *inches*, Width = 29 *inches*

   Ⓒ Height = 8 *inches*, Length = 36 *inches*, Width = 28 *inches*

   Ⓓ Height = 8 *inches*, Length = 36 *inches*, Width = 29 *inches*

   Ⓔ Height = 8 *inches*, Length = 37 *inches*, Width = 29 *inches*

4.

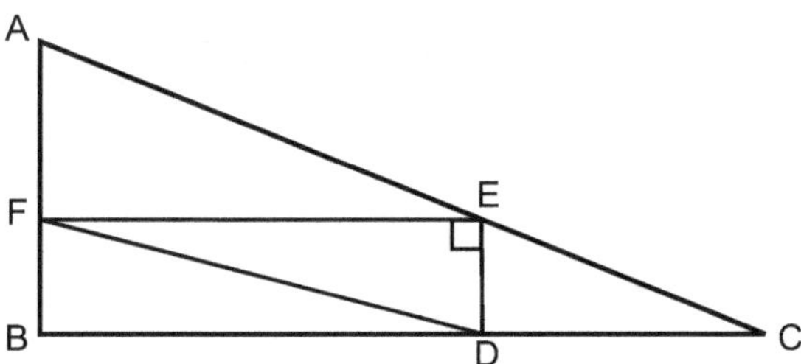


Area of the right triangle $ABC$ is 18. If $BF = \frac{1}{3}$ $(AB)$ and $EF = \frac{2}{3}$ $(BC)$, what is the area of the right Δ DEF?

[ ]

5.

In the $xy$-coordinate plane, the equation of a line is $7x/2+ky=1$, $k$ being a constant.

| Quantity A | Quantity B |
|---|---|
| $x$-intercept of the line | *1* |

(A) Quantity A is greater.

(B) Quantity B is greater.

(C) The two quantities are equal.

(D) The relationship cannot be determined from the information given.

6. If the value of stock $X$ increases 20% on day 1 and further increases 25% on the second day and decreases $33\frac{1}{3}$% on the third day then what is the value of the stock at the end of the third day if the original value of the stock is \$20000.

\$ [ ]

7. Mel is reading a novel that has three volumes and 4,000 pages in total. If the first volume contained 90% less pages than it currently has, the second volume 87.5% less pages and the third volume had 6/7 less pages each of the volumes would have the same number of pages as the others. How many pages does each volume currently have?

(A) 1,750 pages; 1,250 pages; 1,000 pages

(B) 1,440 pages; 1,360 pages; 1,200 pages

(C) 2,000 pages; 1,200 pages; 800 pages

(D) 1,600 pages; 1,400 pages; 1,000 pages

(E) 1,600 pages; 1,280 pages; 1,120 pages

8.

Let $x < 0$, $y > 0$ and $|x| > y$

| Quantity A | Quantity B |
|---|---|
| $\frac{2x^2 + y}{2y + x^3 + 3}$ | $\frac{x + 2y^2}{2y + x^2 + 3}$ |

(A) Quantity A is greater.

(B) Quantity B is greater.

(C) The two quantities are equal.

(D) The relationship cannot be determined from the information given.

9.

Jeremy goes for a walk in the countryside at a speed of 4 *mph*. If he had walked at 6 *mph* he would have walked 9 *miles* more in the same time.

| Quantity A | Quantity B |
|---|---|
| The time that Jeremy walked | The time it would take Jeremy to walk 22 miles at 5 *mph* |

(A) Quantity A is greater.

(B) Quantity B is greater.

(C) The two quantities are equal.

(D) The relationship cannot be determined from the information given.

10.

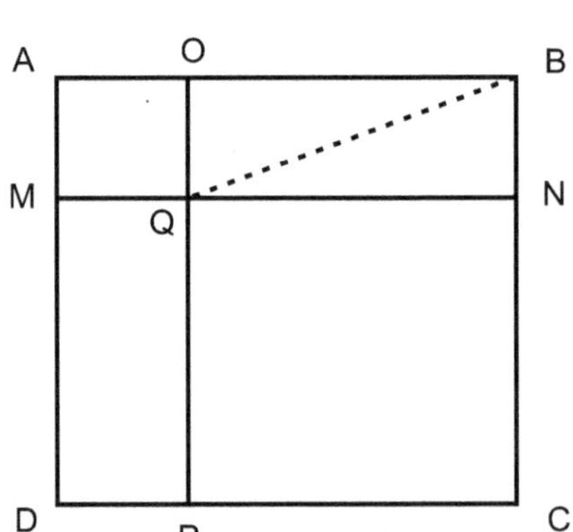


In the following figure, ABCD and AOQN are squares. If AB = 17 and AO = 5, what is the length of the broken line BQP?

**Questions 11 and 12 are based on the following chart:**

The graph below represents the volume of shares traded for a company X in millions at a stock exchange along with the High, Low and Closing prices of shares in dollar. The numbers on the left side along Y – axis represents the volume of shares traded whereas the numbers on the right side along Y – axis represents the prices of shares in dollar.

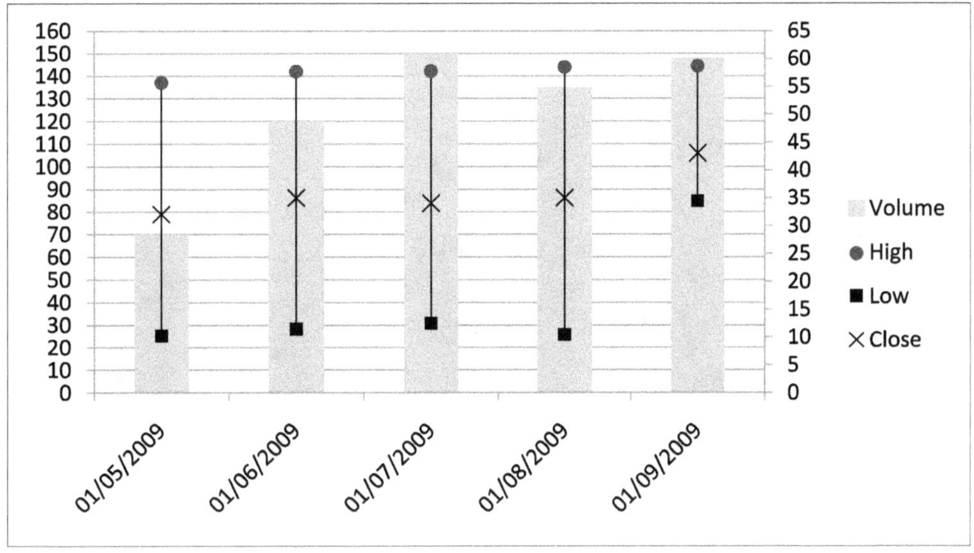


11. On which dates were the closing price of the share same?

- A 01-05-2009
- B 01-06-2009
- C 01-07-2009
- D 01-08-2009
- E 01-09-2009

12. What is the total volume of shares traded over the five days?

- A 613 million
- B 618 million
- C 623 million
- D 628 million
- E 631 million

**For questions 13 and 14 study the following graph and answer the given questions.**

**The following table shows the number of laptops sold by five different shops in three different years.**

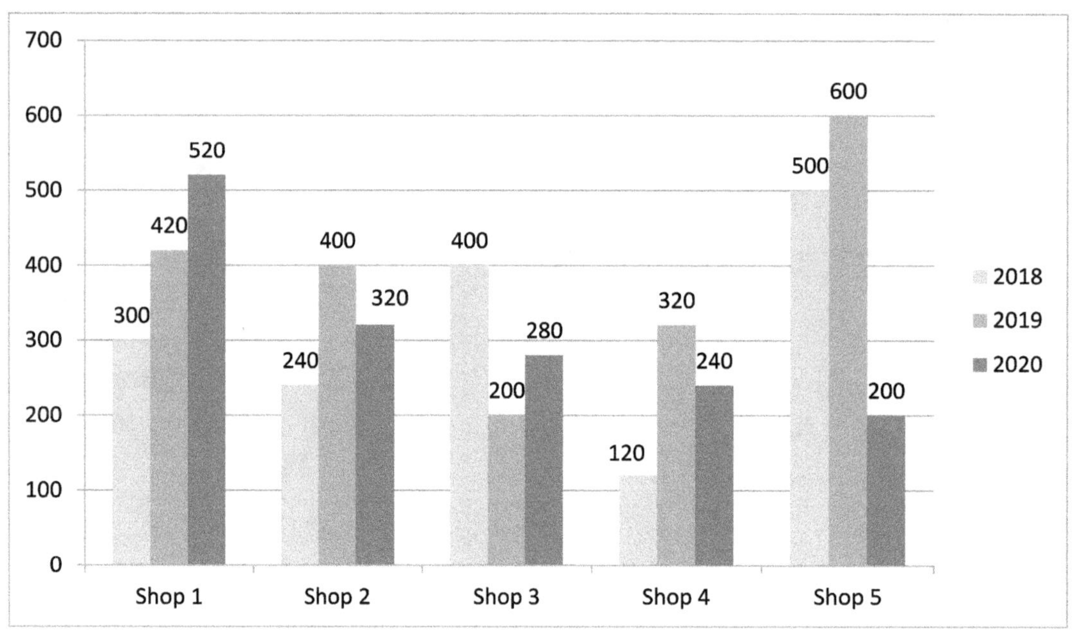


13. What is the ratio between the number of laptops sold by shop 1 in all the years together and the total number of laptops sold in 2019 in all the shops together?

(A) 12:11

(B) 87:62

(C) 62:97

(D) 61:62

(E) 87:88

14. The total number of laptops sold by shop 3 in all the years together is approximately what percentage of the total number of laptops sold by shop 4 in all the years together?

(A) 185.6%

(B) 129.4%

(C) 180.8%

(D) 110.7%

(E) 145.2%

15.

$$x < y \text{ and } y < z.$$

| **Quantity A** | **Quantity B** |
|---|---|
| $\frac{x+y}{2}$ | $z$ |

(A) Quantity A is greater.

(B) Quantity B is greater.

(C) The two quantities are equal.

(D) The relationship cannot be determined from the information given.

16.

$$4^x + 3 \times 4^{x+1} - 52 = 0$$

| **Quantity A** | **Quantity B** |
|---|---|
| One million times $x$, where $x$ is a solution of the equation | The greater of $7^{38}$ and $2^{95}$ |

(A) Quantity A is greater.

(B) Quantity B is greater.

(C) The two quantities are equal.

(D) The relationship cannot be determined from the information given.

17. Which of the following is the equation describing a circle that has as center $C(3, 4)$ and it is tangent to the $Y$-axis?

(A) $x^2 + y^2 + 10 = 0$

(B) $x^2 + y^2 - 2(3x + 4y) + 9 = 0$

(C) $x^2 + y^2 + 4(x + y) + 16 = 0$

(D) $(x-3)^2 + (y - 1)(y - 7) = 0$

(E) $x^2 + y^2 + 2(3x + y) - 7 = 0$

18. A line passes through (6, 9) and intersects the y axis below the x-axis. What could be its slope? Indicate all such values.

A -7

B -1.5

C 3/10

D 9/5

E 15/7

F 5/4

G 2

19. $\Delta ABC$ is defined by the points with the following coordinates: $A(2, 2\sqrt{3})$, $B(4,0)$ and $C(0,0)$. What is the $m\angle BAC$?

A 30°

B 45°

C 60°

D 75°

E 90°

20. 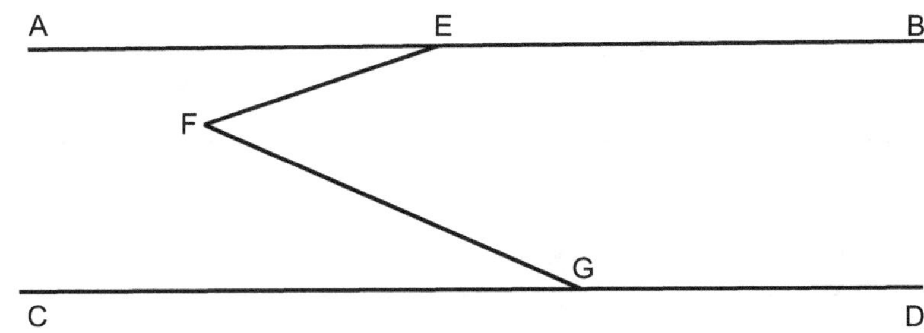


In the above figure line AB is parallel to line *CD*. Also, $\angle BEF=x$, $\angle EFG=y$, $\angle FGD=z$.

Which of the following statements could be true? Indicate all your answers.

A $x+y+z=270^0$

B $x+y+z=360^0$

C $x+z=150^0$

D $x+z=170^0$

E $x+z=180^0$

F $x+z=270^0$

G $x+z=300^0$

H $x+z=360^0$

# Answers Key

## Section 2

1. coetaneously
2. confounded, esoteric, and rudimentary
3. partaking, correlations, and incontrovertible
4. E
5. C
6. A
7. "This ultimately leads to the erection of civil societies that, if examined more closely, are mired in and permeated by the absurd "at every street corner.""
8. craven and impolitic
9. obstinacy and recalcitrance
10. eminence, sprightly and regal
11. latitude, authentic, and purview
12. B
13. C
14. D
15. "Transcendentalism, like all idealistic movements, had its "lunatic fringe," its camp– followers of excitable, unstable visionaries."
16. "If song denotes only sweet melodies such as those of the shama and the nightingale, then indeed flycatcher–warblers are not singers."
17. D
18. reticence and reserve
19. meandering and rambling
20. synergy, cadence, and analogously

## Section 3

1. B and E
2. C
3. C
4. C
5. A
6. B
7. 75
8. C
9. D
10. A
11. C and F
12. A and C
13. C
14. B
15. A
16. A
17. D
18. B, C and F
19. D
20. A

## Section 4

1. polymath
2. affectability, benchmark, and extrapolated
3. incontrovertibly, appreciation, and denigrated
4. debilitate, paucity, and superseded
5. condensed and reduced
6. vilipend and denigrate
7. ousted and superseded
8. villainy and turpitude
9. C
10. vibrant, expunged, and extant
11. calamity, corroborate and communal
12. acrimonious, ruinously, and sagacious
13. B
14. C
15. B
16. A and C
17. B and C
18. "Let us analyze the facts, the habits of thought, the emotions behind competition and determine where and how it may be applied to the task of increasing our own and our employees' efficiency."
19. C
20. E

## Section 5

1. E
2. D and F
3. C
4. 4
5. B
6. $20,000
7. E
8. A
9. A
10. 25
11. B and D
12. C
13. C
14. B
15. B
16. B
17. D
18. D, E and G
19. C
20. B, F and G

# Explanations

## Section 1 – Analytical Writing

### Task 1 – Analyze an Issue

**The sample essay that follows was written in response to the prompt that appeared in the question.**

For most young people, setting long–term, realistic goals is the route to lifetime success. Those who choose this route are less likely to experience failure and become discouraged. However, setting long–term, realistic goals is not the best choice for some, and notable exceptions exist today and throughout history that demonstrate the wisdom of their choices. Those with special talents may be better served by seeking immediate fame and recognition.

The world of professional sports is populated by stellar athletes who made the decision to seek immediate fame and recognition. It used to be that those seeking careers as professional athletes would first complete a college degree and, then, enter the draft. In recent years, it has become more common for those with high–level skills to leave college early or never attend at all and be drafted right out of high school. Kobe Bryant and LeBron James went directly from high school to the NBA. At the ripe old age of eighteen, each was making millions of dollars per year. Would four years of college hoops have made them better players? Perhaps not. They may have run the risk of career–ending injuries, ultimately ending any chance of signing multi–year, multi–million dollar contracts. Seeking immediate fame and recognition was the right decision for these two superstars, both of whom have won multiple NBA championships with their teams.

Examples abound in the world of the arts of those whose talents may not have been recognized or rewarded had they been advised to set realistic goals. Every year, hundreds of thousands of hopefuls audition for American Idol. Rather than testing their talents in small clubs or enduring rounds of auditions, these young singers take a single shot at the big time. Only one of them can win the prize, relegating the remainder to the ranks of also–rans. In the case of the winner and a select few of the top ten, great success ensues. In 2012, Phil Phillips won, and the song written for him to sing in the finale became the theme of the American gymnastics team at the London Olympics.

Still a teenager, Phillips gained immediate fame and recognition. Had he not taken a chance on American Idol, he may have continued to sing in church and the school choir, and singing might have become a pleasant pastime in his adult life.

Situations do exist where long–term, realistic goals are more likely to insure success. Medical research comes to mind. As scientists search for cures or treatments for serious, even deadly, diseases or genetic conditions, they must meticulously test and retest, create scientific trials, and seek FDA approval before releasing new drugs on the market. This process can take many years, and virtually none of those individual scientists gains fame or recognition.

A young woman from my home town set a long–term goal for her life when she was a small child. She wanted to be an astronaut when she grew up. Toward that end, Jessica Meir worked hard in schooland graduated as valedictorian of her class. She wenton to Brown University and obtained her first degree. She completed research at the Scripps Oceanographic institute, becoming an aquanaut. Eventually, she attended the International Space University in Strasbourg, France. At the time of her selection as one of eight in the newest class of NASA astronauts she was an assistant professor of anesthesiology at Harvard. Now in her mid–thirties, Jessica has reached her lifelong goal by systematically setting a course that would lead her there. It is important to note that Jessica was not selected the first time she applied to become an astronaut, but she stayed the course and, eventually, reached her destination.

In reality, the vast majority of us benefit from setting long–term goals. The finish line is far in the future, and we will get there one step at a time. Making long–term, realistic goals will keep us from becoming discouraged or quitting altogether. Even very talented individuals sometimes spurn the chance for early fame and recognition in order to avoid the stress and public scrutiny that attend them. Young people should be encouraged to take the path that best suits their talents and circumstances.

## Task 2 – Analyze an Argument

**The sample essay that follows was written in response to the prompt that appeared in the question.**

Making a profit is the key to remaining in business. The owner of Sunnyside Towers has taken what he declares to be an important step to insuring the solvency of his business. Gathering more evidence about the cost of operations at Sunnyside Towers may lead the owner to decide he could have taken more or other steps to reduce expenses and increase profitability.

Of course, the most helpful piece of evidence, which the owner says is not yet available, is the water usage before and after installing the new shower heads. In the meantime, other evidence may shed light on the savings likely to be incurred by completing the conversion. The owner might begin by determining how much of the total water usage in the buildings is attributed to showers. Other appliances that use water include toilets, dishwashers, and washing machines. Knowing how much water the tenants use to complete these activities may lead the owner to seek savings in other areas. Some tenants may prefer baths to showers, so low–flow shower heads will have little impact in those apartments. In addition to household appliances, the owner may have installed a lawn sprinkler; the complex may have a pool. Those amenities might account for a great deal of total water usage in the complex. If the weather has been warmer and/or drier than normal, the sprinklers and pool may be used more than in an average year.

Another piece of evidence that would be helpful is a maintenance log. Each unit in the complex has a kitchen and at least one bathroom. If only half of them have leaky faucets, gallons of water are wasted every day. The owner may discover that repairing the faucets is more cost–effective both in materials and water saved.The maintenance log may also reveal that several steps, such as repairing leaky faucets, have already been taken and replacing the shower heads is the next logical step.

Knowing the occupancy rates in the buildings would help to evaluate the argument. Low occupancy in the three buildings that have had shower heads replaced might account for the low number of complaints about water pressure. It would be helpful to know if those complainants are taking longer showers to compensate for the reduction in pressure. Full occupancy might lead to more complaints. In fact, knowing the occupancy rates of all twelve buildings would help to make decisions about changes that increase profitability. If several apartments in each building are empty, replacing the shower heads is not likely to have much impact on profits. If most units are full, however, the savings realized from each shower head will be multiplied.

Evidence relating to all operating expenses will help determine what changes, if any, should be made at the apartment complex to increase profits. If the owner pays for heat as well as water, he has likely seen an increase in the cost of doing so. Oil prices have risen, and the owner may find greater savings by turning down the thermostats a couple of degrees or adding insulation to the walls. The cost to mow the lawns or plow the driveways may have risen. Without investigating all costs associated with the apartment buildings, the owner may discover that the money he saves on water usage is offset by greater expenditures in other areas.

Knowing which month the shower heads were in use would help to evaluate the argument. If it was a winter month, overall water usage may be less because sprinklers are idle. During the summer, several residents may be away on vacation, so water used for showers would be reduced. Evidence about rainfall totals and frequency may help him decide to change or reduce the amount of time that the sprinklers are in operation.

Attributing savings to shower heads may be incorrect. In fact, any savings or extra expenditures at any time of the year may be difficult to credit to the installation of the shower heads unless some of the water meters for the complex are dedicated to measuring water used for showering. The owner of Sunnyside Towers needs more evidence about water usage before declaring that new shower heads will create a significant savings.

# Section 2 – Verbal Reasoning

1. **coetaneously**

This sentence says that the conditions early humans lived in can be further understood by studying animals. There is a certain relationship between these animals and early humans that explains why this is a useful approach. We want a word that establishes a logical relationship that could cause animals to be studied. "Inventively" means "creatively." This answer does not make sense in the context of the question. "Transcendentally" means "supernaturally." This answer also does not work. A "supernatural" quality wouldn't shed light on the conditions that distant humans lived in. "Incredulously" means "disbelievingly," but this answer does not explain why studying these animals would help understand ancient conditions. "Mysteriously" means "strangely." This answer does not make sense in the context of the question. "Coetaneously" means of the same age or period. This is the best answer. More information about the conditions early humans lived in would be gleaned from studying animals that lived in the same conditions.

2. **confounded, esoteric, and rudimentary**

This passage states that the man's teachers don't understand how his mind operates. "Conquered" means "dominated." There is no indication in the passage that the young man uses his genius to "dominate" his teachers. "Cohabitated" means "lived together," which does not fit the context of the question. "Confounded" means "confused." The teachers cannot understand how the man's brain works, so he confuses them.

For the second blank, the passage is saying how the young man finds difficult questions easy, but finds ostensibly easy questions difficult. "Palliative" means "calming." The young man would not find questions that confuse him to be calming. "Pellucid" means "clear." The young man would not find difficult questions to be clear, or else he would be able to solve them. "Esoteric" means "cryptic." If the young man is not able to answer a question, he must find it to be cryptic and confusing.

For the third blank, the passage is describing the type of problem that the young man cannot solve. The passage has already stated that his mind works "solely on an advanced level," so it must be simple questions that confuse him. "Rustic" means "rural," which does not fit the context of math problems. "Invective" means "diatribe." This word does not make sense in the context of the question. "Rudimentary" means "basic." If the young man is only capable of working "on an advanced level," then he would have a hard time with basic work.

3. **partaking, correlations, and incontrovertible**

This passage states that there is a direct relationship between religious involvement and good health. "Renunciation" means "rejection." The passage says that it is religious involvement that increases health benefits, so rejection would not work. "Eloquence" means "articulacy." The passage makes no reference to how eloquence within one's religion affects health benefits. "Partaking" means "involvement." This makes sense. The passage states that involvement in religion provides health benefits.

For the second blank, the passage discusses qualifications for the connection between religion and health. "Antagonisms" means "resentments." The passage isn't talking about resentments between religion and health, it is talking about connections. "Contingencies" means "emergencies." Again, the passage is talking about connections between religion and health. "Correlations" means "connections."

This makes sense. The passage is talking about the factors that affect the connection between health and religion, but it is not denying that a connection exists.

For the third blank, the passage is stating that in spite of slight complications in the relationship, there is definitely a connection between religion and health. "Fungible" means "exchangeable." The passage makes no reference to an "exchangeable" bond between religion and health. "Rescindable" means "reversible." Again, while the passage provides qualifications for the relationship between religion and health, it never mentions a reversal of the connection. "Incontrovertible" means "undeniable." This makes sense. The passage is saying that, in spite of some problems that arise, there is still an undeniable relationship between religion and health.

4. **The correct answer is (E).**

Choice E is correct. The only way that local businesses can profit from advertising on the specialty channels is if the people who watch the channels are inspired to buy the products. If the customers have no interest in the type of product offered, then sales will not increase.

Choice A is incorrect. Even if other media offer better ways to increase sales, sales will still go up if by at least some amount if the businesses place television ads.

Choice B is outside the scope of the question. The cost of advertising does not affect the sales generated, and the question refers to sales.

Choice C is incorrect because it does not matter how many cable companies there are; sales can still increase if ads are placed.

Choice D is incorrect because even if residents do not do home improvements or cook meals, they could enjoy watching shows about such topics.

5. **The correct answer is (C).**

Choice C is the best answer. The reader can infer that existentialism is a school of philosophical thought since the passage states that existentialism is a movement in the humanities, particularly in philosophy.

Choice A is incorrect. While the passage states that existentialism is a movement in the humanities, but does not give enough information to infer that existentialism's primary concern is the humanities.

Choice B is incorrect. The passage does not explicitly connect existentialism with the absurdity of modern life. Absurdity is a topic that Camus explores but the reader is not given enough information to infer that absurdity and existentialism are directly linked, particularly since Camus himself shunned being called an existentialist.

Choice D is incorrect. The passage does not give the reader enough information to infer what existentialism teaches, only enough information to infer that it is a branch of philosophy.

Choice E is incorrect. The passage does not indicate existentialism is a method of investigating structures in civil society; the reader is only able to make the inference that existentialism is a branch of philosophy.

6. **The correct answer is (A).**

Choice A is correct. The passage states that the world cannot fulfill the human need for meaning - meaning does not exist.

Choice B is incorrect. The passage does not indicate that humans could understand the world if they had the right analytical tools.

Choice C is incorrect. Whether or not humans pay close enough attention to the structures of civil society has no bearing on whether or not the world ultimately has meaning.

7. **"This ultimately leads to the erection of civil societies that, if examined more closely, are mired in and permeated by the absurd "at every street corner.""**

According to the passage, Camus believed that a direct consequence of human desire for meaning and logic in the world leads to the creation of social structures that are ultimately absurd since life has no inherent meaning.

8. **craven and impolitic**

This question sets up a pair of opposites. The business will not survive with one type of leader, but the business will survive with a strong leader that has enough fortitude to make tough decisions; therefore, the business leader that will not survive must be the opposite of strong and sound. Choice C, "limpid," which means transparent or easily understood, Choice D, "ribald," which means humorously vulgar or coarse, and Choice E, "brusque," which means curt, rough, or abrupt in manner, do not provide opposite meanings of strong or brave. Choice F, "prosaic," meaning uninspired, flat, or dull, likely defines a poor leader but does not reflect an opposite meaning of strong and sound. The correct answers are Choice A, "craven," which refers to a lack of even the rudiments of courage, and Choice B, "impolitic," which refers to being unwise or failing to display prudence.

9. **obstinacy and recalcitrance**

This sentence tells of a prosecution that plans of unleashing a witness whose testimony will surprise the defense, but is surprised themselves at how unwilling to cooperate the witness is. Therefore, we want words that establish a lack of cooperativeness from the witness. "Aimlessness" means pointlessness. We want words that describe the witness as being uncooperative to work with. Aimlessness certainly doesn't help the prosecution, but we need a description of deliberate refusal to help. "Simplicity" means straightforwardness. This quality would help the prosecution therefore it cannot be correct. "Insinuations" means allusions or references. You can't make vehement allusions, therefore this answer is wrong. "Effervescence" means enthusiastic. Again, this quality would help the prosecution, not hurt them. This leaves "Obstinacy" and "Recalcitrance." Both mean stubbornness or resistance. This is exactly the type of behavior that would surprise the prosecution, especially coming from a formerly helpful witness. Therefore, B and E are correct.

10. **eminence, sprightly and regal**

The passage states how airlines haven't just lost their financial standing, but the prestige of the people working within the industry. "Loquaciousness" means "talkativeness." There's no mention in the passage about talkativeness in relationship to the airline industry. "Ire" means "anger." The article doesn't make any reference to any anger that the airline industry used to have. "Eminence" means "prestige." This makes sense. From "picturesque teams of stewardesses" to pilots enjoying high salaries, there clearly used to be prestige within the airline industry.

For the second blank, the passage is talking about how the airline industry has managed to evolve. It takes an agile industry to evolve. "Brusque" means "rude." This is not a quality that would help an industry evolve. "Indolent" means "lazy." This is not a quality that would help an airline evolve, either. "Sprightly" means "lively," or "agile." Being lively and agile would allow an industry to evolve and fix itself.

For the third blank, the passage is talking about how flying experiences have been toned down and become more functional. Therefore, we can infer that they focused on other approaches to the flying experience before toning it down. "Immaterial" means "unimportant." It would be hard to tone down further a flying experience that is "unimportant." "Nominal" means minor. Again, it would be hard to tone down a flying experience from "minor" and get it to "functional." If anything, it would have to be toned up. "Regal" means "magnificent." If the flying experience has been toned down to "functional," then it must have been something better than functional before. "Regal" fits this description.

11. **latitude, authentic, and purview**

The passage is saying that a writer working in "creative nonfiction" has more room to work with than one would think given the genre. "Ire" means "anger." The passage never implies that working within the genre of creative fiction causes the author to be angry. "Solemnity" means "seriousness." Again, the passage does not imply that working within creative nonfiction always makes the work more serious. "Latitude" means "leeway." If the category of "creative nonfiction" is "wide," then it will allow for leeway in the writing.

For the second blank, the passage is stating that a creative nonfiction story must be based on certain types of events in order to be considered "nonfiction." "Contentious" means "combative." The passage does not imply that combative events are necessary to be considered creative nonfiction. "Farcical" means "silly." The passage also makes no reference to "silly" events. "Authentic" means "real." This is the correct answer. The passage mentions history in its first sentence, and history is obviously composed of real events. And "nonfiction" means factual, which further strengthens the argument.

For the final blank, the passage is talking about how as long as the story has a historical backing, the rest of the story may be original. "Antipathy" means "hostility." The passage makes no reference to staying within the "hostility" of real events. "Trepidation" means "apprehension." Again, the passage makes no reference towards staying within the apprehension of true events. "Purview" means "range." This makes sense. In order for a work to qualify as creative nonfiction it must stay within the range of true events.

12. **The correct answer is (B).**

The correct choice is B. The last sentence of the passage identifies ideas from the French Revolution and the unrest of a fermenting age as influences upon the composition of transcendentalism. Since stability and unrest are contradictory states, it is correct to assume that they would not have similar effects on populations.

Emerson, himself a minister, does not reject religion for the sake of transcendentalism but, rather, points out elements of transcendentalism in popular Christian tales, such as the parable of the Sermon on the Mount. Answer choice A is, therefore, incorrect. Additionally, the author points out the contrast between affirming ideals and beliefs or accepting observable phenomenon when he says that an explorer must bring back proof of his journey to the North Pole while we willingly accept on faith an individual's claim of enlightenment. Answer choice C is also incorrect.

13. **The correct answer is (C).**

The correct answer is C. The author states that Jesus' words are pure reason, which distinguishes transcendental thought from secular thinking.

Answer choice A is incorrect because the author makes a distinction between spiritual language and the new vocabulary of transcendentalism. Although Emerson, like his father before him, had been a minister, he strove to reconcile this career with his new ideas that resulted in transcendental thought. Answer choice B is incorrect.

14. **The correct answer is (D).**

The best answer is D. Reason and understanding are two different approaches to an idea. It is helpful to know this to gain some insight into transcendentalism. There is no historical evidence provided about the development of the two concepts, making answer choice A incorrect. Because reasoning and understanding are contrasted in the passage, answer choice B is also incorrect. No mention is made about religion per se, eliminating the possibility that clerics think differently than the laity, so answer choice C is not a correct choice. The author mentions Milton and Coleridge briefly, but does not provide enough information about their thinking to make answer choice E a logical or correct choice.

15. **"Transcendentalism, like all idealistic movements, had its "lunatic fringe," its camp-followers of excitable, unstable visionaries."**

The writer's use of lunatic fringe and unstable visionaries to describe some adherents of any idealistic philosophy suggests that the philosophy itself is perhaps not as important as the thinkers themselves as it attracts adherents that are not to be taken entirely seriously.

16. **"If song denotes only sweet melodies such as those of the shama and the nightingale, then indeed flycatcher-warblers are not singers."**

Beauty is a subjective quality. It is judged –or interpreted–differently based on the sex, age, level of education, or even the geographical location of the observer. In the case of this author, he would agree or disagree with critics of the fly-catcher warbler's song, depending on the definition of song in general. In the case of this passage, a song is in the ear of the listener.

17. **The correct answer is (D).**

The correct answer is D, lighthearted. The author's including the anecdote about the poor pianist lets the reader know that neither he nor we should take too seriously his sketch concerning the warbler's lack of a melodious song. Although lacking gravity, the passage is not frivolous because the number of warblers in this geographical area makes them worthy of mention. Answer choice A is incorrect. Answer choice B is also incorrect. The author uses descriptive language, but he is not fanciful which would include creating imaginary qualities or discipline of the warbler. Lugubrious is mournful, which is the opposite of the writer's obvious delight in describing this little bird; answer choice C is, therefore, incorrect. Although the author's tone is not heavy, it is not flippant or dismissive, either. He respects the warbler and his place in the Himalayas.

18. **reticence and reserve**

This sentence is saying that authors will sometimes write fictional stories in which they imbed the truth because of a certain personality trait they possess. If they're hesitant to tell direct information about themselves it can be inferred that they are shy. "Arrogance" means conceit or egotism. This doesn't make sense because an arrogant person would want to write about themselves. "Bombast" is the desire to talk frequently and fiercely. This doesn't make sense because a bombastic person would want to talk about themselves. "Structure" means order, which does not fit the context.

How could an author overcome his or her own sense of order? "Cynicism" means suspicion. This also doesn't make sense because writing a roman à clef would not necessarily help a writer overcome their own cynicism. Therefore, the remaining choices are "Reticence" and

"Reserve." Both of these words mean a restraint or silence. An author would definitely want to use a roman à clef to overcome their own personal restraint in divulging autobiographical details. Therefore, A and D are correct.

19. **meandering and rambling**

The way in which the proctor is reading the testing information has taken a focused student and caused her mind to wander. Therefore, we want words that talk about lack of focus for our answer. "Wily" means crafty. The proctor is described as "indolent," or lackadaisical, therefore his reading wouldn't be wily. Moreover, a wily reading wouldn't cause her to lose focus. "Craven" means spineless. Again, there's nothing about a spineless reading of testing center rules (if such a thing exists) that would cause a student to lose focus. "Cacophonous" means harsh or jarring. If anything, such a reading would actually pull Janet back towards the test because she wouldn't be able to let her mind wander. "Harrowing" means traumatic or distressing. Like "Cacophonous," this word would actually cause her to focus more because of its intensity. Therefore, we are left with "Meandering" and "Rambling." Both of these two words mean long-winded and tedious. A reading that fits this description would bore a student, especially one who entered the testing center with so much focus, and cause their mind to wander. A and E are the correct answers.

20. **synergy, cadence, and analogously**

This passage is saying that a person can find a connection between basketball and guitar. "Delusion" means "misapprehension." There is nothing delusional about the connection between basketball and guitar. One helps get better at the other. "Deprecation" means "scorn." There is no scorn between basketball and guitar, because they assist each other. "Synergy" means "cooperation." Because each activity helps get better at the other, there is cooperation between the two.

For the second blank, the passage is stating that a skill from music helped a person get better at basketball. "Conjecture" means "guess." Establishing a guess would not help the man get better at basketball. "Clout" means "influence." Establishing an influence would not help someone get better at basketball, either. "Cadence" means "rhythm." Rhythm is a concept that one would learn from guitar, and by utilizing it and not "playing at full speed," a person could also get better at basketball.

For the last blank, the passage is stating that basketball can help with guitar, just like guitar has helped at basketball. "Refreshingly" means "in a way that is invigorating," but there is is no indication given in the passage that the help makes a person feel livelier, just get better. "Exceedingly" means "very much," but there is no indication that the actions must be done a lot. "Analogously" means "similarly." The way in which guitar playing is helped by basketball is similar to the way basketball playing is helped by guitar.

# Section 3 – Quantitative Reasoning

1. **The correct answers are (B) and (E).**

First, determine the percentage of wells exceeding the petroleum limit for each of the site areas, by dividing the number of wells exceeding the limit by the total number of wells in each area :

| Site Area | Number of Wells | Number of Wells with Exceedence of Petroleum Limit | Percent of Wells Exceeding Petroleum Limit |
|---|---|---|---|
| North–1 | 47 | 23 | 48.9% |
| North-2 | 32 | 21 | 65.6% |
| East-1A | 11 | 2 | 18.2% |
| East-1B | 32 | 21 | 65.6% |
| East-2 | 21 | 3 | 14.3% |
| South-1 | 6 | 1 | 16.7% |
| South-2 | 55 | 32 | 58.2% |
| South-3 | 31 | 18 | 58.1% |
| West-1 | 17 | 11 | 64.7% |
| West-2A | 24 | 3 | 12.5% |
| West-2B | 2 | 0 | 0.0% |
| West-2C | 13 | 6 | 46.2% |

Second, determine the total site average for the percent of wells exceeding the petroleum limit:

| Site Area | Number of Wells | Number of Wells with Exceedence of Petroleum Limit |
|---|---|---|
| North–1 | 47 | 23 |
| North-2 | 32 | 21 |
| East-1A | 11 | 2 |
| East-1B | 32 | 21 |
| East-2 | 21 | 3 |
| South-1 | 6 | 1 |
| South-2 | 55 | 32 |
| South-3 | 31 | 18 |
| West-1 | 17 | 11 |
| West-2A | 24 | 3 |
| West-2B | 2 | 0 |
| West-2C | 13 | 6 |
| TOTALS | 291 | 141 |

The total average is 141/291 = 48.5%

Identify those wells with percentages that exceed the average by at least 5% (greater than 53.5%):

| Site Area | Percent of Wells Exceeding Petroleum Limit |
|---|---|
| North–1 | 48.9% |
| North-2 | 65.6% |
| East-1A | 18.2% |
| East-1B | 65.6% |
| East-2 | 14.3% |
| South-1 | 16.7% |
| South-2 | 58.2% |
| South-3 | 58.1% |
| West-1 | 64.7% |
| West-2A | 12.5% |
| West-2B | 0.0% |
| West-2C | 46.2% |

Next, determine which of those areas has a percentage of abandoned wells no greater than 12%

| Site Area | Number of Wells | Number of Abandoned Wells | Percent of Abandoned Wells |
|---|---|---|---|
| North-2 | 32 | 3 | 9.4% |
| East-1B | 32 | 8 | 25.0% |
| South-2 | 55 | 2 | 3.6% |
| South-3 | 31 | 4 | 12.9% |
| West-1 | 17 | 2 | 11.8% |

Finally, determine which of the areas has no more than 25% of the wells deeper than 50'

| Site Area | Number of Wells | Number of Wells Deeper than 50' | Percent of Wells Deeper than 50' |
|---|---|---|---|
| North-2 | 32 | 4 | 12.5% |
| South-2 | 55 | 39 | 70.9% |
| West-1 | 17 | 4 | 23.5% |

The answers are North-2, and West-1; answers b and e.

2. **The correct answer is (C).**

If we add the sales of old and new cars we will get the following information

| Year | Old Cars | New Cars | Total Cars |
|---|---|---|---|
| 2011 | 5 | 6 | 11 |
| 2012 | 6.2 | 7 | 13.2 |
| 2013 | 7 | 8.1 | 15.1 |
| 2014 | 8.1 | 9 | 17.1 |
| 2015 | 9 | 11.8 | 20.8 |
| 2016 | 12 | 12 | 24 |
| 2017 | 11 | 13 | 24 |
| 2018 | 10.5 | 16 | 26.5 |
| 2019 | 9 | 16.5 | 25.5 |
| 2020 | 9.2 | 17 | 26.2 |

From this, we will be able to see the answer as the years 2016 and 2017 (24,000 cars each)

3. **The correct answer is (C).**

The years in which the old car sales was less than the previous year but the new car sales was more than the previous year are 2017, 2018 and 2019. Note that 2020 does not come under this category.

4. **The correct answer is (C).**

We calculate the percentage increase using the formula

Percentage increase =Increase/Original×100

$(A)\ 2012{:}\frac{1}{6}\times 100 = 16.67\%(increase = 7-6=1)$

$(B)\ 2014{:}\frac{0.9}{8.1}\times 100 = 11.11\%(increase = 9-8.1=0.9)$

$(C)\,2015{:}\frac{2.8}{9}\times 100 = 31.11\%(increase = 11{,}8-9=1.69\%)$

$(D)\ 2016{:}\frac{0.2}{11.8}\times 100 = 16.98\%(increase = 12-11.8=0.2)$

$(E)\ 2017{:}\frac{1}{12}\times 100 = 8.33\%(increase = 13-12=1)$

5. **The correct answer is (A).**

Daniel's average speed is = *186 miles/3 hours = 62 mph*

Time taken by Daniel to drive *279 miles = (279 miles)/(62 mph)= 4.5 hours*

In order to calculate Georgia's average speed for her whole journey we need to calculate the overall distance and time taken to cover it.

Time taken by Georgia to drive *73.25 miles = (73.25 miles)/(58.6 mph) = 1.25 hours*

Distance driven by Georgia in *11/2 hour at 58 mph =1.5 hours × 58 mph = 87 miles*

Distance driven by Georgia in *2.5 hours at 64 mph = 2.5 hours × 64 mph = 160 miles*

Total distance driven by Georgia in her journey = *73.25 miles + 87 miles + 160 miles = 320.25 miles*

Total time taken by Georgia to drive *320.25 miles = 1.25 hours + 1.5 hours + 2.5 hours = 5.25 hours*

Georgia's average speed for the whole journey = *320.25 miles/5.25 hours = 61 mph*

Time taken by Georgia to drive *244 miles = (244 miles)/(61 mphh) = 4 hours*

*4.5 hours* is greater than *4 hours*; the left column is greater than the right.

6. **The correct answer is (B).**

The two digit positive integers are all the numbers from 10 to 99

Total number of outcomes = 90

The perfect cubes between 10 and 99 are 27 (= $3^3$) and 64 (= $4^3$)

Number of ways it can happen = 2

The probability of picking a perfect cube when choosing any two digit positive integer = 2/90 = 1/45

Probability (perfect square or divisible by 25) = Probability (perfect square) + Probability (divisible by 25) – Probability (perfect square and divisible by 25)

There are 99 numbers that are positive integers less than 100 (don't forget 0 is not considered a positive integer, 0 is neither positive nor negative)

There are 9 perfect squares < 100 (all squares from $1^2$ to $9^2$)

There are 3 numbers divisible by 25 < 100 (these are 25, 50 and 75)

There is 1 number which is both a perfect square and divisible by 25, i.e. $25 = 5^2$

Probability (perfect square or divisible by 25) = 9/99 + 3/99 – 1/99 = 11/99= 1/9

This can be written as 5/45

5/45 is greater than 1/45

7. **The correct answer is 75.**

We know $a^m \times a^n = a^{m+n}$ *and* $(a^m)^n = a^{mn}$

Consider $(125)^{\frac{2}{3}} = (5^3)^{\frac{2}{3}} = 5^2$

$(729)^{\frac{1}{2}} = (3^6)^{\frac{1}{2}} = 3^3$

$(27)^{\frac{2}{3}} = (3^3)^{\frac{2}{3}} = 3^2$

$$\therefore \frac{(125)^{\frac{2}{3}} \times (729)^{\frac{1}{2}}}{(27)^{\frac{2}{3}}} = \frac{5^2 \times 3^3}{3^2} = 5^2 \times 3^1 = 75$$

8. **The correct answer is (C)**

*DE* is parallel to *BC*. So, the Δs *ADE* and *ABC* are similar. Therefore, the ratio of any side or height of one triangle to the corresponding side or height of the second triangle is constant.

$\frac{AD}{AB} = \frac{DE}{BC}$

We know AD = DB

$\frac{AD}{AB} = \frac{1}{2}$

$\frac{1}{2} = \frac{24}{BC}$

BC = 48 inches

Perimeter $\Delta ABC$ = 128 inches

$AB + AC + BC$ = 128 inches

$AB + AC$ = 128 – 48 inches

$\Delta ABC$ is isosceles

$AB = AC = \frac{80}{2}$ = 40 inches

In order to find the area of $\Delta ABC$ we need to know one of its heights.

First, we draw a height by drawing line segment *AF* as a perpendicular to *BC*.

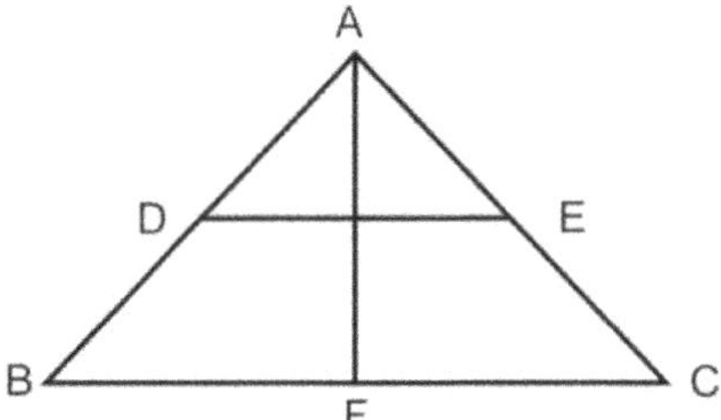


As $\Delta ABC$ is isosceles

$BF = FC$ =BC/2 = 24 inches

We can apply Pythagoras' theorem in either of the Δs *ABF* or *ACF*. Let's apply it in ΔACF:

$AC^2 = AF^2 + FC^2$

$AF^2 = AC^2 - FC^2$

$AF^2 = 40^2 - 24^2 = 1600 - 576 = 1024$

$AF = \sqrt{1024} = 32$ *inches*

$$\textit{Area } \Delta ABC \frac{(AFxBC)}{2} = \frac{(32x48)}{2} = 768 \textit{ square inches}$$

which is answer C.

9. **The correct answer is (D).**

The total weight of the 4 children is as follows:

Total weight of the four children = 4(60) = 240 lb.

The wife's weight a week ago was 210 lb. Since she lost 2 lb each day, so, her weight at present is as follows.

The wife's weight at present = 210 – 7(2) = 196 lb.

Now, we find the total weight of the family members.

Total weight = 196 + 240 + 236 = 672

Dividing the total weight by the number of family members gives the average weight of the family.

Average weight = $\frac{672}{6}$ = 112 lb.

10. **The correct answer is (A).**

We know that the total interest after N years is PNR/100 where P is the invested amount, N is the number of years and R is the rate of interest per annum.

Also total debt after N years =P+PNR/100.

So, according to the data

$$8000+\frac{(8000\times N\times 6)}{100}=6000+\frac{6000\times N\times 10}{100}$$

$$\therefore 8000+480N=6000+600N$$

$$\therefore 120N=2000$$

$$N=16\frac{2}{3}\,years$$

11. **The correct answers are (C) and (F).**

(A) Since $m$ is a negative integer, then $m< 0$. This implies that

(1) $x< 0$

Also, we are given

(2) $y> 0$

These two inequalities do not satisfy the left part of the 3–part inequality in (A). Therefore, we do not need to the compare $x$ and $y$ with $z$. This evidence is sufficient to conclude that (A) is not true.

(B) $z$ is the square of an integer. Thus it is greater than any negative integer. Since $x$ is a negative integer, therefore x>z is not true. This means that the right part of the given inequality is not true. Hence (B) is not true.

(C) Obviously, square of an integer is greater than the square root of that integer. Thus,

(3) z>y

On the other hand, x is a negative number. Therefore, it is smaller than both y and z. Hence,

(4) y>x and z>x

Comparing the inequalities (3)–(4), we can conclude that z>y>x. Therefore, (C) is an answer.

(D) The left side of the inequality is the product of a positive and a negative integer. Therefore, their product is negative. That is,

(5) xy< 0

The right side of the inequality is the sum of two positive integers and one negative integer. We do not know the numerical values of these variables, so we cannot make decision whether their sum is negative or positive. Therefore, there is not precise answer for this inequality.

(E) The left side of the inequality is the product of a positive and a negative integer. Therefore, their product is negative. That is,

(6) xz< 0

The right side of the inequality is the sum of a positive integer (z) and two negative integers (x and -y). We do not know the numerical values of these variables, so we cannot make decision whether their sum is negative or positive. So, we cannot find an answer for this inequality.

(F) Both y and z are positive integers. Therefore, their product is greater than zero.

(7) yz> 0

On the other hand, all the integers x, -y (since y> 0) and -z (since z > 0) are negative integers. The sum of three negative integers is a negative integer. Thus,

x - y - z < 0

The left side of the inequality is greater than zero, and the right side is less than zero. So, the left side is greater than the right side. Hence, this inequality is true, and (F) is also correct.

12. **The correct answers are (A) and (C).**

Let the third number be $x$

The first number = $\frac{10x}{100}=\frac{x}{10}$

The second number = $\frac{60x}{100}=\frac{3x}{5}$

Let $x \cong$ 100%

When it is increased by 25%, the new value of the

third number $\cong 125\% \cong \frac{125}{100}x=1.25x=\frac{5x}{4}$

Let the initial value of the first term, $\frac{x}{10}\cong 100\%$

When it is reduced by 10%, the new percentage will

be $90\% \cong \frac{90}{100}\times\frac{x}{10}=\frac{9x}{100}$

Since the initial value of $x$ is 24,

The new value $=\frac{5x}{4}=\frac{5}{4}\times 24=30$

The value of the new first number is

$$\frac{9x}{100}=\frac{9}{100}\times 24=2.16$$

The value of the new first number is

$$\frac{3x}{5} = \frac{3}{5} \times 24 = 14.4$$

The number within the given range is 3.2 and 14.1.

13. **The correct answer is (C).**

Let $M$ be the amount of milk that was used to produce the 88 *gallons* of butter

$M$ x 22% x 25% = 88 *gallons*

$$M = \frac{88 gallons}{22\% \times 25\%} = \frac{88 gallons}{5.5\%} = 1,600\, gallons$$

It takes 4 gallons of milk to make 90 kg of chocolate

The quantity of chocolate produced from 1,600 gallons of milk

$$= \frac{1600\, gallons \times 90\, kgs}{4\, gallons} = 36,000\, kgs$$

14. **The correct answer is (B).**

Let's assume that pipe A on its own takes x minutes to fill the tank.

Pipe B takes 15 *minutes* more than pipe A.

Pipe B will take *(x + 15)* to fill the tank.

Part of the tank filled by pipe A in 1 *minute*: *1/x*

Part of the tank filled by pipe B in 1 minute: *1/((x+15))*

Pipe A and B used together can a fill a tank in 10 minutes

Part of the tank filled by both pipes together in 1 minute: *1/10*

$1/x + 1/(x+15)= 1/10$

$10(x + 15 + x) = x(x+15)$

$x^2 - 5x - 150 = 0$

$(x - 15)(x + 10) = 0$

$x = 15$ minutes (the solution $x = -10$ minutes would not make sense, hence not valid)

It takes pipe A alone 15 minutes to fill the tank

It takes pipe B: 15 minutes + 15 minutes = 30 minutes to fill the tank alone

It takes pipe C: 30 minutes + 15 minutes = 45 minutes to fill the tank alone

Part of the tank filled by pipe B in 1 minute: 1/30

Part of the tank filled by pipe C in 1 minute: 1/45

Part of the tank filled by pipe B+C in 1 minute:

1/30 +1/45= 5/90 = 1/18

It takes pipes B and C together 18 minutes to fill the tank

18 minutes is greater than 15 minutes.

15. **The correct answer is (A).**

Quantity A is greater

Consider the Triangle Inequality Theorem, which states that the sum of two sides of a triangle must be greater than the third side. In the rectangle above, Triangle $ABC$ is made up of two sides of Rectangle $ABCD$ ($\overline{AB}$,$\overline{BC}$) and one of the diagonals ($\overline{AC}$). The Triangle Inequality Theorem tells us that $\overline{AB}+\overline{BC}>(\overline{AC}$.) Since a rectangle has two pairs of opposite sides that are congruent, you can determine that $2(\overline{AB}+\overline{BC})>2(\overline{AC})$.

16. **The correct answer is (A).**

Use the conjugate identity, squares of sum and difference identities factor both given equations.

(1) $$\frac{(x-2)(x+2)}{(y-3)(x+3)} = m$$

(2) $$\frac{(x+2)(x^2-4x+4)}{(y+3)(y^2-4y+9)} = \frac{1}{n}$$

(3) $$\frac{(x+2)(x-2)^2}{(y+3)(y-3)^2} = \frac{1}{n}$$

Divide (1) by (2) side by side and simplify.

$$\frac{(x-2)(x+2)}{(y-3)(y+3)} \div \frac{(x+2)(x-2)^2}{(y+3)(y-3)^2} = m \div \frac{1}{n}$$

$$\frac{(x-2)(x+2)}{(y-3)(y+3)} \times \frac{(y+3)(y-3)^2}{(x+2)(x-2)^2} = mn$$

The factors (x – 2), (x + 2), and (y – 3), and (y + 3) are cancelled out.

(4) $\frac{y-3}{x-2} = mn$

Inverse both sides of (4)

$$\frac{x-2}{y-3} = \frac{1}{mn}$$

17. **The correct answer is (D).**

The correct answer is Option D.

*Revenue-Cost=Profit.*

For this example,

the revue will be the sales price per unit ($4.00) multiplied by the number of units sold.

The store had a 70% sell-through rate of the 1,500 cases ordered. *Revenue=4(1500× 70%)=4(1500 × 0.7)=4(1050)=4200 Cost=Price × Ordered =2(1500)=3000*

*4200-3000=1200*

18. **The correct answer is (B), (C) and (F).**

Take $\angle POQ=100^0$

Then $\angle QOR=80^0$(Linear Pair)

But $\angle OQR = \angle ORQ$ (Since the (half) diagonals of a rectangle are equal. i. e .$OQ=OR$)

By angle sum property $\angle QOR+2\angle OQR=180^0$

$80^0+2\angle OQR=180^0$

$2\angle OQR=180^0-80^0$

$\angle OQR=50^0$

But it is given as, $40^0$. in the answer choice. hence Option (A) is not correct.

Similarly, we can arrive at the angle pairs as $110^0,55^0$; $120^0,60^0$; $130^0,65^0$; $140^0,70^0$; $150^0,75^0$

So the answer choices B, C, and F are correct.

19. **The correct answer is (D).**

Let's assume that $n$ = the number of trucks that John sold and P = total profit.

We can now write two equations for $n$ and $P$:

$n \times \$3,650 = P$

$(n - 2) \times \$3,550 = P - \$20,000 + \$900$

If we substitute P in the second equation

$(n - 2) \times \$3,550 = n \times \$3,650 - \$20,000 + \$900$

$n(\$3,650 - \$3,550) = \$19,100 - 2 \times \$3,550$

$n = \$12,000/\$100 = 120$ *trucks*

20. **The correct answer is (A).**

In the given fraction, divide each factor of the numerator by a factor of the denominator which has common bases

(1) $\frac{3^x \times 5^y \times 7^{x+z}}{3^y \times 5^x \times 7^{y+z}} = \left(\frac{3^x}{3^y}\right)\left(\frac{5^y}{3^x}\right)\left(\frac{7^{x+z}}{7^{y+z}}\right)$

Apply the quotient rules for exponents, $(a/b)^m = a^m/b^m$

(2) $\frac{3^x \times 5^y \times 7^{x+z}}{3^y \times 5^x \times 7^{y+z}} = (3^{x-y})(5^{y-x})[7^{(x+z)-(y+z)}]$

Remove the parentheses on the exponent of the third factor. Because of the negative sign next to the second parentheses, change the signs of all the terms within the second parentheses.

$$\frac{3^x \times 5^y \times 7^{x+z}}{3^y \times 5^x \times 7^{y+z}} = [(3^{x-y})][(5^{y-x})][7^{(x+z-y-z)}]$$

Factor out –1 from the exponent of the second power, and combine the like terms in the exponent of the third factor.

$$\frac{3^x \times 5^y \times 7^{x+z}}{3^y \times 5^x \times 7^{y+z}} = (3^{x-y})[5^{-(x-y)}](7^{(x-y)})$$

Replace the value of $(x - y)$ given in the stem of the problem.

$$\frac{3^x \times 5^y \times 7^{x+z}}{3^y \times 5^x \times 7^{y+z}} = (3^1)(5^{-1})(7^1)$$

$$(3^1)(5^{-1})(7^1) = \left(\frac{3}{1}\right)\left(\frac{1}{5}\right)\left(\frac{7}{1}\right)$$

Since there is no common factor among the denominators and numerators, multiply the denominators together and multiply the numerators together.

$(3^1)(5^{(-1)})(7^1) = (21/5)$

# Section 4 – Verbal Reasoning

1. **polymath**

This sentence describes a variety of ways that Copernicus contributed to society. "Polymath," is the best answer because it refers to someone who is talented in many fields, so accurately describes someone who works in many fields. "Neophyte," refers to a novice, but Copernicus was not a novice if he created theories that are still used today. "Prognosticator" refers to someone who sees the future, not a scientist making valid contributions about existing phenomena. "Aristocrat," is a person who comes from a noble family. There is no evidence in the passage to support this claim, nor is being noble a reason for him to have been successful in multiple fields. "Magistrate," is also incorrect. It refers to a person who has a public office, but there is no indication that Copernicus was employed by the government.

2. **affectability, benchmark, and extrapolated**

The passage is stating how the construction industry fluctuates very powerfully. As a result, we can infer that it is very reactive. "Frugality" means "thriftiness." The passage talks about how the construction industry fluctuates frequently. It makes no comment on any cheapness or thriftiness of it. "Insignificance" means "lack of worth." The passage talks about how useful the construction industry is in analyzing the overall economy. Therefore, it is not insignificant. "Affectability" means "responsiveness to stimuli."

If the construction industry is "one of the first industries to come to a halt during a recession, and one of the first to regain capital during a recovery," then it must respond very quickly to economic stimuli.

If the construction industry fluctuates with the economy, then it must be a good barometer for the direction the economy is moving in. "Complication" means "problem." The construction industry is not described as being a "problem" for economic health. "Impediment" means "impairment." Again, the construction industry is described as fluctuating with the economy, not being an "impediment" to the economy. "Benchmark" means "standard." Since the construction industry fluctuates so powerfully with the overall state of the economy, one can deduce that if the construction industry is doing well (or poorly), so is the rest of the economy.

The last blank continues the sentiment that has been established in the passage. The construction industry can yield information about the overall economy.

Therefore, inferences about the overall economy can be concluded from looking at the construction industry. "Ameliorated" means "upgraded." Trends about the overall economy can be taken from the construction industry, but the passage never implies that they can be "upgraded." "Enervated" means "lethargic." The passage never states that overall economic health is rendered "lethargic" by the construction industry. "Extrapolated" means "inferred." If the construction industry tends to move in the same direction as the overall economy, just more powerfully, then overall economic movement can be "inferred" from looking at the construction industry.

3. **incontrovertibly, appreciation, and denigrated**

The passage talks about the accomplishments that Sigmund Freud has made in the field of psychology.

Therefore, we can infer that he is considered an important figure in the field. "Allegedly" means "supposedly." If Sigmund Freud was only "supposedly" the father of modern psychology then the passage would not be listing his accomplishments. "Disconcertingly" means "upsettingly." There is no evidence presented in the passage that Sigmund Freud's status as an important figure in the field of psychology should be considered "unsettling." "Incontrovertibly" means "undeniably." If the passage is talking about Sigmund Freud's accomplishments then the speaker must be confident in Sigmund Freud's status as the father of modern psychology.

The second sentence talks about an approach being taken towards "previously ignored" conditions. If these conditions used to be ignored then we can infer this new approach is to not ignore them. "Discounting" means "ignoring." This is the opposite of what we want. "Presumption" means "assumption." Promoting the "assumption" of psychological conditions, whether they were previously ignored or not, does not make any sense. "Appreciation" means "consideration." This makes sense. If these conditions were previously ignored then a change in attitudes towards them would most likely increase the appreciation of their effect upon the human mind.

The passage has been building towards the notion of appreciating formerly dismissed notions about human psychology. The last blank is one last glance back at how various conditions were treated before Sigmund Freud helped to change people's mind.

The way in which people treated these conditions before Sigmund Freud came around were, of course, dismissive. "Alleviated" means "assuaged." These conditions were not "assuaged" before Sigmund Freud came around. They were dismissed. "Conflated" means "brought together." There is no evidence that paranoid schizophrenia and manic depression were "brought together" before Sigmund Freud came around. "Denigrated" means "belittled." This makes sense. Before Sigmund Freud came around and helped the public appreciate the deeper meaning of mental conditions, they may very well have been "belittled" and considered merely the product of a defective mind.

4. **debilitate, paucity, and superseded**

The third sentence talks of the stress that pediatric heart surgeons experience. Therefore, we want a word that expresses the effect that stress can have on a person. "Buttress" means "support." Stress would not "support" a surgeon. "Assuage" means "ease." Again, stress would not "ease" a doctor. We are left with "Debilitate." This word means "weaken," or "incapacitate." This makes sense. Stress would definitely have the potential to weaken a doctor. The last sentence talks about how patients sometimes need to be flown great distances in order to have access to a pediatric heart surgeon. Therefore, they must be hard to come by. "Opalescence" is the quality of being bright. This does not make sense in the context of the question. "Ubiquity" is the state of being everywhere. Of course, if patients need to be flown in from great distances, then these pediatric heart surgeons must not be everywhere. We are left with "Paucity." This word means "rarity." Pediatric heart surgeons being a rarity would mean that patients would have to be flown great distances to receive treatment. The last part of the last sentence implies that the necessity of seeing a pediatric heart surgeon must trump the dangers of flying when ill. We want a word that expresses this sentiment. "Delineated" means "described." Necessity would not "describe" risk of travel. "Critiqued" means "reviewed." Necessity would not "review" travel. "Superseded" means "surpassed." It makes sense that the dangers of flying would be surpassed by the potential benefit of seeing a pediatric heart surgeon.

5. **condensed and reduced**

This passage is saying that String Theory is tremendously complicated a topic, but still one that can be made simpler. Therefore we want answer choices that relate to reduction and streamlining. "Fulminated" means ranted or raved. This does not complete the sentence in any logical fashion and can be thrown out immediately. "Inverted" means reversed. This answer looks tempting because it describes the material being manipulated in some way, but it's not being done in a way that is conducive to teaching. "Interpolated" means added or inserted. This barely makes sense in the context of the question, and even if it did it would mean String Theory had been made more complex, which is the opposite of what we want. "Expanded" means made larger. Once again, this shows the theory becoming more complex and therefore the answer is wrong.

This leaves "Condensed" and "Reduced." Both of these words mean to abbreviate or summarize. This is exactly what a good teacher would need to do to the String Theory in order to make it accessible to students. b and e are the correct answers.

6. **vilipend and denigrate**

This sentence says that carbon is responsible for much more in the natural world than casual viewers give it credit for. If credit is being denied to carbon, then these "casual observers of chemistry" must be talking down to it in some way. Therefore, we want words that stress degrading language. "Question" means to doubt. While this answer seems like it might work it doesn't have the same import as some other choices. To "question" isn't nearly as severe as to insult or degrade. "Corroborate" means to uphold or support. This question states that people doubt carbon as being an important element. To doubt something is the opposite of corroborating it. Therefore, "Corroborate" makes no sense as an answer. "Endorse" means to support or approve, and thus fails for the same reason as "Corroborate" does. The point is that casual observers are speaking against carbon, not for it. "Invigilate" means to observe or check. Again, this doesn't show anybody speaking ill of carbon, so it doesn't work. We are left with "Vilipend" and "Denigrate." Both of these words mean to bitterly speak against. It makes sense that the speaker in the sentence is telling people not to bitterly speak against carbon because it is the foundation for complex creations. Therefore, B and C are correct.

7. **ousted and superseded**

The words should establish the competition between computers and written documents. "Fulminated" means raged against or criticized. Computers obviously did not criticize paper documents. They surpassed them. "Integrated" means unified or combined. Computers can unify and combine written documents, but this passage is stressing that computers are destroying written documents, not rendering them more efficient. "Prioritized" means ordered or ranked. Again, computers can certainly order and rank written documents but this answer doesn't stress the way in which computers have "defeated" written documents. "Galvanized" means spurred or roused. This is a completely wrong sentiment. Computers have not "roused" written documents into life.

They've replaced them. This leaves "Ousted" and "Superseded" as the correct answers. Both of these words mean to succeed or replace something else. This completes the sentence because the sentence is trying to express how computers have made office work easier by abandoning a vestigial idea. If computers are easier to do office work on than written documents, computers must have "ousted" or "superseded" them. B and F are the correct answers.

8. **villainy and turpitude**

The sentence says that if companies focus entirely on making money, then certain ill-desired traits might crop up and hurt their public standing. Therefore, we want answer choices that describe these ill-desired traits. "Velocity" is swiftness. This answer does not describe any type of negative trait that could be associated with a company because it obsesses too much over money. If anything, becoming a "swift" company would be a good thing. "Complaisance" is the tendency to be agreeable. Again, this characteristic would actually be a good thing for the company and would not undermine its legitimacy with the public. "Indolence" means laziness. A "profit at all cost" approach to business would not lead to laziness. It might be dishonest, but it would require hard work to pull off. Either way, there is no other answer choice that means "laziness." "Articulacy" means the ability to explain one's self. This, again, is not a bad thing and would not hurt a company in the public eye. We are left with "Villainy" and "Turpitude." These two words both mean depravity or wickedness. These are the base human instincts that can crop up in a "profit at all cost" environment. A and D are the correct answers.

9. **The correct answer is (C).**

The correct answer is C. The author's criticism of handbooks is their tendency to include any discussion of ritual dance at the end rather than at the beginning, where it belongs chronologically. Answer A choice is incorrect because it is not the author's claim that gaps exist in handbooks that cover the progression of art history, but that they have been covered in the wrong order. Answer choice B is incorrect because there is no concern about the omission of any art form in this passage. Answer choice D is incorrect for the same reason. Answer choice E is incorrect as well. The author does not criticize the handbooks for their treatment of any artistic expression, merely the order in which they are discussed.

10. **vibrant, expunged, and extant**

The passage is saying that the Hundred Schools of Thought was a very lively time in Chinese history. "Inane" means "pointless." The passage talks of the impact that the Hundred Schools of Thought had, so it was not a pointless period. "Avaricious" means "greedy." The passage makes no mention of the Hundred Schools of Thought being greedy. "Vibrant" means "lively." This makes sense. A long period of philosophical and didactic progression could accurately be described as "lively." For the second blank, the passage is stating that there was a campaign of retribution against the Hundred Schools of Thought. This would not be good for the longevity of the schools. "Liberated" means "freed." The schools of thought weren't being freed, they were the targets of "a campaign of bloody retribution." "Inoculated" means "immunized." The schools of thought weren't being immunized against anything, either. "Expunged" means "deleted." This makes sense.

The campaign of retribution against the Hundred Schools of Thought would end up deleting many influences from history.

For the third blank, the passage states that some of the ideas still have influence in our modern world, so they are still alive. "Lamented" means "mourned." Ideas would not be mourned if they were still around, so this answer is wrong. "Defunct" means "obsolete." If the ideas are still around in the modern world, then they are not obsolete. "Extant" means "living." This makes sense. In order to influence the modern world, ideas from the Hundred Schools of Thought would need to still be "living" today.

11. **calamity, corroborate and communal**

The passage states how healthcare costs in the United States are threatening the country's entire economy. "Windfall" means "payout." Obviously, if the healthcare industry is costing the country so much money, it is not any type of payout. "Evolution" means "progress." The passage talks about how pervasive the problems are in the health care industry. It does not mention what progress is being made to deal with it. "Calamity" means "disaster." This makes sense. If the healthcare industry in the United States is causing so many problems then it can accurately be called a "disaster."

For the second blank, the passage shows numbers supporting the assertions being made. "Mitigate" means "lessen." The numbers that the passage provides in regards to American healthcare do not "lessen" the argument being made. They support it. "Exonerate" means "forgive." The numbers do not "forgive" the argument being made. Again, they support it. "Corroborate" means "support." The statistic about healthcare costs causing bankruptcy certainly support the argument being made in the passage.

For the third blank, the passage talks about how healthcare costs are a problem for the entire country, even people who believe themselves to be well–off. "Reserved" means "kept back." Obviously, the problem is not being kept back if it affects so many people. "Counter–intuitive" means "going against intuition." There's nothing in the passage to suggest that the damaging effects of healthcare costs go against anybody's intuition about health care. "Communal" means "collective." This makes sense. If the healthcare problems facing the United States affect the entire country, then it can be described as a "collective" problem.

12. **acrimonious, ruinously, and sagacious**

The entire passage needs to be read before the first blank can be filled in. After reading the whole passage, we learn that the topic of public sector finance has "polarized" private citizens. Therefore, we can infer that the topic does not lend itself to friendly conversation. "Acquiescent" means "submissive." Given the description of "polarized political parties," this is not a good answer. "Frank" means "honest." Although the topic of public sector finance is never specifically described as dishonest, there is no evidence given that it is honest, either. Furthermore, the idea of "polarized political parties" invokes the notion of potential dishonesty far more than honesty. "Acrimonious" means "hostile." This is an accurate description of a topic that leads to "polarized political parties."

The second blank starts off a sentence in which it is said that the number of voices participating in public debate overwhelms certain types of engagements. If public engagement is being overwhelmed then it is certainly a bad thing. "Equally" means "alike." The number of voices participating in public debates is not described as being equal to anything else, so this is wrong. "Pensively" means "thoughtfully." There is nothing thoughtful about voices overwhelming social engagement. "Ruinously" means "disastrously." This makes sense. It would be disastrous if too many voices were allowed to overwhelm public engagement on an issue. The last blank can better be understood after the second has been filled. Now that we know that excessive amounts of voices are "ruinously" overwhelming a certain type of public discourse, we can safely infer that this type of discourse must be preferred. "Sardonic" means "mocking," or "sarcastic." This is not a type of public engagement that we would lament being rid of. "Rancorous" means "bitter." Once again, this is not a type of public engagement that we would lament being rid of. "Sagacious" means "wise," or "learned." It would be "ruinous" if sagacious public engagement was overwhelmed by too many public voices.

13. **The correct answer is (B).**

The correct answer is B. The traditional school winter break is likely to be a busy time for any ski resort.

Parents and children can take advantage of the break to enjoy a family ski vacation. If Mogul Mountain hosted an Olympic trial, one or more of its downhill runs along with the ski lifts would not be available for the public to use. Athletes and coaches would likely be housed in any hotels for the time period, making them also unavailable to the public. Limiting public access to the mountain during this vacation week would have a serious effect on lift ticket sales.

Answer A is incorrect because the reader doesn't know the original prices of tickets at Mogul Mountain or the nearby resort, and if both decreased by the same amount, then there is no obvious incentive to change from one resort to the other based on price.

Answer choice C is incorrect, because the passage says that there was adequate snow, so the snow-making machine was not necessary. New equipment in the rental shop should make skiing at Mogul Mountain more attractive rather than have a negative effect on ticket sales, so answer choice D is incorrect. Choice E is incorrect because changing the meal price does not necessarily affect whether people buy a lift ticket or not; they could buy the lift tickets and go skiing without eating a meal.

14. **The correct answer is (C).**

The correct answer is C. In the same way that his social status increases as the number of his dances increases, so his status declines as he loses his ability to dance. A younger man with greater ability to dance assumes the elder's social status. Answer A is not the best answer because it is not the most logical next step after increasing social status.

Answer B is incorrect because there is no information in the passage to lead the reader to conclude that the aged choose to leave the society in order to die. For the same reason, answer D is incorrect. There is no evidence in the passage that the younger men ignore the elders of the community. Answer E is incorrect.

15. **The correct answer is (B).**

The correct answer is B. The author refers to the people in the passage as primitive, implying that they are preliterate. There is no evidence that these savages are rude or boorish, making choice A incorrect.

These savages do appear to be civilized, as they live in societies and respect their elders. Answer C is, therefore, incorrect. The people are not described as fierce, brutal, or cruel, so answer D is incorrect. There is too little information in the paragraph to conclude that they live in rough circumstances, so option E is incorrect.

16. **The correct answers are (A) and (C).**

Both A and C are correct choices. The author reveals that these people, rather than asking some unseen supreme being to help them obtain life's necessities, they take it upon themselves to create positive outcomes through the creation of their dances which essentially serve as practice for the actions they will take. They are self–reliant. The author does not criticize their performing magical acts, but merely states it as a fact of their existence. Although the author implies in the last sentence of the passage, the loss of social status of aging members of the society, she reveals no concern for their continued existence as members of that society. Answer B is incorrect as a result.

17. **The correct answers are (B) and (C).**

Both B and C are correct choices. The sentence reveals that anthropologists discover something different from their expectations concerning societies they label as heathen. Because it is followed by an explanation of the purpose of the ritual dance in primitive societies, it can be said to introduce that narrative on the part of the author. Answer choice A is incorrect because there is no indication that these primitive societies ever had temples to tear down whether they were temples of their own construction or temples built by societies that preceded them.

18. **"Let us analyze the facts, the habits of thought, the emotions behind competition and determine where and how it may be applied to the task of increasing our own and our employees' efficiency."**

In order to analyze a compound, a chemist must determine its component elements. In the same way, the author states that it is his intention to analyze the elements that contribute to competition. Analysis always means to examine the parts of a whole, whether it is in a lab or when writing an analysis of a poem, or, in this case, competition.

19. **The correct answer is (C).**

The correct answer is C. The author states, in paragraph 3 that, without the struggle for existence, development would scarcely be possible. The reader can infer that competition for food and other necessities led to survival of the strongest or fastest or the possessor of some other superior characteristic, which is a tenet of evolution. The next– to–last paragraph explicitly states that in some few instances, one may compete with himself to improve on a previous performance, so answer choice A is incorrect. The reader can use that same paragraph to show that answer choice B is incorrect, as well. One needs only to compete with his own better self.

20. **The correct answer is (E).**

The correct answer is E, didactic. He is attempting to instruct the reader or listener about the best methods to inspire effective competition. Answer choice A is incorrect because the author is not agreeing with any ideas that the audience might have. He is not disagreeing with anyone else's ideas, so he is not antagonistic, making answer choice B incorrect. Answer choice C is incorrect because he is not talking down to his audience. He assumes that his audience is receptive to his ideas. The author is not repeating conventional ideas. He is introducing what he assumes to be new ideas and examples to his audience. Therefore, answer choice D is incorrect.

# Section 5 – Quantitative Reasoning

1. **The correct answer is (E).**

Set $A$ rearranged in ascending order, excluding $x$: {1, 3, 4, 4}

We know the median is 4. The median of a set is the middle number. $x$ must be greater than 4, otherwise the median would be 3.

A) cannot be true.

If another student with 5 absences is introduced to the set, the set (excluding $x$) becomes:

{1, 3, 4, 4, 5}– In this case, no matter what value is $x$, the median cannot be 5

For example if x was 6, the set would be {1, 3, 4, 4, 5, 6} and the median would still be 4.

However, if $x$ was 2 for instance, the set would be {1, 2, 3, 4, 4, 5}. In this case there are two middle numbers so the median is the average of the two middle numbers = (3+4)/2 = 3.5

B) cannot be true.

The mode is the most frequent number in the set. While this looks like 4, because 4 appears twice, we do not know the value of $x$. $x$ could be 1 or 3, in which case both 4 and $x$ would appear twice

We cannot say with certainty that the mode is 4 no matter what the value of $x$

C) is not always true.

The range is the difference between the largest number and the smallest number in the set. Again, while at a first look this seems to be 4–1 = 3, we do not actually know the value of $x$.

For example, if $x$ was 5, the range would be

5–1 = 4

D) is not always true.

If $x$ was 8, the set becomes {1, 3, 4, 4, 8}

The median is 4 (4 is the middle number) and the mode is also 4 (most frequent)

The mean is the average = (1+3+4+4+8)/5= 20/5= 4

E) is true.

2. **The correct answers are (D) and (F).**

We write $x^2+y^2+2x-4y+1=0$ in its standard form using completing square method

$x^2+y^2+2x\text{-}4y+1=(x^2+2x)+(y^2-4y)+1=0$

$=(x^2+2x+1)+(y^2-4y+4)+1-1-4=0$

$=(x^2+2x+1)+(y^2-4y+4)=4$

$= (x+1)^2+(y-2)^2=2^2$

Comparing with the standard form of an equation of a circle $(x\text{-}a)^2+(y\text{-}b)^2=r^2$ where $(a,b)$ is the center of the circle and r is the radius, we have.

The center of the circle is (–1,2) and the radius is 2 units.

A point will be in the circle if its distance from the center of the circle is less than 2 units. We therefore test all the points

(3,1) Distance=$\sqrt{(3+1)^2+(1-2)^2}$=4.1>2

(1,1) Distance=$\sqrt{(1+1)^2+(1-2)^2}$=2.2>2

(2,–3) Distance=$\sqrt{(2+1)^2+(-3-2)^2}$=5.8>2

(–2,1) Distance=$\sqrt{(-2+1)^2+(1-2)^2}$=1.4<2

(–3,3) Distance=$\sqrt{(-3+1)^2+(3-2)^2}$=2.2>2

(–1,3) Distance=$\sqrt{(-1+1)^2+(3-2)^2}$=1<2

3. **The correct answer is (C).**

The volume of the chest of drawers is equal to *length* × *width* × *height* = 38 × 30 × 42 = 47,880 *cubic inches.*

7,560 cubic inches of the chest's volume are not occupied by drawers.

Total volume of all the drawers = 47,880 – 7,560 = 40,320 *cubic inches.*

The ratio of the drawers *height*: *length* : *width* is 2:9:7.

Let the *height* = *2X, the length* = *9X and the width* = *7X.*

$40{,}320 = 2X \times 9X \times 7X \times 5 = 126X^3 \times 5$

$64 = X^3$ So, $X = 4$

Drawer height = 2 × 4 = 8 *inches*

Drawer length = 9 × 4 = 36 *inches*

Drawer width = 7 × 4 = 28 *inches*

4. **The correct answer is 4.**

We are given

(1) Area of triangle $ABC = 18$

(2) Area of triangle $ABC = 1/2$ (AB)(BC)

Replace the value of the area from (1) in (2).

$1/2(AB)(BC) = 18$

Multiply each side by 2.

(3) $(AB)(BC) = 36$

We are given

(4) $BF = 1/3(AB)$

(5) $EF = 2/3(BC)$

The area of the right triangle DEF in terms of legs is

Area of triangle $DEF = (EF)(BF)$

Replace equivalents of $BF$ and $EF$ from (4) and (5) in this equation.

Area of triangle $DEF = 1/2\ [1/3\ (AB)][2/3\ (BC)] = 1/9(AB)(BC)$

Replace the known value from (3) in this equation, and then simplify.

Area of triangle $DEF = 1/9(36) = 4$

5. **The correct answer is (B).**

The equation of the line is given by

$$\therefore \frac{7x}{2} + ky = 1$$

where $k$ is a constant,

$x$-intercept means the $x$ co-ordinate of the point of intersection of the line with $x$-axis.

That means the $y$-coordinate is zero.

So to find $x$-intercept substitute $y$=0 in the equation of the line.

$$\therefore \frac{7x}{2} + ky = 1$$

$$\text{i.e.}\ \frac{7x}{2} + 0 = 1$$

(Irrespective of the value of $k$)

$$x = \frac{2}{7} < 1$$

6. **The correct answer is $20,000.**

The original value of the stock $X$ =20000

On the first day, the increase is 20%

So the new value will be 120% of the original value.

Value at the end of the first

$$\text{day}=20000\times120\%=20000\times\frac{120}{100}=20000\times1.2=24000$$

Value at the end of the second

$$\text{day}=24000\times125\%=24000\times\frac{125}{100}=24000\times1.25=30000$$

Value at the end of the third day=30000×66

$$\frac{2}{3}\%=30000\times\frac{200}{300}=20000$$

7. **The correct answer is (E).**

Let's assume that:

$X$ = number of pages of the first volume.

$Y$ = number of pages of the second volume.

$Z$ = number of pages of the third volume.

$X + Y + Z$ = 4,000 pages.

$X - 90\%X = Y - 87.5\%Y = Z - 6/7\ Z$

$X/10 = Y/8 = Z/7$ and let assume they all equal $p$

$X = 10p,\ Y = 8p$ and $Z = 7p$

$10p + 8p + 7p = 4{,}000$

$25p = 4{,}000$

$p = 160$ *pages*

The first volume has $X = 10p = 10 \times 160 = 1{,}600$ pages.

The second volume has $Y = 8p = 8 \times 160 = 1{,}280$ pages.

The third volume has $Z = 7p = 7 \times 160 = 1{,}120$ pages.

8. **The correct answer is (A).**

Since $x < 0$, $x^2 > 0$

Given that $|x| > y$, $x^2 > y^2$ and $2x^2 > 2y^2$

Since $x < 0$, $y > 0$, $x < y$ hence $2x^2 + y > 2y^2 + x$

$x < 0$ Implies that $x^3 < 0 > x^2$,

thus $2y + x^3 + 3 < 2y + x^2 + 3$

9. **The correct answer is (A).**

Let the distance that Jeremy walked be $x$

$$\frac{x}{4} = \frac{x+9}{6}$$

$6x = 4x + 36$

$x = 18\ miles$

The time that Jeremy walked =

$$\frac{18\,miles}{4\,mph} = 4\frac{1}{2}\,hours = 4\,hours\ and\ 30\,minutes$$

The time it would take Jeremy to walk 22 miles at 5 mph

$$= \frac{22\,miles}{5\,mph} = 4\frac{2}{5}\,hours = 4\,hours\ and\ 24\,minutes$$

4 *hours* and 30 *minutes* is greater than 4 *hours* and 24 *minutes*

10. **The correct answer is 25.**

We are given

(1) AB = 17

(2) AO = 5

Subtract (2) from (1) side by side.

AB – AO = 17 – 5

AB – AO = 12

From the figure AB – AO = OB. Substitute this into the equation above.

(3) OB = 12

Since *AOQN* and *QPCM* are squares, then *OBMQ* and *NQPD* are congruent rectangles. These facts along with (3) imply that

(4) QP = MQ = OB = 12

Apply the Pythagorean theorem to the right triangle OBQ.

$(BQ)^2 = (OB)^2 + (OQ)^2$

Substitute the length of a side of the square OQNQ for

OQ and 12 the value of OB from (3) in this equation.

$(BQ)^2 = (12)^2 + (5)^2$

Find the products on the right and then add them up.

$(BQ)^2 = 169$

Take square root of each side.

(5) BQ = 13

From the figure

BQP = BQ + QP

Replace the values of QP and BQ from (4) and (5) in this equation

BQP = 13 + 12 = 25

11. **The correct answers are (B) and (D).**

The closing price of share was 35 dollars on 01-06-2009 and 01-08-2009.

12. **The correct answer is (C).**

The total volume of shares traded over five days = 70 + 120 + 150 + 135 + 148 = 623 million

13. **The correct answer is (C).**

The number of laptops sold by shop 1 in all the years together = 300 + 420 + 520 = 1240

The total number of laptops sold in 2019 in all the shops together = 420 + 400 + 200 + 320 + 600 = 1940

Ratio = 1240 : 1940 = 62 : 97

14. **The correct answer is (B).**

The total number of laptops sold by shop 3 in all the years together = 400 + 200 + 280 = 880

Total number of laptops sold by shop 4 in all the years together =120 + 320 + 240 = 680

Required percentage = 880 / 680 × 100 = 129.4%

15. **The correct answer is (B).**

Add the corresponding sides of the given inequalities.

$x + y < y + z$

Subtract y from each side.

(1) $x < z$

We are given

(2) $y < z$

Add the corresponding sides of (1) and (2).

$x + y < z + z$

$x + y < 2z$

Divide each side by 2.

$\frac{x + y}{2} < z$

Answer: Quantity B is greater.

16. **The correct answer is (B).**

First we solve the equation:

$4^x + 3 \times 4^{x+1} - 52 = 0$

$4^x + 3 \times 4^x \times 4 = 52$

$4^x + 12 \times 4^x = 52$

$13 \times 4^x = 13 \times 4$

$4^x = 4$

$x = 1$

One million times $x = 1{,}000{,}000$

Looking at $7^{38}$ and $2^{95}$ it is obvious that we cannot bring the numbers at the same base in order to compare them. We try to bring them to a form where the exponents are the same.

$7^{38} = 7^{2\times19} = (7^2)^{19} = 49^{19}$

$2^{95} = 2^{5\times19} = (2^5)^{19} = 32^{19}$

$49 > 32$

$49^{19} > 32^{19}$

$7^{38} > 2^{95}$

It is obvious that $7^{38}$ (or $49^{19}$) is greater than 1,000,000 (or $10^6$) because both the base and the exponent are greater.

17. **The correct answer is (D).**

The circle is tangent to the Y axis. The radius must be the distance between the center C(3,4) and the Y axis, i.e. the distance between point C(3,4) and a point of coordinates (0,4) which describes a perpendicular from C(3,4) to Y axis

The radius $r = \sqrt{(3-0)^2 + (4-4)^2} = 3$

The standard form for the equation of a circle is $(x-a)^2 + (y-b)^2 = r^2$ where (a,b) are the coordinates of the center and r is the radius. If we substitute the values we find:

$(x-3)^2 + (y-4)^2 = 3^2$

$(x-3)^2 + y^2 - 8y + 16 = 9$

$(x-3)^2 + y^2 - 8y + 16 - 9 = 0$

$(x-3)^2 + y^2 - 8y + 7 = 0$

$(x-3)^2 + (y-1)(y-7) = 0$

18. **The correct answer is (D), (E) and (G).**

The line intersects the y axis below the origin. The x coordinate of the point of intersection will be 0 and the y-intercept will be negative.

Let the point of intersection will be (0, y_1) where y_1<0.

The slope of the line m will be equal to

$m = \frac{y_2 - y_1}{x_2 - x_1} = \frac{9 - y_1}{6 - 0} = \frac{9 - y_1}{6}$

But as y_1 is negative, the numerator will be more than 9.

That means the required line's slope will be more than 9/6=1.5

If we check all the slopes the ones we get the options as (D), (E) and (G)

19. **The correct answer is (C).**

One approach would be to calculate the slopes of lines AB and AC to see if their product equals-1 in which case the lines would be perpendicular

The slope of AB is $\frac{2\sqrt{3}-0}{2-4} = -\sqrt{3}$

The slope of AC is $\frac{2\sqrt{3}-0}{2-0} = \sqrt{3}$

The product of the slopes is -3, which means the lines cannot be perpendicular. The answer E) is definitely wrong.

Next we can calculate the length of the triangle sides to see if that gives a helpful indication.

$AB = \sqrt{(4-2)^2 + (0-2\sqrt{3})^2} = \sqrt{4+12} = 4$

$AC = \sqrt{(0-2)^2 + (0-2\sqrt{3})^2} = \sqrt{4+12} = 4$

$BC = \sqrt{(4-0)^2 + (0-0)^2} = \sqrt{16+0} = 4$

$AB = AC = BC$

ΔABC is equilateral

All angles in ΔABC = 60°, including ∠BAC.

20. **The correct answer is (B), (F) and (G).**

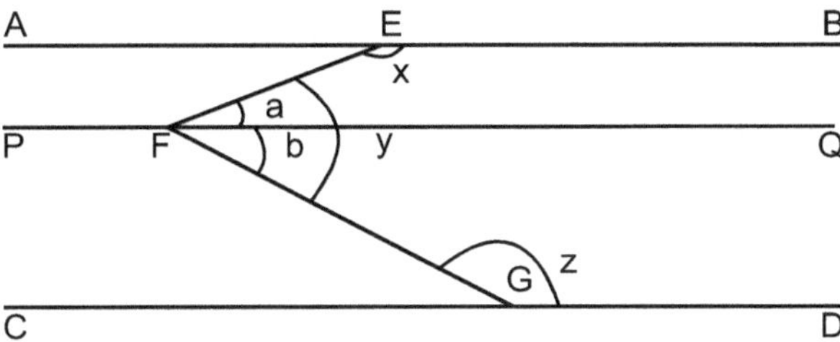


Given AB||CD

Draw a line PFQ parallel to both AB and CD.

Now let ∠EFQ=a and ∠GFQ=b

$x+a=180^0$ (co-interior angles)

$b+z=180^0$ (co-interior angles)

$\angle x+a+b+z=360^0$

But $a+b=y$

Hence $x+y+z=360^0$

Therefore (A) is wrong and (B) is correct.

Now $x+y+z=360^0$

But $y$ is less than $180^0$ (since *EFG* is not a straight line)

$\angle x+z>180^0$

Also, $x+z<360^0$ since $y>0$

Therefore, $x+z$ must lie between $180^0$ and $360^0$

Hence (C),(D), and (E) are not correct as each value is less than or equal to $180^0$

Also, (F) and (G) are correct since the values lie between $180^0$ and $360^0$

(H) is not correct since the value is $360^0$

This page is intentionally left blank

## Chapter 4

# Practice Test 2

You are about to begin a full length Practice Test. The Test has five sections. The time allotted for each section is marked at the beginning of the section. Work on one section at a time. Use a timer to keep track of the time limits for every section.

Try to take the Practice Test under real test conditions. Find a quiet place to work, and set aside enough time to complete the test without being disturbed. At the end of the test, check your answers by referring to the Answer Key and fill in your raw score in the score card below. Also, note down the time taken by you for completing each section.

Pay particular attention to the questions that were answered incorrectly. Read the answer explanations and understand how to solve them.

### My Score Card (Raw Score)

| | Section 2 | Section 3 | Section 4 | Section 5 |
|---|---|---|---|---|
| **Out of** | 20 | 20 | 20 | 20 |
| **My Score** | ________ | ________ | ________ | ________ |
| **Time Taken** | ________ | ________ | ________ | ________ |

# Section 1 – Analytical Writing

Task 1 – Analyze an Issue | 30 mins

*Claim: Any piece of information referred to as a fact should be mistrusted, since it may well be proven false in the future.*

*Reason: Much of the information that people assume is factual actually turns out to be inaccurate.*

*Write a response in which you discuss the extent to which you agree or disagree with the claim and the reason on which that claim is based.*

You may start writing your response here

## Task 2 – Analyze an Argument Task | 30 mins

*The following appeared in a memorandum written by the vice president of Health Naturally, a small but expanding chain of stores selling health food and other health-related products.*

*"Our previous experience has been that our stores are most profitable in areas where residents are highly concerned with leading healthy lives. We should therefore build one of our new stores in Plainsville, which clearly has many such residents. Plainsville merchants report that sales of running shoes and exercise equipment are at all-time highs. The local health club, which nearly closed five years ago due to lack of business, has more members than ever and the weight-training and aerobics classes are always full. We can even anticipate a new generation of customers: Plainsville's schoolchildren are required to participate in a program called Fitness for Life, which emphasizes the benefits of regular exercise at an early age."*

*Write a response in which you discuss what specific evidence is needed to evaluate the argument and explain how the evidence would weaken or strengthen the argument.*

You may start writing your response here

# Section 2 – Verbal Reasoning

20 questions | 30 mins

---

**For Questions 1 and 2, for each blank, select one entry from the corresponding column of choices. Fill all blanks in the way that best completes the text.**

1. __________ forensic scientist understands that the Hollywood interpretation of their field deliberately plays up the sensationalist aspects, and that such an approach is not applicable in reality.

| A judicious |
|---|
| A despondent |
| An imprudent |
| An asinine |
| A daft |

2. Researchers at the University of Michigan have developed a means of focusing high–pressure sound waves into a type of "invisible knife," which can be used to perform  surgery for conditions such as kidney stones and small tumors, allowing for surgery that requires no external wound care and limited risk of infection.

| unobtrusive |
|---|
| impertinent |
| extraneous |
| noninvasive |
| integral |

**For Questions 3 and 4, select the two answer choices that, when used to complete the sentence, fit the meaning of the sentence as a whole and produce completed sentences that are alike in meaning.**

3. Out of fear of __________ business growth — and a desire to remain competitive in a ferocious global marketplace—some nations decide to enact low business tax rates to encourage new investment and to incentivize existing foreign businesses to move their headquarters from their home countries to within their nations' borders.

   A promulgating

   B restricting

   C obstructing

   D averring

   E congealing

   F glowering

4. The pace of the game had slowed to a crawl so when the ________ of an intercepted pass unexpectedly broke the monotony, the lethargic crowd, even those cheering for the losing team, burst into raucous applause.

[A] frisson

[B] immediacy

[C] thrill

[D] folly

[E] rapidity

[F] arrogance

**Questions 5 and 6 are based on the following passage.**

In the first narrative of my experience in slavery, written nearly forty years ago, and in various writings since, I have given the public what I considered very good reasons for withholding the manner of my escape. In substance these reasons were, first, that such publication at any time during the existence of slavery might be used by the master against the slave, and prevent the future escape of any who might adopt the same means that I did. The second reason was, if possible, still more binding to silence: the publication of details would certainly have put in peril the persons and property of those who assisted. The abolition of slavery in my native State and throughout the country, and the lapse of time, render the caution hitherto observed no longer necessary. But even since the abolition of slavery, I have sometimes thought it well enough to baffle curiosity by saying that while slavery existed there were good reasons for not telling the manner of my escape, and since slavery had ceased to exist, there was no reason for telling it. I shall now, however, cease to avail myself of this formula, and, as far as I can, endeavor to satisfy this very natural curiosity. I should, perhaps, have yielded to that feeling sooner, had there been anything very heroic or thrilling in the incidents connected with my escape, for I am sorry to say I have nothing of that sort to tell; and yet the courage that could risk betrayal and the bravery which was ready to encounter death, if need be, in pursuit of freedom, were essential features in the undertaking. My success was due to address rather than courage, to good luck rather than bravery.

**For Questions 5 and 6, select only one answer choice.**

5. Which of the following most closely identifies the author's tone in this passage?

(A) pessimistic

(B) optimistic

(C) apologetic

(D) sarcastic

(E) self–effacing

6. What genre of writing is represented by this passage?

(A) biography

(B) autobiography

(C) journalism

(D) editorial

(E) historical fiction

**For Questions 7 and 8, select the two answer choices that, when used to complete the sentence, fit the meaning of the sentence as a whole and produce completed sentences that are alike in meaning.**

7. Many scholars read ancient legal documents not because they want to adopt those antiquated judicial constructions directly into modern law, but rather because they want to glean the _______ properties of the works.

[A] didactic

[B] infallible

[C] educational

[D] argumentative

[E] vituperative

[F] preposterous

8. There has never been a consensus on what constitutes "good" writing and that would explain the _______ of written works.

[A] incisiveness

[B] plethora

[C] disparity

[D] visibility

[E] multiplicity

[F] incoherence

**Questions 9 and 10 are based on the following passage.**

In consequence of this point of view the Roman government first came to deal with denial of the gods as a breach of law when confronted with the two monotheistic religions which invaded the Empire from the East. That which distinguished Jews and Christians from Pagans was not that they denied the existence of the Pagan gods—the Christians, at any rate, did not do this as a rule—but that they denied that they were gods, and therefore refused to worship them. They were practical, not theoretical deniers. The tolerance which the Roman government showed towards all foreign creeds and the result of which in imperial times was, practically speaking, freedom of religion over the whole Empire, could not be extended to the Jews and the Christians; for it was in the last resort based on reciprocity, on the fact that worship of the Egyptian or Persian gods did not exclude worship of the Roman ones. Every convert, on the other hand, won over to Judaism or Christianity was eo ipso an apostate from the Roman religion, an atheos according to the ancient conception. Hence, as soon as such religions began to spread they constituted a serious danger to the established religion, and the Roman government intervened. Judaism and Christianity were not treated quite alike; in this connexion details are of no interest, but certain principal features must be dwelt on as significant of the attitude of antiquity towards denial of the gods. To simplify matters I confine myself to Christianity, where things are less complicated.

**Consider each of the three choices separately and select all that apply.**

9. Which of the following statements is likely to be true of the Roman empire in the period prior to that described in the passage?

[A] Laws concerning denial of the gods were unnecessary.

[B] Monotheistic religions did not exist to the West of Rome.

[C] Neither the Romans nor the adherents of other pagan religions actively sought converts.

**Select only one answer choice.**

10. What function does the highlighted sentence serve in this passage?

(A) It predicts the content of the successive text.

(B) It reveals the author's attitude toward the Christians' activities during the time of the Roman Empire.

(C) It prepares the reader for a discussion of the contrasts between the behavior of the Jews and the Christians.

(D) It prevents the reader from developing high expectations from the writing to follow.

(E) It reveals the author's greater familiarity with Christianity as opposed to Judaism.

**For Questions 11 and 12, for each blank, select one entry from the corresponding column of choices. Fill all blanks in the way that best completes the text.**

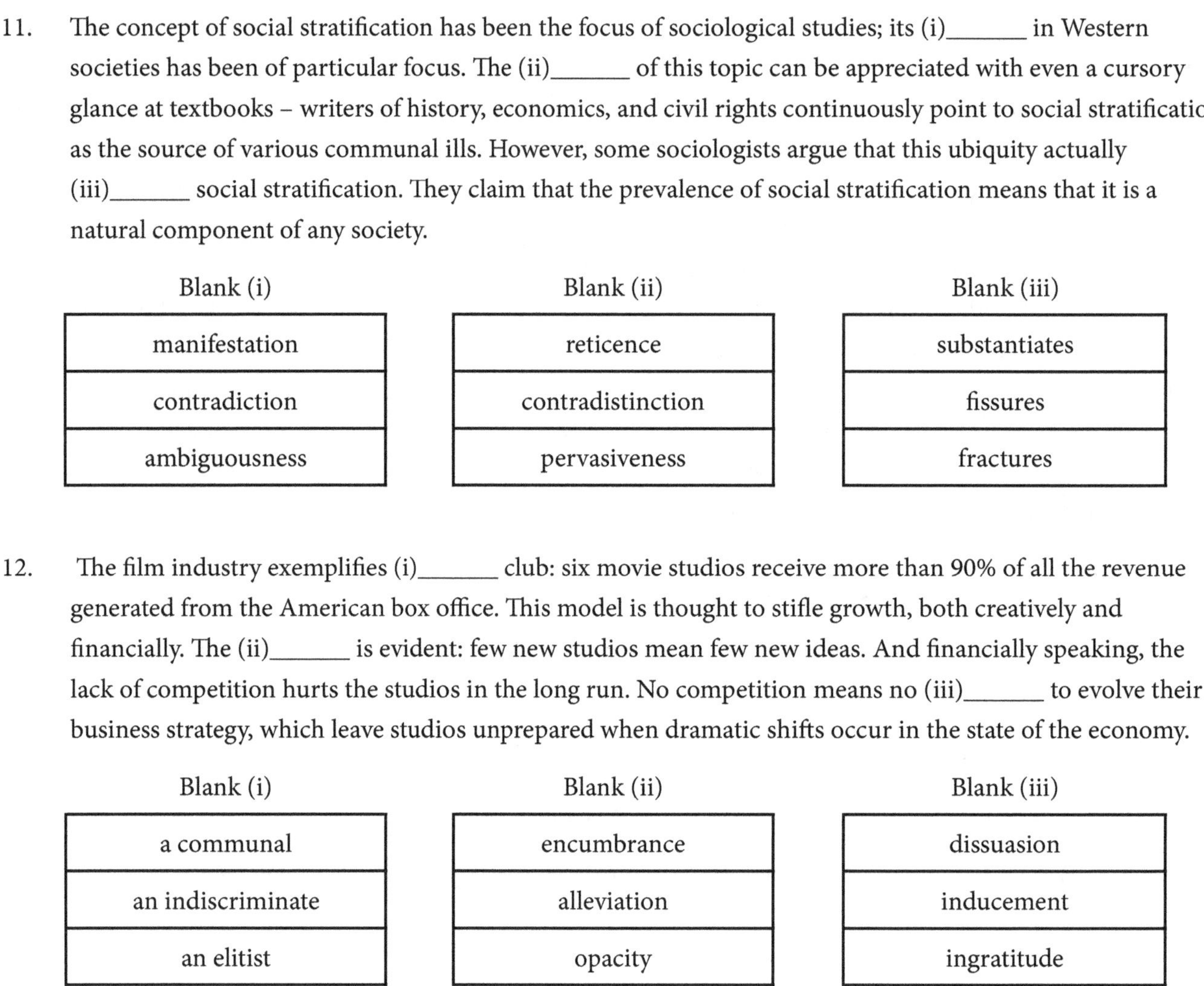

11. The concept of social stratification has been the focus of sociological studies; its (i)______ in Western societies has been of particular focus. The (ii)______ of this topic can be appreciated with even a cursory glance at textbooks – writers of history, economics, and civil rights continuously point to social stratification as the source of various communal ills. However, some sociologists argue that this ubiquity actually (iii)______ social stratification. They claim that the prevalence of social stratification means that it is a natural component of any society.

| Blank (i) | Blank (ii) | Blank (iii) |
|---|---|---|
| manifestation | reticence | substantiates |
| contradiction | contradistinction | fissures |
| ambiguousness | pervasiveness | fractures |

12. The film industry exemplifies (i)______ club: six movie studios receive more than 90% of all the revenue generated from the American box office. This model is thought to stifle growth, both creatively and financially. The (ii)______ is evident: few new studios mean few new ideas. And financially speaking, the lack of competition hurts the studios in the long run. No competition means no (iii)______ to evolve their business strategy, which leave studios unprepared when dramatic shifts occur in the state of the economy.

| Blank (i) | Blank (ii) | Blank (iii) |
|---|---|---|
| a communal | encumbrance | dissuasion |
| an indiscriminate | alleviation | inducement |
| an elitist | opacity | ingratitude |

**Questions 13 to 15 are based on the following passage.**

Perhaps the most celebrated turning–point recorded in history was the crossing of the Rubicon. Suetonius says, “Coming up with his troops on the banks of the Rubicon, he halted for a while, and, revolving in his mind the importance of the step he was on the point of taking, he turned to those about him and said, "We may still retreat; but if we pass this little bridge, nothing is left for us but to fight it out in arms."

This was a stupendously important moment. And all the incidents, big and little, of Caesar's previous life had been leading up to it, stage by stage, link by link. This was the last link—merely the last one, and no bigger than the others; but as we gaze back at it through the inflating mists of our imagination, it looks as big as the orbit of Neptune.

You, the reader, have a personal interest in that link, and so have I; so has the rest of the human race. It was one of the links in your life–chain, and it was one of the links in mine. We may wait, now, with bated breath, while Caesar reflects. Your fate and mine are involved in his decision.

While he was thus hesitating, the following incident occurred. A person remarked for his noble mien and graceful aspect appeared close at hand, sitting and playing upon a pipe. When not only the shepherds, but a number of soldiers also, flocked to listen to him, and some trumpeters among them, he snatched a trumpet from one of them, ran to the river with it, and, sounding the advance with a piercing blast, crossed to the other side. Upon this,

Caesar exclaimed: "Let us go whither the omens of the gods and the iniquity of our enemies call us. THE DIE IS CAST.

So he crossed—and changed the future of the whole human race, for all time. But that stranger was a link in Caesar's life–chain, too; and a necessary one. We don't know his name, we never hear of him again; he was very casual; he acts like an accident; but he was no accident, he was there by compulsion of HIS life–chain, to blow the electrifying blast that was to make up Caesar's mind for him, and thence go piping down the aisles of history forever."

"If the stranger hadn't been there! But he WAS. And Caesar crossed. With such results! Such vast events—each a link in the HUMAN RACE'S life–chain; each event producing the next one, and that one the next one, and so on: the destruction of the republic; the founding of the empire; the breaking up of the empire; the rise of Christianity upon its ruins; the spread of the religion to other lands—and so on; link by link took its appointed place at its appointed time, the discovery of America being one of them; our Revolution another; the inflow of English and other immigrants another; their drift westward (my ancestors among them) another; the settlement of certain of them in Missouri, which resulted in ME.

13. Select the sentence in the passage that the author uses to creates tension in the mind of the reader.

**For Questions 14 and 15, select only one answer choice.**

14. The author has included the account of Caesar's crossing the Rubicon for which of the following purposes?

Ⓐ To illuminate an important event in ancient history.

Ⓑ To compare it to a life–changing event in his own life.

Ⓒ To provide an example in support of his thesis.

Ⓓ To demonstrate how Caesar's actions changed the course of history.

Ⓔ To introduce the reader to the man who actually blew the call to arms.

15. Which choice is the most logical conclusion based on the highlighted portion in the passage?

Ⓐ The pipe player planned to be at that place at that time in order to blow the trumpet.

Ⓑ The gods had called the pipe player to be in that place at that time.

Ⓒ None of the events in a person's life occur by chance.

Ⓓ All of the events in a person's life occur by chance.

Ⓔ People are the masters of their own destinies.

**Question 16 is based on the following passage.**

Candy's Chocolate Shoppe has stores in several malls throughout the state. Sales have increased every year. Her best–selling item is a chocolate–covered cream flavored with locally produced maple syrup. Candy has recently contracted to open stores in two malls in another state next year. She plans to feature the chocolate–covered maple cream and has placed a large order for future delivery to her new stores. She predicts that the popular candy will generate significant sales and profits in these stores.

**Select only one answer choice.**

16. Which of the following conditions could undermine Candy's prediction of sales and profits in her new stores?

- (A) Her lease agreement requires her to pay a percentage of her sales to the mall management.
- (B) These malls have other candy stores that feature their own locally–sourced specialty items.
- (C) The new malls have 20 more stores than the malls where she currently has shops.
- (D) The weather conditions this past spring were not favorable for sap production in the maple trees.
- (E) The unemployment rate in the state where her new stores will be located is lower than the national average.

**For Questions 17 and 18, select the two answer choices that, when used to complete the sentence, fit the meaning of the sentence as a whole and produce completed sentences that are alike in meaning.**

17. Even comparing such extremes as residents of mountains of Tenochtitlan with the aborigines of Australia, it is notable how even in spite of__________ appearances and customs, people the world over have tremendous similarities.

- [A] disparate
- [B] concurrent
- [C] idyllic
- [D] dissimilar
- [E] uniform
- [F] familiar

18. Even though the other members of the board saw the future of the corporation being predicated on raw sales, he knew that the sales themselves were predicated on more human intra–office endeavors such as a quality working _________ between employees.

A turbidity

B condescension

C relationship

D rapport

E despair

F synecdoche

**Questions 19 and 20 are based on the following passage.**

That is the essential. That is the stern condition laid upon all artists touching this luxury of fear. The terror must be fundamentally frivolous. Sanity may play with insanity; but insanity must not be allowed to play with sanity. Let such poets as the one I was reading in the garden, by all means, be free to imagine what outrageous deities and violent landscapes they like. By all means let them wander freely amid their opium pinnacles and perspectives. But these huge gods, these high cities, are toys; they must never for an instant be allowed to be anything else. Man, a gigantic child, must play with Babylon and Nineveh, with Isis and with Ashtaroth. By all means let him dream of the Bondage of Egypt, so long as he is free from it. By all means let him take up the Burden of T y re, so long as he can take it lightly. But the old gods must be his dolls, not his idols. His central sanctities, his true possessions, should be Christian and simple. And just as a child would cherish most a wooden horse or a sword that is a mere cross of wood, so man, the great child, must cherish most the old plain things of poetry and piety; that horse of wood that was the epic end of Ilium, or that cross of wood that redeemed and conquered the world.

**For Questions 19 and 20, select only one answer choice.**

19. Which of the following best identifies the author's purpose in this passage?

A To admonish poets about their approach to their subjects

B To praise the ancient poets

C To change the course of poetic thought

D To remind poets to acknowledge their readers

E To establish a set of criteria for writing poetry

20. Based on the information available, what can the reader infer about the function of this passage in the larger context?

(A) It is an introduction.

(B) It is a preface.

(C) It is conclusion.

(D) It is an epilogue.

(E) It is a glossary entry

# Section 3 – Quantitative Reasoning

20 questions | 35 mins

---

1. In a company, there are 2 sections A and B. The average salary of employees of both the sections put together is $14000.The average salary of employees in section A is $12000 and that of Section B is $24000. If there are 66 employees in both the sections put together, find the number of employees in section B.

   (A) 19

   (B) 17

   (C) 15

   (D) 13

   (E) 11

2. Let *M* and *N* be events such that $P(M) = \frac{1}{2}, P(M\ and\ N) = \frac{1}{6}$ and $P(M\ or\ N) = \frac{3}{4}$. Find *P*(*N*).

   (A) $\frac{1}{12}$

   (B) $\frac{1}{4}$

   (C) $\frac{5}{12}$

   (D) $\frac{5}{6}$

   (E) $\frac{1}{2}$

3. A grandmother was thirteen times the age of her granddaughter five years ago. The grandmother will be five times the age of her granddaughter 5 years hence. What is the sum of the present ages of the grandmother and the granddaughter?

   (A) 75

   (B) 80

   (C) 90

   (D) 95

   (E) 100

4.

There are three classes in happy futures school. There are 20 students in the first class with an average age of 17.06; the second class has an average age of 17.50; and there are 20 students in the third class. The average age of the first and third class combined is 17.18. The ratio of students in the first class to students in the second class is 5:6.

| **Quantity A** | **Quantity B** |
|---|---|
| The average age of students in the first and second classes combined | The average age of students in the third class |

(A) Quantity A is greater.

(B) Quantity B is greater.

(C) The two quantities are equal.

(D) The relationship cannot be determined from the information given.

5.

Anna, Beatrice and Charlotte have $2,200 between them. After Anna spends 50% of her money, Beatrice spends 75% of her money and Charlotte spends 80% of hers, they are each left with similar amounts.

| **Quantity A** | **Quantity B** |
|---|---|
| The initial amount of money owned by Beatrice | The amount of money spent by Charlotte |

(A) Quantity A is greater.

(B) Quantity B is greater.

(C) The two quantities are equal.

(D) The relationship cannot be determined from the information given.

6.

1200 kg of apples is purchased for $3000. It is sold in such a way that after selling the whole quantity, the quantum of loss is equal to the amount obtained by selling 300 kg of apples.

| **Quantity A** | **Quantity B** |
|---|---|
| Selling Price per Kg | $1.90 |

(A) Quantity A is greater.

(B) Quantity B is greater.

(C) The two quantities are equal.

(D) The relationship cannot be determined from the information given.

7. A road test was conducted, and results showed that cars fail the test for two reasons: bad brakes or defective lights. The probability of a car failing due to bad brakes is 0.30, while the probability of a car failing due to defective lights is 0.15. Also, the probability of failure due to having defective lights and bad brakes is 0.10. If any random car is tested, what is the probability that it will fail the road test?

   (A) 0.25

   (B) 0.35

   (C) 0.45

   (D) 0.55

   (E) 0.65

8. Rob and Tom drive independently but take the same route every day. The probability that Rob arrives late for work is 0.12, while the probability that Tom arrives late for work is 0.16. Find the probability that at least one of them arrives on time for work on any given day.

   (A) 0.0192

   (B) 0.2416

   (C) 0.7392

   (D) 0.9808

   (E) 0.9982

9.

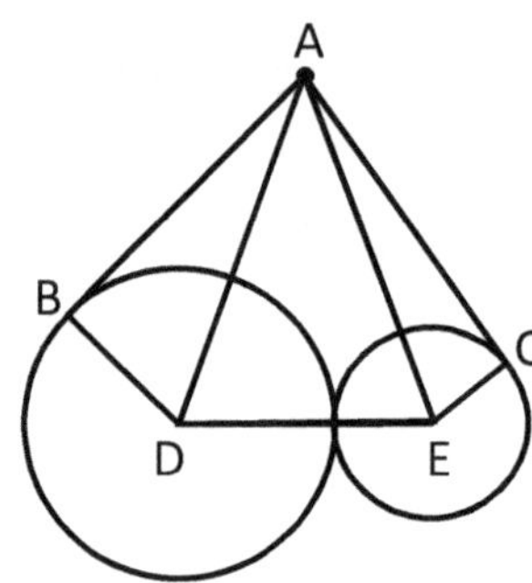


A is a point outside both circles. The two circles touch in one point only. The distance between A and the center of the large circle D is AD = 30. The distance between A and the center of the small circle E is AE = 25. The distance between the two circle's centers is DE = 33. AB is a tangent to the large circle at point B, and AB = 24. AC is a tangent to the small circle at point C. What is the perimeter of ΔACE?(Figure not to scale)

Ⓐ 75

Ⓑ 70

Ⓒ 65

Ⓓ 60

Ⓔ 50

10. From the set of 2–digit positive integers, what is the probability that a number selected at random has 7 in either the units place or tens place?

Ⓐ $\frac{2}{10}$

Ⓑ $\frac{1}{9}$

Ⓒ $\frac{2}{9}$

Ⓓ $\frac{19}{90}$

Ⓔ $\frac{1}{11}$

11. If $0 \le x \le 3$, $3 \le y \le 6$, and $x$ and $y$ are integers, find the probability that $y - x \ge 4$.

(A) $\frac{3}{16}$

(B) $\frac{3}{8}$

(C) $\frac{1}{4}$

(D) $\frac{1}{6}$

(E) $\frac{1}{8}$

12.

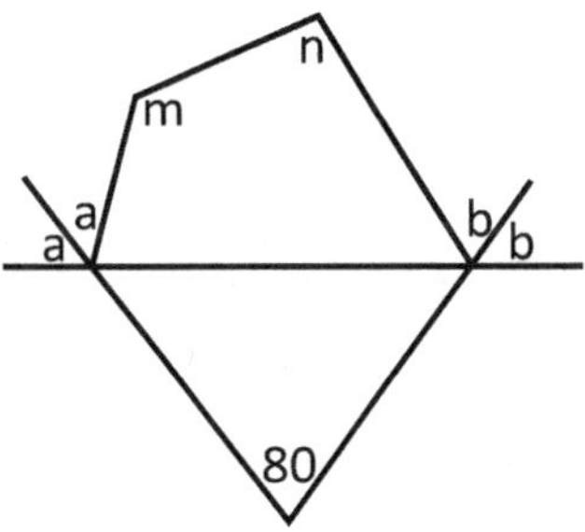


| Quantity A | Quantity B |
| --- | --- |
| $m + n$ | 180 |

(A) Quantity A is greater.

(B) Quantity B is greater.

(C) The two quantities are equal.

(D) The relationship cannot be determined from the information given.

13.

The longer leg of a right-angled triangle is fourteen yards more than the shorter leg. The shorter leg is three yards less than half of the hypotenuse.

| Quantity A | Quantity B |
| --- | --- |
| The length of the hypotenuse. | *28* |

(A) Quantity A is greater.

(B) Quantity B is greater.

(C) The two quantities are equal.

(D) The relationship cannot be determined from the information given.

14.

Solve for $x$ :$4^{2x+6}=8^{6x+12}$

| Quantity A | Quantity B |
|---|---|
| $x$ | -2 |

(A) Quantity A is greater.

(B) Quantity B is greater.

(C) The two quantities are equal.

(D) The relationship cannot be determined from the information given.

15.

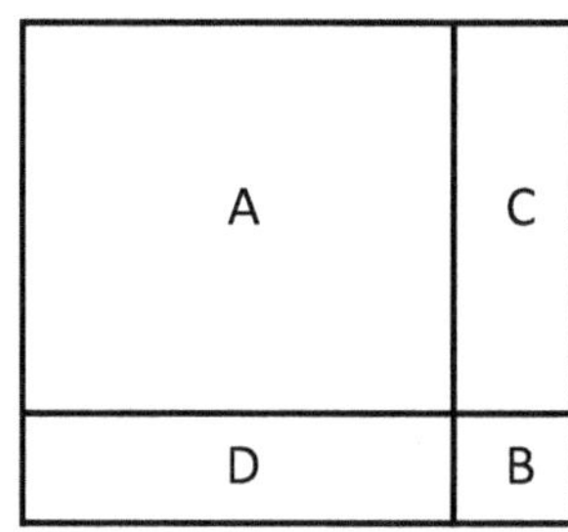


In the given figure areas A and B are squares. The side of the square A is 10 units more than the side of the square B. Sum of the areas of these squares is 625 square units. What is the the sum of the areas of the remaining rectangles C and D?

16. Benjamin invested an amount of $100,000 in a deposit scheme which pays 5% at the end of one year, 10% at the end of two years, and 15% at the end of 3 years. If all the interest payments are reinvested, what would be the amount of interest earned at the end of 3 years?

(A) $30,000

(B) $31,625

(C) $32,825

(D) $36,275

(E) $39,725

17. Peter, a salesman, bought a laptop at $320. While selling the laptop, he offered a 2.5% discount on the marked price. If the discounted price gave him a profit of 21.875%, what was the marked price?

(A) 410

(B) 390

(C) 400

(D) 380

(E) 328

18. A person goes from his company's corporate office to the worksite in three modes. First, he travels 100 km in his car and then 1200 km by airplane and the remaining distance of 300 km by train. If the speed of the airplane is 6 times that of the car and 3 times that of the train, what is the speed of the airplane if it takes 4 hours 30 minutes for the entire journey?

(A) 400 *km/h*

(B) 500 *km/h*

(C) 550 *km/h*

(D) 600 *km/h*

(E) 800 *km/h*

19. The ratio of a to b and c to d and e to f are all equal to 1000. Which of the following ratios is equal to 1000? Indicate all such answers.

[A] $(a+c+e):(f+d+b)$

[B] $(2a+c+e):( b+2d+f)$

[C] $(a-c+e):(b-d+f)$

[D] $(a^3+c+e):(b^3+d+f)$

[E] $(8a-2c-e):(8b-2d-f)$

[F] $(a^2+c^2):(b^2+d^2)$

[G] $(a^2+2c^2):(b^2+4d^2)$

20. A survey of 100 individuals revealed that 96% are actively using Instagram and 85% are active on their Pinterest accounts. If 83% of the surveyed individuals have both Instagram and Pinterest accounts, what percent of these individuals do not use Instagram nor Pinterest?

[ ] %

# Section 4 – Verbal Reasoning

20 questions | 30 mins

---

**For Questions 1 and 2, select one entry for the blank. Fill the blank in the way that best completes the text.**

1. Predicting which way a body should move when acted on by outside forces sounds easy, but the ________ way in which these forces often act makes the process significantly more challenging.

| unequivocal |
|---|
| callow |
| tepid |
| disparate |
| engorged |

2. What we understand about physics on planet Earth can only be applied ________ to distant galaxies – it would be foolish to assume that physical phenomena manifest uniformly across the universe.

| torpidly |
|---|
| dogmatically |
| rancorously |
| assiduously |
| maladroitly |

**For Questions 3 and 4, select the <u>two</u> answer choices that, when used to complete the sentence, fit the meaning of the sentence as a whole <u>and</u> produce completed sentences that are alike in meaning.**

3. Because of the prevalence of the Medieval theory of "spontaneous generation," Darwin's attempt to modernize the alternate "descent with modification" theory had to endure years of ________ before the scientific community would warm to it.

[A] contempt

[B] derision

[C] companionship

[D] competition

[E] egotism

[F] relief

4. The invention and adoption of Magnetic Resonance Imaging in delineating the soft tissues of the heart and brain have made ________ the high quality spatial resolution maps that only a few years ago seemed unattainable.

- [A] ubiquitous
- [B] inconceivable
- [C] relatable
- [D] prevalent
- [E] extreme
- [F] essential

**Questions 5 to 8 are based on the following passage.**

The notion that people can increase self–discipline and decrease fear in the face of adversity by making a small mental change seems like an idea that would make us more positive when we consider the capacity of what we are able to do. However, personal beliefs and self–image, especially in regards to creating lasting changes and improvements, often hold people back. Psychologists who specialise in human development have demonstrated that people who believe certain traits to be unchangeable are more likely to worry about failure and react negatively to critique, which hinders their chances for success. Taking the approach that personal character traits can be altered and improved, however, allows a person to more effectively push beyond his or her existing limitations in order to acquire new abilities.

Recent studies have shown that academic performance and attendance can be improved by helping students understand that intelligence is malleable and persistence is beneficial. Furthermore, these studies also demonstrate that fear does not necessarily reflect weakness or a low level of intellect. Researchers who have studied this subject say that having a mindset that focuses on growth and expansion is beneficial in all areas of life because it allows people to tackle more challenges without giving up.

**For Questions 5 and 6, select only one answer choice.**

5. In regards to the power of perception on one's own mindset and the effect that this view has on the overall outcome of success, the overriding message of this passage is that

- (A) Innate intelligence is an important factor in determining how successful a person will be in life.
- (B) The inability to adapt to new and difficult situations is due to deep–rooted beliefs.
- (C) When a person believes that he or she is skilled in an area of expertise, he or she will be able to handle challenges that may arise, as long as they fall within the boundaries of his or her skill set.
- (D) A constant feeling of struggle and difficulty is often a sign that a person is not employing his or her strongest skills.
- (E) People are born with certain weaknesses and strengths that indicate how they should focus their efforts in order to be successful.

6. What is the function of the highlighted sentence in the passage?

   (A) It explains the detrimental effects that adversity can have on a person's progress towards goals, even if it temporarily makes them more optimistic.

   (B) It defines a hypothetical ideal which serves to contrast the reality of the behavior that most people tend to exhibit.

   (C) It sets up the idea that people can approach obstacles in different ways that can either improve or decrease self–confidence and motivation.

   (D) It introduces the idea that knowledge about how to increase willpower is beneficial for becoming a stronger person.

   (E) It demonstrates the ever–changing nature of human abilities, especially when confronted with difficult or trying situations.

**Consider each of the three choices separately and select all that apply.**

7. The author's attitude towards the power that people tend to have over their own mind and abilities could best be described as

   [A] impartial

   [B] pragmatic

   [C] scientific

8. Select the sentence from the passage which best strengthens the argument that intelligent people will make little progress towards their goal if they think that they are only as good as their current situation allows.

**Questions 9 to 12 are based on the following passage.**

The writer was practising his profession in the city of Albany, his native place, in 1848, when reports came of the discovery of gold in California. In a short time, samples of scales of the metal of the river diggings were on exhibition, sent to friends in the city in letters. Many of Colonel Stevenson's regiment had been recruited in that city. Soon these rumors were exaggerated. It was said that barrels of gold were dug by individuals named. Soon the excitement extended all over the country, and the only barrier to wealth, it seemed, was the difficulty of getting to the Eldorado. Why the discovery of gold there should have produced so much excitement cannot be fathomed. It seemed an era in human affairs, like the Crusades and other events of great importance that occur. Your correspondent became one of its votaries, and organized a company to go to the gold rivers and secure a fortune for all interested in it, and it seemed all that was required was to get there and return in a short time and ride in your carriage and astonish your friends with your riches. Suffice it to say, this company was fully organized (with its by–laws and system of government drawn up by the writer), and sailed from the port of New York on the ship Tarrolinter on the 13th of January, 1849, to go around Cape Horn, arriving in San Francisco on the following July. From that time I became absorbed in all the news from the gold regions, and losing confidence somewhat in the certainty of a fortune from my interest in the company, and reading of the high price of lumber, the scarcity of houses, and the extraordinary high wages of mechanics there, conceived the project of shipping the materials for some houses there, having all the work put on them here that could be done, thus saving the difference in wages, and to have them arrive there before the rainy season set in, and thus realize the imaginary fortune that I had expected from my interest in the company. In the following spring I had twelve houses constructed. The main point upon which my speculation seemed to rest was to get them to San Francisco before the rainy season commenced. I went to New York to secure freight for them in the fastest vessel. Fortunately for me, as I conceived at the time, I found the day before I arrived in New York, the Prince de Joinville, a Havre packet ship, had been put up to sail for the port of San Francisco, and as yet had engaged no freight. I made a bargain with them at once to take my houses at sixty cents per square foot, and had the contract signed, half to be delivered at the side of the ship by such a date and the other half at a subsequent date. I delivered the first half of the houses on the time agreed, sending them down the Hudson River by a barge on a tow. I sent the second half on a barge to get there on the day they were due, apprehending no trouble, I going down myself a few days in advance. They commenced complaining at the ship that they would not have room for the balance of my houses on board, although I had their written contract to take them at sixty cents per foot.

There was great California excitement about this time, and other parties had come to the conclusion that the Prince de Joinville was probably the fastest ship taking freight for San Francisco. I saw them accept of offers at $1.50 per foot, when their contract with me was for less than half that price, which would make a difference of several thousand dollars in their favor. So, if the balance of my houses did not arrive within the time stated in the contract, they would not be taken on that vessel, and my speculation ruined. The time was up the next day at twelve o'clock. I was down on the Battery the next morning early watching for the tow, with the barge with my houses. The ship was at the dock in the East river. About ten o'clock, A.M., I had the good fortune to see the barge rounding the Battery. I cried out to the captain to cut loose from the tow, employ the first steam tug and I would pay the bill, which he did, getting on the side of the vessel by eleven o'clock, thus saving my contract by one hour. But they did not commence taking them on board, so the captain of the barge put a demurrage of $20 per day for detention. In the meantime, I had bought my ticket to sail by the steamer Georgia to the Isthmus to go on the 1st of July which was but a few days off. They, seeing that I had them on my contract, came to me and said that my houses should go on their ship according to contract, if they had to throw other freight out, and that they would sign a regular bill of lading for all the material deliverable to me upon the arrival of the Prince de Joinville at the port of San Francisco, and take my carpenters' specifications for the description of them, which seemed all right to me.

9. Select the sentence in the second paragraph that explains the writer's change from a matter–of–fact tone in the beginning of the passage to one of anxiety or urgency in the second paragraph.

**For Questions 10 and 11, consider each of the three choices separately and select all that apply.**

10. Which of the following familiar adages might apply to the actions described by the writer in the highlighted portion of the first paragraph?

A Don't put all of your eggs in one basket.

B Make sure to cover all the bases.

C Hedge your bets.

11. For which of the following purposes does the author mention the Crusades in the first paragraph?

- [A] As a point of comparison for the fervor displayed by those leaving for the gold fields in California.
- [B] As a point of comparison for the length of the journey the prospective miners must complete.
- [C] As a point of comparison for seeking the Holy Grail.

**Select only one answer choice.**

12. In the context of this passage, which of the following is the best definition of "votary" as it appears in the first paragraph?

- (A) A person bound by solemn vows
- (B) An adherent of a religion or cult
- (C) The worshiper of a particular deity
- (D) A person devoted or addicted to some subject or pursuit
- (E) A devoted follower or admirer

**For Questions 13 to 15, for each blank, select one entry from the corresponding column of choices. Fill all blanks in the way that best completes the text.**

13. Political science, like the entire field of social science, faces challenges in conducting accurate studies. Unlike the physical or natural sciences, which are focused on (i)______ observations, political science must deal with the biases of the human mind. These inconsistencies have lead political scientists to (ii)______ their research approaches in order to mitigate the shortcomings of any one approach. In spite of these obstacles, the field of political science has (iii)______ significantly in recent years.

| Blank (i) | Blank (ii) | Blank (iii) |
|---|---|---|
| dispassionate | coalesce | regressed |
| preconceived | inundate | proliferated |
| psychological | diversify | fulminated |

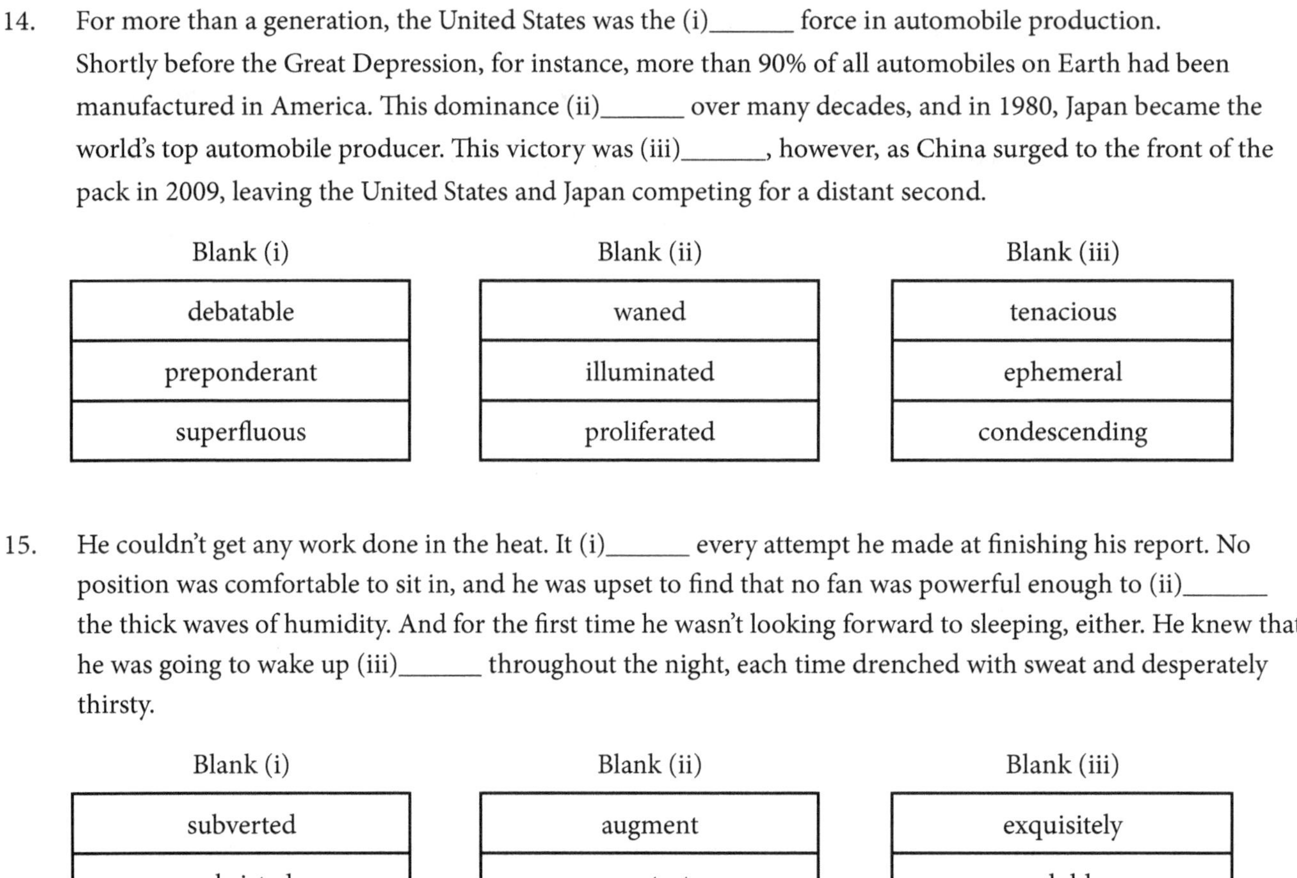

14. For more than a generation, the United States was the (i)______ force in automobile production. Shortly before the Great Depression, for instance, more than 90% of all automobiles on Earth had been manufactured in America. This dominance (ii)______ over many decades, and in 1980, Japan became the world's top automobile producer. This victory was (iii)______, however, as China surged to the front of the pack in 2009, leaving the United States and Japan competing for a distant second.

| Blank (i) | Blank (ii) | Blank (iii) |
|---|---|---|
| debatable | waned | tenacious |
| preponderant | illuminated | ephemeral |
| superfluous | proliferated | condescending |

15. He couldn't get any work done in the heat. It (i)______ every attempt he made at finishing his report. No position was comfortable to sit in, and he was upset to find that no fan was powerful enough to (ii)______ the thick waves of humidity. And for the first time he wasn't looking forward to sleeping, either. He knew that he was going to wake up (iii)______ throughout the night, each time drenched with sweat and desperately thirsty.

| Blank (i) | Blank (ii) | Blank (iii) |
|---|---|---|
| subverted | augment | exquisitely |
| subsisted | penetrate | volubly |
| sanctioned | succor | sporadically |

**Question 16 is based on the following passage.**

In the jungles of India, which preserve a state of things which has existed for immemorial years, lives the tiger, his stripes simulating jungle reeds, his noiseless approach learnt from nature in countless millions of lessons of success and failure, his perfectly powerful claws and execution methods; and, living in the same jungle, and with him as one of the conditions of life, are small deer, alert, swift, light of build, inconspicuous of color, sharp of hearing, keen-eyed, keen-scented-- because any downward variation from these attributes means swift and certain death. To capture the deer is a condition, of the tiger's life, to escape the tiger a condition of the deer's; and they play a great contest under these conditions, with life as the stake. The most alert deer almost always escape.

**Consider each of the three choices separately and select all that apply.**

16. Which of the following events would cause the greatest decline in the number of tigers in the jungles of India?

   A An increase in rain that causes jungle reeds to flourish

   B Destruction of the food source for the deer

   C A mutation increasing the deer's ability to see colors

   D An increase in eco-tourism attracting more people to watch the animals

   E The addition of an invasive new species of deer

**For each blank, select one entry from the corresponding column of choices. Fill all blanks in the way that best completes the text.**

17. There is an immense (i)_______ in the amount of worrying that parents do over violence in their children's movies. They (ii)_______ the use of explicit violence in modern cinema, yet never seem to turn a critical eye towards the movies of their day. The violence may have not been explicit, but it was still there. In many ways it was worse, because this violence was so (iii)_______ that it made cruel acts seem part of everyday life.

| Blank (i) | Blank (ii) | Blank (iii) |
|---|---|---|
| prosperity | authenticate | incisive |
| irony | theorize | gracious |
| singularity | disparage | blasé |

**For Questions 18 and 19, select the two answer choices that, when used to complete the sentence, fit the meaning of the sentence as a whole and produce completed sentences that are alike in meaning.**

18. The two defendants decided to reconceive and re-synthesize their respective stories in light of a growing feeling that their two ________ explanations of what happened the night of the crime would arouse the suspicions of the jury.

   A hilarious

   B harmonious

   C discordant

   D incongruous

   E syphoned

   F dastardly

19. When the particular epoch and theoretical structure of two disparate genres of music are thrown away and all that is considered is the emotional import of the material, one finds that any two genres of music have made essentially ________ contributions to the elevation of the human emotional state.

- [A] fungible
- [B] unequal
- [C] confusing
- [D] unnecessary
- [E] interchangeable
- [F] enlightening

**Question 20 is based on the following passage.**

Let us notice the critical instinct which he brought to the task of creation. His theory of verse is simple, in fact too simple to account for all of the facts. The aim of poetry, according to Poe, is not truth but pleasure—the rhythmical creation of beauty. Poetry should be brief, indefinite, and musical. Its chief instrument is sound. A certain quaintness or grotesqueness of tone is a means for satisfying the thirst for supernal beauty. Hence the musical lyric is to Poe the only true type of poetry; a long poem does not exist. Readers who respond more readily to auditory than to visual or motor stimulus are therefore Poe's chosen audience. For them he executes, like Paganini, marvels upon his single string. He has easily recognizable devices: the dominant note, the refrain, the "repetend," that is to say the phrase which echoes, with some variation, a phrase or line already used. In such poems as "To Helen," "Israfel," "The Haunted Palace," "Annabel Lee," the theme, the tone, the melody all weave their magic spell; it is like listening to a lute–player in a dream.

**Select only one answer choice.**

20. Which of the following is the most appropriate definition of "supernal" as it is used in this passage?

- (A) superior
- (B) celestial
- (C) supernatural
- (D) physical
- (E) natural

# Section 5 – Quantitative Reasoning

20 questions | 35 mins

1. The price of a pen is increased by 20% while the price of a pencil is deceased by 10%. If the pen cost twice as much as the pencil before the changes in price, what is the ratio of the new price of the pen to that of the pencil?

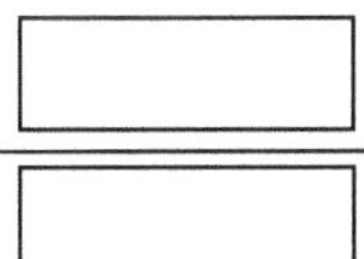

2.

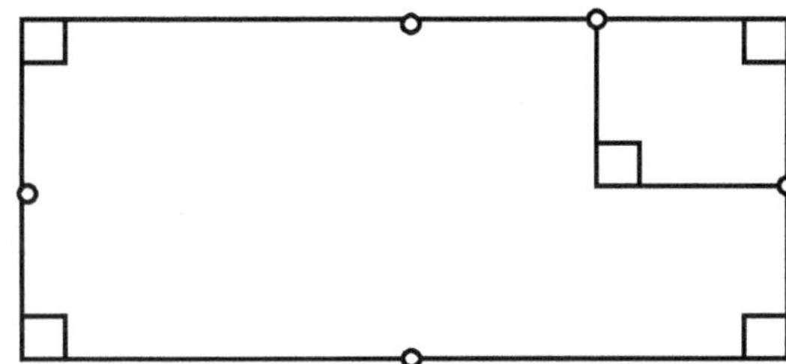

Length of the rectangle is as twice as its width, and the measure of one side of the square is as one half as the width of the rectangle. The perimeter of the square is 8.

| Quantity A | Quantity B |
|---|---|
| Area of Rectangle | 32 |

(A) Quantity A is greater.

(B) Quantity B is greater.

(C) The two quantities are equal.

(D) The relationship cannot be determined from the information given.

3.

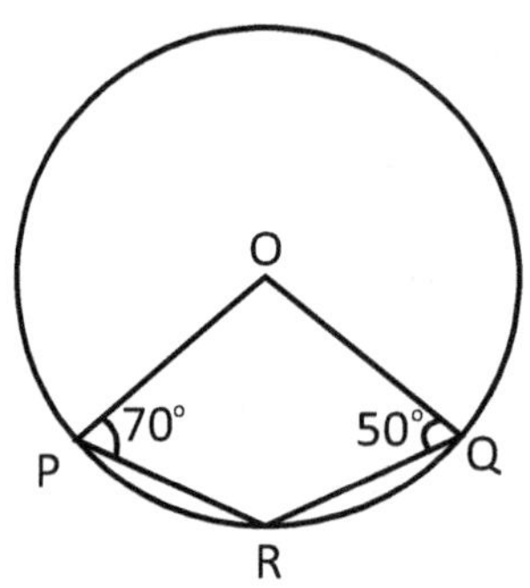


In the above figure, *O* is the center of the circle and $\angle OPR=70^0$ AND $\angle OQR=50^0$

| **Quantity A** | **Quantity B** |
|---|---|
| *Reflex angle ∠POQ* | $240^0$ |

(A) Quantity A is greater.

(B) Quantity B is greater.

(C) The two quantities are equal.

(D) The relationship cannot be determined from the information given.

4.

*632X* is a positive integer divisible by 3, where *X* is a digit. *X7X* is a positive integer divisible by 9, where *X* is the same digit as in *632X*.

| **Quantity A** | **Quantity B** |
|---|---|
| The least common multiple of integers *X5* and *2X* | The greatest common factor of integers *5X* and *X02* |

(A) Quantity A is greater.

(B) Quantity B is greater.

(C) The two quantities are equal.

(D) The relationship cannot be determined from the information given.

5.

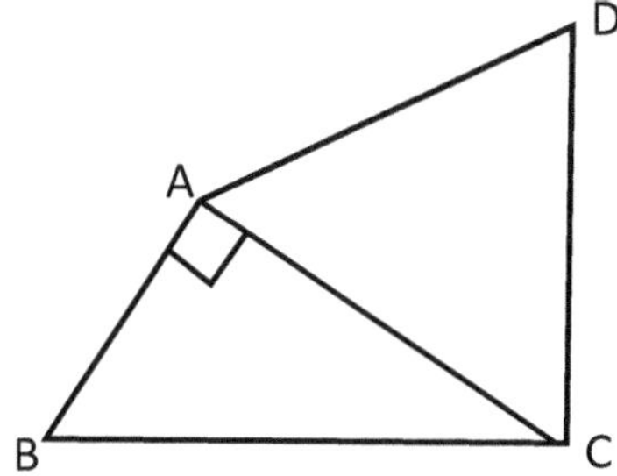


In $\Delta ABC$, $m\angle BAC = 90°$ and $m\angle ACB = 30°$. $\Delta ADC$ is equilateral. (figure not to scale)

| **Quantity A** | **Quantity B** |
|---|---|
| Area of $\Delta ABC$ | Area of $\Delta ADC$ |

(A) Quantity A is greater.

(B) Quantity B is greater.

(C) The two quantities are equal.

(D) The relationship cannot be determined from the information given.

6. Identify the number with the lowest value among the following if a is between 0 and 1.

(A) $10a$

(B) $100a$

(C) $\frac{10}{a}$

(D) $\frac{11}{a}$

(E) $10a^2$

7. Determine the interest rate of the bank if $2,250 is realized from a deposit of $1,500 after 5 years, if it earned simple interest at a rate calculated semi annually.

(A) 2.5%

(B) 10%

(C) 5%

(D) 3.3%

(E) 6.7%

8. Albert rides his bicycle a certain distance at a speed of m miles per hour. His friend walks one-third the distance ( that Albert covers) in six times the length of the time that Albert takes. What is his friend's speed?

Ⓐ $m/3$

Ⓑ $3m$

Ⓒ $m/6$

Ⓓ $18m$

Ⓔ $m/18$

9. Two six–sided dice are rolled. Which of the following events will have a probability of less than $\frac{1}{2}$?

Select all such probabilities.

[A] At least one even number shows up

[B] 3 and another odd number show up

[C] The first die rolled is greater than 3

[D] The sum of the two numbers showing up is less than or equal to 6

10.

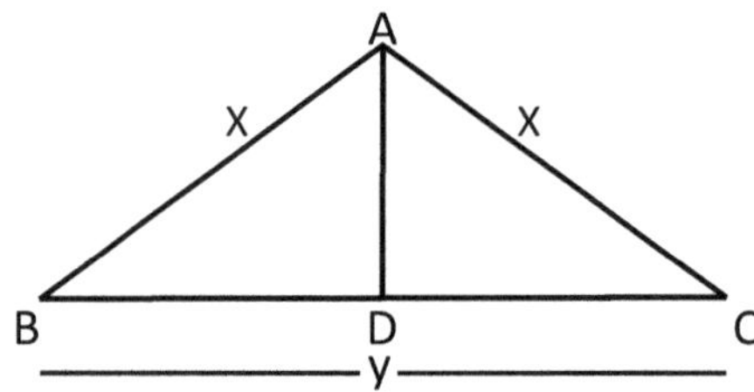


In the following diagram, ABC is an isosceles triangle with AB=AC=x units.

BC= y units. AD is a median.

For triangle ABC which of the following statements must be true? Indicate all such statements.

[A] $y/2<x$

[B] $\angle ABC=\angle BAC$

[C] $\angle ADC$ is a right angle

[D] $\angle BAD=\angle CAD$

[E] $y^2=2x^2$

[F] $2AD>\sqrt{}(4x^2-y^2)$

**For questions 11 and 12, refer to the following bar graph and answer.**

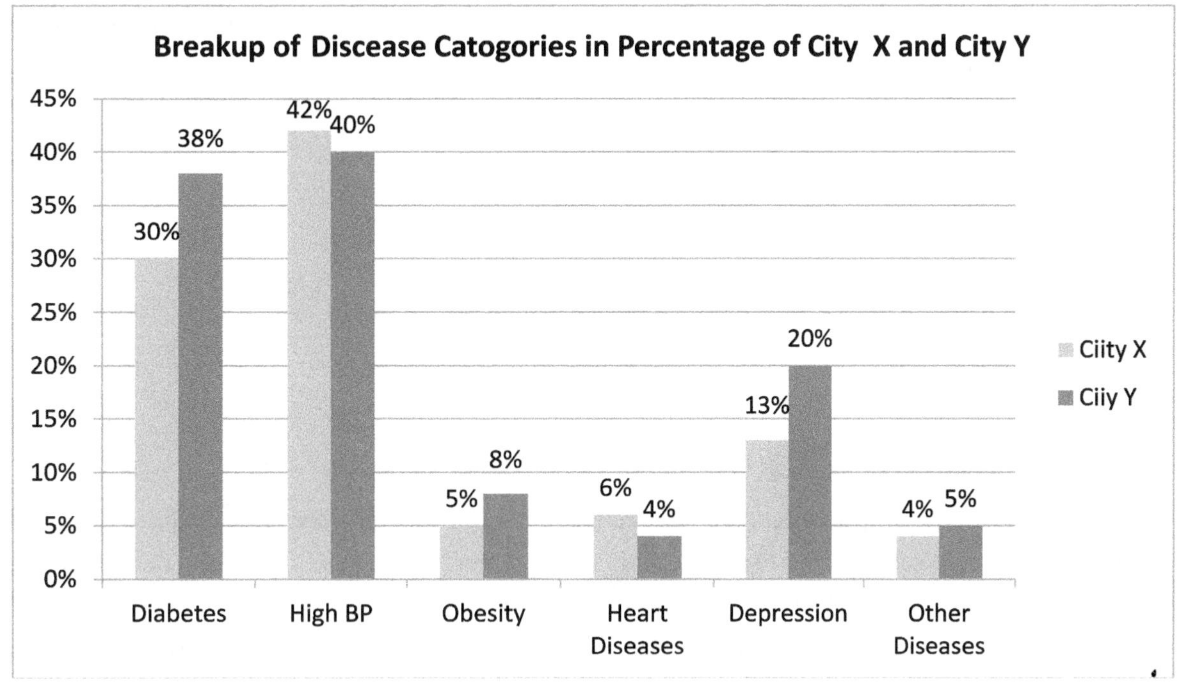


11.

| <u>Quantity A</u> | <u>Quantity B</u> |
|---|---|
| Number of persons with high BP in city *X* | Number of persons with high BP in city *Y* |

(A) Quantity A is greater.

(B) Quantity B is greater.

(C) The two quantities are equal.

(D) The relationship cannot be determined from the information given.

12. From the the above graph it can be inferred

(A) There is a possibility of persons who have multiple diseases in city X.

(B) There is a possibility of persons who have multiple diseases in city Y.

(C) There is a possibility of persons who have multiple diseases in both cities X and Y.

(D) There is a possibility of persons who have no multiple diseases in both cities X and Y.

(E) No inference can be drawn about the possibility of multiple diseases from the given data.

13. A certain gas station's beverage sales constitute 8% of their total profit that quarter. The beverage coolers were extended and a new walk-in cooler was installed. During the next quarter, assume beverage sales double while all other categories are stagnant. What percent of the new quarter's profits does the beverages section represent?

(A) 0%

(B) 8.8%

(C) 10.3%

(D) 14.8%

(E) 16%

14. The company that owns the gas station is conducting market research to determine the feasibility of adding a "made to order" selection at this location. Of the 1,500 individuals surveyed, 54% said they would take advantage of this service on their way to work, 41% said they would take advantage of this service on their way home from work, and 38% said this service does not interest them. How many individuals reported that they would use this service both before and after work?

(A) 300

(B) 400

(C) 500

(D) 600

(E) Not enough information

15. The product of two different non–negative integers less than 10 is the square of another integer less than 10. The difference of these numbers is 6. Which is the larger number?

[ ]

16.

If 8y–4x=5. and y>800.

| **Quantity A** | **Quantity B** |
|---|---|
| The least integer value of $x$ | 1600 |

- (A) Quantity A is greater.
- (B) Quantity B is greater.
- (C) The two quantities are equal.
- (D) The relationship cannot be determined from the information given.

17.

Equation 1: $4^x - 4^{3-x} = 12$

Equation 2: $25^{\sqrt{y}} - 6 \times 5^{\sqrt{y}} + 5^{\sqrt{1}} = 0$

| **Quantity A** | **Quantity B** |
|---|---|
| $x$ | $y$ |

- (A) Quantity A is greater.
- (B) Quantity B is greater.
- (C) The two quantities are equal.
- (D) The relationship cannot be determined from the information given.

18. George requires 10 days to completely build a house, while his friend requires 8 days to do the same job. If two masons who work at the same rate as George are allowed to work together with him and his friend, how long will it take them to complete the same job?

- (A) 2.5 days
- (B) 2.4 days
- (C) 9.8 days
- (D) 18 days
- (E) 38 days

19. Carl leaves his house at 6:00 am and drives due west at a speed of 50 mph. Joseph leaves the same house at 7:30 pm and drives due west at a speed of 70 mph. At what time will Joseph have gone exactly 55 miles past Carl?

(A) 11:00 am

(B) 12:00 pm

(C) 1:00 pm

(D) 2:00 pm

(E) 3:00 pm

20.

A cistern has three discharge pipes of differing sizes. When the tank is full, Pipes R and T can empty the cistern in three hours, whereas pipes R and Y can empty the cistern in four hours.

| **Quantity A** | **Quantity B** |
|---|---|
| The length of time it takes Pipe Y to empty the full cistern alone. | The length of time it takes Pipe T to empty the full cistern alone. |

(A) Quantity A is greater.

(B) Quantity B is greater.

(C) The two quantities are equal.

(D) The relationship cannot be determined from the information given.

# Answers Key

## Section 2

1. A judicious
2. D
3. restricting and obstructing
4. frisson and thrill
5. E
6. B
7. didactic and educational
8. disparity and multiplicity
9. A and C
10. A
11. manifestation, pervasiveness, and substantiates
12. elitist, encumbrance, and inducement
13. "We may wait, now, with bated breath, while Caesar reflects."
14. C
15. C
16. D
17. disparate and dissimilar
18. relationship and rapport
19. A
20. C

## Section 3

1. E
2. C
3. B
4. C
5. C
6. A
7. B
8. D
9. D
10. A
11. B
12. B
13. B
14. B
15. 525 square units.
16. C
17. C
18. D
19. A, C and E
20. 2%

## Section 4

1. disparate
2. assiduously
3. contempt and derision
4. ubiquitous and prevalent
5. B
6. B
7. B
8. "Psychologists who specialise in human development have demonstrated that people who believe certain traits to be unchangeable are more likely to worry about failure and react negatively to critique, which hinders their chances for success."
9. "So, if the balance of my houses did not arrive within the time stated in the contract, they would not be taken on that vessel, and my speculation ruined."
10. A, B and C
11. A and B
12. D
13. dispassionate, diversify and proliferated
14. preponderant, waned, and ephemeral
15. subverted, penetrate, and sporadically
16. B
17. irony, disparage, and blase
18. discordant and incongruous
19. fungible and interchangeable
20. B

## Section 5

1. $\frac{8}{3}$
2. C
3. C
4. A
5. B
6. E
7. C
8. E
9. B and D
10. A, C and D
11. D
12. B
13. D
14. C
15. 8
16. B
17. A
18. B
19. D
20. A

# Explanations

## Section 1 – Analytical Writing

### Task 1 – Analyze an Issue

**The sample essay that follows was written in response to the prompt that appeared in the question.**

A healthy dose of skepticism is recommended when digesting a meal of facts delivered by someone else. In most cases, however, one should trust that those who have expertise in a specific field have done due diligence before making claims they presume to be true. Over time and with improved technology, new discoveries may appear that alter or contradict the current facts, but that doesn't mean they weren't true for the time and conditions under which they were espoused.

Some facts are true in the context in which they appear, but the reporters of such facts have cherry–picked them to serve their own purposes. This is never more obvious than during a presidential election. Social media makes these "facts" spread like wildfire, and the uninformed willingly accept them as gospel, especially if they coincide with their own political leanings. One of the most pervasive claims during the last presidential election was based on a chart depicting the yearly salaries of the President and members of Congress. The chart intended to inflame readers by stating that those individuals get that salary for life. While the dollar amounts were correct, the duration of said salaries was not. The President, senators and representatives get a pension based on their salaries. Another fact intended to shame Michelle Obama for having 26 assistants. What a waste of taxpayer money! A little research reveals that Laura Bush and other First Ladies had similar numbers of assistants. Displaying a little mistrust concerning facts presented for political purposes is wise.

Gossip is, perhaps, the most egregious misuse of facts. Generally repeated sotto voce, gossip can easily be misheard or misinterpreted. The listener then hurries off to spread the facts as he or she understood them. By the time the inflammatory remarks return to the subject of them, there is little truth remaining. In the case of gossip, the issue's original claim and reason hold true, not just for the sake of accuracy but for the protection of those subjected to vicious gossip. Rumors have characteristics in common with gossip. However, while gossip is never intended to spread good news, rumors may be used to disseminate both good and bad information, and their effect can be just as harmful as gossip. I live in a small city that was devastated when a nearby Air Force base closed. It had been rumored that the base would close several times over the years. Each time that the rumors began, local citizens would become despondent with worry over their futures. A Save Loring Committee worked tirelessly to keep the base from closing and succeeded twice. When the rumors began the third time, the locals refused to believe them,

and believed the more positive rumors that, once again, the base would remain open. It was like the little boy whocried wolf. As in the fable, the wolf, in the form of BRAC, did finally make an appearance, and the citizens of

Some facts that have been disproved have little or no effect, either positive or negative, on the course of human development. In recent history, Pluto has lost its status as a planet. It was always a little suspect, anyway. So our solar system is reduced to eight planets. This fact reversal has no effect on the way the world proceeds or stands as an argument that one should mistrust factual information. A much earlier astronomical reversal, however, did have an impact on the world. The Catholic Church believed the Earth to be the center of the universe. Since God had created the Earth and all of the creatures in it, it must be the most important of His creations. Hence, the sun and other planets must be inferior and show obeisance to the Earth by revolving around it. In the sixteenth century, Copernicus developed a model that disproved the geocentric theory and validated the heliocentric theory that had been proposed centuries before. Even though the Church was wrong about the solar system, one should not necessarily mistrust everything that the Church proclaims to be fact.

Every day begins with the immutable fact that the sun will rise in the East and ends when the sun sets in the West. Much of what happens in that span of time is open to interpretation, but the average human will not question the events that occur or the facts they hear. Those who do so relinquish the ability to simply enjoy the day that they have been given. The habit of mistrusting those in authority leads to a life filled with uncertainty.

## Task 2 – Analyze an Argument

**The sample essay that follows was written in response to the prompt that appeared in the question.**

Health Naturally is expanding, and, like any well–run company, has researched existing conditions before deciding which towns to select for its new stores. Using past experience, Health Naturally has determined that Plainsville is a suitable location. The company vice president has loaded his memo with highly charged words in an effort to persuade others to adopt his recommendation. "All–time high", "more than ever", and "always full" make the future in Plainsville sound very promising. These descriptors mean little or nothing when taken out of context.

When Plainsville merchants claim that sales of running shoes are at an all–time high, they don't reveal by how much in dollars or how many units sold. Sales in total dollars would just have to be one dollar higher than the previous best year to be considered an all–time high. The high dollar amount might be a result of an increase in the prices of running shoes. The merchants may actually have sold fewer pairs of shoes. The number of units sold might be a better measure of greater–than–ever success, but, again, selling one more pair of shoes than in the previous best year should not determine the health consciousness of Plainsville residents. If the conditions stated here are true, they do not support the argument put forth by Health Naturally's vice president.

The health club in Plainsville also appears to be thriving, claiming more members than ever before. A total membership of one more than the previous best year supports this claim, but one additional member is not sufficient to justify the expense of building a Health Naturally store in this location. In fact, this company should seek to know why the health club had so little business five years ago. There may have been several other clubs in the area that actually have closed in the intervening years, leaving this club as the only one still standing. When members of the closed clubs sought another place to exercise, they had no other choice but the club in Plainsville. This same situation explains why the aerobics and weight–training classes are always full. On the other hand, the health club may have reduced the number of classes, causing those who want to attend to crowd in to those available. Membership in the health club may fluctuate throughout the year. Some of the most popular New Year's resolutions are to lose weight and to adopt a healthier life style. If Health Naturally interviewed the merchants and the health club owner shortly after the beginning of the New Year, their numbers may be inflated. If those interviews took place in May or September, for example, the numbers reported could be a reason for optimism.

A presumption in this argument is that people who exercise will buy health foods, and they will buy them at a Health Naturally store. If the residents of Plainsville buy natural foods, they must already have a source for it, maybe even the local grocery store. Getting people to change their shopping habits is expensive and time consuming and, ultimately, may not be possible. Knowing the socioeconomic status of Plainsville residents would help Health Naturally make a decision about locating there. Natural foods are generally more expensive than foods carried in typical grocery stores. If the income levels in Plainsville are too low, the new health store will probably fail.

Finally, the vice president of the company assumes that the children of Plainsville are sure to become future customers of the store. Because the children must participate in a Fitness for Life program, they will continue to practice what they learn. A piece of information that would help determine the veracity of this assumption is the employment picture in Plainsville. Unless today's children can be assured of employment as adults, they will have to leave to seek their fortunes elsewhere.

The vice president of Health Naturally needs more detailed evidence to support his proposal to establish one of the company's new stores in Plainsville. It may turn out that this town is indeed health conscious and would welcome a store offering products that enhances their lifestyle choice. In contrast, further evidence may reveal the shallow nature of the apparent healthy behavior in Plainsville, and the decision to locate a new store in another location would be the wisest one.

# Section 2 – Verbal Reasoning

1. **A judicious**

This sentence states that Hollywood exaggerates the flashier aspects of forensic science. It also says that certain types of forensic scientists are smart enough to avoid believing in the sensationalist depiction of their work. Therefore, we want a word that stresses this quality of reservation and common sense. "Despondent" means "depressed." Being depressed would not cause a forensic scientist to ignore Hollywood sensationalism. "Imprudent" means "irresponsible." Being irresponsible would increase a forensic scientist's chances of getting caught up in Hollywood sensationalism, so this answer is wrong. "Asinine" means "foolish." Once again, if anything this would increase a forensic scientist's chances of getting caught up in Hollywood sensationalism. "Daft" means "unintelligent." An unintelligent forensic scientist would have a greater chance of being caught up in Hollywood sensationalism. Therefore, we are left with "Judicious." This word means "sensible." A sensible forensic scientist is the exact type that would not allow himself to get caught up in Hollywood sensationalism.

2. **The correct answer is (D).**

This question comes down to the difference between unobtrusive, meaning inconspicuous, and noninvasive, which in its medical application means that medical tools are not introduced into the body. Impertinent refers to something that is done rudely or without consideration, and cannot be applied to a description of a surgical technique that does not require incisions or surgical tools within the body. Something described as extraneous is unrelated or tangential. It is nonsensical that one would perform an unrelated surgery when treating a patient for kidney stones or small tumors. Integral refers to that which is impossible to do without. It would not be impossible to complete these surgeries without the invisible knives.

3. **restricting and obstructing**

The sentence points out that some nations have implemented low tax rates to bring businesses into their countries. As they are attempting to encourage more business growth, they would fear the opposite action – discouraging business investment. The correct answers must reflect the idea of stopping business investment. None of the incorrect answers refers to the idea of stopping or discouraging: Choice A, "promulgating," means putting a law into effect by formal declaration. Choice D, "averring, refers to formally declaring something to be true, and Choice, "congealing," means mean solidifying in a similar manner to liquid freezing. Choice F, "glowering," refers to staring angrily or sullenly. The correct answers are therefore Choice B, "restricting," because it refers to placing limitations, and Choice C, "obstructing," which refers to blocking the natural progression of something.

4. **frisson and thrill**

The sentence is saying that the game was going slowly until something happened that woke the crowd up. This "something" had to have been an exciting moment. "Immediacy" means proximity. We know the moment was immediate; it happened in the stadium. That doesn't mean it possessed the necessary excitement to make the crowd cheer. "Folly" means silliness. Silliness would not cause a crowd to erupt in cheers during a sporting event. It would need to be something exciting. "Rapidity" means speediness. While this answer looks acceptable, rapidity does not necessarily promise excitement. And even if the answer was closer, it has no match in the answer choices. "Arrogance" means egotism. There's nothing about the moment that can justify the use of "arrogance." The athlete merely made a play. Therefore we are left with "Frisson" and "Thrill." Both of these words mean a moment of excitement or thrill. This is exactly what would be needed to get the crowd on their feet. Therefore, the answers are A and C.

5. **The correct answer is (E).**

The correct answer is E. The author downplays the level of courage or exceptionality in his actions. Although the author left a bad situation for a better one, he reveals neither optimism for the future nor pessimism for his past. He reports the transition in a rather matter–of–fact manner; neither answer choice A nor B is correct. The writer does apologize for not having anything heroic or thrilling to tell, but this does not color the entire passage, making answer choice C incorrect. He is not sarcastic about any of the individuals involved in either his captivity or his freedom, so answer choice D cannot be correct.

6. **The correct answer is (B).**

The correct answer is B, autobiography. The use of the first person indicates that the author is telling his own story. If he were writing a biography, he would have used the third person, referring to the escaped slave as he instead of I. Answer choice A is incorrect. This passage would have to be newspaper article to be considered journalism. Since journalism is generally devoted to reporting recent events, this passage, referring to an event in the past, would not appear in a newspaper. Answer choice C is, therefore, incorrect. The purpose of an editorial is to express a point of view or opinion on a controversial topic. This passage does not do that, making answer choice D incorrect. This passage could be considered historical fiction, but the reader would need more information to make that determination, so answer choice E is not correct.

7. **didactic and educational**

The scholars who read ancient documents are trying to take something instructive away from the experience, not trying to adopt the documents wholesale. Therefore, we want words that establish these scholars as trying to learn something. "Infallible" means unfailing. If these documents were unfailing then scholars would want to adopt them directly, so this can't be an answer. "Argumentative" means challenging. This answer does fit (because the scholars could want to see how ancient cultures argued for legal concepts) but there is no second choice that matches it. "Vituperative" means scathing or malicious. Reading the malicious properties of ancient works would not be of any benefit to modern scholars. "Preposterous" means absurd or outrageous. Scholars looking to learn new ideas from old documents would not be concerned with the absurd properties of said documents. This leaves "Didactic" and "Educational." These terms both mean instructive. It makes sense that, even though the scholars don't want the word–for–word adoption of ancient law, they do want to learn from it for the benefit of modern law. Therefore, A and C are correct answers.

8. **disparity and multiplicity**

This passage is saying that there is a lack of consensus on what qualifies as "good" writing, therefore implying that written works are often vastly different from one another. Therefore, we want answers that stress how different written works can be. "Incisiveness" means brutality. Written works might sometimes be brutal, but a lack of consensus on what is "good" writing would not cause this to happen. "Plethora" means an excess. A public that never agrees on what is good writing could lead to a plethora of written works, because everybody is trying to push their own opinion. However, this requires assumptions to be made; namely, that people would write not just different works but a lot of them in order to forward an opinion. Because this answer relies on assumptions not explicitly stated in the passage it is not a good one. "Visibility" is prominence, or clarity. This word does not fit with the sentiment of the passage. How would lack of consensus make written works more prominent? It could happen, but it's not a strict requirement. "Incoherence" means unintelligibility. Again, it's possible that changing public perception could render some written works incoherent, but a clear line of cause and effect cannot be drawn. So, the remaining answers are "Variety" and "Diversity." Both of these two words mean a varied assortment. It makes sense that a lack of consensus on what constitutes "good" writing would lead to a variety of different works, because people would always be writing to fit their particular definition of "good." Therefore, C and E are the correct answers.

9. **The correct answers are (A) and (C).**

Both answer choices A and C are correct. The first sentence of the passage explicitly states that the Romans had no need to deal with denial of the gods as a breach of the law until the appearance of Christians and Jews in the empire. Because practitioners of other pagan religions across the Roman Empire and Romans themselves demonstrated mutual respect, they were unlikely to expend much energy converting observers of one set of beliefs to their own. There is no information in the passage to determine if answer choice B is correct or not, therefore making it the wrong answer.

10. **The correct answer is (A).**

The correct answer is A. By confining himself to Christianity, the author will not, at this time, provide a discussion of the Jews during the Roman Empire. Answer choice B is incorrect, as the sentence does not reveal his attitude toward the Christians. It appears that he has chosen to discuss them because it will be an easier task. He does not even mention the Jews in this sentence, so assuming that he will contrast them with the Christians is incorrect, making answer choice C the wrong one. The sentence gives no indication that the following information will be dull or uninteresting or scanty, so the reader's expectations about quality are not affected, making answer choice D incorrect. There is no evidence that the author is more familiar with Christianity rather than Judaism, so answer choice E is also incorrect.

11. **manifestation, pervasiveness, and substantiates**

The passage opens by talking about the general idea of social stratification, and then by giving a specific example. This example can be seen as an "expression" of the general idea. "Contradiction" means "inconsistency." There is no evidence given that social stratification is built on an "inconsistency." "Ambiguousness" means "vagueness." If a particular example of social stratification is being provided then it must not be suffering from "vagueness." "Manifestation" means "expression." This makes sense. The upper–middle–lower class dynamic of Western societies can be considered a "manifestation" of the general idea of social stratification. The second blank is in a sentence that lists all of the fields of study in which social stratification can be seen. This implies that it is an omnipresent idea. "Reticence" means "silence." If the issue is being seen so often then it must not be "silent." "Contradistinction" means "distinction by way of contrast." Social stratification is not being compared by way of contrast to any other topic, so this is wrong. "Pervasiveness" means "universality." This makes sense. If social stratification is seen in history, economics, and other fields of study then it must have a universal quality to it. The last blank comes in a sentence that immediately follows another sentence in which social stratification is condemned. Since the sentence containing the last blank starts with "However," we can infer that it is going to provide something positive that can be taken away from the previous sentence. "Fissures" and "Fractures" both mean "splits," or "breaks." This doesn't make any sense. The sentence is trying to list something positive that the pervasiveness of social stratification implies. "Breaking" is not something positive. "Substantiates" means "validates." This makes sense. The pervasiveness of social stratification could possibly mean that it is the natural state of human existence. The very fact that it frequently exists could mean that it is supposed to.

12. **elitist, encumbrance, and inducement**

The passage states that only 6 movie studios control more than 90% of film revenue. Therefore, we know that the film industry's wealth is in the hands of a small group. "Indiscriminate" means "uncritical." If so much wealth is concentrated in so few companies, they cannot be described as "indiscriminate." "Communal" means "shared." If so few companies control so much wealth, the film industry is not a commune. "Elitist" means "selective." This accurately describes the film industry as it is described in the passage. For the second blank, the passage goes on to list all of the ways that the exclusive nature of the film industry hurts it, both creatively and financially. "Alleviation" means "easing." The business model of the film industry does not "ease" its problems, it creates them. "Opacity" means "lack of clarity." The passage is critical of the business model of the film industry for a variety of reasons, but it never accuses it of lack of clarity. "Encumbrance" means "burden." This makes sense. The passage lists all of the ways the business structure of the film industry limits it, so this model can be described as a "burden."

For the third blank, the passage ends by talking about how lack of competition leaves studios "unprepared."

This must be because competition causes studios to evolve their business strategy. "Dissuasion" means "deterrence." Competition wouldn't dissuade film studios from evolving their business mode,

it would persuade them. "Ingratitude" means "thanklessness." The passage makes no reference as to how competition would use "thanklessness" to cause film studios to upgrade their business model. "Inducement" means "incentive." This word makes sense. Competition would provide an "incentive" for film studios to evolve their business model.

13. **"We may wait, now, with bated breath, while Caesar reflects."**

The author interrupts his narrative about Caesar in much the same way that a television commercial interrupts a show at a moment of high drama in order to create tension or anticipation concerning the events to follow. The phrase "bated breath" means that he and the reader are holding their breath to see what happens next.

14. **The correct answer is (C).**

The correct answer is C. The author's premise is that every event leads to another inevitable event, and that no event stands alone as the ultimate one in a person's life. His selection of Caesar's crossing the Rubicon is arbitrary. He could as easily have chosen Ferdinand and Isabella's decision to send Columbus to discover the new world and listed the effect of it.

The purpose of the essay is not to point out important events in history for their own sake, so answer choice A is incorrect. Answer choice B is incorrect because the author fails to mention an important, life–changing event in his own life. Although the author lists the far–reaching effects of Caesar's decision, he does so only to support his thesis, not to show how Caesar affected history. Answer choice D is incorrect. Although the author includes the detail about the piper, his identity is not central to the author's purpose for including the account of Caesar's crossing the Rubicon. Answer choice E is incorrect.

15. **The correct answer is (C).**

The correct answer is C. The author says that the piper appears to have been there by accident, but his appearance was no accident. The previous events in the piper's life led him to be in that place at that time. In that same way, every event in a person's life have led him to be where he is at this moment, such as your being here to take this test. The author does not reveal that the piper planned to be there at that time, or, if he did, that he knew Caesar and his troops would arrive at the same place at that time. Answer choice A is incorrect. Although Caesar says that the omens of the gods call us, the writer does not suggest that as the reason for his fate having been determined, so answer choice B is incorrect. Answer D implies that people have no control over their destinies. The author states that all of the events in one's life, often occurring by choice, lead them to their present situations, so that answer is incorrect. The author does not believe that people are the masters of their own destinies, even though they are free to make choices. The choices we make may influence events in others' lives, just as their choices may influence our lives, so answer choice E is also incorrect.

16. **The correct answer is (D).**

The correct answer is D. Candy is predicting that sales of the maple–flavored creams will insure significant sales and profits in her new stores. If she cannot get enough maple syrup to provide sufficient inventory, her sales will fail to live up to expectations. Answer A is incorrect because she may be paying a percentage of her sales to the management of the malls where she currently has stores. The only way this can affect her expected profits is if the percentage is too high. Answer B is incorrect because the sales of candy in other stores will have no direct bearing on her sales. In fact, customers at the mall may be looking for something new, and Candy's maple creams may draw customers from the other stores in the mall. The new malls having more stores than the malls where Candy currently has stores should only help her business succeed as there are likely to be more customers in the mall on a daily basis. Therefore, answer choice C is incorrect. The lower unemployment rate may affect Candy's ability to find salespeople to work in her store. However, the reader doesn't know how many employees Candy needs. A lower unemployment rate also implies that more people have discretionary income and are able to purchase Candy's candy.

17. **disparate and dissimilar**

This sentence conveys that different-looking people are still the same on a fundamental level. "Concurrent" means parallel, or coexisting, rather than different, so "concurrent appearances" doesn't work. "Idyllic" means calm or peaceful. "Idyllic appearances" says nothing about the similarity or differences between appearances and is therefore incorrect. It offers no comparison. "Uniform" means the same, so is incorrect for the same reasons as "concurrent." "Familiar" means acquainted. Again, this word in no way stresses the similarities or differences between cultures. The correct answers are "Disparate" and "Dissimilar," which both mean unlike or different. This is exactly how we want to describe these two cultures: looking different and unlike in spite of their similarities inside. A and D are the correct answers.

18. **relationship and rapport**

The financial aspirations of this company are being compared to more human aspects of business life. Therefore, we want words that stress human interaction. "Turbidity" means a muddled or confused state. Establishing a confused state between coworkers doesn't make much sense and wouldn't help them connect to each other. "Condescension" means disdain. This would of course create a negative working environment and would not be desirable. "Despair" means misery. Again, this is not the type of interaction that an employer would want to create with their employees. "Synecdoche" is a figure of speech in which a part is made to represent the whole. This answer does not make any sense in this context. This leaves "Relationship" and "Rapport" as the correct answers. They both mean bond or connection, which is exactly what employers would want to cultivate in their employees. c and d are correct.

19. **The correct answer is (A).**

The correct answer is A. The author gives poets permission to choose subjects of their liking but warns them about giving those subjects too much importance, revealed by his use of the word but at the end of his list of permissions. Answer B is incorrect because the writer merely makes an allusion to the ancient poet, Homer, at the end of the passage. The author, in essence, gives poets permission to employ any subject in their writing. His goal is not to change what poets write about, making answer choice C incorrect. The only reader of poetry mentioned in the passage is the author himself, so answer choice D is not correct. The list of permissions by the author negates the idea of his establishing criteria for writing poetry. His chief concern is the seriousness with which poets approach their subjects. Answer E is incorrect.

20. **The correct answer is (C).**

The correct choice is C. The author appears to be making his final point. The reader knows that it is not an introduction because the first sentence refers to something the author has already written. Answer choice B is incorrect. A preface prepares the reader for the content of the larger text that he has written. A preface is similar to an explanation. Answer B is incorrect. An epilogue appears after the author has finished writing the primary text. It may reveal events that have occurred since he sat down to write. Answer D is incorrect. A glossary appears at the end of a text and its entries generally include definitions of terms or translations of foreign words or phrases. Answer E is also incorrect.

# Section 3 – Quantitative Reasoning

1. **The correct answer is (E).**

Total salary = 14000 × 66 = 524000

Let $x$ and $y$ be the number of employees in section A and section B.

$12000x + 24000y = 524000$

i.e $x + 2y = 77$-----(1)

Also $x + y = 66$ ------(2)

(Total number of employees)

Subtracting (2) from (1)

$y = 11$.

2. **The correct answer is (C).**

For combined events, the formula is

$P(A \text{ or } B) = P(A) + P(B) - P(A \text{ and } B)$

Substituting the given values,

$$\frac{3}{4} = \frac{1}{2} + P(N) - \frac{1}{6}$$
$$\frac{9}{12} = \frac{6}{12} P(N) - \frac{2}{12}$$
$$\frac{9}{12} = \frac{4}{12} P(N)$$
$$P(N) = \frac{5}{12}$$

3. **The correct answer is (B).**

Let the ages of grandmother and granddaughter be $x$ and $y$.

Five years ago the ages would have been $x$-5 and $y$-5.

As per data $x-5=13(y-5)$

i.e. $x-13y= -60$-----(1)

Five years hence

$x+5=5(y+5)$

i.e. $x-5y=20$-------(2)

Subtracting (1) from (2) we get

$8y=80$

$y=10$

Substituting in (2)

$x-50=20$

$x=70$

$x+y = 80$

4. **The correct answer is (C).**

The ratio of students in the first class to students in the second class is 5:6 and there are 20 students in the first class. Number of students in the second class = (20 × 6)/5 = 24

The key point for this question is to make sure you calculate the weighted average.

The average age of the first and second classes

combined is: $\dfrac{20 \times 17.06 + 24 \times 17.50}{20 + 24}$

$$= \frac{341.2 + 420}{44} = 17.3$$

The average age of the first and third classes combined is 17.18. Let the average age of the third class be $X$.

$$\frac{20 \times 17.06 + 20 \times X}{20 + 20} = \frac{341.2 + 20X}{40} = 17.18$$
$$341.2 + 20X = 40 \times 17.18$$
$$20X = 687.2 - 341.2$$
$$X = \frac{346}{20} = 17.3$$

The average age of the first and second classes combined is the same as the average age of the third class (=17.3).

5. **The correct answer is (C).**

Let's assume:

$a$ = initial amount of money owned by Anna

$b$ = initial amount of money owned by Beatrice

$c$ = initial amount of money owned by Charlotte

$a + b + c = \$2,200$

Anna spends 50% of her money

Amount left = $a$ – 50% $a$ = 50% $a$ = $a/2$

Beatrice spends 75% of her money

Amount left = $b$ – 75% $b$ = 25% $b$ = $b/4$

Charlotte spends 80% of her money

Amount left = $c$ – 80% $c$ = 20% $c$ = $c/5$

We know that after spending some money they are each left with identical amounts of money

$a/2 = b/4 = c/5$

Let $x = a/2 = b/4 = b/4$

$a = 2x$, $b = 4x$ and $c = 5x$

We can now substitute in the first equation

$2x + 4x + 5x$ = \$2,200

$11x$ = \$2,200

$x$ = \$200

The initial amount of money owned by Beatrice is

$b = 4x$ = \$800

The initial amount of money owned by Charlotte is

$c = 5x$ = \$1,000

The amount of money spent by Charlotte =

80% × \$1,000 = \$800

The initial amount of money owned by Beatrice (\$800) is the same as the amount of money spent by Charlotte (\$800).

6. **The correct answer is (A).**

Let the selling price of each *Kg* be *\$x*

*Loss=Cost Price-Selling Price*

According to the question, It is sold in such a way that after selling the whole quantity, the quantum of loss is equal to the amount obtained by selling 300 *kg* of apples

$3000 - 1200x = 300x$

$3000 = 1500x$

$x$ = \$2

7. **The correct answer is (B).**

Let B be the event of failing due to bad brakes, and L be the event of failing due to defective lights. The probability of failing can be represented as:P(B or L). Using the formula for combined events:

*P(B or L)=P(B)+P(L)-P(B and L)*

*P(B or L)=0.30+0.15-0.10*

*P(B or L)=0.35*

8. **The correct answer is (D).**

The probability that at least one of them arrives on time for work is the combination of the following events: Rob arrives on time but Tom arrives late, Rob arrives late but Tom arrives on time, and both Rob and Tom arrive on time. These 3 events combined are the complement of the event that both Rob and Tom arrive late for work.

P(at least one arrives on time)

=1-P(both Rob and Tom arrive late)

P(at least one arrives on time)=1-(0.12×0.16)

P(at least one arrives on time)=1-0.0192

P(at least one arrives on time)=0.9808

9. **The correct answer is (D).**

We are told that AB is a tangent to the large circle. It is known that the tangent to a circle is perpendicular to the radius at the point of tangency.

AB and BD are perpendicular (BD is the radius) so we can use Pythagoras theorem in ΔABD

$AD^2 = AB^2 + BD^2$

$BD^2 = 30^2 - 24^2$

BD = 18

The radius of the large circle = 18

D and E are the centers of the two circles. It is known that if two circles touch in one point only the distance center to center is the sum of the two radiuses.

DE = radius of the large circle + radius of the small circle

DE = 33 and we calculated the radius of the large circle = 18

The radius of the small circle = 15

The same logic applies to ΔACE as to ΔABD (i.e. EC and AC are perpendicular, EC is the radius)

$AE^2 = AC^2 + CE^2$

$AC^2 = 25^2 - 15^2$

AC = 20

Perimeter of ΔACE = AE + AC + CE = 25 + 20 + 15 = 60

10. **The correct answer is (A).**

The set of 2–digit positive integers includes a total of 90 numbers. The numbers with 7 in either the units place or tens place are the following: 17, 27, 37, 47, 57, 67, 70, 71, 72, 73, 74, 75, 76, 77, 78, 79, 87, and 97 – total of 18 numbers. Therefore, the probability is 18 out of 90 is 18/90=2/10.

11. **The correct answer is (B).**

Set x includes 0, 1, 2, and 3. Set y includes 3, 4, 5, and 6. To list all possibilities for y-x, the following grid method can be used:

| | 3 | 4 | 5 | 6 |
|---|---|---|---|---|
| 0 | 3 | 4 | 5 | 6 |
| 1 | 2 | 3 | 4 | 5 |
| 2 | 1 | 2 | 3 | 4 |
| 3 | 0 | 1 | 2 | 3 |

The grid shows the 16 combinations for y-x. Out of all the results, there are 6 combinations that will result in a difference of greater than or equal to 4. Hence, the probability is 6/16=3/8

12. **The correct answer is (B).**

Angles a and b are vertical with two angles of the triangle. Using the angle sum postulate in a triangle, we obtain

$a + b + 80 = 180$

Subtract 80 from each side of this equation, and combine numbers on each side.

$a + b + 80 - 80 = 180 - 80$

(1) $a + b = 100^\circ$

In any quadrilateral, the sum of the interior angles is 360. Applying this rule to the quadrilateral above the horizontal line we obtain

$m + n + x + y = 360$

Subtract $x + y$ from each side of this equation, and cancel out the opposite terms.

$m + n + x + y - (x + y) = 360 - (x + y)$

(2) $m + n = 360 - (x + y)$

The sum of the angles formed above the horizontal line around each point of intersection is 180. Thus,

(3) $x + a + a = 180$

(4) $y + b + b = 180$

Subtract $2a$ from each side of (3), and subtract $2b$ from each side of (4).

$x + a + a - 2a = 180 - 2a$

$y + b + b - 2b = 180 - 2b$

Combine the like terms on the left side of each equation.

$x = 180 - 2a$

$y = 180 - 2b$

Add these equations side by side and then factor out 2 on the right side.

(5) $x + y = 360 - 2(a + b)$

Replace (1) in (5).

(6) $x + y = 360 - 2(80) = 200$

In any quadrilateral, the sum of the interior angles is $360^\circ$.

(7) $m + n + x + y = 360$

Replace (6) in (7) and solve for ($m$ + n).

$m + n + 200 = 360$

$m + n = 360 - 200 = 160$

13. **The correct answer is (B).**

Let the shorter leg be $x$ yards.

The longer leg is $x$+14 yards

If h is the hypotenuse then $x=h/2-3$

$h/2=x+3$

$h=2(x+3)=2x+6$

By the Pythagoras theorem, the square of the hypotenuse is equal to the sum of the squares of the legs.

Now $(2x+6)^2=x^2+(x+14)^2$

$4x^2+24x+36=x^2+x^2+28x+196$

$\therefore 2x^2-4x-160=0$

$\therefore x^2-2x-80=0$

$\therefore x^2-10x+8x-80=0$

$\therefore x(x-10)+8(x-10)=0$

$\therefore (x-10)(x+8)=0$

$\therefore x=10$ OR $x=-8$

Hence we get $x$=10, eliminating the negative value.

Therefore $h$=2$x$+6=20+6=26

14. **The correct answer is (B).**

Given: $4^{3x+6}=8^{6x+12}$

$4^{3x+6}$ can be written as $2^{2(3x+6)}=2^{6x+12}$

And $8^{6x+12}$ can be written as $2^{3(6x+12)}=2^{18x+36}$

$\therefore 2^{6x+12}=2^{18x+36}$

Since bases are the same exponents also will be the same.

Hence $6x+12=18x+36$

$\therefore 12x=-24$

$\therefore x=-2$

15. **The correct answer is 525 square units.**

Let the side of the small square be $x$ units. Then the side of the larger square $A$ will be ($x$+10) units.

Now the sum of the areas of $A$ and $B$ = 625 *square units* (Given)

$\therefore (x+10)(x+10)+x \times x=625$

$\therefore x^2+20x+100+x^2=625$

$\therefore 2x^2+20x=525$ --------(1)

Now length of each rectangle=($x$+10)

Width of each rectangle=$x$

Area of one rectangle =$(x+10)x=x^2+10x$

Sum of the areas of the two rectangles C and D=$2(x^2+10x)=2x^2+20x=525$ from (1)

16. **The correct answer is (C).**

Principal for the first year =100,000.

Interest for the first year =100000×5%=100000×5/100=5000

Principal for the second year =100000+5000=105000

Interest for the second year =105000×10%=10500

Principal for the third year =105000+10500=115500

Interest for the third year=115500×15%=17325

Total interest earned=5000+10500+17325=32825

17. **The correct answer is (C).**

The buying price = \$320 = 100%

Selling price percentage = buying price + profit = 100% + 21.875% = 121.875%

The selling price = 121.875/100×320=\$390

The selling price is 100% – 2.5% = 97.5% of the marked price

If the marked price percentage = 100%,

The marked price =100/97.5×390=\$400

18. **The correct answer is (D).**

Let the speed of the car be $s$.

Speed of airplane = 6 times the speed of the car

Speed of airplane = 6s

Speed of airplane = 3 times that of the train.

∴ Speed of the train = 2$s$

Time = distance/speed

Total time taken = Sum of the individual times

$$=\left(\frac{100}{s}+\frac{1200}{6s}+\frac{300}{2s}\right)=\frac{600+1200+900}{6s}=\frac{2700}{6s}=\frac{450}{s}$$

But the total time taken = 4 hours 30 minutes = 4 1/2 hours

$$\therefore \frac{450}{s}=4\frac{1}{2};$$

$$\frac{450}{s}=\frac{9}{2};$$

$$s=\frac{900}{9};$$

$$s=100$$

Speed of the airplane= 6$x$ = 600 *km/h*

19. **The correct answers are (A), (C) and (E).**

Explanation: To solve this problem let's pick some numbers so that it is easy to solve.

Let $a$=1000, $b$=1, $c$=2000, $d$=2, $e$=3000, $f$=3

(A) $(a+c+e) : (f+d+b)$ = (1000+2000+3000) ; (3+2+1) = 6000 : 6 = 1000 : 1

(B) $(2a+c+e) : (b+2d+f)$ = (2000+2000+3000) : (1+4+3) = 7000 : 8 ≠ 1000 : 1

(C) $(a-c+e) : (b-d+f)$ = (1000-2000+3000) = (1-2+3) = 2000 : 2 = 1000 : 1

(D) $(a^3+c+e) : (b^3+d+f)$ = (1000000000+2000+3000) :

(1+2+3) = 1000005000 : 6 ≠ 1000 : 1

(E) ($8a$-$2c$-$e$) : ($8b$-$2d$-$f$) = (8000-4000-3000) : (8-4-3) = 1000 : 1

(F) ($a^2$+$c^2$) : ($b^2$+$d^2$) = (1000000+9000000) : (1+9) = 10000000 : 10 = 1000000 : 1 ≠ 1000 : 1

($a^2$+$2c^2$) : ($b^2$+$4d^2$) = (1000000+18000000) : (1+36) = 19000000:37 ≠ 1000 : 1

20. **The correct answer is 2%.**

Those who do not use Instagram or Pinterest can be represented as P(A ∪ B)'. First, let's solve for

P(A ∪ B)=P(A)+P(B)-P(A ∩ B)

Substituting the given values,

P(A ∪ B)=0.96+0.85-0.83=0.98

P(A ∪ B)'=1-P(A ∪ B)

P(A ∪ B)'=1-0.98=0.02

Therefore, P(A ∪ B)' is 2%.

# Section 4 – Verbal Reasoning

1. **disparate**

This sentence says that making a prediction of where a body will move seems easy, but in reality, is not. It specifically says that it's not easy because of a certain way in which forces act on the body in question. This "certain way" must be a discordant way of acting. If they moved in a uniform way predictions would be easier. "Unequivocal" means "clear." Forces interacting in a "clear" way would not make the prediction process more difficult. "Callow" means "inexperienced" or "immature." Physical forces cannot act in an "immature" way, so this answer is wrong. "Tepid" means lukewarm, or lacking in intensity. Again, the tepid action of forces would make the prediction process easier. "Engorged" means enflamed. This word does not make sense in the context of the question. "Disparate" means unequal, or unlike. Forces acting in an unequal fashion would be difficult to make predictions about because they would be interacting with each other in a variety of confusing ways.

2. **assiduously**

This sentence states that there is a certain way in which our understanding of physics on planet Earth should be applied to distant galaxies. Given that the assumption of physics in different galaxies being identical to Earth's is described as "foolish," we can infer that this "certain way" must be judiciously. What words enforce this idea? "Torpidly" means sluggishly. Applying our physical laws on Earth "sluggishly" to the rest of the universe would not help in any way. "Dogmatically" means strictly. This is the opposite of what we want. The entire passage infers that strict application of Earth physics would be a bad idea. "Rancorously" means "with resentment." Applying our Earth logic with resentment would not make it more likely to apply in distant galaxies. "Maladroitly" means "awkwardly." An awkward application of our understanding of physics on Earth would not help to apply it elsewhere. "Assiduously" means "carefully." This is exactly how you would want to apply Earth logic to different galaxies. It is logical to base future endeavors on the models you know, but not to assume that the model will be translated perfectly.

3. **contempt and derision**

Darwin is described as going against Medieval and Christian theory; therefore his ideas were presumably not quickly adopted. To this end we want answer choices that focus on the conflict he experienced. "Companionship" means company or friendship. Nothing about this sentence implies that Darwin's ideas granted him exceptional amounts of company or friendship. "Competition" means rivalry. This answer choice does work, as there were obviously rival theories on this matter, but there is no matching answer choice for it. Therefore it cannot be chosen. "Egotism" means arrogance. Like "Competition," this answer choice works on its own. Darwin certainly had to deal with the egos of other scientists who scoffed at his theory. However, much like "Competition," this answer choice does not have a partner in the answer list. "Relief" means respite. If Darwin had to fight so hard against entrenched theories, then he could not have had too much respite. The remaining answers are "Contempt" and "Derision." These two choices mean scorn or mockery. It makes sense that Darwin and his theory would experience scorn and mockery from the scientific establishment, who had held the same ideas for hundreds of years. Therefore, a and b are correct.

4. **ubiquitous and prevalent**

This sentence is trying to say that something (the high-quality spatial resolution maps) that used to be difficult to obtain is now easier to obtain. Therefore, we want words that stress how something has become commonplace. "Inconceivable" means unthinkable or implausible. This is the exact opposite sentiment that we want to express in this sentence. The sentence is trying to say that high quality spatial maps have become less unattainable – calling them inconceivable means they've become more unattainable. "Relatable" means relevant or applicable. There's no reason to believe that high quality spatial resolution maps were not applicable to medicine before the MRI was invented. The difficulty was making the maps easier to obtain. "Extreme" means risky or dangerous. There's no reason to believe that the MRI would render the imaging maps risky or dangerous. "Essential" means vital or crucial. Again, we want answers which show that the imaging maps have become less difficult to obtain. "Essential," if anything, has the opposite effect. This leaves "Ubiquitous" and "Prevalent," which both mean widespread. They both work in the sentence because they state how the imaging maps that used to be difficult to obtain are now commonplace in a medical setting. Therefore, A and D are correct.

5. **The correct answer is (B).**

"B" is a correct rendition of the main idea of the passage because it reiterates the idea that beliefs about how much or how little one can accomplish is a more significant factor in determining success than ability, which can be increased with practice and education. Thinking that abilities are "unchangeable", as the passage states, is a mental process that 'hinders' productivity.

"A" is incorrect because although intelligence may indeed be a big part of what determines success, this idea is not supported in this particular passage, as the main idea deals more with attitude towards intelligence rather than the amount of intelligence that a person possesses.

"C" is incorrect because only the first part of this answer is true, yet the second part is not supported by the passage; it is not true that a person is limited by the boundaries of their current skill set and that challenges must fall within these limitations, as the passage argues that anyone can surpass their current skills with the belief that they can change.

"D" is incorrect because if someone feels like they are struggling, this text claims that it is more likely due to feelings of not knowing how to change or not thinking they can; it's not because they are not employing the skills that they already have. Also, if a person does not have the necessary skills to reach a goal, then, according to the passage, they can learn them no matter how much they lack to begin with.

"E" is also incorrect because success should have nothing to do with what a person is born with, just as the studies aimed to prove that "intelligence is malleable".

6. **The correct answer is (B).**

"B" is correct because this opening sentence does not say what people tend to do but rather what would happen if people did indeed display this behavior.

The contrast is identified in the beginning of the next sentence which begins with "however" to show that although the aforementioned situation would be desirable, it is not what most people tend to do.

"A" is incorrect because although this sentence mentions adversity, it does not focus on how it is challenging.

"C" is incorrect because this sentence does not outline different ways of approaching adversity but rather simply focuses how to decrease fear.

"D" is incorrect because this sentence fails to provide methods for increasing self-discipline. Though this sentence does state that believing in the possibility of increased self-discipline would be empowering, it does not provide specific instructions on how to do it.

"E" is incorrect because there is no mention of abilities or certain skills; though the sentence implies that knowledge is empowering and that it can enable us to remain courageous in the face of adversity, it does not mention whether skills are necessary in those times.

7. **The correct answer is (B).**

"B" is a correct option because the author takes a practical approach to utilizing the power of the mind. By offering ways to improve mental capacity and explaining some of the possible results of doing so, the author gives 'real world' applications for this advice.

"C" is another possibility for the author's tone because the stance of the passage is supported with scientific research; thus, the message is not simply based on opinion but on evidence as well.

"A" is incorrect because the author is not without bias; he presents an argument that demonstrates the many benefits of adopting the idea that a person can control their mind through their beliefs.

8. **"Psychologists who specialise in human development have demonstrated that people who believe certain traits to be unchangeable are more likely to worry about failure and react negatively to critique, which hinders their chances for success."**

This sentence explains that having only one way of viewing personal skills causes debilitating emotions such as worry, and that such a mindset 'hinders' success.

By focusing on the negative consequences of holding onto certain beliefs instead of discussing the positive impact of intelligence, this sentence maintains the idea that innate skills are irrelevant to a person's ability to handle failure and criticism, no matter how smart that person may be.

9. **"So, if the balance of my houses did not arrive within the time stated in the contract, they would not be taken on that vessel, and my speculation ruined."**

The writer has some concerns about his houses arriving at the contracted time to be loaded onto the ship. He is aware that others who have goods to ship to California have offered higher rates of payment, and he fears that, if his barge is too late, he will miss the boat and lose his investment.

10. **The correct answers are (A), (B) and (C).**

All three answers are suitable choices. If one puts all of his eggs in one basket and then drops the basket, all of the eggs will break, and he or she will have nothing. The writer has divided his "eggs" between two baskets by speculating in gold and houses. Even if there is no gold, the miners will still need places to live. Covering all the bases refers to the game of baseball. If any of the bases is not protected, a runner can steal a base or score a run. The writer has effectively covered his bases by diversifying his interests and even by going to California himself to take delivery of his cargo. Hedging one's bets is similar to putting one's eggs in more than one basket. If one places all of his money on one horse to win a race, he loses it all if the horse doesn't come in first. A wary bettor would choose the horse to win, place, or show in order to save some money. The writer has wagered on both the quantity of gold in California and supplying homes for the miners. He is bound to win at least one of the bets.

11. **The correct answers are (A) and (B).**

Both choices A and B are correct answers. Fervor is passion or zeal. Those choosing to cross the country to seek their fortunes in California would have needed both emotions to complete their journey as did the Crusaders in their desire to restore the Holy Land. The journey for both the miners and the Crusaders was long. The actual Holy Grail is believed to be the cup from which Jesus drank at the last supper, and the search for it was not the goal of the Crusades. Therefore, it cannot be a suitable point of comparison for the miners' quest. Answer C is incorrect.

12. **The correct answer is (D).**

The best answer in this context is D. The writer is devoted to the pursuit of gold in California. The evidence to support this is his investment in the company which he helped to create. Answers A, B, and C have religious connotations. The writer has not taken any solemn vows in this activity, nor is the quest for gold the objective of a cult, making all of those choices incorrect. Answer choice E refers to someone on the sidelines, not an active participant, so it is incorrect.

13. **dispassionate, diversify and proliferated**

The first blank is comparing the subjects of study of the natural sciences versus political science. Since political science is described both as having to deal with "biases" and as being "unlike" the natural sciences, we know that natural sciences must not have "biases." "Preconceived" means "predetermined." If physical sciences had "predetermined" observations then they would have bias, so this answer is wrong. "Psychological" means "of or relating to the mind." Political science, not natural science, is described as dealing with the human mind, so this answer cannot be correct. "Dispassionate" means "unemotional." This makes sense. Physical scientists deal with the natural world. Therefore, they don't have to worry about emotions creeping into their research; they work in quantifiable data.

The second blank tells of how political scientists need to "mitigate the shortcomings of any one approach." This indicates that one approach to research is inadequate. Therefore, multiple approaches are most likely taken. "Coalesce" means "merge." This is the opposite of what we want. "Inundate" means "overwhelm." "Overwhelming" their research methods would not aid scientists conducting research. "Diversify" means "vary." This makes sense. In order to mitigate the shortcomings of any one research method, scientists would vary their research methods.

The third blank talks of how political science has managed to do "something" in spite of obstacles.

If political science is doing "something" in spite of obstacles, it most likely is growing, or developing. "Regressed" means "backslid." The field of political science would not do this in spite of obstacles; it would do it because of them. This answer is incorrect. "Fulminated" means "ranted." This answer makes no sense in the context of the question. "Proliferated" means "thrived." It makes sense that if the field of political science was doing "something" in spite of obstacles, it would be thriving.

14. **preponderant, waned, and ephemeral**

This passage is stating that America used to be the world leader in automobile production, before falling off in later years. "Debatable" means "doubtful." If the United States was producing more than 90% of all automobiles on the planet, its force would not be debatable. "Superfluous" means "unnecessary." Again, if America was producing almost all of the motor vehicles on the planet, its auto industry would not be described as "unnecessary." "Preponderant" means "pre-eminent." If the United States was providing the world with automobiles, then its auto industry could accurately be described as "pre-eminent." For the second blank, the passage is talking about how the dominance of the United States has gone down in recent years. "Illuminated" means "brightened." The dominance of the United States did not become more illuminated over the years, it decreased. "Proliferated" means "thrived." Again, the dominance of the United States went down. It did not "thrive." We are left with "Waned." This word means "faded." If the United States went from being the world's dominant automobile producer to looking up at the competition, then its influence has certainly "faded."

For the third blank, the passage talks of how Japan's ascension to the top of the automobile industry was short-lived. "Tenacious" means "persistent." Japan lost its number one spot, so it can't be described as persistent. "Condescending" means "arrogant." This answer does not have support anywhere in the passage. The passage never refers to the Japanese as being "arrogant." "Ephemeral" means "short-lived." If the Japanese surged to the top of the automobile world, only to be supplanted by China, then their dominance was short-lived.

15. **subverted, penetrate, and sporadically**

The passage is saying that the heat is preventing the man from getting comfortable and working. "Subsisted" means "lived." The heat isn't "living" any attempts at work, so this answer is wrong. "Sanctioned" means "authorized." The heat isn't authorizing his work, it is preventing it, so this is wrong. "Subverted" means "undermined." If the heat is preventing the man from working then it is clearly undermining him.

For the second blank, the passage is stating that the fan cannot provide him respite. "Augment" means "increase." The man would not be concerned with the fan failing to "increase" the heat. He would want it to fail at increasing the heat. It's supposed to keep him cool. "Succor" means "help." The man would not be upset if the fan was failing to help the heat, because it is supposed to cool him off. "Penetrate" means "pierce." The man would be upset to find out that fan was unable to pierce the heat, because he needs it to do that to make him cool.

For the last blank, the passage talks about "each time" the man wakes up during the night. Therefore, he must wake up multiple times. "Exquisitely" means "divinely." Given the harsh conditions, the man will not be waking up divinely throughout the night. "Volubly" means "articulately." Being articulate has nothing to do with waking up because of heat, so this is wrong. "Sporadically" means "intermittently." If the man is waking up throughout the night, then he is waking up sporadically.

16. **The correct answer is (B).**

Choice B is correct because, if the deer do not have an adequate food supply, they will die. If there are fewer deer reproducing, there will be a decline in successive generations. A smaller deer population means a reduction in the food supply for the tigers, and they will not survive in traditional numbers. Choice A is incorrect because the tigers hide in the reeds. If there are more reeds, then they can hide from the deer better. Choice C is incorrect because, if the deer can see the tigers better, they will be able to flee. The tigers will weaken without a food source. Choice D is unrelated to the problem; ecotourism, if anything, may include management methods to ensure that animal populations remain high for visitors to see. Choice E is incorrect because the tigers have a new food source that has not adapted to avoid them, so they can potentially eat more food.

17. **irony, disparage, and blase**

This passage is saying that parents who criticize the violence of their children's movies don't appreciate the level of violence in the films of their own generation. "Prosperity" means "wealth." Parents being offended by violence in their children's movies while not recognizing it in their own would not lead to wealth. "Singularity" means "uniqueness." Parents criticizing violence in their children's movies while not recognizing it in their own would not lead to any type of uniqueness, either. "Irony" is the incongruity of expected results versus actual results. It would be expected that parents would find violence in both their children's movies and their own to be offensive. Parents only finding offense in one group of films would be ironic.

For the second blank, the passage is saying how parents do not like the use of violence in modern cinema. "Authenticate" means "endorse." The parents are not endorsing the violence of modern cinema, they are criticizing it. "Theorize" means "conjecture." The parents are not theorizing anything about violence in modern cinema, they are openly criticizing it. "Disparage" means "ridicule." The parents "worry" that their children have too much violence in their movies, so they must be disparaging the use of violence in cinema. For the third blank, the passage is stating that older movies do not use violence explicitly, but it is still present. "Incisive" means "keen." The passage is saying that violence in older movies is done less explicitly, not that it is done "keenly." "Gracious" means "kind." The passage is clearly not implying that there was something kind about violence in older movies. "Blasé" means "nonchalant." If the violence in older movies was not done explicitly, but rather as "part of everyday life," then it must have been done nonchalantly.

18. **discordant and incongruous**

If the two defendants are redoing, and more importantly resynthesizing, their stories then there must be something about their interaction that would raise suspicion. We want words that illustrate two ideas not working together. "Hilarious" means extremely funny. The hilarity of their stories would not cause the jury to suspect they were lying. "Harmonious" means in-tune. This word has the exact opposite meaning as what the sentence is trying to suggest. We want words that show the stories not working together, but two harmonious stories do just that. "Syphoned" means drawn off. This word doesn't make sense in this context. "Dastardly" means immoral. While an immoral story would displease the jury, if they were both immoral the story would still pass as consistent. We want words that stress lack of consistency. Therefore, "Discordant" and "Incongruous" are the correct answers. They both mean incompatible. Obviously, two incompatible stories would rouse the suspicion of the jury because the two men would be giving two different versions of the crime.

19. **fungible and interchangeable**

This sentence is saying that although the period and structure of music changes its superficial qualities, all music elevate the human spirit in the same way. This sameness is the operative idea. We want words that stress the interchangeable effects of these genres. "Unequal" means uneven distribution. This answer cannot work because the whole idea of the sentence is that the emotional elevation of the material is equal. "Confusing" means unclear. This word does not in any way complete the sentiment of sameness between disparate genres of music. "Unnecessary" means not needed. Again, the sentence is not trying to argue of the necessity of these emotional elevations, it's trying to say that they can come from different sources. Therefore "Unnecessary" is incorrect. "Enlightening" means informative. Again, "Enlightening" does not complete the sentiment of the passage. We're trying to establish a quality of computability between these two hypothetical genres, not discuss their philosophical import. Therefore, we are left with "Fungible" and "Interchangeable." Both of these two words mean substitutable. This is the exact sentiment we want. When all of the superficial structures are torn away all genres of music have substitutable contributions to emotional elevation; i.e. the same contributions. a and e are correct.

20. **The correct answer is (B).**

The correct answer is choice B. One generally thirsts for something that is difficult to obtain; humans describe something pleasurable that cannot otherwise be quantified as heavenly, or celestial. Superior is a comparative adjective; to use it, one must have some point of comparison which is lacking in this passage. Answer A is, therefore, incorrect. Supernatural describes something that is magical or mystical or supernormal. One most often associates it with ghosts or the occult, not with beauty, making answer choice C incorrect. One might describe another's physical beauty as supernal, thereby assigning them heavenly status, but the purpose of poetry would not be to satisfy a thirst for physical beauty. Answer choice D is incorrect. Natural beauty is not created by quaintness or grotesqueness, making answer choice E incorrect.

# Section 5 – Quantitative Reasoning

1. **The correct answer is $\frac{8}{3}$**

If we let the cost of pencil be $x$, the cost of the pen will be $2x$.

The ratio begins as $\frac{2x}{x}$.

When the price of the pen is increased by 20%, $2xx$ $1.2 = 2.4x$.

When the price of the pencil is decreased by 10%, $xx$ $0.9 = 0.9x$, so the new ratio is $\frac{2.4x}{0.9x}$

Converting the sides of the ratio to whole numbers, we get $\frac{8}{3}$.

2. **The correct answer is (C).**

Use the following notation in solution process:

$m$ = Length of the rectangle

$n$ = Width of the rectangle

$a$ = Side of the square

$P$ = Perimeter of the square

Translate the given facts in the same order listed above.

(1) $m = 2n$

(2) $n = 2a$

(3) $P = 8$

Also, using the formulas of perimeters of square and rectangle, we have

(4) $P = 4a = 2(2a)$

(5) $Q = 2(m + n)$

Replace (2) and (3) in (4)

(6) $8 = 2n$

Divide each side by 4.

(7) $n = 4$

Apply (7) in (1), and simplify.

$m = 2(4)= 8$

Having measures of a length and a width of the rectangle, calculate its area.

$P = mn= (4)(8)= 32$

The two quantities are equal.

3. **The correct answer is (C).**

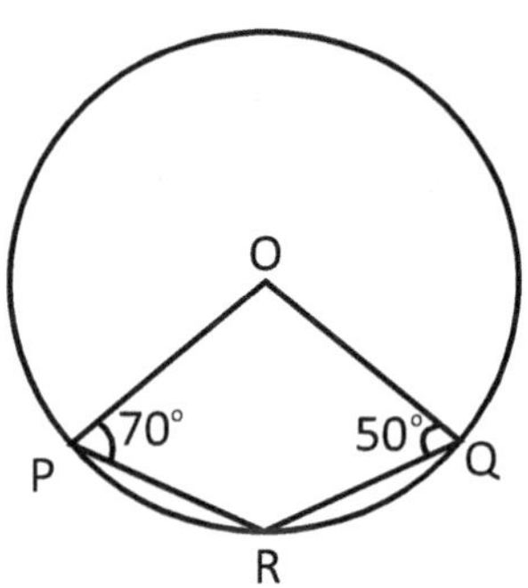


Join $OR$.

Now $OP=OR$ (Radii)

∴ ∠OPR= ∠ORP( angles opposite to equal sides)

∴ ∠ORP=$70^0$

Similarly ∠ORQ = ∠OQR (angles opposite to equal sides).

In triangle OPR

∠OPR+ ∠ORP+∠POR= $180^0$

i.e.$70^0$+$70^0$+∠POR= $180^0$

∠POR= $180^0$-$140^0$=$40^0$

Similarly

∠QOR= $180^0$-$100^0$=$80^0$

∴ ∠POQ=∠POR+∠QOR=$40^0$+$80^0$=$120^0$

∴ Reflex ∠POQ=$360^0$-$120^0$=$240^0$

4. **The correct answer is (A).**

We first must find $X$.

If 632$X$ is a multiple of 3

$6 + 3 + 2 + X$ must be a multiple of 3

There are three possible solutions for $X$:

$X$ = 1 or 4 or 7, so the sum $6 + 3 + 2 + X$ = 12 or 15 or 18

In order for an integer to be a multiple of 9, the sum of its digits must be a multiple of 9

If $X = 1$

$X7X = 171$

1 + 7 + 1 = 9; which is a multiple of 9

If $X = 4$

$X7X = 474$

4 + 7 + 4 = 15 which is not multiple of 9

If $X = 7$

$X7X = 777$

7 + 7 + 7 = 21 which is not multiple of 9

Only X = 1 satisfies both the condition that 632$X$ is divisible by 3 and that $X7X$ is divisible by 9

$X5 = 15 = 3 \times 5$ and $2X = 21 = 3 \times 7$

The least common multiple is 105 (= 3 × 5 × 7)

$5X = 51$ and $X02 = 102 = 2 \times 51$

The greatest common factor is 102

105 is greater than 102, so the left column is greater than the right column.

5. **The correct answer is (B).**

In ΔABC, m∠BAC = $90^0$ and m∠ACB = $30^0$

$$\sin(\angle ACB) = \frac{AB}{BC}$$

$$\sin(30^\circ) = \frac{1}{2} = \frac{AB}{BC}$$

$$\cos(\angle ACB) = \frac{AC}{BC}$$

$$\cos(30^\circ) = \frac{\sqrt{3}}{2} = \frac{AC}{BC}$$

Let BC = s

AB = s/2 and AC = (s√3)/2

As per the formula for the area of an equilateral triangle, the area of $ADC = \frac{(AC^2 \times \sqrt{3})}{4}$

$$Area\ ADC = \frac{\left(\frac{s\sqrt{3}}{2}\right)^2 \times \sqrt{3}}{4} = \frac{s^2 3\sqrt{3}}{16}$$

(If you do not remember the formula for the area of an equilateral triangle, you can still arrive at the correct result by drawing a height in $\Delta ADC$ and using Pythagoras'theorem)

$$Area\,\Delta\,ABC = \frac{(AB \times AC)}{2}$$

$$Area\,\Delta\,ABC = \frac{\frac{s}{2} \times \frac{s\sqrt{3}}{2}}{2} = \frac{s^2\sqrt{3}}{8}$$

which can also be written as $\frac{s^2 2\sqrt{3}}{16}$ $\frac{s^2 3\sqrt{3}}{16}$ is greater than $\frac{s^2 2\sqrt{3}}{16}$, so Area ADC is greater than Area ABC.

6. **The correct answer is (E).**

a is between 0 and 1, so when you multiply it by any number, it reduces the value of that number.

For any value between 0 and 1, dividing by that number is always larger than the numerator.

A squared number between 0 and 1 is always less than 1, and also less than the original number.

When you multiply by $a^2$, you always get a smaller number than your result after multiplying by a. The lowest value expression for a, then, is $a^2$.

7. **The correct answer is (C).**

Amount = \$2,250

Deposit/ principal (P) = \$1,500

Simple interest (I) = Total amount – Principal = \$2,250 – \$1,500 = \$750

Interested is computed semi–annually, or twice a year, so in 5 years it is calculated 10 times.

$\text{Time}(t)=10$

$I = Prt$

$$r = \frac{I}{Pt} = \frac{750}{1500 \times 10} = 0.05 = 5\%$$

8. **The correct answer is (E).**

We shall tabulate the data as follows:

| | Speed = distance / time | Distance | Time |
|---|---|---|---|
| Albert | *m* | *d(say)* | *t(say)* |
| His Friend | *x(say)* | *d/3* | *6t* |

$$Speed = \frac{Distance}{Time}$$

Now $m$=Albert's speed=$\frac{d}{t}$

$$Speed = \frac{Distance}{Time}$$

His Friend's speed=

$$x = \frac{\left(\frac{d}{3}\right)}{6t} = \frac{d}{18t} = \left(\frac{1}{18}\right)\left(\frac{d}{t}\right) = \left(\frac{1}{18}\right)m = \frac{m}{18}$$

$$x = \frac{m}{18}$$

9. **The correct answers are (B) and (D).**

For choice A: Having at least one even number showing can be calculated as follows:

$P$(at least 1 even) = $P$(1st even) + $P$(2nd even) – $P$(both even).

Solving,

$$P(atleast 1\ even) = \frac{18}{36} + \frac{18}{36} - \frac{9}{36} = \frac{27}{36} = \frac{3}{4}$$

which is greater than 1/2.

For choice B:

$$P(3 \cap odd) = P(1st:3, 2nd:odd) + P(1st:odd, 2nd:3) - P(both 3)$$

Solving, $P(3 \cap odd) = \frac{3}{36} + \frac{3}{36} - \frac{1}{36} = \frac{5}{36}$, which is less than 1/2.

For choice C: The condition is only for the first die and it should be greater than 3. So the probability is 1/2×1=1/2, which is not a correct answer since the question is looking for probabilities less than, not equal to, 1/2.

For choice D: This requires the sum of both dice to be less than or equal to 6, which will happen when the sums are 2, 3, 4, 5 or 6. The different combinations per sum are as follows:

2: 1+1 -> 1

3: 1+2, 2+1 -> 2

4: 1+3, 2+2, 3+1 -> 3

5: 1+4, 2+3, 3+2, 4+1 -> 4

6: 1+5, 2+4, 3+3, 4+2, 5+1 -> 5

Adding all the combinations, 1 + 2 + 3 + 4 + 5 = 15. Therefore, the probability of getting a sum less than or equal to 6 is 15/36, which is less than 1/2. Hence, the only correct choices are B and D.

10. **The correct answers are (A), (C) and (D).**

Since Triangle *ABC* is isosceles, median *AD* will also be altitude (perpendicular to *BC*) and angle bisector of $\angle BAC$

(A) $BD = \frac{y}{2}$

In the right-angled triangle *ADB*, *AB* is the hypotenuse.

Hence side $BD < AB$

i.e. $y/2 < x$. A is true.

(B) Only we know $\angle ABC = \angle ACB$.

Hence $\angle ABC$ is not necessarily equal to $\angle BAC$. B is false.

(C) $\angle ADC$ is a right angle, from the concept that *AD* is the altitude, C is true.

(D) $\angle BAD = \angle CAD$ from the concept that *AD* is the angle bisector of $\angle A$. D is true.

(E) $y^2=2x^2$ is false since *y* and *x* values can be any value. E is false.

(F) In the right-angled triangle *ADB*, *AB* is the hypotenuse.

Hence

$$AD^2 = x^2 - \left(\frac{y}{2}\right)^2 = \frac{(4x^2 - y^2)}{4}$$

Hence $4AD^2=(4x^2-y^2)$

$\therefore 2AD = \sqrt{4x^2 - y^2}$.

Hence F is false.

11. **The correct answer is (D).**

Since we do not have **the total number** of persons in each of the cities we will not be able to calculate the exact number of persons who have high BP in the cities and hence no inference can be drawn.

12. **The correct answer is (B).**

In order to find the possibility of persons having multiple diseases, we will add the percentages of diseases and find that for city X it is 30+42+5+6+13+4=100%. For city Y it is 38+40+8+4+20+5=115% which is possible only if some persons have more than one disease.

13. **The correct answer is (D).**

During the second quarter, beverage sales doubled, going from 8% to 16%. This is an additional 8% that was not present in the first quarter, so total sales had an 8% increase.

Quarter 1: Beverages=8/100

Quarter 2: Beverages=(8+8)/(100+8)=16/108=0.14814...=14.8%

14. **The correct answer is (C).**

Since 38% of those surveyed said they would not use this service, 62% said they would. 100%-38%=62%

Of those 62%, 54% would use it before work, which means 8% would not use it before work. 62%-54%=8% that would not use it before work.

Likewise, since 41% said they would use it after work, that indicates 21% would not use it after work. 62%-41%=21%.

Of the 62% surveyed that said they would use the, 8% would not use it before work, and 21% would not use it after work. The difference is the overlap. 62%-(21%+8%)=62%-29%=33%

33% of 1,500 is 500.

15. **The correct answer is 8.**

Let the two numbers be x and y with x<10 and y<10.

Since their difference is 6, the possible pairs are 1 and 7, 2 and 8, or 3 and 9.

$1 \times 7 = 7$, $2 \times 8 = 16$ and $3 \times 9 = 27$. Of these three sets, only 2 and 8 have a product that is the square of another integer ($4^2 = 16$).

Since the problem asks for the larger number, the solution is 8.

16. **The correct answer is (B).**

Given $8y$-$4x$=5

$$8y = 4x + 5$$

$$y = \frac{4x+5}{8}$$

Now $y$>800

$$\therefore \frac{4x+5}{8} > 800$$

$$\therefore 4x + 5 > 6400$$

Hence $4x$>6395

$$\therefore x > \frac{6395}{4}$$

$$\therefore x > 1598.75$$

So the least integer value of $x$= 1599

17. **The correct answer is (A).**

First we solve Equation 1:

$$4^x - x^{3-x} = 12$$

$$4^x - 4^3 \times 4^{-x} = 12$$

$$4 \ \ - 4^3 \times \frac{1}{4^x} = 12$$

$$4^x \times 4^x - 4^3 = 12 \times 4^x$$

$$4^{2x} - 12 \times 4^x - 4^3 = 0$$

Let $4^x = t$

If we substitute in the equation, it becomes

$t^2 - 12t - 64 = 0$

This can be factorized into $(t+4)(t-16) = 0$

One solution is $t = -4$, but $4^x$ cannot be negative

$t = -4$ is not a valid solution

Second solution is $t = 16$

$4^x = 4^2$

$x = 2$

Now, we solve Equation 2:

$$25^{\sqrt{y}} - 6 \times 5^{\sqrt{y}} + 5^{\sqrt{1}} = 0$$

$$5^{2\sqrt{y}} - 6 \times 5^{\sqrt{y}} + 5 = 0$$

Let $5^{\sqrt{y}} = u$

If we substitute in the equation, it becomes

$u^2 - 6u + 5 = 0$

This can be factorized into $(u-1)(u-5) = 0$

One solution is $u = 1$

$$5^{\sqrt{y}} = 1 = 5^0$$

$$y = 0$$

Second solution is $u = 5$

$$5^{\sqrt{y}} = 5 = 5^1$$
$$y = 1$$

The unique solution of Equation 1 (i.e. $x = 2$) is greater than any of the solutions of Equation 2 (i.e. 0 and 1)

18. **The correct answer is (B).**

We have three masons with a rate of 10 days, so each mason completes 1/10 of the work in one day

George's friend takes 8 days to complete the job, so he completes 1/8 of the work in one day

If all the masons begin to work together on that particular house, they will complete $(1/10\times3)+1/8=17/40$ in one day. So, the total time required to complete the job is $40/17=2.4$ days.

19. **The correct answer is (D).**

To solve this equation, we need to use the formula *d=rt (distance=rate × time)*. We need to write an equation to represent Carl's and Joseph's distance driven. If we assume that Carl drove for time t, then Joseph drove for t−1.5, since he left an hour and a half after Carl left.

Carl: d_c=(50*mph*)(t)

Joseph: d_J=(70*mph*)(t-1.5)

We want to know when Joseph will be 55 miles beyond Carl, so the difference between their distances will be 55 miles. We then solve the equation for *t*.

$$d_J - d_c = 55$$
$$70(t-1.5) - 50t = 55$$
$$70t - 105 - 50t = 55$$
$$20t - 105 = 55$$
$$20t = 160$$
$$t = 8 \text{ hours}$$

If Carl started at 6:00am and he drove 8 hours, Joseph will be 55 miles beyond him at 2:00pm.

20. **The correct answer is (A).**

Pipes *R* and *T* can empty the cistern in three hours, whereas pipes *R* and *Y* can empty the cistern in four hours.

This can be represented by the inequality $3<4$, where $3=r+t$ and $4=r+y$. In that case, $r+t<r+y$.

The Subtraction Property of Equality tells us that if $a=b$, then $a-c=b-c$.

The same holds true for inequalities, if $a<b$, then $a-c<b-c$.

Therefore, $r+t-r<r+y-r$, showing us that $t<y$.

## Chapter **5**

# Practice Test 3

You are about to begin a full length Practice Test. The Test has five sections. The time allotted for each section is marked at the beginning of the section. Work on one section at a time. Use a timer to keep track of the time limits for every section.

Try to take the Practice Test under real test conditions. Find a quiet place to work, and set aside enough time to complete the test without being disturbed. At the end of the test, check your answers by referring to the Answer Key and fill in your raw score in the score card below. Also, note down the time taken by you for completing each section.

Pay particular attention to the questions that were answered incorrectly. Read the answer explanations and understand how to solve them.

### My Score Card (Raw Score)

| | **Section 2** | **Section 3** | **Section 4** | **Section 5** |
|---|---|---|---|---|
| **Out of** | 20 | 20 | 20 | 20 |
| **My Score** | ________ | ________ | ________ | ________ |
| **Time Taken** | ________ | ________ | ________ | ________ |

# Section 1 – Analytical Writing

## Task 1 – Analyze an Issue | 30 mins

*The primary goal of technological advancement should be to increase people's efficiency so that they have more leisure time.*

*Write a response in which you discuss the extent to which you agree or disagree with the statement and explain your reasoning for the position you take. In developing and supporting your position, you should consider ways in which the statement might or might not hold true and explain how these considerations shape your position.*

You may start writing your response here

## Task 2 – Analyze an Argument Task | 30 mins

*The following appeared in an e-mail sent by the marketing director of the Classical Shakespeare Theatre of Bardville.*

*"Over the past ten years, there has been a 20 percent decline in the size of the average audience at Classical Shakespeare Theatre productions. In spite of increased advertising, we are attracting fewer and fewer people to our shows, causing our profits to decrease significantly. We must take action to attract new audience members. The best way to do so is by instituting a 'Shakespeare in the Park' program this summer. Two years ago the nearby Avon Repertory Company started a 'Free Plays in the Park' program, and its profits have increased 10 percent since then. If we start a 'Shakespeare in the Park' program, we can predict that our profits will increase, too."*

*Write a response in which you discuss what questions would need to be answered in order to decide whether the recommendation is likely to have the predicted result. Be sure to explain how the answers to these questions would help to evaluate the recommendation.*

You may start writing your response here

# Section 2 – Verbal Reasoning

20 questions | 30 mins

---

**For Questions 1 and 2, select one entry for the blank. Fill the blanks in the way that best completes the text.**

1. The usefulness of sulfuric acid in producing everything from detergents to fertilizers seems to supersede what would otherwise be considered __________ levels of risk in utilizing such a volatile chemical.

| garish |
|---|
| propitious |
| exorbitant |
| obsequious |
| fastidious |

2. It's hard to believe that a field of study as _________ as inorganic bond angles is so essential for the comprehension and manipulation of chemical compounds.

| pedestrian |
|---|
| prevalent |
| torpid |
| applicable |
| parsimonious |

**Questions 3 to 6 are based on the following passage.**

Consciousness is like a stream, which, so far as we are concerned with it in a psychological discussion, has its rise at the cradle and its end at the grave. It begins with the babe's first faint gropings after light in his new world as he enters it, and ends with the man's last blind gropings after light in his old world as he leaves it. The stream is very narrow at first, only as wide as the few sensations which come to the babe when it sees the light or hears the sound; it grows wider as the mind develops, and is at last measured by the grand sum total of life's experience.

**This mental stream is irresistible.** No power outside of us can stop it while life lasts. We cannot stop it ourselves. When we try to stop thinking, the stream but changes its direction and flows on. **While we wake and while we sleep, while we are unconscious under an anaesthetic, even, some sort of mental process continues.** Sometimes the stream flows slowly, and our thoughts lag—we "feel slow"; again the stream flows faster, and we are lively and our thoughts come with a rush; or a fever seizes us and delirium comes on; then the stream runs wildly onward, defying our control, and a mad jargon of thoughts takes the place of our usual orderly array.

**For Questions 3 and 4, select only one answer choice.**

3. What is the function of the two bold–faced sentences in the passage?

   (A) The first introduces a new argument, and the second provides evidence to support that idea.

   (B) The first explains the author's argument, and the second provides a conclusion.

   (C) The first presents the author's main point, and the second provides an alternate view.

   (D) The first provides evidence, and the second explains the evidence.

   (E) The first explains a new idea, and the second concludes that idea.

4. Based on the passage, what is the main idea that the author strives to convey regarding the power of consciousness?

   (A) Thoughts can be silenced with the right amount of mental concentration.

   (B) Consciousness is a mental entity that has a life and energy of its own.

   (C) The types of thoughts that a person has can be halted more easily at a younger age, as they have not gained as much momentum as they have in the mind of an older person.

   (D) A person's energy level is not directly proportionate to their thoughts, as neither one can be consciously controlled.

   (E) Consciousness has its own energy that is separate from life experiences.

**Consider each of the three choices separately and select all that apply.**

5. What can be inferred from the passage regarding the author's attitude towards the ability to control thought processes?

   [A] The author has met with frustration at attempting to control his thoughts and not being able to.

   [B] The author has spent many years studying mental control by observing numerous people and tracking their mental activity.

   [C] The author believes that a person's feelings can provide a direct reflection of their inner thoughts.

6. Select the sentence that best demonstrates the adaptive energy of a person's mental activity despite any attempt to stop the flow of thoughts.

**Question 7 is based on the following passage.**

Anthropologists have found stories showing that Tezcatlipoca guided the Nahua, and especially the people of Tezcuco, from a more northerly clime to the valley of Mexico. But he was not a mere local deity of Tezcuco; his worship was widely celebrated throughout the country. His exalted position in the Mexican pantheon seems to have won for him especial reverence as a god of fate and fortune. The place he took as the head of the Nahua pantheon brought him many attributes which were quite foreign to his original character. Fear and a desire to exalt their tutelar deity will impel the devotees of a powerful god to credit him with any or every quality, so that there is nothing remarkable in the spectacle of the heaping of every possible attribute, human or divine, upon Tezcatlipoca considering the supreme position he occupied in Mexican mythology. As a result of his importance, __________ .

7. Which choice most effectively completes the passage?

(A) there are very few extant representations of Tezcatlipoca, and many are associated with the color black.

(B) he is the most famous of the four sons of Ometecuhtli and Omecihuatl.

(C) his right foot is often replaced in drawings with the image of a snake or obsidian mirror.

(D) his worship was originally introduced by the Nahua people in the 10th century A.D.

(E) his priestly caste far surpassed in power the priesthoods of the other Mexican deities.

**For Questions 8 to 12, select the two answer choices that, when used to complete the sentence, fit the meaning of the sentence as a whole and produce completed sentences that are alike in meaning.**

8. The legendary teacher possessed unparalleled learning but nobody could ask him to elucidate any of his theories because, in spite of the communal nature of his works, his ________ outmatched even his brilliance.

[A] superciliousness

[B] popularity

[C] reclusiveness

[D] obtuseness

[E] unimportance

[F] solitariness

9. While he was familiar with the complexities of magnetic flux, the relationship between alternating and direct currents, and the study of electromagnetism, he still found the Earth's abilities to combine these principles in its geomagnetic reversal to be __________.

[A] impenetrable

[B] opaque

[C] pellucid

[D] clear

[E] self–effacing

[F] insidious

10. Even the most cunning of corporate executives will try to mask his ________ with an effervescent personality in order to remain in the public's good graces.

A guile

B acquiescence

C wiliness

D obstinacy

E friendliness

F vicariousness

11. In order to lure his business rival into a false sense of security, the corporate executive would ask deliberately ________ questions during the rival's presentation even while relentlessly prodding it for holes.

A refractory

B benign

C transparent

D gentle

E insensitive

F meandering

12. The wave phenomena can be observed travelling through solid media and the vacuum of space; it can also take the form of compression and rarefactions or be measured through the transfer of energy and momentum; this __________ often confuses and overwhelms students.

A ubiquity

B uniformity

C pervasiveness

D conformity

E expressivity

F petulance

**Question 13 is based on the following passage.**

Knowing that we can improve our willpower and become grittier in the face of obstacles should make us more optimistic about what we are capable of. Unfortunately, we are often held back by our own beliefs about ourselves and our capacity for change. Developmental psychologists have shown that having a fixed mindset -- viewing attributes such as intelligence and personality as set in stone -- causes people to fear failure, react badly to criticism and avoid new or difficult assignments, hardly a recipe for success. The belief that your traits are malleable, on the other hand, makes you more willing to stretch yourself and learn new skills.

Over the last decade, a team led by Carol Dweek at Stanford University has improved the grades and attendance records of thousands of school and college students across the US simply by teaching them that intelligence isn't fixed, that hard work can make you smarter, and that struggling to adjust to college is a normal learning process and not a sign of poor intellect. A "growth" mindset is advantageous at all stages of life, says Dweek. "It allows you to take on more challenges, and you don't get discouraged by setbacks or find effort undermining."

**Select only one answer choice.**

13. In regards to the power of perception on one's own mindset and the effect that this view has on the overall outcome of success, the overriding message of this passage is that

(A) innate intelligence is an important factor in determining how successful a person will be in life.

(B) the inability to adapt to new and difficult situations is due to deep-rooted beliefs.

(C) when a person believes that he or she is skilled in an area of expertise, he or she will be able to handle challenges that may arise, as long as they fall within the boundaries of his or her skill set.

(D) a constant feeling of struggle and difficulty is often a sign that a person is not employing his or her strongest skills.

(E) people are born with certain weaknesses and strengths that indicate how they should focus their efforts in order to be successful.

**Questions 14 to 17 are based on the following passage.**

Susan B. Anthony did not forget her unfinished business in New York State. The refusal of the legislature to amend the property laws had doubled her determination to continue circulating petitions until married women's civil rights were finally recognized. It took courage to go alone to towns where she was unknown to arrange for meetings on the unpopular subject of woman's rights. Not knowing how she would be received, she found it almost as difficult to return to such towns as Canajoharie where she had been highly respected as a teacher six years before. In Canajoharie, however, she was greeted affectionately by her uncle Joshua Read. He and his friends let her use the Methodist church for her lecture, and when the trustees of the academy urged her to return there to teach, Uncle Joshua interrupted with a vehement "No!" protesting that others could teach but it wasSusan's work "to go around and set people thinking about the laws."

Returning to the scene of her girlhood in Battenville and Easton, visiting her sisters Guelma and Hannah, and meeting many of her old friends, Susan realized as never before how completely she had outgrown her old environment. In her enthusiasm for her new work, she exposed "many of her heresies," and when her friends labeled

William Lloyd Garrison an agnostic and rabble rouser, she protested that he was the most Christlike man she had ever known. "Thus it is belief, not Christian benevolence," she confided to her diary in 1854, "that is made the modern test of Christianity."

After eight strenuous months away from home, she was welcomed warmly by a family who believed in her work. She found abolition uppermost in everyone's mind. Her brother Merritt, fired by Daniel's tales of the West and the antislavery struggle in Kansas, was impatient to join the settlers there and could talk of nothing else. While he poured out the latest news about Kansas, he and a cousin, Mary Luther, helped Susan fold handbills for future woman's rights meetings. Susan listened eagerly and approvingly as he told of the 750 free–state settlers who during the past summer had gone out to Kansas, traveling up the Missouri on steamboats and over lonely trails in wagons marked "Kansas." Most of them were not abolitionists but men who wanted Kansas a free–labor state which they could develop with their own hard work. She heard of the ruthless treatment these "Yankee" settlers faced from the proslavery Missourians who wanted Kansas in the slavery bloc. There was bloodshed and there would be more. John Brown's sons had written from Kansas, "Send us guns. We need them more than bread." Merritt was ready and eager to join John Brown.

The Anthony farm was virtually a hotbed of insurrection with Merritt planning resistance in Kansas and Susan reform in New York. Susan mapped out an ambitious itinerary, hoping to canvass with her petitions every county in the state. With her father as security, she borrowed money to print her handbills and notices, and then wrote Wendell Phillips asking if any money for a woman's rights campaign had been raised by the last national convention. He replied with his own personal check for fifty dollars. His generosity and confidence touched her deeply, for already he had become a hero to her second only to William Lloyd Garrison. This tall handsome intellectual, a graduate of Harvard and an unsurpassed orator, had forfeited friends, social position, and a promising career as a lawyer to plead for the slave. He was also one of the very few men who sympathized with and aided the woman's rights cause.

Horace Greeley too proved at this time to be a good friend, writing, "I have your letter and your programme, friend Susan. I will publish the latter in all our editions, but return your dollars." Her earnestness and ability made a great appeal to these men. Thirty–four years old now, not handsome but wholesome, simply and neatly dressed, her brown hair smoothly parted and brought down over her ears, she had nothing of the scatterbrained impulsive reformer about her, and no coquetry. She was practical and intelligent, and men liked to discuss their work with her. William Henry Channing, admiring her executive ability and her plucky reaction to defeat, dubbed her the Napoleon of the woman's rights movement. Parker Pillsbury, the fiery abolitionist from New Hampshire, broad–shouldered, dark–bearded, with blazing eyes and almost fanatical zeal, had become her devoted friend. He liked nothing better than to tease her about her idleness and pretend to be in search of more work for her to do.

**For Questions 14 and 15, select only one answer choice.**

14. Based on the passage, if Susan B. Anthony went to speak to an all-male school board who opposed having girls on the football team and told her not to talk as her name was not included on the agenda, what action would she most likely have taken?

   (A) Pound on the table, raise her voice and tell them they should be ashamed of their decision.

   (B) Excuse herself and ask to be included on the next meeting's agenda.

   (C) Rattle off whatever came to mind in attempt to persuade them to allow girls' participation.

   (D) Insist on being allowed to speak anyway and pass out papers showing her research of other schools that have allowed women to participate on football teams.

   (E) Ask the men to give their reasons for the decision and tell them she would report this to the state school athletic association.

15. What role does the highlighted portion play in the understanding of Susan B. Anthony's actions throughout the passage?

   (A) This displays contradictory information between the old and new William Lloyd Garrison.

   (B) This displays a conclusive statement about the characters with whom Anthony associates.

   (C) This displays contradictory information between Anthony's feelings and "the real William Lloyd Garrison"

   (D) This displays contradictory information about William Lloyd Garrison, showing the value of Anthony's contact with William Lloyd Garrison to know him better.

   (E) This displays contradictory information about William Lloyd Garrison, illuminating the difference between some of the views of Anthony's traditional upbringing and her own enlightenment having traveled and worked on her own.

**For Questions 16 and 17, consider each of the three choices separately and select all that apply.**

16. Which statements are not supported by the passage?

   [A] Women should be allowed to be pastors if they choose, and this should not be a controversy.

   [B] Anthony had many financial supporters that contributed to her efforts to bring about reform for women.

   [C] Anthony greatly longed to appear attractive to men and wanted to be married as soon as possible to help her career.

17. Which of the following statements would are supported by this passage?

   [A] Anthony's nature could be described as "intrepid and methodical."

   [B] Men feared Anthony and resisted becoming involved with the issues she confronted.

   [C] Anthony's appearance was very physically unattractive, plain and neat.

**For Questions 18 to 20, select one entry for the blank. Fill the blank in the way that best completes the text.**

18. The closer scientists investigate the sources of life in our macroscopic world, the more they see and appreciate just how _________ our origins really are.

| vapid |
|---|
| caustic |
| culminated |
| calamitous |
| infinitesimal |

19. The _________ nature of the American automotive industry has led to periods of panic when a foreign producer overtakes it and periods of euphoria when it introduces new models that sweep the world with their popularity.

| baroque |
|---|
| indulgent |
| recurrent |
| immutable |
| steadfast |

20. Literary techniques are ______ to creating a unique work of literature – two otherwise identical plots, if written with widely different literary devices, will not be recognizable to each other in any way.

| indispensable |
|---|
| antagonistic |
| allegorical |
| anachronistic |
| insufficient |

# Section 3 – Quantitative Reasoning

20 questions | 35 mins

---

1.

A pack of candies contains 5 yellow, 3 pink and 7 white candies. Two candies are taken from the pack without replacement.

| Quantity A | Quantity B |
|---|---|
| Probability of drawing a yellow candy, followed by a 1 pink candy | Probability of drawing 2 white candies |

(A) Quantity A is greater.

(B) Quantity B is greater.

(C) The two quantities are equal.

(D) The relationship cannot be determined from the information given.

2.

Two dice are thrown and the numbers facing up are added.

| Quantity A | Quantity B |
|---|---|
| Probability of getting a sum of 5 | Probability of getting a sum of 9 |

(A) Quantity A is greater.

(B) Quantity B is greater.

(C) The two quantities are equal.

(D) The relationship cannot be determined from the information given.

**Questions 3 and 4 are based on the following diagram:**

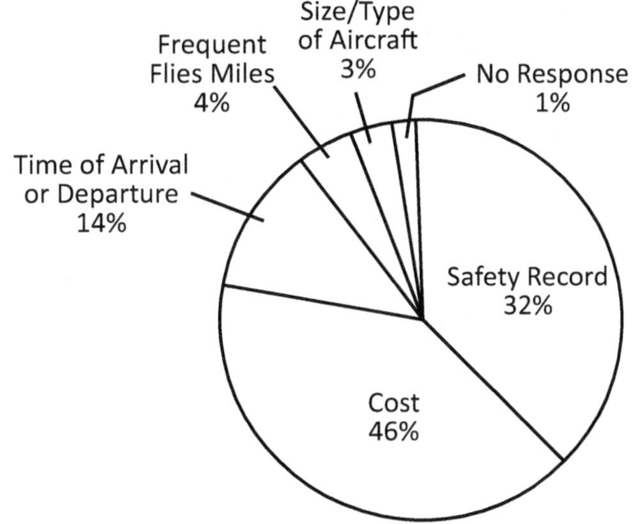


3. What percentage of passengers is not concerned with the Time of Arrival or Departure?

(A) 14%

(B) 54%

(C) 32%

(D) 78%

(E) 86%

4. What percentage of passengers is not concerned with Frequent Filer Miles, Safety Record, or Size/Type of Aircraft?

(A) 39%

(B) 71%

(C) 32%

(D) 61%

(E) 46%

**Questions 5 and 6 are based on the following diagram:**

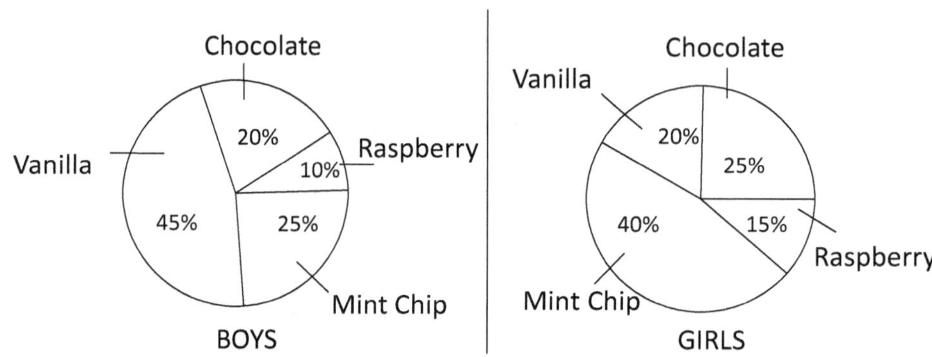


5. If there are twice as many girls as there are boys, which flavor ice cream is preferred by most?

   (A) Vanilla

   (B) Mint Chip

   (C) Raspberry

   (D) Chocolate

   (E) Not enough information is given.

6. Twelve boys like mint chip more than any of the other flavors. How many boys are there in total?

   (A) 37

   (B) 100

   (C) 60

   (D) 30

   (E) 48

7. Dolly deposited $8,050 in a bank which offered simple interest at a rate of 2.25% quarterly for 6 years. Determine the total amount of money in the bank after this period.

   $- [ ]

8. If $-5x+2y=9$ and $3x-4y=-4$, then what is the value of $7x+10y$?

Ⓐ -19

Ⓑ -17

Ⓒ -9

Ⓓ 9

Ⓔ 19

9. At the beginning of the day, Carla had $y$ dollars in her pocket. She spent \$5.00 on breakfast and half of what was left on lunch. She got lucky and found \$2.00 on the ground. Write an algebraic expression that describes how much she has to spend for dinner?

Ⓐ $\frac{1}{2}y-\frac{1}{2}$

Ⓑ $y-5\frac{1}{2}$

Ⓒ $\frac{1}{2}y-2\frac{1}{2}$

Ⓓ $\frac{3}{2}y-\frac{1}{2}$

Ⓔ $\frac{3}{2}y+\frac{1}{2}$

10.

| **Quantity A** | **Quantity B** |
|---|---|
| Probability of drawing a diamond suit from a deck of cards | Probability of drawing a face card from a deck of cards |

Ⓐ Quantity A is greater.

Ⓑ Quantity B is greater.

Ⓒ The two quantities are equal.

Ⓓ The relationship cannot be determined from the information given.

11. Lian took algebra exam five times during the past academic year. For exams 1 through 3, her score increased 10% with respect to the previous one. Her score in the second exam was 44, and the average of all five exams was 58. The difference between scores of the last two exams was 7.6.

Which of the following statements are true?

[A] Score of first exam = 40

[B] Score of first exam = 44

[C] Score of third exam = 44.8

[D] Score of third exam = 48.4

[E] Score of fourth exam = 82.8

[F] Score of fifth exam = 67

[G] Sum of the last two exams = 157.6

12. Two vehicles, a car and a bus, are traveling directly towards each other at the speed of 68 mph and 30 mph, respectively. If the distance between them is 792 feet, determine how much time (in seconds) it will take for them to meet.

[ ] *seconds*

13. What is the value of g in the equation $5x - 2g = 5 - 7zg$ ?

(A) $g = \frac{5z + 5x}{3}$

(B) $g = \frac{5x + 5}{7x + 2}$

(C) $g = \frac{5(x-1)}{2-7z}$

(D) $g = \frac{5x - 5}{-5z}$

(E) $g = \frac{5x + 5}{7x - 2}$

14. What is the product of $4.23 \times 10^4$ and $8.53 \times 10^5$ in scientific notation?

(A) $3.608 \times 10^9$

(B) $3.608 \times 10^{10}$

(C) $36.08 \times 10^9$

(D) $360.8 \times 10^8$

(E) $3.608 \times 10^8$

15.

A fair coin is tossed 5 times.

| **Quantity A** | **Quantity B** |
| --- | --- |
| Probability of getting 3 tails | Probability of getting 2 tails |

(A) Quantity A is greater.

(B) Quantity B is greater.

(C) The two quantities are equal.

(D) The relationship cannot be determined from the information given.

16.

Events *A* and *B* are independent. $P(A)=0.5$

| **Quantity A** | **Quantity B** |
| --- | --- |
| $P(A)'$ | $P(B)$ |

(A) Quantity A is greater.

(B) Quantity B is greater.

(C) The two quantities are equal.

(D) The relationship cannot be determined from the information given.

17. Find the roots of the quadratic equation $f(x) = -3x^2 + 4x + 7$

(A) $\frac{4+\sqrt{88}}{6}, \frac{4-\sqrt{88}}{6}$

(B) $\frac{2+\sqrt{22}}{3}, \frac{2-\sqrt{22}}{3}$

(C) $\frac{7}{3}, -1$

(D) $\frac{2+\sqrt{88}}{3}, \frac{2-\sqrt{88}}{3}$

(E) $\frac{-2+\sqrt{22}}{3}, \frac{-2-\sqrt{22}}{3}$

18. On a sale, John bought one tie at 60% off and one pair of shoes at 30% off. If he paid $64 less for the tie than for the shoes and he spent a total of $104, what was the initial price of the tie?

(A) 46

(B) 50

(C) 52

(D) 54

(E) 56

19. After 4 years, Henry will be four times as many years old as Jacob is now. If Henry were thrice as old as he was 4 years ago, and if Jacob were twice as old as he was one year ago, the sum of their ages would be 30. What will be the sum of their ages after 5 years?

(A) 20

(B) 22

(C) 24

(D) 26

(E) 28

20. Magazine A has a total of 28 pages, 16 of which are advertisements and 12 of which are articles. Magazine B has a total of 35 pages, all of them either articles or advertisements. If the ratio of the number of pages of advertisements to the number of pages of articles is the same for both magazines, then magazine B has how many more pages of advertisements than magazines A?

(A) 2

(B) 3

(C) 4

(D) 5

(E) 6

# Section 4 – Verbal Reasoning

20 questions | 30 mins

---

**For Questions 1 and 2, select one entry for the blank. Fill the blank in the way that best completes the text.**

1. Some religions are deliberately ______; others believe that all living things, whether or not they even practice a religion, are still part of the spiritual family.

| inane |
|---|
| exclusive |
| facetious |
| technophobic |
| indolent |

2. Even though his doctor warned him that running would not be good for his knees, the middle–aged man found that the emotional ______ of exercise justified any subsequent stiffness.

| catharsis |
|---|
| indolence |
| exacerbation |
| calamity |
| inanity |

**Questions 3 to 5 are based on the following passage.**

Mrs. Archer, who was fond of coining her social philosophy into axioms, had once said: "We all have our pet common people—" and though the phrase was a daring one, its truth was secretly admitted in many an exclusive bosom. But the Beauforts were not exactly common; some people said they were even worse. Mrs. Beaufort belonged indeed to one of America's most honoured families; she had been the lovely Regina Dallas (of the South Carolina branch), a penniless beauty introduced to New York society by her cousin, the imprudent Medora Manson, who was always doing the wrong thing from the right motive. When one was related to the Mansons and the Rushworths one had a "Droit de cité" (as Mr. Sillerton Jackson, who had frequented the Tuileries, called it) in New York society; but did one not forfeit it in marrying Julius Beaufort?

The question was: who was Beaufort? He passed for an Englishman, was agreeable, handsome, ill–tempered, hospitable and witty. He had come to America with letters of recommendation from old Mrs. Manson Mingott's English son–in–law, the banker, and had speedily made himself an important position in the world of affairs; but his habits were dissipated, his tongue was bitter, his antecedents were mysterious; and when Medora Manson announced her cousin's engagement to him it was felt to be one more act of folly in poor Medora's long record of imprudences.

But folly is as often justified of her children as wisdom, and two years after young Mrs. Beaufort's marriage it was admitted that she had the most distinguished house in New York. No one knew exactly how the miracle was accomplished. She was indolent, passive, the caustic even called her dull; but dressed like an idol, hung with pearls, growing younger and blonder and more beautiful each year, she throned in Mr. Beaufort's heavy brown–stone palace, and drew all the world there without lifting her jewelled little finger. The knowing people said it was Beaufort himself who trained the servants, taught the chef new dishes, told the gardeners what hot–house flowers to grow for the dinner–table and the drawing–rooms, selected the guests, brewed the after–dinner punch and dictated the little notes his wife wrote to her friends. If he did, these domestic activities were privately performed, and he presented to the world the appearance of a careless and hospitable millionaire strolling into his own drawing–room with the detachment of an invited guest, and saying: "My wife's gloxinias are a marvel, aren't they? I believe she gets them out from Kew."

Mr. Beaufort's secret, people were agreed, was the way he carried things off. It was all very well to whisper that he had been "helped" to leave England by the international banking–house in which he had been employed; he carried off that rumour as easily as the rest—though New York's business conscience was no less sensitive than its moral standard—he carried everything before him, and all New York into his drawing–rooms, and for over twenty years now people had said they were "going to the Beauforts'" with the same tone of security as if they had said they were going to Mrs. Manson Mingott's, and with the added satisfaction of knowing they would get hot canvas–back ducks and vintage wines, instead of tepid VeuveCliquot without a year and warmed–up croquettes from Philadelphia.

**For Questions 3 to 5, select only one answer choice.**

3. The passage most clearly addresses which of the following issues regarding the social implications of being linked, whether inextricably or temporarily, to Mr. Beaufort?

   (A) How anyone who marries him can enjoy a lavish lifestyle without ever having to worry about entertaining guests.

   (B) Whether marrying him indelibly tarnishes his wife's formerly favorable reputation.

   (C) Whether a rise in social status will pose a burden to the new wife who will then have to spend more time catering to her husband and his friends.

   (D) How people will perceive the Beauforts in regards to their lavish spending.

   (E) How the duality of Mr. Beaufort's personality creates doubt among his peers as to whether he is genuine or deceitful.

4. The author provides textual support in this passage for all of the following statements EXCEPT:

(A) Mr. Beaufort leads a duplicitous existence, purposely presenting himself as a relaxed, carefree person yet all the while fussing over the details of his surroundings.

(B) Mrs. Beaufort, amidst her lavish and affluent lifestyle, is most known for her impeccable sense of style.

(C) Many people doubt the validity of Mr. Beaufort's English background despite his charm and wealth.

(D) Medora Manson is known to make questionable decisions despite her honorable intent to please others.

(E) Mrs. Beaufort was well–respected as a wealthy socialite until she married Mr. Beaufort.

5. What function does the highlighted phrase serve in the passage?

(A) To predict that Medora Manson will always continue to commit a social 'faux–pas' every time that she associates with the Beauforts.

(B) This phrase implies that people tend to take pity on Medora, and that she is often the bearer of unfortunate news.

(C) It demonstrates the widely–shared opinion of Mr. Beaufort's questionable social standing and predicts the negative effect that he will have on everyone with whom he associates.

(D) To explain that Medora is much more outspoken than her cousin, who does not express her own feelings about the important events in her life.

(E) People in New York only hear about important events through 'word of mouth' rather than reading about them in the newspaper.

**For Questions 6 to 9, select the two answer choices that, when used to complete the sentence, fit the meaning of the sentence as a whole and produce completed sentences that are alike in meaning.**

6. As he watched his inheritance pour into his bank account and the __________ urges begin pulsing through his veins, Stephen knew that he would have a difficult road ahead of him if he wanted to maintain his pre–wealth humility.

[A] enlightened

[B] supercilious

[C] chic

[D] vacuous

[E] haughty

[F] violent

7. Aspiring business owners may wait until their government ________ that corporations are entities separate from their owners before they registering their businesses to ensure that they will not lose their personal wealth if their businesses are sued or undergo bankruptcy proceedings.

A emends

B palavers

C gibes

D promulgates

E avers

F inveighs

8. Understanding the mechanics of removing retinoblastomas via ocular surgery must be complimented with ________ in order to successfully complete such a technically demanding procedure.

A tenacity

B predilection

C awareness

D doggedness

E contempt

F sensitivity

9. Preparing for a complex reaction synthesis such as the sharpless epoxidation often overwhelms the mind of an organic chemistry lab student and causes him or her to forget more _______ yet still–necessary things such as proper distillation apparatus setup.

A perfunctory

B riveting

C sympathetic

D adroit

E mechanical

F inexplicable

**Questions 10 to 12 are based on the following passage.**

Now, of all the various responsibilities, expressed, implied, or assumed by the United States in Haiti, it would naturally be supposed that the financial obligation would be foremost. Indeed, the sister republic of Santo Domingo was taken over by the United States Navy for no other reason than failure to pay its internal debt. But Haiti for over one hundred years scrupulously paid its external and internal debt--a fact worth remembering when one hears of "anarchy and disorder" in that land--until five years ago when under the financial guardianship of the United States interest on both the internal and, with one exception, external debt was defaulted; and this in spite of the fact that specified revenues were pledged for the payment of this interest. Apart from the distinct injury to the honor and reputation of the country, the hardship on individuals has been great.

**For Questions 10 and 11, select only one answer choice.**

10. This passage discusses which of the following issues regarding the United States' policies toward Haiti?

(A) The unfairness of the U.S.'s treatment of Haiti in comparison to its actions toward Santo Domingo.

(B) The comparative importance of internal vs. external debt to Haiti's financial infrastructure.

(C) The reasons that the United States assumed financial guardianship in Haiti.

(D) The role of the United States in regard to Haiti's financial crisis.

(E) The reasons that designated revenues were not used to pay Haiti's debts.

11. Based on the passage, with which of the following statements would the author probably agree?

(A) Haiti's default on its debts can be attributed to anarchy and disorder in the country.

(B) Haiti defaulted on its debts despite the best efforts of the United States.

(C) Haiti does not fully deserve its reputation for "anarchy and disorder".

(D) Revenues set aside for interest payments should have instead been used to pay down internal debt.

(E) While the United States was primarily concerned with the issue of internal debt, Haiti erred by attempting to pay down internal and external debts simultaneously.

**Consider each of the three choices separately and select all that apply.**

12. The passage implies which of the following about the country of Haiti?

[A] Many people assume that Haiti's economic crisis is its own fault.

[B] Financial insolvency is not typical of Haiti.

[C] Haitian citizens have suffered in tangible ways from the default.

**For each blank, select one entry from the corresponding column of choices. Fill all blanks in the way that best completes the text.**

13. Music and theater have been (i)______ for millennia. Even the legendary Athenian tragedies, known for their high drama, utilized choruses that were often accompanied by musical instruments. This tradition has (ii)______ into the modern age of theater. Some of the most famous stage tragedies of our time express their (iii)______ through the use of music.

| Blank (i) | Blank (ii) | Blank (iii) |
|---|---|---|
| intertwined | perished | avarice |
| antagonistic | glided | aplomb |
| extraneous | lurched | pathos |

**Question 14 is based on the following passage.**

What a given amount of energy will do depends only upon its form, that is, the kind of motion that embodies it. The energy spent upon a stone thrown into the air, giving it translatory motion, would, if spent upon a tuning fork, make it sound, but not move it from its place; while if spent upon a top, would enable the latter to stand upon its point as easily as a person stands on his two feet, and to do other surprising things, which otherwise it could not do. One can, without difficulty, form a mechanical conception of the whole series without assuming imponderables, or fluids or forces.

**Select only one answer choice.**

14. All of the following statements identify assumptions on which the author's argument relies EXCEPT:

Ⓐ The energy that a person spends in throwing an object can be applied to a different object with the same amount of force.

Ⓑ The amount of energy needed to throw an object can be transferred to a different object without hurling the object through the air.

Ⓒ A person who ponders the mechanics of energy can easily comprehend the basic knowledge associated with this subject matter.

Ⓓ It is just as easy to throw a stone as it is to spin a top.

Ⓔ Creating a sound in a tuning fork is as simple as throwing a stone, though may require two people to do so simultaneously.

**Questions 15 to 17 are based on the following passage.**

There seem to be two literary factions pitted against each other. Those of one class employ their best effort in dissuading young writers from writing; those of another set forth an author's life in glowing colors. **One faction will tell you that half the manuscripts sent to editors are not even accorded the courtesy of an examination unless signed by a well-known name.** Another says that editors are keenly on the outlook for original matter, seizing with avidity anything that promises to make a new element in current literature.

A noted author writes to a young aspirant: "Sweet and natural though your utterance seems to be, let me ask you in the friendliest spirit not to write at all. The toil is great, the pursuit incessant, the reward not outward." To the same young woman writes another equally well-known writer: "Your work is excellent; you can and will succeed."

**For Questions 15 and 16, select only one answer choice.**

15. This passage primarily sets out to prove which of the following ideas?

    (A) Accomplished writers view work with a critical eye and have differing opinions on the rhythm and cadence in a writer's work.

    (B) Authors are opinionated and base their criticism of aspiring writers' works on their own experiences.

    (C) The profession of writing is difficult and toilsome, yet can also be rewarding.

    (D) The opinions of established writers differ greatly and can be distinguished by their outlook on the perceived difficulty of writing as a profession.

    (E) In order to earn money, aspiring authors must make their own decisions regarding how to submit their work to editors so that pessimistic people will not dissuade them from reaching their goals.

16. What is the primary effect of the sentence in boldface type on the passage's overall message?

    (A) To indicate the severity with which editors express their opinion of work that does not meet the high standards of publishing companies.

    (B) This sentence demonstrates the clout that well-known authors have in the publishing world; without a good reputation, it is very difficult to solicit an editor for advice on completed works.

    (C) It indicates the fragility of amateur writers' careers and the detrimental effects that harsh criticism can have on their aspirations.

    (D) To explain that editors rudely ignore at least fifty percent of submitted manuscripts without so much as a cursory glance unless the work comes highly recommended by one of their colleagues.

    (E) It establishes the opinion of one group of people in the writing business who warn about the regimented approach that editors often take to critiquing unpublished manuscripts.

17. Select a sentence from the passage that provides support for the author's viewpoint that writing is too subjective for one person to determine the fate of an aspiring writer's career.

**For Questions 18 to 20, for each blank, select one entry from the corresponding column of choices. Fill all blanks in the way that best completes the text.**

18. Calculating the habitability of distant planets is an inexact science. Because of the immense distances involved, astronomers are forced to rely on (i)__________ about distant solar systems. Moreover, the more astronomers look at these solar systems, the more they realize that the solar system around our Sun might not be the (ii)________ it was assumed to be. This is because most neighboring solar systems actually reverse the structure of our own – their gas giants close to their sun, while rocky planets are farther away.

| Blank (i) |
| --- |
| fauna |
| inferences |
| ambiguities |

| Blank (ii) |
| --- |
| liability |
| archetype |
| recidivist |

19. Einstein's theory of relativity is so (i)________ that it has not been disproven. It is the rare theory that crosses through many disciplines. (ii)________, many of the experiments that have been conducted to challenge the theory of relativity have actually served to reinforce its validity. It has seen slight tweaks in recent years, but its central tenets are unequivocal.

| Blank (i) |
| --- |
| axiomatic |
| equivocal |
| arcane |

| Blank (ii) |
| --- |
| Disparagingly |
| Ironically |
| Redundantly |

20. Biogerontology, the study of the biological causes of aging, is a field in rapid development. The science continues to creep forward and caress answers out of formerly (i)________ issues. Even if some of biogerontology's loftier goals are never reached, any (ii)________ increases in our understanding of human aging will yield tremendous dividends in the fields of chemistry and biology.

| Blank (i) |
| --- |
| intractable |
| acquiescent |
| vituperative |

| Blank (ii) |
| --- |
| specious |
| substantive |
| unexplainable |

# Section 5 – Quantitative Reasoning

20 questions | 35 mins

---

1. Four people (Stephanie, Caroline, Brenda and Simon) take 5 *minutes*, 3 *minutes*, 4 *minutes* and 6 *minutes* respectively to wash a certain amount of clothes. Which combination(s) would do more than half of the job in one *minute*?

   [A] Stephanie and Brenda

   [B] Stephanie and Caroline

   [C] Stephanie and Simon

   [D] Brenda and Caroline

   [E] Simon and Caroline

   [F] Brenda and Simon

2. Bill has to type a paper that is $P$ pages long, with each page containing $w$ words. If Bill types an average of $x$ words per *minute*, how many *hours* will it take him to finish the paper?

   (A) $60wpx$

   (B) $\frac{wx}{60p}$

   (C) $\frac{60wp}{60x}$

   (D) $\frac{wpx}{60}$

   (E) $\frac{wp}{60x}$

3. If $x$ ,$y$, and $z$ are such that $xyz$=385 what is the value of $x$+$y$+$z$?

   [ ]

4. If Seymour drove 120 *miles* in *x hours* at constant speed, how many *miles* did he travel in the first 20 *minutes* of his trip?

(A) $60x$

(B) $3x$

(C) $\frac{120}{x}$

(D) $\frac{40}{x}$

(E) $\frac{6}{x}$

5.

A box of chocolates has 3 with mint cream filling, 5 with strawberry cream filling, and 9 with an almond center. Three pieces of chocolate were taken, and the first 2 chocolates were both almond–centered.

| **Quantity A** | **Quantity B** |
|---|---|
| Probability that the 3rd chocolate has either mint cream or strawberry cream filling | Probability that the 3rd chocolate is almond centered |

(A) Quantity A is greater.

(B) Quantity B is greater.

(C) The two quantities are equal.

(D) The relationship cannot be determined from the information given.

6. If a sweater sells for $48 after a 25 percent markdown, what was its original price?

(A) $56

(B) $60

(C) $64

(D) $65

(E) $72

7.

Using the set of integers from 1 to 100, inclusive:

| **Quantity A** | **Quantity B** |
|---|---|
| Probability that a given number is a multiple of 6 | Probability that a given number is a multiple of 5 |

(A) Quantity A is greater.

(B) Quantity B is greater.

(C) The two quantities are equal.

(D) The relationship cannot be determined from the information given.

8. Three people stop for lunch at hot dog stand. If each person orders one item and there are three items to choose from, how many different combinations of food could be purchased? (Assume that order doesn't matter, e.g., a hot dog and two sodas are considered the same as two sodas and a hot dog.)

(A) 6

(B) 9

(C) 10

(D) 18

(E) 27

9.

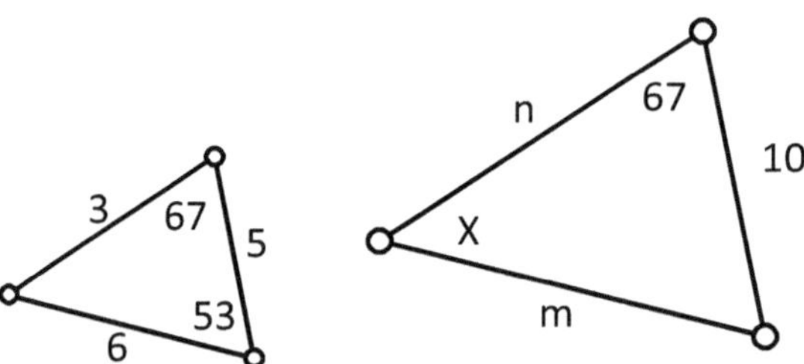


What is the value of $2x+m+2n$ if the triangles are similar?

10.

| Quantity A | Quantity B |
|---|---|
| The measure of the greatest angle out of two complementary angles $\angle A$ and $\angle B$, where $m\angle A - m\angle B = 50°$ | The measure of the greatest angle in a triangle with the sides *a*, *b* and *c* that satisfy: $a^6 + b^6 = c^6 - 3a^2b^2(a^2 + b^2)$ |

(A) Quantity A is greater.

(B) Quantity B is greater.

(C) The two quantities are equal.

(D) The relationship cannot be determined from the information given.

11. Consider the function $f(x) = \dfrac{13}{-2-x}$. Which of the following input values renders the function undefined?

(A) -2

(B) 13

(C) 0

(D) 2

(E) None of the above

12.

The students of Goodwill School are electing their student union president. There are 450 students at Goodwill but 8% of them are currently taking a gap year and hence not entitled to vote. Another 19 are currently in the process of transferring to a new school, so not entitled to vote either. Out of those who are allowed to vote only 60% voted. Richie Ambitious got 15/19 th of the total votes, Albert Aspirant received 75% of the remaining votes and Bobby Content got the rest.

| Quantity A | Quantity B |
|---|---|
| Votes received by Richie Ambitious | Votes received by Bobby Content |

(A) Quantity A is greater.

(B) Quantity B is greater.

(C) The two quantities are equal.

(D) The relationship cannot be determined from the information given.

13.

The ratio of the length and the width of a rectangle is 4:3. The area of the rectangle is 108 *square inches.*

| **Quantity A** | **Quantity B** |
|---|---|
| The width of the rectangle | The square of the difference between the length and the width |

(A) Quantity A is greater.

(B) Quantity B is greater.

(C) The two quantities are equal.

(D) The relationship cannot be determined from the information given.

14.

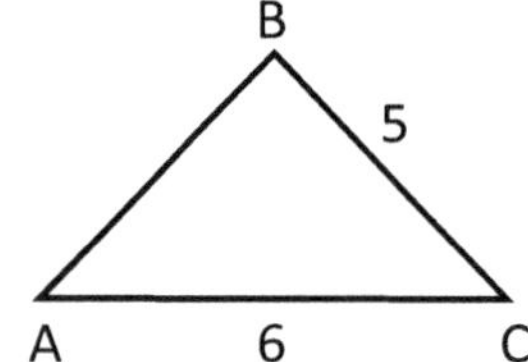


If the perimeter of ΔABC is 16, what is its area?

(A) 8

(B) 9

(C) 10

(D) 12

(E) 15

15. Cars X and Y traveling at uniform speed, reach points P and Q respectively at 9 pm. The distance between P and Q is 2 miles. The cars are traveling in the same directions. Car X catches car Y at 9:24 pm. What could the speed of the cars be in miles/hour? Indicate all answers.

[A] 68, 63

[B] 65, 60

[C] 64, 58

[D] 60, 55

[E] 59, 53

[F] 57, 52

[G] 55, 55

[H] 52, 47

16.

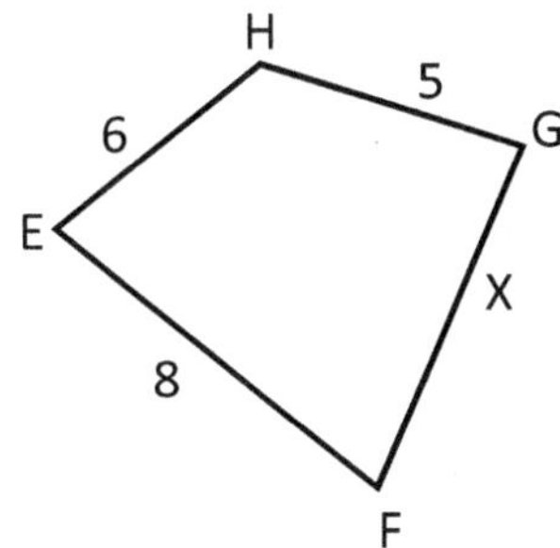


What is the value of $x$ in the figure above?

(A) 4

(B) $3\sqrt{3}$

(C) $3\sqrt{5}$

(D) $5\sqrt{3}$

(E) 9

17. In a medical study of 100 people the effectiveness of a drug was tested. Twenty–five participants saw no improvement after taking the drug for the duration of the trial. Sixteen participants saw some improvement after the study and the remaining felt like they were completely recovered after the study. Assuming that the study's result was taken to large scale, how many people saw some improvement or no improvement. Mark all that apply.

[A] 328 people if 800 people were involved in the study

[B] 200 people if 620 people were involved in the study

[C] 225 people if 550 people were involved in the study

[D] 902 people if 2,200 people were involved in the study

[E] 797 people if 1,350 people were involved in the study

**Questions 18 to 20 are based on the following table:**

| 1 | 4 | 5 | 5 | 6 | 6 | 9 | 9 | 9 | 10 | 10 |
|---|---|---|---|---|---|---|---|---|---|---|

18.

| Quantity A | Quantity B |
|---|---|
| The mean of the data set | The median of the data set |

(A) Quantity A is greater.

(B) Quantity B is greater.

(C) The two quantities are equal.

(D) The relationship cannot be determined from the information given.

19.

| Quantity A | Quantity B |
|---|---|
| Average of the mean and median of the data set | The mode of the data set |

(A) Quantity A is greater.

(B) Quantity B is greater.

(C) The two quantities are equal.

(D) The relationship cannot be determined from the information given.

20.

| Quantity A | Quantity B |
|---|---|
| 1/2 of the range of the data set | Interquartile range of the data set |

(A) Quantity A is greater.

(B) Quantity B is greater.

(C) The two quantities are equal.

(D) The relationship cannot be determined from the information given.

# Answers Key

## Section 2

1. exorbitant
2. pedestrian
3. A
4. C
5. B and C
6. "When we try to stop thinking, the stream but changes its direction and flows on."
7. E
8. Reclusiveness and Solitariness
9. impenetrable and opaque
10. guile and wiliness
11. benign and gentle
12. ubiquity and pervasiveness
13. B
14. D
15. E
16. B and C
17. A
18. infinitesimal
19. recurrent
20. indispensable

## Section 3

1. B
2. C
3. E
4. D
5. B
6. E
7. $12,397.
8. A
9. A
10. A
11. A, D, E, and G
12. 5 seconds.
13. C
14. B
15. C
16. D
17. C
18. B
19. D
20. C

## Section 4

1. exclusive
2. catharsis
3. B
4. E
5. C
6. supercilious and haughty
7. promulgates and avers
8. tenacity and doggedness
9. perfunctory and mechanical
10. D
11. C
12. A, B and C
13. intertwined, glided, and pathos
14. E
15. D
16. E
17. "To the same young woman writes another equally well–known writer: "Your work is excellent; you can and will succeed."
18. inferences and archetype
19. axiomatic and ironically
20. intractable and substantive

## Section 5

1. B and (D
2. E
3. 23
4. D
5. A
6. C
7. B
8. C
9. 144
10. B
11. A
12. B
13. C
14. D
15. A, B, D, F, and H
16. D
17. A, C and D
18. A
19. B
20. B

# Explanations

## Section 1 – Analytical Writing

### Task 1 – Analyze an Issue

**The sample essay that follows was written in response to the prompt that appeared in the question.**

To presume that technological advancements should serve the desires of humans for leisure is, at the very least, self–serving. Greater efficiency should make it possible for humans to accomplish more in a given period of time, However, advances in technology should improve not only the lives of humans in a variety of ways but also other life forms and the Earth itself. If any aspect of daily life on the planet is ignored by improvements in technology, some other aspect will suffer.

The advent of mechanization in the nineteenth century undoubtedly improved the efficiency of human activity. The cotton gin and the McCormack reaper changed agriculture forever by replacing backbreaking human labor with machine power. These advances enabled farmers to plant more crops and accomplish more work in less time. The steam engine enabled people to travel more quickly along the length of America's great rivers and across the country by train. Because more goods could move more efficiently, new factories arose and the demand for raw materials increased. Rather than creating more leisure time, mechanization created more jobs and a boost to the economies in countries that adopted it. In the twentieth century, mechanization entered the home, making it possible for housewives to complete household chores with greater efficiency. The vacuum cleaner eliminated the need to beat rugs hanging on a line in the backyard. The automatic washing machine replaced washboards and hand wringing of wet clothes. Eventually, the dishwasher and microwave would make short shrift of other kitchen chores. The upshot of these advances in technology had an effect contrary to creating more leisure time. Instead, women were able to enter the workforce. Greater efficiency in the home made possible the foray of housewives into the world of education, medicine, and business. Efficiency created by technological advances created time to complete more tasks rather than creating more leisure time.

Leisure time is not important when other aspects of life have not been improved by technological advances. The ability to spend leisure time traveling, for example, would have fewer benefits if all forms of travel had not been made safer. The frequency with which airliners crash and scores of people are killed has greatly diminished despite the fact that more planes and people take to the air every day. Going on vacation in the family car is safer because of air bags that make it more likely for passengers to survive a crash. Thanks to advances in communication technology, families can spend their leisure time enjoying any type of entertainment on their high– definition televisions.

More leisure time would be meaningless if technology had not made it possible to live longer, healthier lives. Implantable pacemakers and defibrillators enable people with heart disease to pursue active lifestyles. Those who previously were affected by debilitating osteoarthritis can have damaged joints replaced and enjoy their leisure time pain free. More children live to become healthy adults as a result of advances in vaccinations and treatment of childhood cancers.

Advances in technology have allowed scientists to monitor the climate conditions on Earth. We know that human activity has contributed to the depletion of natural resources that affect the environment. The hole in the ozone layer caused by greenhouse gases has created an alarming increase in the incidence of skin cancer. Deforestation in the rain forests has led to the extinction of important plant and animal species. Climate change is melting the ice caps, imperiling the existence of polar bears and causing water levels to rise in coastal areas. Technological advances must address these conditions, or human leisure time will become meaningless.

# Task 2 – Analyze an Argument

**The sample essay that follows was written in response to the prompt that appeared in the question.**

Declining audience numbers is a legitimate concern for Classical Shakespeare Company. Efforts on the part of the company appear to have been ineffective, so they propose to duplicate the actions of Avon Repertory Company whose success appears to be on the rise. There is always danger associated with abandoning what one has always done. Change may be necessary, but the shape of that change must be carefully considered. One size does not always fit all. The marketing director needs answers to several questions before making the suggested changes.

An average is derived by adding a specific number of figures and dividing the total by that number. Some numbers are higher than the average, and some are lower. There may be a significant span between the highest and lowest numbers. Have some of Classical Shakespeare Theatre's productions had very poor attendance while others have standing–room–only attendance? This theater company may be able to solve attendance problems by discontinuing production of the plays that draw small audiences and increasing the number of performances of the plays that draw large audiences. The company may also benefit from changing the times of the performances. Are the largest reductions in attendance occurring consistently for performances on certain days of the work or specific times of the day? Changing days and times would be a relatively simple fix for the attendance problem. Avon Repertory Company may have been paying attention to these details and plays to full houses as a result.

Virtually all commercial enterprises use advertising to encourage the public to buy its product or use its service. Classical Shakespeare Company has used advertising in the past and has recently expanded its advertising in an effort to increase attendance at its productions. This tactic appears to have failed. Has the company changed the type of advertising it does or advertised in different publications? This theater company should research the reach of the advertising, perhaps by surveying their audience members. They may need to shift advertising dollars from print sources to radio or television. If the company has increased its television advertising, its ads may be appearing at times in the station's rotation when theater goers are not tuned in. If they are advertising upcoming productions that historically have had low attendance, they are likely to have wasted their money. The company may have changed advertising agencies, and the new agency has no experience creating ads for the entertainment industry.

Rather than look outside of the theater to improve attendance, Classical Shakespeare Company might look at the condition of the theater itself. Has the company taken steps to ensure that the audience enjoys attending performances at its theater? The seats may be worn and uncomfortable. The heating and cooling system may work inefficiently. If the audience finds it difficult to sit in the seats, or they are too cold or too warm, they may abandon this company for another that has renovated, making the theater experience more pleasurable. In fact, the condition of its theater may be the reason that Avon Repertory Company has increased profits rather than its Free Plays in the Park.

Is the company's payroll too large? Employees are a big expense, and producing plays requires a variety of skilled workers in addition to the actors themselves. On– stage talent usually receive the biggest paychecks. This can be a double–edged sword. A theater company can hire better actors in an effort to draw bigger audiences, or it can hire lesser–known actors to reduce the overall payroll. If the payroll is smaller, the company's bottom line looks better. The risk is smaller audiences. Theater companies must strike a delicate balance when casting its productions.

A theater company experiencing financial uncertainty may only ensure its demise by taking on a project that has no proven benefit. Before imitating Avon Repertory Company's Free Plays in the Park, the Classical Shakespeare Company should ask if that program directly contributes to Avon's increase in profits. Classical Shakespeare Company should scrutinize its past and current practices and answer some tough questions before adopting the suggestion in the argument.

# Section 2 – Verbal Reasoning

1. **exorbitant**

This passage states that sulfuric acid is useful, and that usefulness outweighs its risk. Therefore, the blank must specify that, without the usefulness of sulfuric acid in various production capacities, it would be too risky to use. In other words, the correct choice should refer to being "unreasonable." "Garish" means loud or tasteless, so doesn't fit the context. "Propitious" means favorable. The speaker would not be concerned with a "favorable" level of risk; he would be concerned with an excessive one. "Obsequious" means servile, which does not make sense when referring to a level of risk. "Fastidious" means choosy, so also does not fit when referring to a level of risk. The correct answer is "Exorbitant." This word means "excessive" and describes exactly how the risk of using sulfuric acid would be considered if it were not for the wide range of benefits.

2. **pedestrian**

This sentence says that the study of inorganic bonds is essential for understanding the nature of chemical compounds. The sentence also says that this fact is hard to believe. Therefore, the correct answer should stress the understated nature of inorganic bond study. "Prevalent" means widespread. This is the opposite of understated. "Torpid" means lazy or sleepy. A field of study can't be described as "sleepy," so this doesn't work. "Applicable" means relevant. It wouldn't be hard to believe that inorganic bond angles were essential to understanding chemical compounds if the field of study was "relevant."

"Parsimonious" means frugal. This quality has nothing to do with a field of study. Therefore, the correct answer is "Pedestrian." This word means dull or ordinary. It would make sense that a "dull" field of study wouldn't be expected to yield insight into the manipulation of chemical compounds.

3. **The correct answer is (A).**

"A" is correct; the first sentence, though continuing with the previously introduced comparison of the mind as a stream, introduces a new concept: that this 'stream' or mental consciousness is unavoidable. The next sentence then provides a specific example of what this means, explaining how the mind continues producing thoughts even when in a state of anaesthesia. This example can be categorized as evidence because it is stated as a fact.

"B" is incorrect because the first sentence, though presenting the author's point in this paragraph, does not explain his message but rather simply introduces it.

"C" is incorrect because the second sentence does not provide an alternate view but rather supports the author's argument.

"D" incorrectly states that the first sentence provides evidence, though it is not in fact factually based and instead presents the author's argument. Also, the second presents evidence rather than explaining evidence.

"E" is almost correct, though not quite; the first sentence does not provide a new idea altogether but rather presents a new view of the idea that has already been introduced. Also, the second sentence provides support for the author's argument but does not conclude it.

4. **The correct answer is (C).**

"B" most accurately identifies the author's main point; the author begins by comparing consciousness to a stream in order to provide a mental image of a force that carries its own 'flow' and goes on to explain that this 'stream' cannot be controlled. All of the examples that the author provides serve to further this notion, that a person cannot stop this flow no matter what their mental state.

"A" incorrectly refutes the idea that thoughts can be controlled; no amount of mental concentration can, according to the author, stop thoughts completely, as they will simply change course but will not dissipate completely.

"C" is almost correct; it identifies the difference between a young mind and an older mind in comparing the more narrow scope that a baby's mind has based on the limited perspective of the world that a baby has. The passage does not, however, indicate that this limited scope affects the ability to control thoughts.

"D" incorrectly states that a person's energy does not match their thoughts; the passage explains that when a person's thoughts slow down, so does their energy, and vice–versa.

"E" is also incorrect in attempting to separate life experiences from consciousness; the passage states that a baby has a smaller 'stream' due to lack of experience, thus directly drawing a connection between development of the mind and "the grand sum total of life's experience".

5. **The correct answers are (B) and (C).**

"B" and "C" are both possible options based on what can be inferred from this passage. Based on the confidence with which the author states that thoughts cannot be altogether controlled, it seems as if he has been able to draw this conclusion based on some sort of scientific research, rather than simply forming this opinion based on personal experience, thus supporting "B" as an option. The specificity that the author uses to demonstrate the power of thoughts further supports the idea that his argument is based on research, such as when he says that "while we are unconscious under an anaesthetic, even, some sort of mental process continues." It would be difficult to make such a claim as this without having found conclusive evidence that thoughts continue to flow even when a person is under anaesthesia, thus supporting the idea that this author has based his argument on scientific research.

"C" is also possible, as the author provides direct comparisons between a person's thoughts and feelings in saying that when "the stream flows slowly, and our thoughts lag—we "feel slow"; again the stream flows faster, and we are lively and our thoughts come with a rush". By connecting the energy of the 'stream' of mental activity with the way that it affects a person's energy, the author links thoughts to feelings, and it can thus be inferred that if a person appears or feels slow, their thoughts are likely to be slow as well. Conversely, if a person feels "lively", as the author puts it, then it is likely that their thoughts are coming in a "rush".

"A" is not likely, as this passage is more scientific and factually–based than an emotional response such as frustration would imply. The author also discusses the human mind in terms that seem more general and broad than the limited scope of his own personal experience would suggest.

6. **"When we try to stop thinking, the stream but changes its direction and flows on."**

This sentence explains how the mind avoids being controlled by demonstrating the mental reaction that occurs when a person attempts to impose control on his or her thoughts. By reacting to this attempt at control by changing direction, the mind demonstrates its ability to alter its course without being silenced or halted. Just as water can adapt to any surface, so too can thoughts continue on their path regardless of any attempt to stop them.

7. **The correct answer is (E).**

The passage describes how important the god Tezcatlipoca is in the Mexican pantheon. Choice E offers a logical addition to this discussion by showing that as a result of his importance, the "priestly caste" or "those who worshipped him" had the most power. None of the other choices offers a logical conclusion based on the "result of his importance." Choice A says that there are few images of the god, but if he were very important, it would be more likely that there were many images. There is no apparently connection between the color black and the lack of images or the fact he was important. Choice B includes the idea that he was famous or important, but if the reader does not know who Ometecuhtli and Omecihuatl are, that fact does not help understand his importance. It is already established that he is the most important god, so it is logical that he is the most important son of someone. Choice C also has no apparent connection with importance. Even if his right foot is often replaced in drawings with the image of a snake or obsidian mirror, it is unclear whether this is a good or bad thing. Choice D relates to his introduction, not about a result of his increasing importance, so also does not logically complete the text.

8. **Reclusiveness and Solitariness**

This sentence is saying that the legendary scholar cannot be accessed for a certain reason. Because this reason contradicts his pro–community writing, it must have something to do with being private.

Therefore, we want words that express the notion of keeping to one's self. "Superciliousness" means arrogance. While this answer looks good at a glance it must be remembered that the answer needs to contradict the teachings of a pro–community writer. "Superciliousness" does not accomplish this. "Popularity" means fame. Again, this would not contradict the notion of him being a pro–community writer. If anything, it would support it. "Obtuseness" means dullness or dimwittedness. A brilliant teacher wouldn't be obtuse, so this is automatically out. "Unimportance" means pettiness or triviality. Again, this is a legendary teacher we're talking about, so "unimportance" shouldn't work on any level. This leaves "Reclusiveness" and "Solitariness." These words both mean tending to keep to one's self. This would be an ironic, and appropriately contradictory, characteristic for a pro–community writer to have.

Therefore, c and f are correct.

9. **impenetrable and opaque**

This sentence is saying that the student has tremendous knowledge of magnetism and electric currents but he still finds something frustrating about the geomagnetic reversal of the Earth's poles. For a well–read student this frustration would come from not understanding. "Pellucid" means easily understood, as does "Clear." Therefore both of these answers are out because the student's problem is that the process isn't clear. "Self–Effacing" means humble. This makes no sense in the context of the question. The process doesn't have a personality. "Insidious" means sinister or treacherous. Once again, this answer makes no sense in the context of the question. A natural process can't be sinister. We are left then with "Impenetrable" and "Opaque." These two words both mean unclear or difficult to understand. This is exactly how an overwhelmed student would find a topic such as geomagnetic reversal. Therefore, a and b are correct.

10. **guile and wiliness**

This sentence is saying that executives need to play both sides of the game: they need to appear friendly while also masking an undesirable characteristic. This undesirable characteristic can be inferred from the context to be craftiness or sneakiness. "Acquiescence" means passive assent. This doesn't make any sense: that's what the executives would want to show publicly, so it's not the quality they would want to mask. "Obstinacy" means stubbornness. This is a flimsy fit: there are much better examples of qualities that executives would want to mask from the public. Moreover, there is no other answer choice that means "stubborn." "Friendliness" means openness and sociability. This doesn't work for the same reason as "Acquiescence": this is the facade that the executive must put on in public. It does the executive no good to try to mask this characteristic. "Vicariousness" means the quality of living through another. This does not complete the sentence in a logical way.

This leaves "Guile" and "Wiliness." These both mean slyness and craftiness. This is the exact personality type that the executive would try to mask from the public. a and c are correct.

11. **benign and gentle**

This sentence is saying that the corporate executive isn't just asking questions, he's asking them in a certain way to lure his rival into a false sense of security. Therefore, we want words that characterize the questions as being kind, because a question that appears kind would not arouse the suspicion of the person being interrogated. "Refractory" means headstrong. The executive is going for a quiet attack, therefore this does not work. "Transparent" means clear and easily seen through. This sentiment is the opposite of what the sentence is trying to convey: the executive is working quietly, not clearly. "Insensitive" means cruel or not regarding emotions. Insensitive questions would call attention to themselves and not succeed in being subtle and subversive. "Meandering" means unfocused. This looks like a good answer. But there's no other answer to pair it with. Therefore we come to "Benign" and "Gentle." These words both mean kind and friendly. Asking questions in a seemingly gentle way would be a good way to catch a presenter off–guard and subvert their presentation. b and d are correct.

12. **ubiquity and pervasiveness**

Waves are described as existing anywhere and calculated in many ways, so the correct answer should reflect this diversity and range. "Uniformity" means consistency, but the sentence implies that waves travel in different ways depending on the situation.

"Conformity" means conventionalism. This doesn't work for the same reason that "Uniformity" doesn't work: the waves are different, not the same.

"Expressivity" means articulateness, but wave don't express themselves in fluent speech. "Petulance" is sullenness, which is a personality The remaining words are "Ubiquity" and "Pervasiveness." These two words both mean extensiveness. The waves are obviously seen in an extensive array of mediums. Therefore, A and C are correct.

13. **The correct answer is (B).**

"B" is a correct rendition of the main idea of the passage because it reiterates the idea that beliefs about how much or how little one can accomplish is a more significant factor in determining success than ability, which can be increased with practice and education. The "fixed mindset" or thinking that abilities are "set in stone" is, as the passage says "hardly a recipe for success".

"A" is incorrect because although intelligence may indeed be a big part of what determines success, this idea is not supported in this particular passage, as the main idea deals more with attitude towards intelligence and not the amount of intelligence.

"C" is incorrect because only the first part of this answer is true, yet the second part is not supported by the passage; it is not true that a person is limited by the boundaries of their current skill set and that challenges must fall within these limitations, as the passage argues that anyone can surpass their current skills with the belief that they can change.

"D" is incorrect because if someone feels like they are struggling, this text claims that it is more likely due to feelings of not knowing how to change or not thinking they can; it's not because they are not employing the skills that they already have. Also, if a person does not have the necessary skills to reach a goal, then, according to the passage, they can learn them, no matter how much they lack to begin with, as long as they think it is possible to do so.

"E" is also incorrect because success should have nothing to do with what a person is born with, just as the study by D week aimed to prove that "intelligence isn't fixed" and can be improved with hard work.

14. **The correct answer is (D).**

Choice D is the best answer because the final paragraph describes Anthony's organizational skills and possession of "executive ability." It would have been most like her to "have done her homework" and had literature available to present. Based on the places she went to speak on women's rights, she would not give up easily.

Choice A is incorrect because it would be typical of a fiery personality. Anthony was much more "in control" even though she was passionate. She also would have had more "substance" to her comments.

Choice B is incorrect because she traveled places where she was not completely welcome, suggesting that she would not have left the meeting that quickly. Anthony was very determined.

Choice C is incorrect because "rattle off whatever came to mind" implies that her thoughts were presented at random. The article presented her as very organized and having good "executive ability," not one to present thoughts at random.

Choice E is incorrect because the use of threats would not have been her main tactic. She would more likely have had a convincing, organized presentation.

15. **The correct answer is (E).**

Choice E is the best answer because Anthony learned one definition of Christianity (through benevolence); William Lloyd Garrison showed her another quality of Christianity through his behavior.

Choice A is incorrect because, while there is contradictory information, there is not an "old and new" William Lloyd Garrison. He has not changed.

Choice B is incorrect because some conclusions could be drawn from this statement, like " Anthony associates with some tough individuals." However, that is not the most important purpose of the statement in bold.

Choice C is incorrect because Anthony's understanding of William Lloyd is accurate. She knows him well. The contradiction is between her perception and the limited knowledge of her friends.

Choice D is incorrect as an answer because, although it is true, the greater purpose is to illustrate the new ways of thinking that Anthony is encountering, contradictory with her friends' views.

16. **The correct answers are (B) and (C).**

Choice B is correct. The article does mention some of the people that supported Anthony financially, such as her father and Wendell Phillip. However, they were just a few people. When she asked if the national convention brought about support on her behalf, Mr. Phillip just had his own check to offer her.

Choice C is correct. This statement is refuted by the sentence in the last paragraph which refers to her as having "no coquetry."

Choice A is incorrect because it is supported by the article's discussion of women's equal rights. However, the question asks for those statements that are not supported.

17. **The correct answer is (A).**

Choice A is correct. Intrepid means "bold and courageous". The first paragraph describes Anthony as being someone who went even where she was not welcome, and ready to go "out of her comfort zone."

Choice B is incorrect because the passage does not imply that Anthony was feared by men. Most likely many did not agree with her, and maybe some did fear her, but those topics are not in the passage.

Choice C is incorrect. The passage does describe Anthony as being neat or being plainly dressed. The passage does not describe her as being very attractive, but it does not imply that she was extremely homely, either. The word "very" is too strong for this context.

18. **infinitesimal**

This sentence talks about how the large (macroscopic) world originates somewhere else. These "origins" are being deliberately contrasted with something large, so we can infer that they are small. "Vapid" means "bland." The sentence does not imply "bland" origins of life. "Caustic" means "corrosive." The sentence makes no mention of anything being corroded. "Culminated" means "concluded." This answer does not make sense in the context of the sentence. "Disastrous" means "ruinous." The sentence does not imply that our origins are "ruinous." "Infinitesimal" means "tiny." It makes sense that the closer scientists looked at the macroscopic world the more "tiny" things they would see.

19. **recurrent**

This sentence is saying that the American automotive industry sees frequent highs and lows. "Baroque" means "ornate." The level of intricacy in the American auto industry would not clearly cause periods of panic followed by periods of euphoria. "Indulgent" means "lenient." A lenient character would not explain the highs and lows of the American automotive industry. "Immutable" means "unchallengeable." Of course, if foreign auto makers periodically overtake the American auto industry it cannot be described as "unchallengeable." "Steadfast" means "unwavering." Again, if the American auto industry was unwavering then it would not be occasionally passed by foreign auto makers. "Recurrent" means "periodic," or "cyclical." A cyclical nature would explain why the American auto industry waxes and wanes in terms of global power.

20. **indispensable**

This sentence expresses the importance of literary devices. It says that stories with identical plots can look very different to one another if different literary techniques are used. "Antagonistic" means "opposed." Literary devices help to create a unique work of literature, so this word is wrong. "Allegorical" means "symbolic." This answer might be tempting because an allegory is a literary device, but literary techniques are not described as being "symbolic" of anything in this sentence. "Anachronistic" means "out of chronological order." Literary devices are never described as being out of chronological order, so this answer is wrong. "Insufficient" means "lacking." Literary devices are described as being very useful in crafting stories, so this answer is wrong. "Indispensable" means "essential." Given the effects that literary devices can have on a story, they can accurately be described as "essential."

# Section 3 – Quantitative Reasoning

1. **The correct answer is (B).**

For Quantity A, the probability of drawing a yellow candy, then a pink candy without replacement is

$$\left(\frac{5}{15}\right)\times\left(\frac{3}{14}\right)=\frac{15}{210}$$

For Quantity B, the probability of getting 2 white candies without replacement is

$$\left(\frac{7}{15}\right)\times\left(\frac{6}{14}\right)=\frac{42}{210}$$

For quicker comparison, since the denominators of the two probabilities are known to be the same (i.e.: 15 and 14), there's no need to compute actual values of the denominators. Just compare the numerators: 5×3=15, and 7×6=42. Therefore, Quantity B is greater than Quantity A.

2. **The correct answer is (C).**

A sum of 5 is obtained from the following combinations: 1–4, 2–3, 3–2, 4–1. That means a probability of 4 out of 36. A sum of 9 is obtained from the following combinations: 3–6, 4–5, 5–4, 6–3, which is also a probability of 4 out of 36. Therefore, the two quantities presented are equal.

3. **The correct answer is (E).**

The percentage of passengers who are concerned with time of arrival or departure is 14%; thus, the percentage of passengers not concerned with time of arrival or departure is 100% - 14% = 86%.

4. **The correct answer is (D).**

Percentage of passengers who are concerned with frequent flier miles or safety record or size or type of aircraft is 4% + 32% + 3% = 39%. Hence the percentage of passengers not concerned with frequent flier miles or safety record or size or type of aircraft is 100% - 39% = 61%.

5. **The correct answer is (B).**

Since there are twice as girls as there are boys, the proportions preferred by the girls are counted twice when calculating the combined averages for both boys and girls. The proportions then are:

Vanilla, $\frac{45+20+20}{3}=28\frac{1}{3}\%$

chocolate, $\frac{20+25+25}{3}=23\frac{1}{3}\%$

Raspberry, $\frac{10+15+15}{3}=13\frac{1}{3}\%$ ;and

mint chip, $\frac{15+40+40}{3}=35\%$

Since mint chip is preferred by most. (B) is the correct answer.

6. **The correct answer is (E).**

25% of the boys like mint chip mud 12 boys make up 25% of the total number of boys. The total number of boys $x$ the percentage who prefer mint chip = the number of boys who prefer mint chip.

Therefore $T \times 25\% = 12$

Solving for $T$.

$\frac{12}{25\%}=T$

So $T$=48.

7. **The correct answer is \$12,397.**

*Deposit* = *Principal* = \$8,050

*Rate* ($r$) = 2.25% quarterly

*Period* ($t$) = 6 years; since the rate is given on quarterly basis, the period is

4 × 6 *years* = 24 *quarters.*

Simple interest = $Prt$ = \$8050 × 0.0225 × 24 = \$4,347

Total amount = \$8050 + \$4347 = \$12,397

The solution is \$12,397.

8. **The correct answer is (A).**

To determine the value of $7x + 10y$, we need to solve the system of equations for $x$ and $y$ using the linear combination or elimination method.

$2(-5x+2y=9)$
$1(3x-4y=-4)$

$-10x+4y=18$
$3x-4y=-4$

$-7x=14$
$x=-2$

Substituting $x = -2$ in the first equation, we get:

$-5(-2)+2y=9$
$10+2y=9$
$2y=-1$
$y=-\frac{1}{2}$

$\left(-2,-\frac{1}{2}\right)$

To solve for $7x + 10y$, plug the values of x and y into the equation.

$7(-2)+10\left(-\frac{1}{2}\right)$
$-14-5$
$-19$

9. **The correct answer is (A).**

Here is a chart to help write the algebraic equation:

Step 1: Beginning of the day: $y$

Step 2: Breakfast was \$5.00: $y$ - 5

Step 3: Lunch is half of what was left: $y-5-\frac{1}{2}(y-5)$

Step 4: Found \$2.00: $y-5-\frac{1}{2}(y-5)+2$

Simplify the algebraic expression: $y-5-\frac{1}{2}(y-5)+2$

$=y-5-\frac{1}{2}y+\frac{5}{2}+2=\frac{1}{2}y-\frac{1}{2}$

10. **The correct answer is (A).**

There are 52 cards in a deck of cards: 4 suits with 13 cards for each suit. There are 3 face cards – King, Queen, and Jack – per suit, which gives a total of 12 face cards in one deck. The probability of drawing a diamond suit is 13 out of 52, while the probability of drawing a face card is only 12 out of 52.

11. **The correct answers are (A), (D), (E), and (G).**

Let $x$ be her score on the first exam, $y$ be her score on the second exam, and $z$ be her score on the third exam.

We can write

(A1) $y = x + (10\%)(x)$

$= x + 0.1x = 1.1x$

(A2) $z = y + (10\%)(y)$

$= y + 0.1y = 1.1y$

Replacing $y = 44$ in (A1), we get

$44 = 1.1x$

$x = 40$

Replacing $y = 44$ in (A2), we get

$z = 1.1(44) = 48.4$

Form the average of all exams, we conclude that

$a + b + c + d + e = 5 \times 58 = 290$

$40 + 44 + 48.4 + d + e = 290$

$d + e = 157.6$

$d - e = 7.6$

$d = 82.6$ and $e = 75$

12. **The correct answer is 5 seconds.**

The effective speed that will cover the distance in between the two vehicles is:

$68 + 30 = 98$ *mph*.

Converted to *miles / second*:

$$\frac{98mi}{3600s} = \frac{3}{10} miles / second$$

Converting the distance to miles:

$$795\ feet = \frac{792\,ft}{5280\,ft / mile} = \frac{3}{20} miles$$

$$\text{Time taken} = \frac{3}{20} / \frac{3}{100} = \frac{3}{20} \times \frac{100}{3} = 5 seconds$$

13. **The correct answer is (C).**

To solve this equation, we need to isolate the g on one side, factor and solve.

$5x-2g=5-7zg$

$5x-5=2g-7zg$

$5(x-1)=g(2-7z)$

$\frac{5(x-1)}{2-7z}=g$

14. **The correct answer is (B).**

Multiply using the properties of exponents.

$(4.23\times10^4)(8.53\times10^5)=(4.23\times8.53)x(10^4\times10^5$

$36.08\times10^9=3.608\times10^{10}$

15. **The correct answer is (C).**

This is a probability distribution question. Using the formula for probability distribution, the probability of getting 3 tails is

$10\left(\frac{1}{2}\right)^3\left(\frac{1}{2}\right)^2=0.3125$

The probability of getting 2 tails is

$10\left(\frac{1}{2}\right)^3\left(\frac{1}{2}\right)^2=0.3125$

Even if a calculator isn't used here, by setting up the equations you can observe they will give the same result.

16. **The correct answer is (D).**

The only given information is that the two events are independent. *P(A)'* and *P(B)* can be equal if the two events are mutually exclusive and *P(A ∪ B)=1. P(A)'* can be more or less than *P(B)* if *P(A ∩ B)≠0*. There are multiple relationships that are possible based on the given information.

17. **The correct answer is (C).**

To solve this equation, we need to set $f(x)=0$, and solve using the quadratic formula $\left(\frac{-b\pm\sqrt{b^2-4ac}}{2a}\right)$

$0=-3x^2+4x+7 \quad a=-3, b=4, c=7$

$x=\frac{-(4)\pm\sqrt{(4)^2-4(-3)(7)}}{2(-3)}$

$=\frac{-4\pm\sqrt{16+84}}{-6}$

$=\frac{-4\pm\sqrt{100}}{-6}$

$=\frac{-4\pm10}{-6}$

$=\frac{2\pm5}{3}$

18. **The correct answer is (B).**

Let the initial price of a tie be $\$x$ and that of one pair of shoes be $\$y$.

Let the discounted price of a tie be $\$t$ and that of pair of shoes be $\$s$.

Now $t+s=104$-(1)

$t+64=s$----(2)

Also $t=0.4x$---(3)

and $s=0.7y$---(4)

Substituting (3) and (4) in (1) and (2) we get

$0.4x+0.7y=104$---(5)

$0.4x+64=0.7y$----(6)

Substituting (6) in (5) we get

$0.4x+0.4x+64=104$---(7)

i.e.$0.8x+64=104$

i.e.$0.8x=40$

$\therefore x=\frac{40}{0.8}=50$

19. **The correct answer is (D).**

Let the present ages of Jacob and Henry be $j$ and $h$.

$h+4=4j$----(1)

Four years ago, Henry was $h$-4 years old.

One year ago, Jacob was $j$-1 years old

By the given data

$3(h-4)+2(j-1)=30$----(2)

$3h-12+2j-2=30$-----(3)

$3h+2j=44$---------(4)

Multiplying (4) by 2 we get

$6h+4j=88$---------(5)

Substituting (1) in (4)

$6h+h+4=88$--------(6)

$7h=84$

$h=12$

$12+4=4j$

$J=4$

Five years after, the sum of their ages=12+5+4+5=26

20. **The correct answer is (C).**

The Part / Whole ratio of advertisements (16) to total pages (28) in magazine A is 16/28 or 4/7. Magazine B has the same ratio, so if there are 35 pages in magazines B, $4/7 \times 35$ or 20 pages are advertisements. Therefore there are four more pages of advertisements in magazine B than in magazine A.

# Section 4 – Verbal Reasoning

1. **exclusive**

This sentence is contrasting two different types of religions. The second type is described as being inclusive. We know this because the passage describes the second type of religion as considering "all living things" to be "part of the spiritual family." Therefore, we can infer that the first type of religion must be exclusive. "Inane" means "pointless." The sentence makes no commentary on the usefulness of religion, so this answer is wrong. "Facetious" means "silly." The sentence makes no commentary on how serious or silly these religions are. "Technophobic" means "fear of technology." Again, the sentence makes no reference to the relationship between technology and religion. "Indolent" means "lazy." There is no commentary made on the laziness or work ethic of the religions, either. "Exclusive" means "selective." This makes sense. If two types of religion are being explicitly contrasted against one another, and the second one is described as being inclusive, then it makes sense that the first one could be considered "exclusive," or "selective."

2. **catharsis**

The sentence is saying that something good that happens emotionally more than offsets the physical strain of running. "Indolence" means "laziness." The middle–aged man would not be sacrificing his body in order to become emotionally lazy. "Exacerbation" is the act of making something worse. Again, the man would not insist on running if it was making him feel worse emotionally. "Calamity" means "disaster." Again, the man would not be sacrificing his body to achieve emotional disaster. "Inanity" means "pointlessness." This, also, is not something the man would be striving for. "Catharsis" means "purification." This makes sense. The man would consider emotional purification to be worth the physical pain that would result from running.

3. **The correct answer is (B).**

"B" is correct because though it is clear by the end of the passage that the Beauforts are well–respected by their 'upper crust' peers for their fancy house and the high caliber of the food and beverage that they serve, many people were at first doubtful of how Regina Dallas' engagement to Mr. Beaufort would affect her, and, whether, though she came from a good social standing (through her relationship to her cousin) she would possibly "forfeit it in marrying Julius Beaufort".

"A" is incorrect because although Mr. Beaufort's wife does enjoy a lavish lifestyle, it's not what the passage is mainly about and it is not true that she does not have to entertain guests; though she does not have to do the preparation involved, it is implied that she is present for those visits nonetheless.

"C" is incorrect because the passage does not discuss in depth any burden incurred from marrying Mr.Beaufort, and she also does not have to worry about any of the details to please his friends, as he takes that upon himself.

"D" is incorrect because people respect the Beauforts because of their expensive house and food and clothes, but their spending is not directly mentioned.

"E" is incorrect because although Mr. Beaufort's duplicitous personality is mentioned, his peers do not seem to mind and in fact it is implied that his false presentation of things gains him respect, though again, it is not the main point of the passage. Also, his integrity is not in question as no one seems to be offended but rather impressed by his ability to present himself in a way that is different than what has gone on 'behind the scenes'.

4. **The correct answer is (E).**

"E" is the correct answer because it is the only statement that is technically incorrect (as the question asks for the one that is not true); Mrs. Beaufort, formerly Regina Dallas, was once "penniless" and therefore was not always wealthy.

"A" is true because Mr. Beaufort would like to appear not to have 'lifted a finger' though really he is the one who has put in effort to arrange his house in a certain way

"B" is true because the main image of Mrs. Beaufort that is presented in the passage is of her beauty and clothing; she "dressed like an idol, hung with pearls, growing younger and blonder and more beautiful each year" and it is this description that follows the explanation of her personality after the word 'but', dissipating the importance of her character traits with the stunning and impressive qualities that others perceive in her appearance.

"C", which states that people doubt Mr. Beaufort's background, is supported by the part of the passage that mentions his 'mysterious antecedents'.

"D" is supported by the observation that Medora "was always doing the wrong thing from the right motive".

5. **The correct answer is (C).**

"C" is correct because the sentence states that being engaged to Mr. Beaufort is a 'folly' or mistake, thus representing the opinion that marrying him will not be a good idea and that becoming associated with him due to his mysterious and questionable background will cause a downturn in reputation for all who are attached to him socially.

"A" is incorrect because it speaks of Medora's past history of mistakes yet does not make any predictions about her future.

"B" is incorrect because though it may imply, by saying 'poor Medora', that people take pity on her, it does not suggest that they take pity because of her having to impart bad news but rather by her association with Mr. Beaufort through her cousin's engagement to him. Also, her past 'follies' are not specified in this passage, so it is unclear why exactly people take pity on her.

"D" is incorrect because it does not mention anything about whether Regina is shy or not. It also does not indicate an 'outspoken' quality as being the reason that Medora is the one to make the announcement.

"E" is irrelevant and also is not supported by this text; though this one instance recounts a time when the people in this particular social circle in New York are receiving news via 'word of mouth', there is nothing to suggest that this is always the case, and the way that the announcement is made is also not the main point of this sentence.

6. **supercilious and haughty**

This sentence talks of a person receiving a lot of money and feeling subsequent urges that drag him away from his previous disposition. This disposition is described as being a state of "composure." So we want words that stress how Steven might be giving in to the urges of the wealthy. "Enlightened" means rational or tolerant. Steven was already like that, as the sentence explains, so he wouldn't be worried that wealth was making him more like that. "Chic" means attractive or elegant. Steven may have very well been elegant and fashionable before he became wealthy, so this also does not work. "Vacuous" means hollow or empty. "Hollow urges" doesn't make much sense unless you try to justify it with an incredibly figurative meaning, which makes this answer choice very weak. Moreover, there is no other term that matches it, so it can't be an answer. "Violent" means vicious or forceful. It's doubtful that wealth would immediately make one violent, and once again, this answer choice has no partner in the answer tree. This leaves "Supercilious" and "Haughty." Both of these words mean snooty or self-important. It makes perfect sense that Steven would be afraid that wealth would make him self-important, and that it would cause him to lose his "pre-wealth composure." b and e are the correct answers.

7. **promulgates and avers**

Aspiring business owners might worry about registering their businesses, but do not because of a government action, so the correct answer must support the idea of the government taking action. Choice A, emends, means to make improvements or corrections to something, but it is unclear whether the action taken was an improvement on an old law or if it is a completely new law. Choice B, palavers, means to talk unnecessarily at length, and Choice C, gibes, means to laugh with contempt and derision, so these are not positive actions for a government. Choice F, inveighs, meaning to rail against or protest strongly, is a possible government action, but the government is clearly in support of – not against – making corporations separate entities from their owners; if they were not, there would still be a reason for business owners to be worried.

The correct answers are Choice D, promulgates, because it means to widely advertise, and Choice, E, avers, which means to formally declare something to be true. These choices show that owners are more comfortable registering businesses once the information that the action is safe is spread to them by the government.

8. **tenacity and doggedness**

This sentence is saying that ocular surgery of the eye is a very difficult procedure, and that textbook knowledge needs to be coupled with something else in order to be successful in it. "Predilection" means taste or preference. Whether or not a doctor has preference does not change how the surgery will be performed. How "Predilection" would be used in the sentence doesn't even specify what the doctor would have a preference for, so that answer choice is clearly wrong. "Awareness," means mindfulness. While this answer choice technically makes sense both grammatically and logically, it can be assumed that all doctors have awareness. Furthermore, there is no matching answer choice for "Awareness," making it wrong either way. "Contempt" means dislike. There's no reason to believe that dislike for something (and that "something" wouldn't be specified if this answer was chosen) would cause a doctor to be better at their job. "Sensitivity" means compassion. While compassion is a good trait for a doctor to have there's no reason to believe that it will allow them to complete a technically demanding procedure. Furthermore, like "Awareness," there is no matching answer choice for "Sensitivity." This leaves "Tenacity" and "Doggedness." Both of these words mean resolve and perseverance. These are the characteristics that would be indispensable in completing a difficult procedure. A and D are the correct answers.

9. **perfunctory and mechanical**

This sentence talks about difficult intellectual concepts in the laboratory causing students to overlooking more bland procedural concepts, so the correct answer should establish how distillation apparatus setup is less interesting than the mechanism of the Sharpless epoxidation. "Riveting" means exciting. This word does not complete the sentiment of the sentence because we want to show the apparatus being less interesting than the Sharpless epoxidation. "Sympathetic" means compassionate.

This word does not complete the sentence in any logical way. It doesn't address the relative intrigue of the two topics at hand. "Adroit" means skillful. If the distillation technique is given less consideration by the students, then it cannot require more skill than the epoxidation. "Inexplicable" means mysterious. If the setting up of a distillation apparatus was mysterious then students would be less likely to forget it, not more. This leaves "Perfunctory" and "Mechanical." These words mean routine or automatic. It would make sense that routine, automatic procedures are overlooked by students who are focusing on a more complex topic. Therefore, a and e are correct.

10. **The correct answer is (D).**

D is the correct answer. The first sentence mentions the responsibility of the United States in regard to Haiti, while a later sentence asserts that Haiti was under the U.S.'s financial guardianship, implying that the U.S. shares some responsibility. A is incorrect The passage does compare the treatment of the two countries but does not imply that one policy was fairer than the other. B is incorrect. The passage discusses internal and external debt but does not explain how they operate in Haiti's infrastructure. C is incorrect. The passage states that the United States had guardianship at a certain point, but does not explain its reasons for doing so. E is incorrect. The passage makes a pointed reference to the fact that designated funds were set aside but does not explore why they were not used.

11. **The correct answer is (C).**

C is correct. The purpose of the passage is to point out the culpability of the United States for Haiti's financial condition. Haiti's reputation is mentioned so that the author can rebut it with a counter- example, the country's previous fiscal responsibility. A is incorrect. The author downplays Haiti's chaotic reputation by noting its history of financial responsibility. B is incorrect. The author strongly implies that the United States did not live up to its responsibilities to Haiti by continually reminding the reader that the U.S. was in charge when problems occurred. D is incorrect. The author mentions the designated revenues but does not suggest an alternate way to use them. E is incorrect. The author does not draw this conclusion or suggest that Haiti diverged from the U.S.'s wishes.

12. **The correct answer is (A), (B), and (C).**

All three choices are correct. A is correct because the entire point of the passage is to disabuse the reader of this notion and point out the culpability of the United States in the matter. B is covered when the author points out Haiti's history of successful debt management, and C is found in the last sentence when the author notes the hardships that individuals have suffered.

13. **intertwined, glided, and pathos**

The passage is saying that there is a strong relationship between music and theater. "Antagonistic" means "unfriendly." If theater has utilized music for so long then it's hard to believe they have an "antagonistic" relationship. "Extraneous" means "superfluous." If music and theater have persisted for so long, they cannot be described as "superfluous." "Intertwined" means "linked," or "connected." If music and theater are so often seen together then they can be described as "connected" to one another. For the second blank, the passage talks about how music and theater are still seen today. "Perished" means "died." If music and theater "perished" then they would not be around today. "Lurched" means "staggered." Considering that music and theater combine for some of the "most famous stage dramas of our time," they haven't lurched into the modern age but have done quite well. "Glided" means "moved gracefully." Since music and theater are still around, they have certainly survived. Moreover, since they are involved in famous stage dramas, they have arrived in the modern age very gracefully. For the last blank, the passage is talking about what stage dramas are trying to convey. "Avarice" means "greed." The passage makes no reference to "greed" in relation to music or theater. "Aplomb" means "composure." Again, a tragedy would not be looking to express composure as much as it would be looking to express other, more powerful ideas. "Pathos" means "Despair." This makes sense. A tragedy would want to express despair to its audience.

14. **The correct answer is (E).**

Choice E is the correct answer, as it is the only choice that does not accurately represent an assumption relied upon by the author. Mentioning how many people it would take to conduct two actions is irrelevant to this passage, as is the implied simplicity of creating a sound and throwing a stone, which is also what this choice discusses. Choices A and B are both assumptions that deal with the idea that a person is able to expend his or her energy in a way that is accurate to the needs of the experiment and that the situation surrounding these actions (making noise, throwing objects) is not brought on by external motivators other than gathering data. Choice C represents the assumption made clear by the author's assertion that a person can, without difficulty, form a mechanical conception of the whole series without assuming imponderables" which based on the generalization that this type of thought process is easy for anyone—a fact that may not be true amongst certain groups of people who are perhaps uneducated or young.

Choice D also incorrectly assumes that a person throwing a stone can expend his or her energy just as easily to apply that force to spinning a top, which relies on the basis that every person has the skill and ability to apply energy in this specific way.

15. **The correct answer is (D).**

The correct answer is "D" because the question asks for the main idea of the passage, which is that people have different opinions on the trials that aspiring writers will face in their attempt to make a career of writing.

"A" focuses too closely on the details of written work; the passage makes no mention of specific details regarding what makes a writer good or bad.

Though "B" may be true, the idea of the passage as a whole does not focus on how established authors and editors form their opinions. It simply states that people have differing opinions but does not attempt to state why that is so.

While the passage mentions, in one author's opinion, the toilsome nature of the writing business, it does not discuss ways in which success can be rewarding. The writers who offer encouraging advice simply focus on expressing the possibility for success rather than the benefits that will come with it. Therefore "C" is incorrect.

"E" is inaccurate as the passage does not supply advice to writers on how to make money from writing. While differing opinions are set forth, the author does not outline any explicit advice to young writers.

16. **The correct answer is (E).**

"E" is the correct answer; this sentence outlines the opinion of the more pessimistic people who focus on the harsh reality of the writing business.

"A" is inaccurate as it expresses a stronger opinion than

what the passage supplies; while the author indicates that there are people who understand that editors do not read all submitted manuscripts, the passage does not intend to make such a claim.

While this sentence mentions that manuscripts without a recommendation may not be read by an editor, "B" is incorrect because it focuses too

closely on the benefits of being well-established. The sentence serves to outline reasons why a manuscript may not be read, not to explain the benefits of having connections in the business.

"C" goes beyond what is stated in the passage; though perhaps implied, the text does not support any claims that describe the effects that lack of attention from an editor would have on aspiring writers.

"D" though true, goes too far in bringing emotion into the actions of editors who do not read certain works, calling them 'rude'. While the sentence does indeed indicate that there is a lack of courtesy in this process, the purpose of the sentence is not to create judgment of the editors but rather to state that some people would use this fact to argue that the writing business is a tough one to break into.

17. **"To the same young woman writes another equally well-known writer: "Your work is excellent; you can and will succeed."**

This sentence indicates the unreliability of judging a writer's potential on only one opinion. By indicating that the work being judged was written by the 'same' girl, the author establishes a controlled variable. Also, by pointing out that the differing opinion of this same work was that of an 'equally well-known writer', the author of this passage upholds the credibility of both judgments, thus demonstrating the subjective nature of writing and the unreliability of a single opinion.

18. **inferences and archetype**

The passage states that understanding the habitability of distant galaxies is an inexact science. Therefore, scientists cannot rely on precise data. They must use something else. "Fauna" means wildlife. This answer makes no sense in the context of the question. "Ambiguities" means "contradictions." Scientists would not base their understanding on contradictions. Therefore, we are left with "inferences." This word means "extrapolations." It makes sense that, in lieu of exact data, scientists would base their predictions of habitability on logical interpretations of observable facts. The third sentence talks about how the Milky Way is not a something that we used to believe it was. This "something" is clarified in the next sentence – it says that most nearby galaxies actually invert the structure of the Milky Way. Therefore, the Milky Way is not the standard model that we used to think it was.

"Liability" means "responsibility," which does not fit the context of the sentence. "Recidivist" means "repeat offender," which does not describe an inanimate object like the Milky Way. "Archetype" means standard model. It makes sense that

the Milky Way is no longer considered a standard model of a typical galaxy if scientists keep finding other galaxies with different structures.

19. **axiomatic and ironically**

This is another example of being unable to fill the blanks before reading the entire passage. Upon reading the entire thing, it becomes apparent that Einstein's theory of relativity is the foundation on which modern science is built. This of course leads to ironic situations when physicists try to disprove it, because the very experiments designed to disprove

it are based on the tenets established in the theory. After reading the entire passage and understanding this, we can answer the questions. The first blank is talking about the theory of relativity's relation to science. We have learned that it is self-evident within the scientific community, and should answer accordingly. "Equivocal" means "vague." If the theory is so manifest then it cannot be "vague." "Arcane" means "mysterious." Again, if the theory is so universally-understood then it cannot be mysterious. "Axiomatic" means "accepted," or "manifest." The passage stresses that the "central tenets" of the theory of relativity are "unequivocal" so the theory can safely be called "axiomatic."

The second sentence comments on the inherent contradiction of trying to disprove a theory while using the same tenets that have been established by the theory. "Disparagingly" means "disapprovingly." This answer does not make sense in the context of the sentence. "Redundantly" means "superfluously." Once again, this answer does not make sense in the context of the sentence. "Ironically" means "paradoxically."

It would be paradoxical to try to disprove a theory while using that same theory as an intellectual foundation.

20. **intractable and substantive**

The second sentence talks of how bio gerontology has managed to develop rapidly and solve issues. If these issues weren't solved before then they must have been difficult, or stubborn, so the word needs to fit that description. "Acquiescent" means "agreeable," but the correct word should be the opposite.

"Vituperative" means "insulting." This answer does not make sense. It is not close enough to the desired definition of "stubborn." We are left with "Intractable." This word does, in fact, mean stubborn. This describes formerly unconquerable issues perfectly. The next sentence talks about how lofty accomplishments are not needed in the field, and other types of accomplishments can still provide insight. These other types must be of a lesser magnitude. We want a word that expresses that idea. "Specious" means "misleading." Misleading increases in our understanding would not benefit the scientific community. "Unexplainable" means "incapable of being accounted for." Of course, unexplainable increases in our understanding would not benefit the scientific community, nor would they be an adequate substitute for "lofty" ones. "Substantive" means "practical." This is not as impressive as a "lofty" goal but still fits the sentence's description of a useful one.

# Section 5 – Quantitative Reasoning

1. **The correct answers are (B) and (D).**

In one minute, they will do the following fractions of the work:

Stephanie: $\frac{1}{5}$ Caroline: $\frac{1}{3}$

Brenda: $\frac{1}{4}$ Simon: $\frac{1}{6}$

Computing the combinations from the answer choices, we have

Stephanie and Brenda: $\frac{1}{5}+\frac{1}{4}=\frac{9}{20}$

Stephanie and Caroline: $\frac{1}{5}+\frac{1}{3}=\frac{8}{15}$

Stephanie and Simon: $\frac{1}{5}+\frac{1}{6}=\frac{11}{30}$

Brenda and Caroline: $\frac{1}{4}+\frac{1}{3}=\frac{7}{12}$

Simon and Caroline: $\frac{1}{6}+\frac{1}{3}=\frac{1}{2}$

Brenda and Simon: $\frac{1}{4}+\frac{1}{6}=\frac{5}{12}$

The combinations that do more than half of the job in one minute are Stephanie and Caroline, and Brenda and Caroline.

2. **The correct answer is (E).**

Pick numbers for $p$, $w$, and $x$ that work well in the problem. Let $p$=3 and $w$ =100. So there are three pages with 100 words per page, or 300 words total. Say he types five words a minute, so $x$ = 5. So he types 5 times 60, or 300 words an hour. Therefore it takes him one hour to type the paper. The only answer choice that equals 1 when $p$ = 3, $w$ = 100, and $x$= 5 is choice (E).

3. **The correct answer is 23.**

385 is a composite number. It can be factorized into prime factors such that

$385=5\times77=5\times7\times11$

The factorization is unique.

So the possible values of $x$, $y$ and $z$ can be written as

| Value of $x$ | Value of $y$ | Value of $z$ | Value of $x+y+z$ |
|---|---|---|---|
| 5 | 7 | 11 | 23 |
| 5 | 11 | 7 | 23 |
| 7 | 5 | 11 | 23 |
| 7 | 11 | 5 | 23 |
| 11 | 5 | 7 | 23 |
| 11 | 7 | 5 | 23 |

It can be seen that in all cases $x+y+z=23$

4. **The correct answer is (D).**

Let $x$ =4. That means he drove 120 miles in four hours, so his speed was 120 *miles*/(4 *Hours*) or 30 *mph*. Since 20 *minutes* = 1/3 of an hour, the distance he travelled in the first 20 *minutes* is = 1/3 *hours* x 30 *mph* = 10 *miles*. The only answer choice that equals 10 when $x$ = 4 is choice (D).

5. **The correct answer is (A).**

The total number of chocolates in the box is 17. But since there were already 2 almond–centered chocolates taken, only 15 are left. All 3 mint cream and 5 strawberry cream filled chocolates remain, but only 7 almond–centered chocolates remain. Quantity A is mint cream filled OR strawberry cream filled, so the probability is:

$$\frac{3}{15}+\frac{5}{15}=\frac{8}{15}$$

Quantity B is for almond–centered chocolates, which is 7/15. Therefore, Quantity A is greater than Quantity B.

6. **The correct answer is (C).**

We want to solve for the original price, price before the markdown. The percent markdown is 25 percent, so \$48 is percent of the whole.

*Percent* × *Whole* = *Part*

75 *Percent* × *Original price* = \$48

*Original price* = \$48/0.75=\$64

7. **The correct answer is (B).**

The set consists of 100 elements (integers 1 to 100). There are 16 numbers that are multiples of 6 in the given set; thus, the probability of this (Quantity A) is 16/100. There are 20 numbers that are multiples of 5 in the given set; thus, the probability of this (Quantity B) is 20/100.

8. **The correct answer is (C).**

To find the number, let's call the three items they can purchase *A*, *B*, and *C*. The possibilities:

All three order the same thing: *AAA, BBB, CCC.*

Two order the same thing: *AAB, AAC, BBA, BBC CCA, CCB*

All three order something different: *ABC*

So there are ten different ways the items could be ordered.

9. **The correct answer is 144.**

In this problem, we are using properties of similar triangles. The sides of the smaller triangle are proportional to the sides of the larger triangle.

*Smaller Triangle* 3 : 5 : 6

*Larger Triangle* $n$ : 10 : $m$

Based on the middle side, the sides of the smaller triangle are multiplied by two to get the sides of the larger triangle. Therefore, the

$n=3\times2=6$ and $m=6\times2=12$

All three interior angles of a triangle have a sum of 180°. We can use this property to solve for x.

$x + 67 + 53 = 180$

$x + 120 = 180$ or $x = 60°$

We know $x$=60, $m$=6,and $n$=12

Substitute these values into the expression.

$2x + m + 2n$

$2(60) + 12 + 2(6)$; $120 + 12 + 12$;

$120 + 24 = 144$

10. **The correct answer is (B).**

If angles $\angle A$ and $\angle B$ are complementary,

$m\angle A + m\angle B = 90°$

We also know that $m\angle A - m\angle B = 50°$

If we add the two equations

$2m\angle A = 90° + 50°$

$m\angle A = 70°$

$m\angle B = 70° - 50° = 20°$

The measure of the greatest angle out of two complementary angles $\angle A$ and $\angle B$ is 70°

In order to find the greatest angle in the triangle whose sides satisfy

$a^6+b^6 = c^6-3a^2\, b^2(a^2+b^2)$, we must remember the formula:

$(a+b)^3 = a^3+b^3 + 3ab\,(a+b)$

$(a^2+b^2)^3 = a^6+b^6 + 3a^2\, b^2(a^2+b^2)$

This means that we can write the equation as

$(a^2+b^2)^3 = c^6$

$a^2+b^2 = +^2$ which is Pythagoras theorem

The triangle whose sides satisfy this is a right angled triangle

The greatest angle is 90°. 90° is greater than70°.

11. **The correct answer is (A).**

An input of -2 will have a denominator of zero, which is undefined.

12. **The correct answer is (B).**

First we need to find how many students are entitled to vote:

450 – 450 × 8% – 19 = 450 – 36 – 19 = 395 *students*

Students who actually voted = 395 × 60% = 237

Richie Ambitious got 15/79[th] of the total votes

Richie got 15/79 × 237 = 45 *votes*

Albert Aspirant received 75% of the remaining votes

Albert got (237–45) × 75% = 144 *votes*

Bobby Content got the rest

Bobby got 237 – 45 – 144 = 48 *votes*

48 votes is greater than 45 votes

13. **The correct answer is (C).**

Let the length be l and the width be *w*; l:*w* = 4:3, so

$$\frac{l}{w}=\frac{4}{3}$$

Expressing the length in terms of the width, we have

$$l=\frac{4}{3}w$$

The area is $l\times w=\frac{4}{3}w\times w=108$

$$\frac{4}{3}w^2=108$$

$$w^2=108\times\frac{3}{4}=81;\quad w=\pm 9$$

Since the length of a side must be a positive value, *w = 9 inches*

Length, $l=\frac{4}{3}w=\frac{4}{3}\times 9=12 inches$

Quantity A: The width of the rectangle = 9 inches

Quantity B: The square of the difference between the length and the width = $(12 - 9)^2 = 3^2 = 9$ *inches*

14. **The correct answer is (D).**

To find the area you need to know the base and height. If the perimeter is 16, then AB+ BC+AC=16; that is, AB= 16 – 5 – 6 = 5. Since AB= BC, this is an isosceles triangle. If you drop a line from a vertex B to AC, it will divide the base in half. This divides up the triangle into two smaller right triangles:

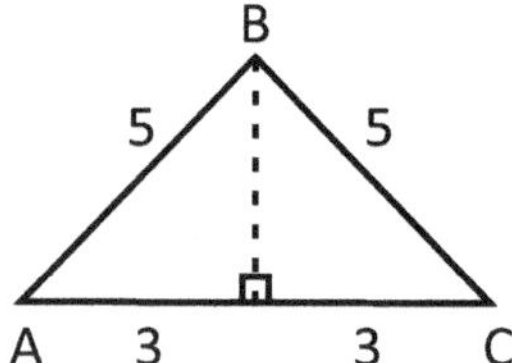


These right triangles each have one leg of 3 and a hypotenuse of 5; therefore they are 3 – 4 – 5 right triangles. So the missing leg (which is also the height of ΔABC) must have length 4. We now know that the base of ABC is 6 and the height is 4, so the area is 1/2 × 6 × 4, or 12, answer choice (D).

15. **The correct answers are (A), (B), (D), (F), and (H).**

*X*: 9:00 AM:*P*

*Q*: *Y*:9:00 AM

The distance between *P* and *Q* is 2km.

*X* catches *Y* at 9:24 PM.

We know that *speed=Distance/time*

Here distance= 2 *miles* and *time* =24 *minutes*=24/60 *hours*=2/5 *hours*

The speed here is the relative speed of *X* and *Y*(*Speed* of *X*- *speed* of *Y*)

Relative speed =2/((2/5))=5 *miles per hour.*

Now relative speed – 5 *mph* means that the speed of *X* is 5 *miles* more than that of *Y*.

So the possible combination of speeds is

: A, B, D, F, and H

16. **The correct answer is (D).**

Draw a straight line from point H to point F, to divide the figure into two right triangles.

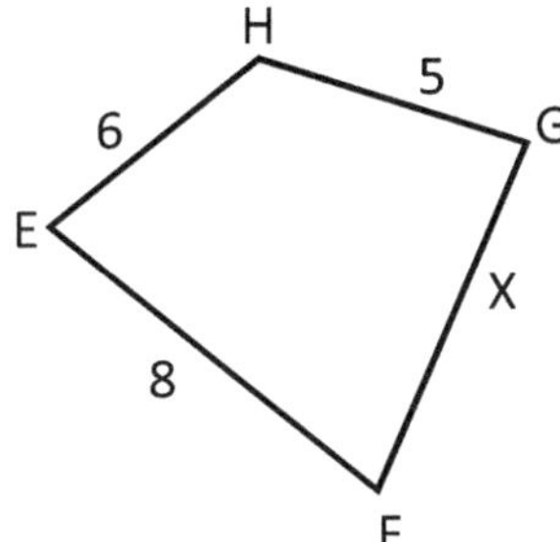


$\Delta EFH$ is a *3 – 4 – 5 right triangle* with a hypotenuse of length 10.

Use the Pythagorean Theorem in $\Delta FGH$ to find $x$:

$x^2 + 5^2 = 10^2$

$x^2 + 5^2 = 100$

$x^2 = 75$

$x = \sqrt{75}$

$x = \sqrt{25}\sqrt{3}$

$x = 5\sqrt{3}$

17. **The correct answers are (A), (C) and (D).**

In the study of 100 people, 25+16 or 41 saw little or no improvement at the end of the study. We will check if the proportions given in the answers are equivalent

to $\frac{41}{100}$ *or* 0.41

A $\frac{328}{800} = 0.41$

B $\frac{200}{620} = 0.32$

C $\frac{225}{550} = 0.41$

D $\frac{902}{2200} = 0.41$

E $\frac{797}{1350} = 0.59$

The only proportions that are equivalent are A, C, and D.

18. **The correct answer is (A).**

Quantity A is greater.

Mean of the data set

$= \frac{\{1(1) + 1(4) + 2(5) + 2(6) + 3(9) + 2(10)\}}{11}$

$= \frac{74}{11} = 6.72$

Median of the data set = 6

Clearly the mean of the data set is greater than the median of the data set.

19. **The correct answer is (B).**

Quantity B is greater.

Mean of the data set

$= \frac{\{1(1) + 1(4) + 2(5) + 2(6) + 3(9) + 2(10)\}}{11}$

$= \frac{74}{11} = 6.72$

Median of the data set = 6

Average of the mean and median of the data set =

$\frac{(6.72 + 6)}{2} = 6.36$

Mode of the data set = 9

Clearly the mode of the data set is greater than the average of the mean and median of the data set.

20. **The correct answer is (B).**

Quantity B is greater.

Range of the data set = 10 – 1 = 9

1/2 of range of data set = 1/2 x 9 = 4.5

Q2(Second quartile of the data set) = median of the data set = 6

The median divides the whole data into two groups of data which are as below

| | | | | | |
|---|---|---|---|---|---|
| First Group: | 1 | 4 | 5 | 5 | 6 |
| Second Group: | 9 | 9 | 9 | 10 | 10 |

$Q_1$ (First quartile of the data set) = median of the first group = 5

$Q_3$(Third quartile of the data set) = median of the second group = 9

Inter quartile range = $Q_3$- $Q_1$ = 9 – 5 = 4

Clearly 1/2 the range of the data set is greater than the interquartile range of the data set.

Chapter **6**

# Practice Test 4

You are about to begin a full length Practice Test. The Test has five sections. The time allotted for each section is marked at the beginning of the section. Work on one section at a time. Use a timer to keep track of the time limits for every section.

Try to take the Practice Test under real test conditions. Find a quiet place to work, and set aside enough time to complete the test without being disturbed. At the end of the test, check your answers by referring to the Answer Key and fill in your raw score in the score card below. Also, note down the time taken by you for completing each section.

Pay particular attention to the questions that were answered incorrectly. Read the answer explanations and understand how to solve them.

## My Score Card (Raw Score)

| | Section 2 | Section 3 | Section 4 | Section 5 |
|---|---|---|---|---|
| **Out of** | 20 | 20 | 20 | 20 |
| **My Score** | ________ | ________ | ________ | ________ |
| **Time Taken** | ________ | ________ | ________ | ________ |

# Section 1 – Analytical Writing

## Task 1 – Analyze an Issue | 30 mins

*In order to become well–rounded individuals, all college students should be required to take courses in which they read poetry, novels, mythology, and other types of imaginative literature.*

*Write a response in which you discuss the extent to which you agree or disagree with the recommendation and explain your reasoning for the position you take. In developing and supporting your position, describe specific circumstances in which adopting the recommendation would or would not be advantageous and explain how these examples shape your position.*

You may start writing your response here

## Task 2 – Analyze an Argument | Task 30 mins

*The council of Maple County, concerned about the county's becoming overdeveloped, is debating a proposed measure that would prevent the development of existing farmland in the county. But the council is also concerned that such a restriction, by limiting the supply of new housing, could lead to significant increases in the price of housing in the county. Proponents of the measure note that Chestnut County established a similar measure ten years ago and its housing prices have increased only modestly since. However, opponents of the measure note that Pine County adopted restrictions on the development of new residential housing fifteen years ago, and its housing prices have since more than doubled. The council currently predicts that the proposed measure, if passed, will result in a significant increase in housing prices in Maple County.*

*Write a response in which you discuss what questions would need to be answered in order to decide whether the prediction and the argument on which it is based are reasonable. Be sure to explain how the answers to these questions would help to evaluate the prediction.*

You may start writing your response here

# Section 2 – Verbal Reasoning

20 questions | 30 mins

---

**For Questions 1 to 3, for each blank, select one entry from the corresponding column of choices. Fill all blanks in the way that best completes the text.**

1. Ecology has recently exploded in popularity. This can be considered a natural consequence of our ability to investigate the world on smaller and smaller scales: eventually, so many people started concerning themselves with the microscopic picture that the macroscopic became forgotten. The study of ecology (i)________ this. It focused on the flow of energy and materials on the macroscopic level to provide (ii)________within which microscopic observations can better be made.

| Blank (i) |
|---|
| ameliorated |
| exacerbated |
| purloined |

| Blank (ii) |
|---|
| a milieu |
| an ambiguity |
| a privation |

2. Marine biologists experience tremendous obstacles when creating their models of aquatic life. They are not granted the (i)_________ that workers in most branches of science take for granted. Their subjects of study travel greater distances and greater depths, and often settle in regions of the ocean that are completely inaccessible to humans. (ii)_________ those problems are the difficulties faced when trying to construct tracking devices that can withstand the environments that subjects will be swimming through.

| Blank (i) |
|---|
| Amenities |
| Recalcitrance |
| Biliousness |

| Blank (ii) |
|---|
| Insinuating |
| Exacerbating |
| Alleviating |

3. The early Chinese made the first unofficial attempts at (i)______ risk, as they transferred their wares on many different ships. Doing so ensured that the loss of one ship would not destroy their entire inventory. The first use of (ii)______ insurance, however, belongs to the Babylonians. They had laws that permitted merchants to purchase insurance on their loans in case they were not able to repay it. In the (iii)______ world of trade, this was often a necessity.

| Blank (i) |
|---|
| alleviating |
| exacerbating |
| annunciating |

| Blank (ii) |
|---|
| sardonic |
| schematized |
| quiescent |

| Blank (iii) |
|---|
| guileless |
| portly |
| tumultuous |

**Questions 4 and 5 are based on the following passage.**

In the year 1885, the Eiffel firm, which also had an extensive background of experience in structural engineering, **undertook a series of investigations of tall metallic piers based upon its recent experiences with several lofty railway viaducts and bridges.** The most spectacular of these was the famous Garabit Viaduct (1880–1884), which carries a railroad some 400 feet above the valley of the Truyere in southern France. While the 200–foot height of the viaduct's two greatest piers was not startling even at that period, **the studies proved that piers of far greater height were entirely feasible in iron construction.** This led to the design of a 395–foot pier, which, although never incorporated into a bridge, may be said to have been the direct basis for the Eiffel Tower.

Preliminary studies for a 300–meter tower were made with the 1889 fair immediately in mind. With an assurance born of positive knowledge, Eiffel in June of 1886 approached the Exposition commissioners with the project. There can be no doubt that only the singular respect with which Eiffel was regarded not only by his profession but by the entire nation motivated the Commission to approve a plan which, in the hands of a figure of less stature, would have been considered grossly impractical.

**For Questions 4 and 5, select only one answer choice.**

4. Based on the passage, with which of the following statements would the author be most likely to agree?

   (A) The Eiffel firm's impressive reputation in France allowed them to initiate more grandiose projects than they would have otherwise been permitted.

   (B) In order to know how high an iron pier can successfully be constructed, it is necessary to design several test structures first in order to gain credibility amongst fellow engineers.

   (C) The Eiffel firm demonstrated an unprecedented ambition in regards to the projects that they designed, and their unwavering optimism was based on their desire to surpass other firms in their field.

   (D) 200–foot viaducts have never been considered impressive, even when they boasted the tallest height of their time.

   (E) Despite the Eiffel firm's successful collection of past construction projects, many of their ideas were considered to be overly ambitious and impractical.

5. What is the primary function of the boldface type phrases in the passage?

   (A) To indicate that the Eiffel firm researches their construction projects before creating designs rather than drawing on their own knowledge of engineering, which would have been inadequate.

   (B) To show the possibility of using iron instead of other materials for constructing piers and viaducts that will far surpass the size of other similar construction projects.

   (C) These phrases draw attention to the ability of construction companies that preceded the Eiffel firm and were able to erect structures that were superior to anything else of that time.

   (D) They explain that the piers and viaducts that had already been constructed at the time of these studies were not as ambitious as the current engineering capabilities could have allowed.

   (E) To demonstrate the inefficiency of using materials other than iron to build bridges that were considered unsafe, regardless of their impressive height.

**For Questions 6 and 7, select the two answer choices that, when used to complete the sentence, fit the meaning of the sentence as a whole and produce completed sentences that are alike in meaning.**

6. The flavored–water company made sure to avoid the use of any specific language in their advertising campaign so they could make __________ claims about the supposed vitamin content of their product.

   [A] disingenuous

   [B] obdurate

   [C] factual

   [D] duplicitous

   [E] lucid

   [F] trivial

7. Rapidly spreading diseases can cause a person to disproportionally weigh the __________ potentials of various New Age medicines over their metaphysical foundation, resulting in a susceptibility to scams.

   [A] prohibitive

   [B] palliative

   [C] luxurious

   [D] alleviative

   [E] intercalated

   [F] illegal

**For Questions 8 and 9, for each blank, select one entry from the corresponding column of choices. Fill all blanks in the way that best completes the text.**

8. The concept of uncertainty dominates the field of economics. Simply put, uncertainty is the unknown potential for gain or loss in a given transaction. This simple concept has tremendous ramifications, however. Potential risk for gain or loss cannot be easily (i)______. As a result, the governments and households that want to have a concrete idea of the risk involved in a given endeavor don't always have data to go by. But this uncertainty is a necessary (ii)______that must be made in order to enjoy the benefits of a market economy.

| Blank (i) |
| --- |
| perturbed |
| enumerated |
| aggrieved |

| Blank (ii) |
| --- |
| frankness |
| flaccidity |
| price |

9. The (i)______ of the modern food industry in America is impressive. Only a small section of the country's population exists outside of its structure. Employing more than 16 million people (and providing more than 10% of American's GDP), changes in the food industry can be felt across the entire country. The (ii)______ task of regulating such a dynamic and widespread industry falls to the Food and Drug Administration, or FDA.

| Blank (i) |
|---|
| extensiveness |
| lethargy |
| bankruptcy |

| Blank (ii) |
|---|
| arduous |
| ridiculous |
| pernicious |

**Questions 10 to 12 are based on the following passage.**

When the schemes started during a commercial bubble begin to be carried out, great quantities of materials are required for building, and the prices of these materials rise rapidly. The workpeople who produce these materials then earn high wages, and they spend these wages in better living and in pleasure. Thus the demand for commodities increases, and tradespeople make large profits and with no sufficient reason, the prices of the remaining commodities usually rise. Every trader now wants to buy, because he believes that prices will rise higher and higher, and that, by selling at the right time, the loss of any subsequent fall of prices will be thrown upon other people.

This state of things, however, cannot go on very long. Those who have subscribed for shares in new companies have to find the capital which they promised. They are obliged to draw out the money which they had formerly deposited in banks, and then the bankers have less to lend. Manufacturers, merchants, and speculators, who are making or buying large stocks of goods, wish to borrow more and more money, in order that they may have a larger business, the profit seeming likely to be so great. Then according to the laws of supply and demand, the price of money rises, which means that the rate of interest for short loans, from a week to three or six months in duration, is increased. The bubble goes on growing, until the more venturesome and unscrupulous speculators have borrowed many times as much money as they themselves really possess.

But the sudden rise which, sooner or later, occurs in the rate of interest, is very disastrous to such speculators. When they began to speculate the interest was perhaps, only two or three percent, but when it becomes seven or eight percent, there is fear that much of the profit will go in interest paid to the lenders of capital. Moreover, those who lent the money, by discounting the speculators' bills, or making advances on the security of goods, become anxious to have it paid back. Thus, the speculators are forced to begin selling their stocks at the best prices they can get. As soon as some people begin to sell in this way, others who hold goods think they had better sell before the prices fall seriously; then there arises a sudden rush to sell, and buyers being alarmed, refuse to buy except at much reduced rates. The bad speculators now find themselves unable to maintain their credit, because, if they sell their large stocks at a considerable loss, their own real capital will be quite insufficient to cover this loss. They are thus unable to pay what they have engaged to pay and become bankrupt. This is very awkward for other people, like manufacturers, who had sold goods to the bankrupts on credit and they do not receive the money they expected, and as they also perhaps have borrowed money while making the goods, they become bankrupt likewise. Thus, the discredit spreads, and firms even which had borrowed only moderate sums of money, in proportion to their capital, are in danger of failing.

This state of things is called a commercial collapse, because there is a sudden falling in of prices, credit, and enterprise. No sooner has such a crisis arrived, than everything changes. No one ventures to propose a new scheme, or a new company, because he knows that people in general have great difficulty in paying up what they promised to the schemes started during the bubble. This bubble is now burst.

**For Questions 10 and 11, select only one answer choice.**

10. The author would most likely support which of the following?

(A) Tougher regulations on speculators

(B) Larger supply of companies

(C) More access to goods

(D) More expensive capital and credit

(E) Abandoning the stock market

11. What is the meaning of the highlighted word “unscrupulous” as it is used in the passage?

(A) destitute

(B) cruel

(C) shady

(D) ill–mannered

(E) ignorant

12. Select the sentence that states the threefold cause of commercial collapse.

**Questions 13 to 16 are based on the following passage.**

Of course you know my friend the squirting cucumber. If you don’t, that can be only because you’ve never looked in the right place to find him. On all waste ground outside most southern cities-Nice, Cannes, Florence; Rome, Algiers, Granada; Athens, Palermo, Tunis, where you will-the soil is thickly covered by dark, trailing vines which bear on their branches a queer, hairy, green fruit, much like a common cucumber at that early stage of its existence when we know it best in the commercial form of pickled gherkins. As long as you don’t interfere with them, these hairy, green fruits do nothing out of the common in the way of personal aggressiveness. Like the model young lady of the books on etiquette, they don’t speak unless they’re spoken to. But if peradventure you chance to brush up against the plant accidentally, or you irritate it of set purpose with your foot or your cane, then, as Mr. Rider Haggard would say, "a strange thing happens": off jumps the little green fruit with a startling bounce, and scatters its juice and pulp and seeds explosively through a hole in the end where the stem joined on to it. The entire central part of the cucumber, in short (answering to the seeds and pulp of a ripe melon), squirt out elastically through the breach in the outer wall, leaving the hollow shell behind as a mere empty windbag.

Naturally, the squirting cucumber knows its own business best, and is not without sufficient reasons of its own for this strange and, to some extent, unmannerly behavior. By its queer trick of squirting, it manages to kill at least two birds with one stone. For, in the first place, the sudden elastic jump of the fruit frightens away browsing animals, such as goats and cattle. Those meditative ruminants are little accustomed to finding shrubs or plants take the aggressive against them; and when they see a fruit that quite literally flies in their faces of its own accord, they hesitate to attack the uncanny vine which bristles with such magical and almost miraculous defenses. Moreover, the juice of the squirting cucumber is bitter and nauseous, and if it gets into the eyes or nostrils of man or beast, it impresses itself on the memory by stinging like red pepper. So the trick of squirting serves in a double way as a protection to the plant against the attacks of herbivorous animals and other enemies.

But that's not all. Even when no enemy is near, the ripe fruits at last drop off of themselves, and scatter their seeds elastically in every direction. This they do simply in order to disseminate their kind in new and unoccupied spots, where the seedlings will root and find an opening in life for themselves. Observe, indeed, that the very word "disseminate" implies a general vague recognition of this principle of plant-life on the part of humanity. It means, etymologically, to scatter seed; and it points to the fact that everywhere in nature seeds are scattered broadcast, infinite pains being taken by the mother-plant for their general diffusion over wide areas of woodland, plain, or prairie.

**Consider each of the three choices separately and select all that apply.**

13. Which of the following examples of adaptation is similar to that of the squirting cucumber?

[A] The camel's ability to go for long periods of time without water

[B] The remora's ability to establish a host relationship with a shark

[C] The chameleon's ability to camouflage itself

**For Questions 14 and 15, select only one answer choice.**

14. Consider the style elements in this passage to determine the writer's tone.

(A) Satiric

(B) Sarcastic

(C) Admiring

(D) Awestruck

(E) Antagonistic

15. Which of the following designate the main points of this passage?

(A) Repulsion and reproduction

(B) Accident and intention

(C) Offense and defense

(D) Adaptation and mutation

(E) Allusion and illusion

16. Select the sentence that expresses the same warning as the familiar adage, "Let sleeping dogs lie."

**Question 17 is based on the following passage.**

The Way became the Pilgrims' Way in 1174, four years after Thomas à Becket was murdered in Canterbury Cathedral. His tomb in the Cathedral became the second shrine in Christendom, and pilgrims came to it along the old trackway through Surrey, from Farnham east of the Hog's Back along the hills to Canterbury in Kent. Henry the Second, one of the earliest pilgrims of all, made his act of repentance a few days after landing at Southampton from France, on February 8, 1174. Or so legend relates, and adds that he swore to walk barefoot; history is less precise. After Henry, the stream of devotees multiplied.

**Select only one answer choice.**

17. Which of the following would, if true, most effectively strengthen the passage's argument?

(A) A detailed definition of the term "pilgrim" from the relevant period.

(B) A document showing that Henry the Second was not related to Thomas à Becket's murder.

(C) Receipts showing that Henry the Second stayed at an inn near Farnham.

(D) A description of a newspaper article that recorded Henry the Second's journey with a reference to the name Pilgrim's Way.

(E) A private journal which explains Henry the Second's alleged refusal to wear shoes.

**For Questions 18 and 19, select the two answer choices that, when used to complete the sentence, fit the meaning of the sentence as a whole and produce completed sentences that are alike in meaning.**

18. The interplay of supply and demand in a marketplace is not ____________ to any one culture or class; the buying and selling of fabrics in a village square and the buying and selling of stocks on Wall Street are both examples of the reciprocal forces of supply and demand at work.

    [A] anomalous

    [B] unorthodox

    [C] incongruous

    [D] apocryphal

    [E] tendentious

    [F] sententious

19. In human physiology the _______ neural response takes care of precise, immediate action in direct response to pressure from the environment while the hormonal response utilizes slow, indirect action to coordinate the development and homeostasis of the body.

    [A] inglorious

    [B] instantaneous

    [C] violent

    [D] explosive

    [E] rapid

    [F] somatic

**For each blank, select one entry from the corresponding column of choices. Fill all blanks in the way that best completes the text.**

20. Many people view philosophy as the (i)______ expansion of what humans are capable of perceiving. Transcendental idealism, however, (ii)______ this. Crafted in part to alleviate the growing tension between empiricism and rationalism, transcendental idealism postulates that human perception is not absolute. There are certain things that are simply outside the realm of human understanding, too esoteric for human brains to understand.

| Blank (i) |
| --- |
| fallible |
| perpetual |
| restricted |

| Blank (ii) |
| --- |
| repudiates |
| collaborates |
| invigorates |

# Section 3 – Quantitative Reasoning

20 questions | 35 mins

1.

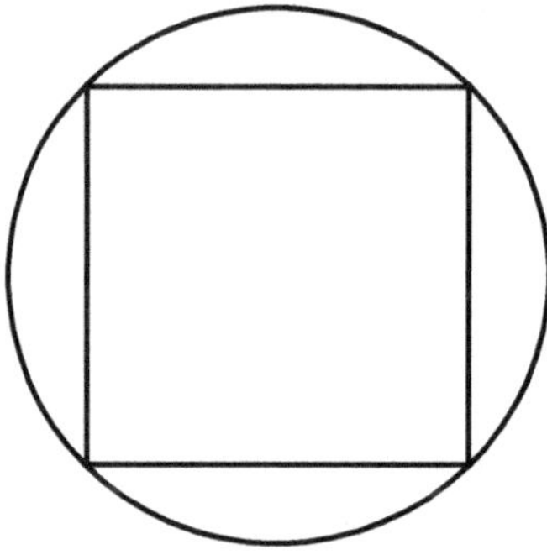

If the circle above has radius of 5 units, then what is the side length of the square inscribed within it?

[ ] units.

2.

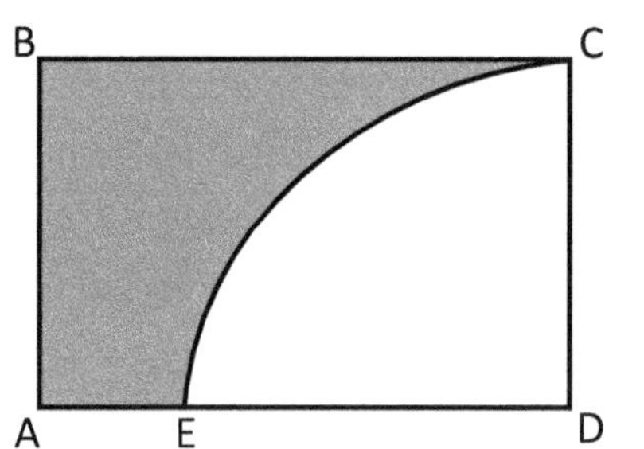


In the figure above, the quarter circle with center D has a radius of 4 and rectangle ABCD has a perimeter of 20. What is the perimeter of the shaded region?

(A) $20 - 80\pi$

(B) $10 + 2\pi$

(C) $12 + 2\pi$

(D) $12 + 4\pi$

(E) $4 + 8\pi$

3. Which of the following algebraic expressions are equivalent to $2x^2 - 2$?

[A] $4(x^2 - 2) - 2(x^2 - 3)$

[B] $2(x^2 - 2) - 4(x^2 + 3)$

[C] $2(x - 1)(x + 1)$

[D] $(x + 6)(x + 1) + (8 + x)(1 - x)$

[E] $2(x + 4)(x - 1) - 3(2x + 5)$

4.

$x < 0$, $a > 0$ and $y > 0$

| Quantity A | Quantity B |
|---|---|
| $xy$ | $-a$ |

(A) Quantity A is greater.

(B) Quantity B is greater.

(C) The two quantities are equal.

(D) The relationship cannot be determined from the information given.

**For Questions 5 and 6 refer to the following chart:**

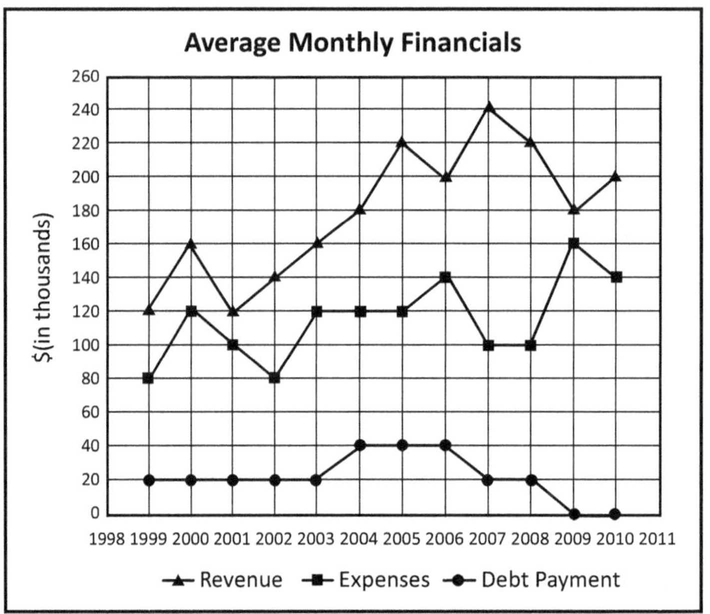


5. Erin has a monthly salary of $3,750, and earns 10% commission on all of her sales. Last year she earned a total of $64,000, with 24% coming from March. What were her total sales in March?

Ⓐ $15,360

Ⓑ $153,600

Ⓒ $11,610

Ⓓ $116,100

Ⓔ $3,750

6. There was an error in calculating the monthly average expenses for 2008, and the value must be increased by $20,000 for that year. The overall average expenses per month from 1999 through 2010 BEFORE the correction was approximately $115,000. What is the approximate increase in thousands of dollars in the overall average of expenses from 1999 through 2010 after the correction was made?

Ⓐ 20

Ⓑ 4

Ⓒ 10

Ⓓ 2

Ⓔ 40

7.

| MARKETS | MONTHS | | | | |
|---|---|---|---|---|---|
| | Jan | Feb | Mar | April | May |
| **Alameda** | 19 | 24 | 23 | 26 | 27 |
| **Brimfield** | 23 | 24 | 24 | 25 | 25 |
| **Brooklyn** | 24 | 26 | 25 | 24 | 25 |
| **Daytona** | 56 | 55 | 58 | 57 | 59 |

The data above shows the revenue (in hundred thousands of dollars) collected from different market places in different years to this year.

Daytona market collected 5% less this year in the first five months that the sum of what Alameda and Brimfield markets collected the previous year in the first five months. If Alameda market collected 8% more this year in the first five months than last year in the first five months, by how many dollars did Brimfield market collect in the first five months of the previous year than Brooklyn market?

- (A) \$300, 000
- (B) \$6,600,000
- (C) \$6,100,000
- (D) \$3,700,000
- (E) \$1,800,000

8.

In a microfinance institution, Regan deposited \$1,000 in one account and \$1,200 in a second account. The accounts earn simple interest over two years.

| Quantity A | Quantity B |
|---|---|
| Interest at a rate of 9.5% at the end of two years in the second account | Interest at a rate of 11.5% at the end of two years in the first account |

- (A) Quantity A is greater.
- (B) Quantity B is greater.
- (C) The two quantities are equal.
- (D) The relationship cannot be determined from the information given.

9. Which of the following are equivalent to $\frac{5x}{3y^2}$ ?

[A] $\dfrac{(15x^3)(x^{-2}y^3)^2}{\left(\frac{1}{3}xy^{-4}\right)^{-2}}$

[B] $\dfrac{(3x^3)(3x^2y^3)^2}{\left(\frac{1}{5}xy^{-4}\right)^{2}}$

[C] $\dfrac{(5x^2)^2(y^2)^2}{(15x^3)(y^2)^3}$

[D] $\dfrac{(3x^5y^2)^{-2}}{(5x^4y)^{-2}x^3}$

10.

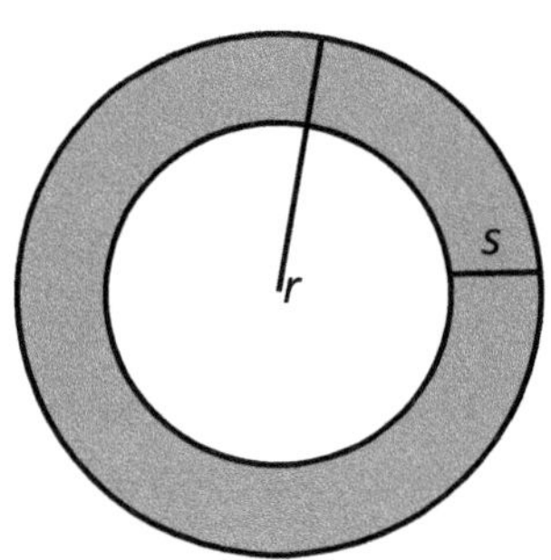


If $r = 15$ and $s = 7$, then what is the area of the shaded portion? Round to the nearest tenth.

[ ]

11. Mike's coin collection consists of quarters, dimes, and nickels. If the ratio of the number of quarters to the number of dimes is 5:2, and the ratio of the number of dimes to the number of nickels is 3:4, what is the ratio of the number of quarters to the number of nickels?

(A) 5:4

(B) 7:5

(C) 10:6

(D) 12:7

(E) 15:8

12.

A bus left Dallas en route to Houston (195 miles away), traveling at an average speed of 39 mph. Later, a car left Houston for Dallas at an average speed of 65 mph. Both vehicles reached their destinations at the same time. They take the same route/ cover the same distance.

| **Quantity A** | **Quantity B** |
|---|---|
| The distance covered by the bus before the car left Houston | The distance remaining for the bus to cover when the car was halfway the journey |

(A) Quantity A is greater.

(B) Quantity B is greater.

(C) The two quantities are equal.

(D) The relationship cannot be determined from the information given.

13. A car traveled from A to B at an average speed of 40 mph, and then immediately traveled back from B to A at an average speed of 60 mph. What was the car's average speed for the round trip, in mph?

(A) 45

(B) 48

(C) 50

(D) 52

(E) 54

14.

It takes 5 hours for Jean to clean a compound and 2 less hours for Jean and John both to clean the same compound.

| **Quantity A** | **Quantity B** |
|---|---|
| Time taken for only John to clean the compound | Time taken for only Jean to clean the compound |

(A) Quantity A is greater.

(B) Quantity B is greater.

(C) The two quantities are equal.

(D) The relationship cannot be determined from the information given.

15.

A train leaves a station in San Francisco at 9:00 am heading south. A second train leaves San Francisco at 11:00 am heading east. The first train travels at a speed of 120 mph while the second train travels at a speed of 150 mph.

| **Quantity A** | **Quantity B** |
|---|---|
| The shortest distance between the two trains at 3.00 pm. | The sum of the distance both trains have traveled by 3:00 pm. |

(A) Quantity A is greater.

(B) Quantity B is greater.

(C) The two quantities are equal.

(D) The relationship cannot be determined from the information given.

16. If $x$ is an odd integer and if $y$ is an even integer, then $x^2 - y^2$ is always which of the following?

I An odd integer

II An even integer

III The square of an integer

(A) I only

(B) II only

(C) III only

(D) I and III

(E) II and III

17. In the last 5 years, the price of new Brand $x$ car increased 30 percent. If it is assumed that the percent increase in the next 5 year period will be the same, then what will be the percent increase in the price of a new Brand $x$ car over the entire 10 year period?

(A) 15%

(B) 30%

(C) 39%

(D) 60%

(E) 69%

18. If $2 \leq y \leq 3$ and $4 \leq z \leq 5$, then what is least possible average of $\frac{1}{y}$ and $\frac{1}{z}$ ?

(A) $\frac{3}{8}$

(B) $\frac{4}{15}$

(C) $\frac{1}{4}$

(D) $\frac{1}{6}$

(E) $\frac{1}{16}$

19.

The cost of 5 pencils is 85 cents, while the cost of 4 pens is $1.20.

| Quantity A | Quantity B |
|---|---|
| The cost of 2 pencils and 3 pens | The cost of 8 pencils and 2 pens |

(A) Quantity A is greater.

(B) Quantity B is greater.

(C) The two quantities are equal.

(D) The relationship cannot be determined from the information given.

20.

If $a > b > c > 0 > d$, and $a$, $b$, $c$ and $d$ are integers, then which of the following is true?

| Quantity A | Quantity B |
|---|---|
| $ab - cd$ | $ad - cb$ |

(A) Quantity A is greater.

(B) Quantity B is greater.

(C) The two quantities are equal.

(D) The relationship cannot be determined from the information given.

# Section 4 – Verbal Reasoning

20 questions | 30 mins

**For questions 1 and 2, for each blank, select one entry from the corresponding column of choices. Fill all blanks in the way that best completes the text.**

1. While the number of motor vehicle fatalities per year has decreased substantially over the past decade, airline passage is still the _______ to which all forms of transportation aspire.

| |
|---|
| exemplar |
| contrarian |
| subversion |
| reprobate |
| scoundrel |

2. Atheism and agnosticism are not as (i)_______ opposed to religion as people often think. In reality, there is a spectrum that runs from religious to irreligious, with many gray areas in between. There is no hard and fast line distinguishing any two groups that fall between "religious" and "irreligious." For instance, some religions (such as Buddhism) actually describe their followers as being atheistic. Instances like this disprove the existence of a strict (ii)_______ between religious affiliations.

| Blank (i) |
|---|
| frugally |
| diametrically |
| judiciously |

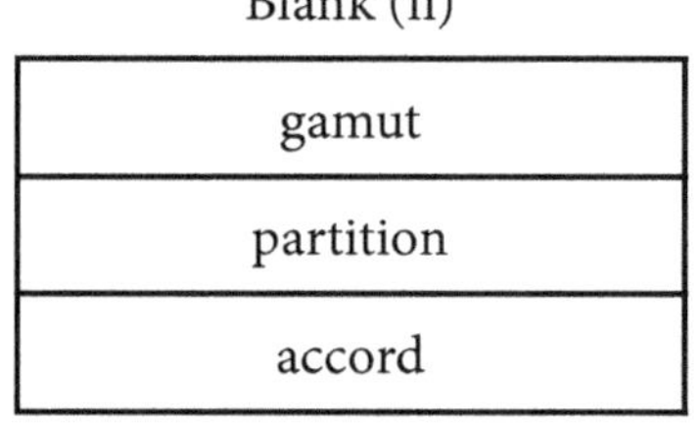

| Blank (ii) |
|---|
| gamut |
| partition |
| accord |

**Questions 3 to 5 are based on the following passage.**

Let us suppose that a colony of twenty or thirty families establishes itself in a wild district, covered with underbrush and forests; and from which, by agreement, the natives consent to withdraw. Each one of these families possesses a moderate but sufficient amount of capital, of such a nature as a colonist would be apt to choose – animals, seeds, tools, and a little money and food. The land having been divided, each one settles himself as comfortably as possible, and begins to clear away the portion allotted to him. But after a few weeks of fatigue, such as they never before have known, of inconceivable suffering, of ruinous and almost useless labor, our colonists begin to complain of their trade; their condition seems hard to them; they curse their sad existence.

**For Questions 3 and 4, select only one answer choice.**

3. Based on the passage, which of the following contributes to the colonists' dissatisfaction with their lot?

   (A) A lack of sufficient monetary funds

   (B) A lack of cooperation among the settlers

   (C) The departure of the native population

   (D) Difficult and unproductive land-clearing

   (E) The division of land into portions

4. According to the passage, all of the following are true of the colonists EXCEPT

   (A) The colonists were divided into family units.

   (B) The colonists did not bring the provisions they needed to clear the land.

   (C) The colonists did not appreciate some of the difficulties they would face.

   (D) The colonists did not suffer in silence.

   (E) The colonists brought an appropriate supply of livestock with them.

**Consider each of the three choices separately and select all that apply.**

5. The passage implies which of the following about the colonists' experience?

   [A] The experience described is typical of that encountered by most early pioneers.

   [B] The settlers should have sought help from the natives rather than seeking their withdrawal.

   [C] The colonists made reasonable preparations for their endeavor.

**For Questions 6 and 7, for each blank, select one entry from the corresponding column of choices. Fill all blanks in the way that best completes the text.**

6. The subtlety that goes into the construction of poems makes them difficult to (i)______. Without strict use of genre conventions, every poem seems to be completely unique. Therefore, unlike prose writing, one rarely sees works of poetry divided (ii)______ into genres. While everybody can identify a science fiction novel, or a romance novel, such distinctions are difficult to make in the field of poetry.

| Blank (i) |
|---|
| inoculate |
| inculcate |
| catalog |

| Blank (ii) |
|---|
| incontrovertibly |
| libidinously |
| debatably |

7. The size of the shadow banking industry may (i)______ previous predictions. What was once estimated as a 25 trillion dollar industry may now be pushing 75 trillion. The very definition of "shadow bank" is still debatable – needless to say, this makes the industry a headache for regulators. Attempts have been made recently to (ii)______ the risks inherent with these shadow banks by discouraging their owners from making large financial gambles.

| Blank (i) |
|---|
| equiponderate |
| outstrip |
| endorse |

| Blank (ii) |
|---|
| obdurate |
| conflate |
| mitigate |

**Questions 8 and 9 are based on the following passage.**

A living organism is such that, though it is continually changing its substance, its identity, as a whole, remains essentially the same. This definition is incomplete, but it gives us a first essential approximation, it indicates the continuance of the whole, with the unceasing change of the details. Were this definition complete, a river would furnish us with a perfect example of a living organism, because, while the river remains, the individual drops of water are continually changing. **There is then something more in the living organism than the continuity of the whole, with the change of the details.**

An analogy, given by Max Verworn, carries us a step further. He likens life to a flame, and takes a gas flame with its butterfly shape as a particularly appropriate illustration. Here the shape of the flame remains constant, even in its details. Immediately above the burner, at the base of the flame, there is a completely dark space; surrounding this, a bluish zone that is faintly luminous; and beyond this again, the broad spread of the two wings that are brightly luminous. The flame, like the river, preserves its identity of form, while its constituent details—the gases that feed it—are in continual change. **But there is not only a change of material in the flame; there is a change of condition.** Everywhere the gas from the burner is entering into energetic combination with the oxygen of the air, with evolution of light and heat.

**For Questions 8 and 9, select only one answer choice.**

8. What information about living organisms does the author aim to express in this passage?

Ⓐ That all living organisms display both unchanging and ever–changing qualities and that there is not much more to it than that.

Ⓑ Living organisms can be defined in regards to the differences that they display when compared to non–living organisms.

Ⓒ Analogies are the easiest way to describe the scientific criteria that define living versus non–living organisms by creating a visual imagery that is much easier to grasp than scientific data.

Ⓓ A flame is different than a river, scientifically speaking, in regards to the organisms that make up their composition, yet both a flame and river contain the same molecular structure.

Ⓔ All living organisms have certain qualities in common, though some are more complex than others in the way that they alter their surrounding conditions, which surpasses the way that most people perceive the identity of these organisms.

9. What function do the boldface type sentences serve in the passage's main message about how to define living organisms?

   (A) The first sentence introduces the complexity of how to define living organisms, and the second serves as an example to illustrate that complexity.

   (B) The first sentence defines the qualities that all living organisms possess, and the second introduces yet another factor in how living organisms are characterized.

   (C) Both sentences explain the main scope of how living organisms can be identified.

   (D) Both sentences express the inconsistency that living organisms display in nature and why no two organisms are the same.

   (E) The first sentence introduces the idea that all living organisms have constant qualities, and the second sentence refutes the first.

**For Questions 10 and 11, select the two answer choices that, when used to complete the sentence, fit the meaning of the sentence as a whole and produce completed sentences that are alike in meaning.**

10. Although it ostensibly works just like any of the other Newtonian forces encountered in the laboratory environment, the application of friction often appears to be _______, and therefore challenging for students.

    [A] ironic

    [B] straightforward

    [C] inconsistent

    [D] deliberate

    [E] complaisant

    [F] unpredictable

11. The rigid, often counter–intuitive machinations of science and the unassailable foundation on which it is built frequently chase away would–be practitioners of research and lead them to look for comfort in the _______ of the arts.

    [A] contradictions

    [B] flexibility

    [C] craftiness

    [D] mutability

    [E] expressivity

    [F] innovation

**For Questions 12 and 13, for each blank, select one entry from the corresponding column of choices. Fill all blanks in the way that best completes the text.**

12. The sub–discipline of socio cultural anthropology can best be understood by looking at its two (i)______ topics. Cultural anthropology is the study of how the people of a culture make sense of the world around them. Conversely, social anthropology seeks to understand the relationship between the members of a culture. By understanding what (ii)______ these two topics, it becomes much easier to understand the ways in which they work together.

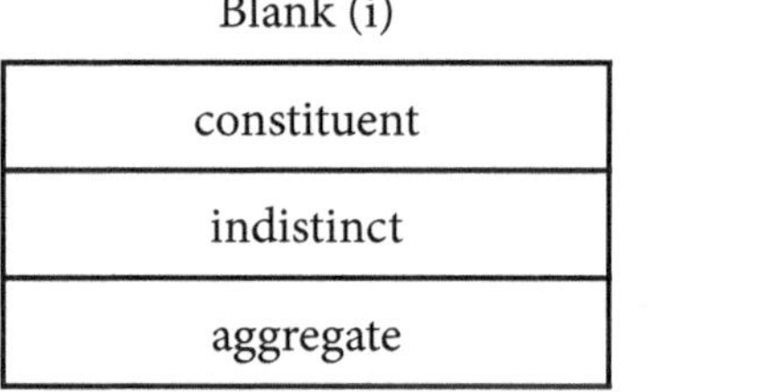

| Blank (i) |
| --- |
| constituent |
| indistinct |
| aggregate |

| Blank (ii) |
| --- |
| demarcates |
| amalgamates |
| denigrates |

13. Early attempts at studying human anatomy relied on (i)________ more than anything. Lacking advanced technologies like x–rays and MRI, early doctors simply dissected corpses to understand placement and function of organs. Although great strides were made with this approach from the macroscopic level, the details of microscopic human anatomy escaped surgeons for generations. The pathogeneses of diseases like cancer were too (ii)________ to be detected in these early days of surgery.

| Blank (i) |
| --- |
| fortitude |
| artifice |
| precision |

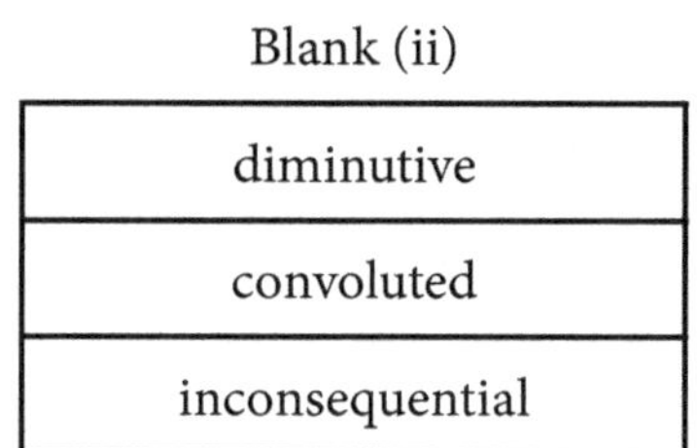

| Blank (ii) |
| --- |
| diminutive |
| convoluted |
| inconsequential |

**Questions 14 to 16 are based on the following passage.**

How are our customary ideas of space and time related to the character of our experiences? The experiences of an individual appear to us arranged in a series of events; in this series the single events which we remember appear to be ordered according to the criterion of "earlier" and "later," which cannot be analysed further. There exists, therefore, for the individual, an I–time, or subjective time. This in itself is not measurable. I can, indeed, associate numbers with the events, in such a way that a greater number is associated with the later event than with an earlier one; but the nature of this association may be quite arbitrary. This association I can define by means of a clock by comparing the order of events furnished by the clock with the order of the given series of events. We understand by a clock something which provides a series of events which can be counted, and which has other properties of which we shall speak later. By the aid of speech different individuals can, to a certain extent, compare their experiences. In this way it is shown that certain sense perceptions of different individuals correspond to each other, while for other sense perceptions no such correspondence can be established. We are accustomed to regard as real those sense perceptions which are common to different individuals, and which therefore are, in a measure, impersonal. The natural sciences, and in particular, the most fundamental of them, physics, deal with such sense perceptions. The conception of physical bodies, in particular of rigid bodies, is a relatively constant complex of such sense perceptions. A clock is also a body, or a system, in the same sense, with the additional property that the series of events which it counts is formed of elements all of which can be regarded as equal. The only justification for our concepts and system of concepts is that they serve to represent the complex of our experiences; beyond this they have no legitimacy. I am convinced that the philosophers have had a harmful effect upon the progress of scientific thinking in removing certain fundamental concepts from the domain of empiricism, where they are under our control, to the intangible heights of the a priori. For even if it should appear that the universe of ideas cannot be deduced from experience by logical means, but is, in a sense, a creation of the human mind, without which no science is possible, nevertheless this universe of ideas is just as little independent of the nature of our experiences as clothes are of the form of the human body. This is particularly true of our concepts of time and space, which physicists have been obliged by the facts to bring down from the Olympus of the a priori in order to adjust them and put them in a serviceable condition.

**For Questions 14 to 16, select only one answer choice.**

14. What can be inferred from this passage regarding the author's view on how people perceive reality?

(A) The author believes that reality can be measured based on how two or more people view certain events that certain sense perceptions of different individuals correspond to each other.

(B) Events can only be accurately documented by trained scientists, whereas philosophers do not have the skills necessary to conduct the proper types of experiments needed for such studies.

(C) Clocks are useful tools for experiments in physics and can represent all sorts of scientific findings.

(D) By assigning a fixed numerical value to events in life, the passage of time can be calculated with strong accuracy.

(E) An individual' sensory perception can be objective when measured through scientific research.

15. Which of the following words best summarizes the author's attitude towards "a priori" as can be inferred from the passage?

(A) reverent

(B) mocking

(C) disdainful

(D) dissatisfied

(E) patronising

16. Based on this passage, the author could likely be any of the following EXCEPT:

(A) A well–educated scientist who specializes in quantum physics.

(B) A professor who teaches science and philosophy courses at a university.

(C) A member of a debate team.

(D) A philosopher who has begun to take interest in science.

(E) A university student who was required to write a report about physics.

**Question 17 is based on the following passage.**

The newspaper is a private enterprise. Its object is to make money for its owner. Whatever motive may be given out for starting a newspaper, expectation of profit by it is the real one, whether the newspaper is religious, political, scientific, or literary. The exceptional cases of newspapers devoted to ideas or "causes" without regard to profit are so few as not to affect the rule. Commonly, the cause, the sect, the party, the trade, the delusion, the idea, gets its newspaper, its organ, its advocate, only when some individual thinks he can see a pecuniary return in establishing it.

**Select only one answer choice.**

17. Which statement, if true, provides the most strength for the validity of the conclusion?

(A) Many religious groups publish newspapers to tell about missionary support.

(B) Newspapers are designed to be attractive and interesting for the reader.

(C) Newspaper printing is one of the most dependable sources of income because there is always news happening somewhere.

(D) The price of newspaper subscriptions has risen 25% in the past 10 years.

(E) The new owners of the local newspaper are seeking the most relevant issues facing the community because they hope to increase the number of subscribers.

**For Questions 18 and 19, select the two answer choices that, when used to complete the sentence, fit the meaning of the sentence as a whole and produce completed sentences that are alike in meaning.**

18. In response to overwhelming physiological damage from the environment, the human body will go to amazing lengths to protect its vital organs, even to the point of sacrificing ________ appendages.

[A] mandatory

[B] inessential

[C] identical

[D] dispensable

[E] asymmetrical

[F] embryological

19. In order to ensure their own survival fitness, organic molecules must establish _______ between their propensities to grow via chemical reaction and their need to maintain the geometric simplicity that is essential for life.

    [A] a synthesis

    [B] an algorithm

    [C] an equation

    [D] a deduction

    [E] a fission

    [F] a unity

**Question 20 is based on the following passage.**

Is there any knowledge in the world which is so certain that no reasonable man could doubt it? This question, which at first sight might not seem difficult, is really one of the most difficult that can be asked. When we have realized the obstacles in the way of a straightforward and confident answer, we shall be well launched on the study of philosophy—for philosophy is merely the attempt to answer such ultimate questions, not carelessly and dogmatically, as we do in ordinary life and even in the sciences, but critically, after exploring all that makes such questions puzzling, and after realizing all the vagueness and confusion that underlie our ordinary ideas.

In daily life, we assume as certain many things which, on a closer scrutiny, are found to be so full of apparent contradictions that only a great amount of thought enables us to know what it is that we really may believe. In the search for certainty, it is natural to begin with our present experiences, and in some sense, no doubt, knowledge is to be derived from them. But any statement as to what it is that our immediate experiences make us know is very likely to be wrong.

**Select only one answer choice.**

20. Which of the following statements best reiterates the author's main point in the passage?

    (A) Any question in life can be conclusively answered either with scientific facts or philosophical research.

    (B) Science takes a methodical approach to gathering information that uses experimentation and facts to compile data, and is a much more regimented procedure for finding answers than other methods that display more casual approaches.

    (C) It is easier to understand our own beliefs about life if we take into account the basic truths that are evident and unquestionable.

    (D) Our senses and beliefs, though seemingly unwavering and certain, may still hide numerous contradicting factors that dispel the assumptions that many people accept as absolute truths.

    (E) Philosophy is the process that people use when they want to arrive at a level of certainty about life that is not possible in other areas of education, such as science.

# Section 5 – Quantitative Reasoning

20 questions | 35 mins

1.

$x > 1$ and $0 < y < 1$

| Quantity A | Quantity B |
|---|---|
| $\dfrac{(xy)^4}{x^3}$ | $\dfrac{\left(\dfrac{x}{y}\right)^4}{x^3}$ |

(A) Quantity A is greater.

(B) Quantity B is greater.

(C) The two quantities are equal.

(D) The relationship cannot be determined from the information given.

2.

| Quantity A | Quantity B |
|---|---|
| $24.6 \times 10^3$ | $0.246 \times 10^5$ |

(A) Quantity A is greater.

(B) Quantity B is greater.

(C) The two quantities are equal.

(D) The relationship cannot be determined from the information given.

**Questions 3 to 5 are based on the following diagram:**

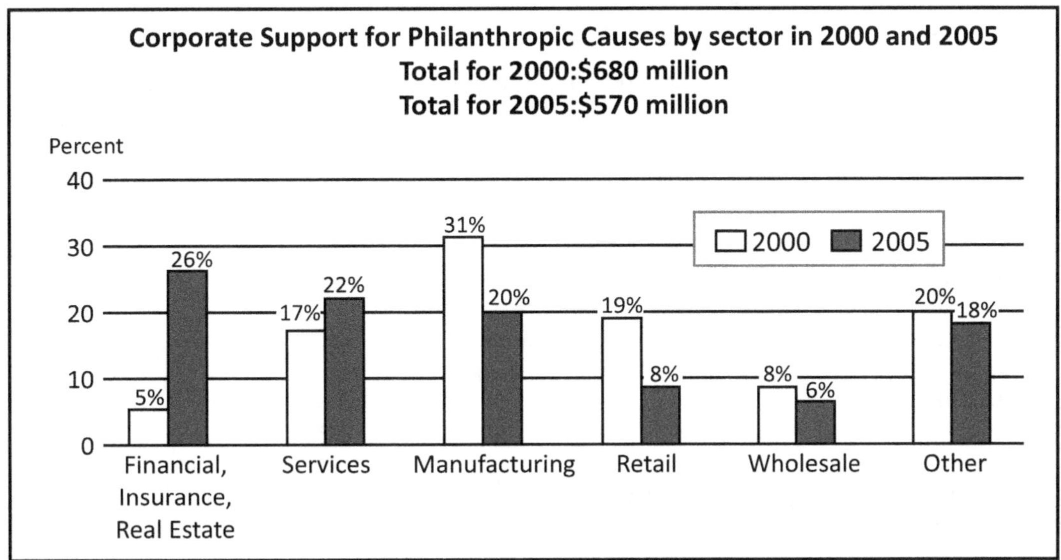


3. What was the total contribution in 2005 (approximately in millions of dollars) by the corporate sectors that decreased their support for Philanthropic causes from 2000 to 2005?

(A) 150 million dollars

(B) 200 million dollars

(C) 250 million dollars

(D) 300 million dollars

(E) 350 million dollars

4. What is the average amount contributed by those sectors who contributed more than $100 million each to the Philanthropic Causes in both 2000 and 2005?

(A) $114 million

(B) $238.6 million

(C) $263.13 million

(D) $324.8 million

(E) $342.6 million

5. Of the Financial, Insurance and Real Estate Sector's 2005 contribution to Philanthropic Causes, one-third went for rebuilding homes lost due to Hurricane Katrina and one-fourth of the remainder went to providing medical aid to the injured. Approximately how many millions of dollars more did the Financial, Insurance and Real Estate Sector contribute towards rebuilding homes that year than to providing medical aid?

(A) $20 million

(B) $25 million

(C) $30 million

(D) $35 million

(E) $40 million

6. In the equation $216^{a+2} = 6^{2-a}$, what is the value of $a$?

[ ]

7. The absolute value of the difference between the values of x satisfying the equation $\frac{1}{x-3} - \frac{3}{x+5} = \frac{1}{5}$ is

[ ]

8. Line A passes through the points (0,–2) and (1, 0). Line B passes through the points (1, b) and (2,1). Line C passes through the points (c,–4) and (–b,–2). For which values of b and c are the three lines parallel?

(A) b = 0, c = –2

(B) b = 1, c = –1

(C) b = –1, c = 2

(D) b = 2, c = 0

(E) b = –1, c = 0

9. If $\frac{x^2}{y^2}$ is a positive integer which of the following statements is always true

(A) If $4x + 5y + 3$ is an odd integer, $\frac{x^2}{y^2}$ is an odd integer

(B) $x$ is divisible by y but not by $y^2$

(C) $x$ and y can only be integers or rational numbers

(D) Its reciprocal is also a positive integer

(E) If $xy + 3$ is a multiple of 3, then $x$ is also a multiple of 3

10.

There was a group of students going on the train for an excursion. When a co-passenger asked one of the students how many of them were going for the excursion, the student replied "If you add twice the number of us and half the number and half of the number of us and yourself it will be 100 people".

| **Quantity A** | **Quantity B** |
|---|---|
| The number of students traveling | 42 |

(A) Quantity A is greater.

(B) Quantity B is greater.

(C) The two quantities are equal.

(D) The relationship cannot be determined from the information given.

11. Which of the following equations have an even integer as the solution?

[A] $3x - 5 = 5x + 1$

[B] $5(2x - 3) = 3x - 1$

[C] $2x + 7 = 5x - 8$

[D] $7 + 3x = 7x - 9$

[E] $2x - 7 = 5x + 2$

[F] $-10x - 9 = 2x + 3$

12.

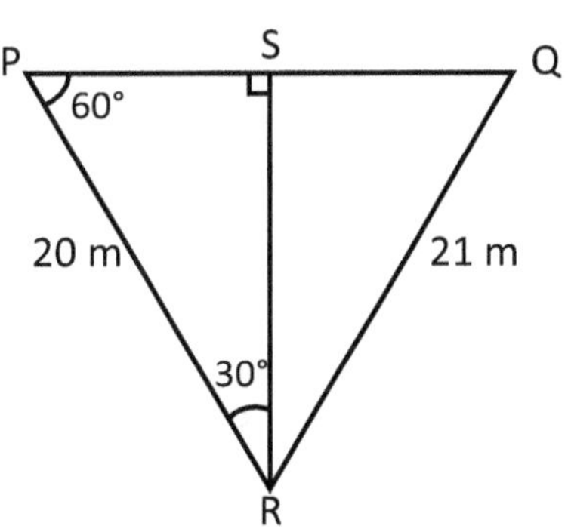


Study the figure shown above.

What is the length of the segment PQ to the nearest tenth of a meter?

[ ] meters

13. Let A be the set of all the ages of the students attending Maths classes {19, 17, 18, 15, 17, 16, 17, 16}. Which of the following statements is not true?

(A) The median and the mode are the same

(B) The range is 4

(C) If a new student aged 18 is joining the class, the new mean is 17

(D) The mode and the mean are the same

(E) If a new student aged 18 is joining the class, the mode does not change

14.

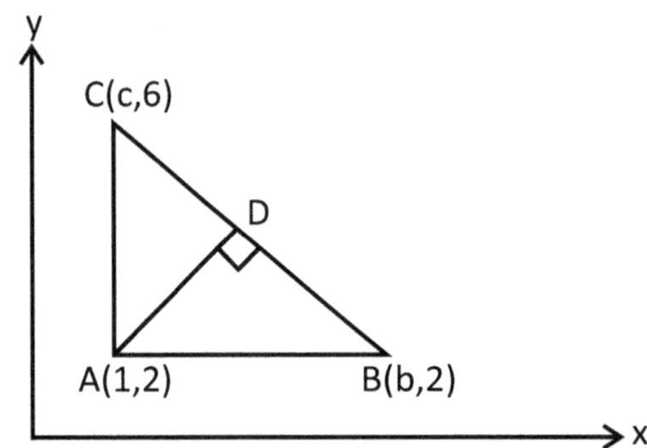


$\Delta$ABC is an isosceles right triangle with hypotenuse *BC*. *AD* is perpendicular to *BC*. Points *A*, *B* and *C* are defined by their coordinates. What is the length of *AD*?

(A) $4\sqrt{2}$

(B) $2\sqrt{2}$

(C) $3\sqrt{2}$

(D) 2

(E) 3

15.

Manny's weekly income is 72 percent of Fran's weekly income. Manny's weekly income is $648.

| **Quantity A** | **Quantity B** |
|---|---|
| Fran's weekly income | $900 |

(A) Quantity A is greater.

(B) Quantity B is greater.

(C) The two quantities are equal.

(D) The relationship cannot be determined from the information given.

16. Two workers produce the same part. For the first worker, it takes 5 minutes longer than second worker to complete the manufacturing of a part. Within 8 hours, the second worker produces 16 parts more than the number of parts the first worker makes. How many parts does the first person make in 8 hours?

(A) 28

(B) 32

(C) 33

(D) 45

(E) 48

17. Richard sold a valuable painting for $1,395, and he incurred a loss. Had he bought it for 3% less and sold it for $351 more, he would have made a 20% profit. What is the loss percentage that Richard incurred?

(A) 2%

(B) 5%

(C) 7%

(D) 10%

(E) 12%

18.

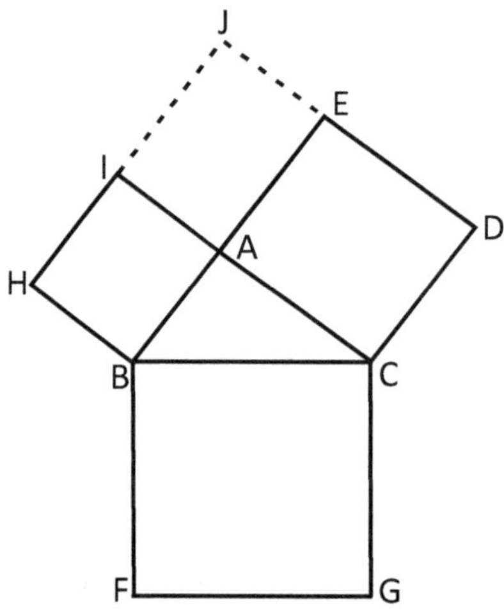


ABC is a triangle with $m\angle BAC = 90^\circ$ and $m\angle ACB = 30^\circ$. Three squares (*ACDE, BCGF* and *ABHI*) were built using the sides of $\Delta ABC$ as basis. *HIJ* and *DEJ* are line segments.

What is the area of quadrilateral AEJI?

(A) Area $AEJI = (Area\ BCGF - Area\ ABHI) \times \sqrt{3}$

(B) Area $AEJI = \dfrac{(Area\ BCGF - Area\ ABHI)}{\sqrt{3}}$

(C) Area $AEJI = \dfrac{(Area\ BCGF - Area\ ACDE)}{\sqrt{3}}$

(D) Area $AEJI = \dfrac{\sqrt{(Area\ ACDE)}}{2}$

(E) Area $AEJI = Area\ ACDE \times \sqrt{3}$

19. Two inlet pipes P and Q take 20 minutes and 30 minutes respectively to fill a tank. Which of the following must be true?

Indicate all such statements.

[A] When the pipes are opened together, the tank will be filled in less than 15 minutes.

[B] The pipes have to be kept open for 14 minutes for the tank to be full.

[C] When the pipes are opened together and pipe P is closed after 10 minutes, the tank will be full in 15 minutes.

[D] When the pipes are opened together and pipe Q is closed after 7.5 minutes, the tank will be full in 15 minutes.

20. Which of the following conclusions are true of the graph $f(x) = 2x^2 - 7x + 3$?

[A] The parabola opens down.

[B] The parabola has a minimum of 3.

[C] The roots can be calculated using factoring.

[D] The axis of symmetry is located at the graph of the linear equation $x = \frac{7}{4}$.

[E] The $x$–intercepts of the graph are located at $x = -3$ and $x = -\frac{1}{2}$.

[F] The graph of the parabola intersects the $y$ axis at $y = 3$.

# Answers Key

## Section 2

1. ameliorated and milieu
2. amenities and exacerbating
3. alleviating, schematized, and tumultuous
4. A
5. D
6. disingenuous and duplicitous
7. palliative and alleviative
8. enumerated and forfeiture
9. extensiveness and arduous
10. A
11. D
12. "This state of things is called a commercial collapse, because there is a sudden falling in of prices, credit, and enterprise."
13. C
14. C
15. A
16. "As long as you don't interfere with them, these hairy, green fruits do nothing out of the common in the way of personal aggressiveness."
17. D
18. anomalous and tendentious
19. instantaneous and rapid
20. perpetual and repudiates

## Section 3

1. $5\sqrt{2}$ units
2. C
3. A and C
4. D
5. D
6. D
7. B
8. B
9. A and C
10. 505.8
11. E
12. A
13. B
14. A
15. B
16. A
17. E
18. B
19. B
20. A

## Section 4

1. exemplar
2. diametrically and partition
3. D
4. B
5. C
6. catalogue and incontrovertibly
7. outstrip and mitigate
8. E
9. A
10. inconsistent and unpredictable
11. flexibility and mutability
12. constituent and demarcates
13. fortitudes and diminutive
14. A
15. D
16. D
17. E
18. inessential and dispensable
19. synthesis and unity
20. D

## Section 5

1. B
2. C
3. D
4. C
5. B
6. −1
7. 16
8. E
9. E
10. B
11. B and D
12. 21.9 meters
13. D
14. B
15. C
16. B
17. C
18. B
19. A, C and D
20. B, C, D and F

# Explanations

## Section 1 – Analytical Writing

### Task 1 – Analyze an Issue

**The sample essay that follows was written in response to the prompt that appeared in the question.**

It is impossible to identify well–rounded individuals on the street, in the workplace, or at the gym. It is unlikely that anyone is choosing his or her friends based on their being well–rounded. It is probably impossible to define well–rounded; everyone would have a point of view. It is true that in the early days of higher education, one aimed to become a "man of letters", knowledgeable to some degree in a variety of subjects. That luxury is not longer desirable or practical. University students are entering a different world.

I like to think of myself as well–rounded. I am interested in a variety of topics, and I participate in a variety of activities. I carry on conversations easily with my friends and family as well as people I meet in the grocery store or at an airport. My seatmates on trains and planes find me engaging. I answer most of the questions on Jeopardy! correctly, and I can complete the New York Times crossword puzzle. I like and can cook food from a variety of cuisines. I can order correctly from a menu written in French. I like HGTV, the Food Network, and action movies. My friends think I'm funny, and I cry over sappy commercials on TV. None of my self–perceived well–roundedness is a result of courses that I either did or did not take in college.

My mother taught me to knit and sew. I got my love of gardening from my father. I think I taught myself to read. My sister taught me how to see different perspectives on an issue. I learned to swim during lessons on cold mornings at the local pool. I learned to play the piano from an older lady who tapped out the measures with a plastic knitting needle on the top of the piano. I learned to drive from a kind and patient man who did not use deodorant and wouldn't let his students roll down the car windows in the heat of the summer. My friends taught me about friendship. I obtained all of these skills before I went to college.

So, what did college teach me? College taught me how to live in close quarters with hundreds of other girls from different states and backgrounds. College taught me to understand football, to party on the weekends, and how to join the best sorority on campus. College taught me to sign up for classes that ended by 1:00 pm and met on Mondays, Wednesdays, and Fridays, so I'd have two full days off from classes. College eventually taught me how to manage my time. It taught me the classes I would need to get a degree in my major.

High school seniors plan to enter colleges and universities with the goal of getting a job after graduation, and that is what college should do. When today's high–school seniors graduate from college, they will have enormous debt. While in college, they must focus on courses that serve practical purposes. They will need immediate employment in order to meet their financial obligations. They will become well–rounded by living their lives after college.

### Task 2 – Analyze an Argument

**The sample essay that follows was written in response to the prompt that appeared in the question.**

In a backlash against urban sprawl, counties have created restrictions and parameters for development that requires expanding their infrastructure and broadening the scope of their services. When a developer presents a plan for a new residential subdivision, he relies on the community to extend its water and sewer lines and lay down new streets. There are more structures for the fire department to cover, more area for police cruisers to patrol, and more roadways for plows to clear in winter. If families with children move into the new homes, the schools may become overcrowded. The expansion of the tax base may not offset increased costs to the city. Despite these additional demands, an expanded housing inventory tends to keep prices affordable and encourages people to move to the area. The council of Maple County would be wise to consider several questions before deciding either course of action regarding development.

The main objection to restricting development appears to be a fear that housing prices will increase dramatically. This is a likely consequence only if conditions exist in Maple County that are very similar to those in Pine County. Why did housing prices more than double in Pine County? It may be that Pine County is a more desirable place to live, and there is a greater demand for homes there. Supply and demand always influence the price of any commodity. Pine County may be home to a large city that provides great career opportunities and cultural activities that make its suburbs attractive to upper middle class citizens. Pine County may have award–winning schools that attract young families desiring a high quality education for their children. If Pine County does, indeed, possess these attributes, a lack of housing inventory would inflate the prices of existing homes.

In contrast, Chestnut County may lack the desirable characteristics that make an area attractive to people seeking a new place to live. Why did the prices of homes in Chestnut County experience only a moderate increase when officials limited development there? This county may be rural in nature, with significant distances between homes, eliminating the neighborhood structure that families find appealing. It may be that Chestnut County lacks opportunities for shopping, recreation, and cultural activities that attract well–educated, affluent families. Its schools may not be stellar, discouraging families with children from settling there. Even though Chestnut County has limited housing inventory, the demand for the homes that do exist simply isn't as high as it is in Pine County. As a result, any increases in prices there are likely due to inflation.

How does Maple County settle the argument about restricting development? Members of the council should complete a thorough analysis of the three counties to determine how Maple County is similar to or different from the other two. If Maple County has more in common with Pine County, they may want to lift restrictions on development and allow more homes to be built in an effort to keep housing prices affordable. On the other hand, if Maple County has more in common with Chestnut County, restricting development for the time being may be the wisest course. They will not have expended county funds to expand infrastructure and services for a county that is not likely to attract sufficient numbers of new residents to offset the cost of such improvement.

# Section 2 – Verbal Reasoning

1. **ameliorated and milieu**

This passage talks of how scientists became increasingly concerned with small scale investigations, until "the macroscopic picture became forgotten." It then goes on to say how ecology provided a macroscopic frame for these scientists. Therefore, ecology must have fixed this problem, so the answer should express the idea of "making better." "Exacerbated" means to "worsen." This is the opposite of what ecology is described as having done. "Purloined" means "stole," but ecology has not "stolen" anything. Ameliorated" means "improved." This is exactly what ecology is described as having done to science's over–reliance on small- scale thinking. The last sentence talks about how this new macroscopic picture provided "something" that microscopic observations could be made within. This must be some kind of frame to work within. "Ambiguity" means "doubt." Increasing doubt would not facilitate microscopic observations. "Privation" means "neediness," which does not fit the context of the question. "Milieu" means "background." A solid background would allow microscopic observations to better be made.

2. **amenities and exacerbating**

The second sentence says that marine biologists are not given something that other scientists take for granted. The passage then goes on to talk of the difficulties in working in an aquatic environment. Therefore, we can infer this "something" that marine biologists are not granted is convenience. "Recalcitrance" means "stubbornness." Marine biologists would not be suffering for lack of stubbornness, so this answer is wrong. "Biliousness" means "sickness." This answer makes no sense in the context of the question. "Amenities" means "conveniences." A lack of conveniences would explain why working in an aquatic environment is more difficult than on land. The last sentence lists even more difficulties that marine biologists face.

Therefore, the second blank must be introducing issues that make a situation worse. "Insinuating" means "implying." This answer does not make sense in the context of the question. The difficulties faced in making durable tracking devices do not "insinuate" problems, they make them. "Alleviating" means to "assuage." This is the opposite of what we want. These problems make matters worse, not better. "Exacerbating" means "making worse." This is exactly what added difficulties do to a situation. They make them worse.

3. **alleviating, schematized, and tumultuous**

The passage states that the Chinese were the first group to attempt to lessen risk in the trade business. "Exacerbating" means "worsening." The Chinese were trying to lessen risk, not increase it. "Annunciating" means "announcing." The Chinese aren't described as "announcing" anything about risk. They are just trying to control it. "Alleviating" means "lessening," or "easing." By transporting their goods on a variety of ships instead of just one, the Chinese would be lessening their risk.

For the second blank, the passage is stating how the Babylonians made the first attempt to incorporate insurance into their official business practices. "Sardonic" means "sarcastic." There is no insinuation made within the passage that the Babylonian insurance program was sarcastically done. "Quiescent" means "calm." No reference as to the speed of the insurance program is ever made in the passage. "Schematized" means "structured." This makes sense. By including insurance in loan purchases, there was a "structured" application of insurance.

For the third blank, the passage states that insurance was necessary in the world of trade. We can then infer that the world of trade was dangerous. "Guileless" means "honest," or "straightforward." If ancient trade required insurance, then it would not be considered a "straightforward" business. "Portly" means "overweight." This answer makes no sense in the context of the question. "Tumultuous" means "wild." Insurance would certainly be necessary in a world that was wild.

4. **The correct answer is (A).**

Choice A is the correct answer because this passage deals mainly with the way that the Eiffel firm was able to initiate projects based on their reputation and the way that "Eiffel was regarded not only by his profession but by the entire nation". Were it not for this favorable reputation, the Eiffel firm's project would likely not have been approved, which supports the statement that their proposed project to build the Eiffel Tower was 'grandiose' as there was no proof that it would succeed based on similar undertakings.

Choice B is incorrect because in determining the possibility for high iron structures, Eiffel conducted investigations on structures that were not as tall as the intended projects, and found evidence to suggest that higher ones were possible; however, they did not build them before determining that it was possible.

There is no mention, as Choice C suggests, that the Eiffel firm was in direct competition with other construction companies.

Choice D states that the 200-foot viaducts were never impressive structures, though the passage simply states that they were not startling. They were, however, as the passage states, "spectacular."

Choice E is partially true in its assertion that some of Eiffel's projects may have appeared to be overly ambitious, but the passage focuses on their reputation to lend credibility, not past projects.

5. **The correct answer is (D).**

Choice D is the correct answer; these sentences introduce the studies that focused on existing piers and the potential that these investigations brought to light. Although nothing as tall as Eiffel planned to build had yet been constructed, these studies made it apparent that such structures were possible.

Choice A is incorrect because, while it is true that Eiffel conducts preliminary research, it is unclear whether relying on engineering alone would have been insufficient.

Choice B is also too vague to be proven by the passage; the text does not explicitly mention which materials were used for the piers that were studied. It says that they were metallic but is unclear about whether they are in contrast to iron structures.

Choice C focuses too strongly on the abilities of other construction companies and their superiority. These sentences serve to explain how the Eiffel firm prepared their plans rather than looking at the specifics of how the other firms arrived at their ideas, which this answer implies.

Choice E is incorrect because there is no mention of safety issues with the structures that were investigated.

6. **disingenuous and duplicitous**

This sentence is saying that the flavored-water company is trying to get away with claiming something that ostensibly isn't true, so the answer should refer to deceit. "Obdurate" means stubborn. They are not trying to make stubborn claims about their water; they are trying to make deceitful ones. "Factual" means accurate. The entire aim of the company is to use language that allows them to avoid making accurate claims, so this cannot be true. "Lucid" means coherent. This is the opposite of what they are doing. They're not being clear, they're being vague. "Trivial" means minor or unimportant. Considering that the company is trying to get away with making these claims they must be a big deal in the advertising campaign and therefore not trivial. We are left with "Disingenuous" and "Duplicitous."

Both of these two words mean deceitful, which correctly characterizes the quality of their advertising campaign. A and D are correct.

7. **palliative and alleviative**

This sentence states that a person may become so desperate that he or she can only focus on one potential good of dangerous medicine rather than the many ills. A potential benefit that would cause someone to forget the problems must be the ability to lessen suffering. "Prohibitive" means unaffordable, which would be a bad rather than good characteristic of the New Age medicine. "Luxurious" means lavish, which doesn't fit the context of desperation. "Intercalated" means added or interposed, which doesn't make sense in the context of the question. "Illegal" means illicit, which would be considered negative, not the one possible benefit of the New Age medicine. The remaining words "Palliative" and "Alleviative" mean calming or soothing. It makes sense that someone desperate to be soothed from pain would only focus on a product's potential to provide that service rather than the plethora of problems that would come with it, including falling for a scam. Therefore, B and D are the correct answers.

8. **enumerated and forfeiture**

The first blank can best be understood by reading the sentence that comes after it. The sentence says that households don't always have "data to go by" when it comes to assessing risk. Therefore, it must be difficult to quantify risk. “Perturbed” means “worried.”

The concept of the potential for gain or loss being “worried” does not make any sense in this context. “Aggrieved” means “distressed.” This answer suffers from the same problem as “Perturbed.” “Enumerated” means “tallied,” or “computed.” This answer makes sense. If we cannot generate data by which to assess risk then risk must not be easily “enumerated.”

The second blank talks of how certainty must be given up in order to enjoy the benefits of a market economy. We want a word that expresses the idea of giving something up. “Frankness” means “honesty.” This word does not express any idea of giving things up. “Flaccidity” means “slackness.” Again, this word does not express the idea of giving things up. “Forfeiture” means “abandonment.” This answer makes sense. In order to enjoy the benefits of a market economy one must be willing to “abandon” some semblance of certainty.

9. **extensiveness and arduous**

The passage is saying that the modern food industry in America is very large. “Lethargy” means “tiredness.” The modern food industry is described as being large, not lazy. “Bankruptcy” means “insolvency.” If the modern food industry is 10% of America’s GDP then it must be doing fine financially. “Extensiveness” means “comprehensiveness.” This makes sense. An institution as large as the modern food industry would certainly be described as “extensive.”

The passage also talks of how this “dynamic and widespread” industry must be regulated. It can be inferred that regulating a “dynamic and widespread” industry must be difficult. “Ridiculous” means “absurd.” The passage makes no claim that regulating the food industry is an “absurd task.” It certainly states that the industry is large, but it never insinuates that it’s too large to logically regulate. “Pernicious” means “evil.” Again, the passage talks about the size of the food industry. It makes no comment as to its morality, or the morality of trying to regulate it. “Arduous” means “difficult.” This makes sense. Regulating such a large industry would certainly be a difficult task.

10. **The correct answer is (A).**

Choices B and C are incorrect, as having more companies or goods would only exacerbate the problem. Choice D is incorrect, as more expensive capital and credit would make it even harder to pay for things. Choice E is incorrect, as the author never proposes using an alternate way of exchanging stock. Choice A is correct, as regulating speculators more might help weaken commercial collapse.

11. **The correct answer is (D).**

Choice A is incorrect; the passage does not state or imply that these investors have no money. B is incorrect. Cruelty is not stated or implied. Choice C is correct, as shady is the closest synonym to unscrupulous. D is incorrect. The manners of such individuals are not relevant to the passage. E is incorrect. The passage does not state or imply ignorance on the part of such investors.

12. **"This state of things is called a commercial collapse, because there is a sudden falling in of prices, credit, and enterprise."**

The first sentence of the last paragraph states that credit, prices, and enterprise can cause commercial collapse.

The passage describes the complex land laws of England. The author does not present an argument or opposing views.

13. **The correct answer is (C).**

The squirting cucumber has developed a defense against animals or others who would intentionally or accidentally destroy its ability to survive. Although both the camel and the remora have adapted in order to survive, their adaptations are not defenses against their enemies. Neither A nor B are correct answers. The chameleon, on the other hand, changes its colors to make it invisible to predators. The chameleon is the only animal on the list to adapt as a means of defense, making C the only correct answer.

14. **The correct answer is (C).**

The writer's use of the words "my friend" sets a positive tone. Neither sarcastic nor antagonistic has a positive connotation; answer choices B and E cannot be correct.

Satire frequently uses sarcasm to ridicule a person, institution, or idea. This is not the writer's intention here, making answer choice A incorrect.Awestruck is a bit extreme to describe the attitude of the writer toward the squirting cucumber, but it is reasonable to conclude that the writer admires the feisty little plant. C is the best answer choice.

15. **The correct answer is (A).**

The correct answer is A. The fruit expels its interior to repel predators and to reproduce itself. In its own time, the fruit eventually drops off the vine and expels its seeds; this is not done intentionally, eliminating

B as a correct choice. The fruit does defend itself when disturbed, but it does not seek to be aggressive or offensive, making C an incorrect choice as well. Mutation is a form of adaptation, but there is no discussion of this likelihood in the passage; D cannot be the correct choice. Although the writer does allude to books of etiquette and another writer, he does so to make his point about the cucumber, not as a focus of the passage. E is not the correct answer.

16. **"As long as you don't interfere with them, these hairy, green fruits do nothing out of the common in the way of personal aggressiveness."**

A sleeping dog will not bite or cause any other problems. In other words, leave well enough alone. Like the sleeping dog, this fruit will do nothing aggressive if you do not disturb it.

17. **The correct answer is (D).**

Choice D is the correct answer. The first sentence of this passage introduces the argument that needs strengthening: when the Pilgrim's Way was created. Choice D effectively supports the idea by showing that the term was used at the date suggested in the passage, as it was printed in a newspaper.

None of the other choices establish when the name and concept of the Pilgrim's Way came into use. Choice A is incorrect because the meaning of "pilgrim" is not essential, as long as the name was used at the time. Choice B is not related to the topic of the Way, only Henry the Second, so can be eliminated. Choice C establishes that Henry the Second used the Way, but does not show what it was called at the time. Choice E is also unrelated to the name, only to details of one person who walked there.

18. **anomalous and tendentious**

The process of supply and demand is present in such different cultural spaces as a village squares and stock exchanges. The message is the forces of supply and demand is not limited to or not unique to any one type of environment; since the missing word comes after "not", the correct answer will mean similarly to limited or unique. Choice(D)- apocryphal (meaning being of doubtful authenticity or fictional) and Choice (F) – sententious (meaning given to pompous moralizing) are off-topic for this sentence. Choice(B) unorthodox(meaning deviating from the norm), and Choice(C)-incongruous (meaning out of place or absurd) do have the connotations needed, but neither choice is grammatically correct when inserted into the sentence. The answers that fit the needed meaning and are grammatically correct are Choice(A) anomalous (meaning peculiar or unique) and Choice(E) tendentious (meaning biased or promoting a specific point of view).

19. **instantaneous and rapid**

In this sentence the neural response is being contrasted with the hormonal response. The hormonal response is being characterized as being slow and indirect; therefore, the correct answer should express the opposite meaning for the neural response. "Inglorious" means shameful. This word does not describe the neural response in any capacity, least of all when compared to the hormonal response. "Violent" means fierce or vehement. The neural response is also described as being precise and immediate. A violent action is not a precise one. "Explosive" means volatile. This answer does not work for the same reason that "Violent" does not work: it contradicts the "precise" description given to the neural response. Keep in mind that even though "Violent" and "Explosive" work well in a pair they do not complete the sentiment of the sentence and therefore are not a correct answer pair. "Somatic" means relating to the body. While the neural response is a component of the body the word "somatic" does not in any way distinguish the neural response from the hormonal response, which is also a part of the human body. This leaves "Instantaneous" and "Rapid." Both of these words mean quick or speedy. These words describe the contrast between the neural response and the hormonal response, which is described as slow and indirect. Therefore, B and E are the correct answers.

20. **perpetual and repudiates**

This passage is stating that transcendental idealism argues that human perception is limited. This is clearly implied to run contrary to what "many people view philosophy" as being. So people must have viewed philosophy as limitless before transcendental idealism was invented. "Fallible" means "weak." If many people viewed philosophy as being limitless, they would not describe it as "weak." "Restricted" means "constrained." If people viewed philosophy as being limitless then they would not describe it as being "constrained." We are left with "perpetual." If people viewed philosophy as being limitless then they would certainly consider it to be the "perpetual expansion of what humans perceive."

For the second blank, look at what transcendental idealism introduces into philosophy. It introduces the argument that human perception is not limitless. Therefore, transcendental philosophy runs contrary to what most people view philosophy as. "Collaborates" means "works together."

Transcendental idealists do not work together with typical understandings of philosophy, they denounce them. "Invigorates" means "enlivens." Transcendental idealism does not "enliven" common perceptions of philosophy, it denounces them. "Repudiates" means "rejects." This makes sense. By arguing that human perception is limited, transcendental idealists are rejecting what most people think about philosophy.

# Section 3 – Quantitative Reasoning

1. **The correct answer is $5\sqrt{2}$ units.**

The radius is half the diameter D = 10. This diameter is also the diagonal of the inscribed square. Use Pythagorean Theorem to solve for the side length, where side length is *s* and the hypotenuse is 10. Therefore, $s^2+s^2= 10^2$. Thus, $100 = 2s^2$ ; so $s=\sqrt{50}=5\sqrt{2}$

2. **The correct answer is (C).**

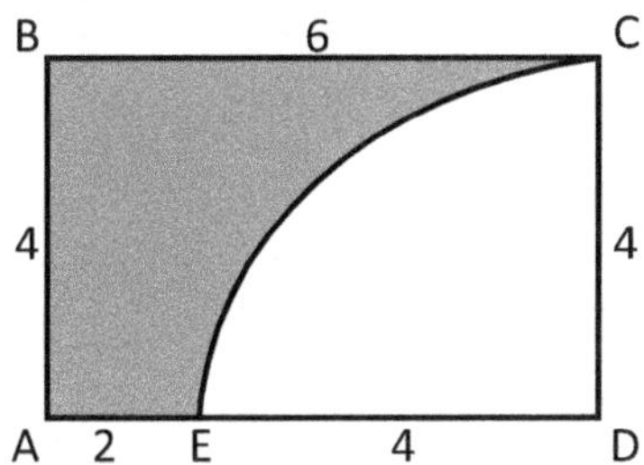


Opposite sides of a rectangle are equal, so AB is also 4. The perimeter of the rectangle is 20, and since the two short sides account for 8, the two longer sides must account for 12. The radius of the circle is CD. Therefore, BC = 6 and AD = 6. To find AE, subtract the length of ED, another radius of length 4, from the length of AD, which is 6; AE = 2.

Since arc EC is a quarter circle, the length of the arc EC is $\frac{1}{4}$ of the circumference of a whole circle with radius 4: $\frac{1}{4}\times 2\pi r=\frac{1}{4}\times 8\pi=2\pi$

So the perimeter of the shaded region is 6 + 4 + 2 + 2π = 12 + 2π.

3. **The correct answers are (A) and (C).**

We need to simplify each expression to determine if it is equivalent to $2x^2 - 2$ using the distributive property and FOIL method.

**A.** $4(x^2 - 2) - 2(x^2 - 3) = 4x^2 - 8 - 2x^2 + 6$

$=2x^2 - 2$

**B.** $2(x^2 - 2) - 4(x^2 + 3) = 2x^2 - 4 - 4x^2 - 12$

$=-2x^2 - 16$

**C.** $2(x - 1)(x + 1) = 2(x^2 - x + x - 1) = 2(x^2 - 1)$

$=2x^2 - 2$

**D.** $(x + 6)(x + 1) + (8 + x)(1 - x)$

$=x^2 + x + 6x + 6 + 8 - 8x + x - x^2 = 14$

**E.** $2(x + 4)(x - 1) - 3(2x + 5)$

$= 2(x^2 - x + 4x - 4) - 6x - 15$

$= 2(x^2 + 3x - 4) - 6x - 15$

$= 2x^2 + 6x - 8 - 6x - 15$

$= 2x^2 - 23$

The only answers that simplify to $2x^2 - 2$ are A and C.

4. **The correct answer is (D).**

Since $x < 0$, $x$ is less than zero, or a negative number

$y > 0$, $y$ is greater than zero, or a positive number

Thus, $xy$ is a product of a negative number and a positive number; hence it is a negative number of unknown value.

$a > 0$, $a$ is greater than zero, or a positive number.

Thus, $-a$ makes the number negative; hence it is a negative number of unknown value.

Since both expressions are negative but have unknown values, a comparison cannot be made.

5. **The correct answer is (D).**

If 24% of her $64,000 from last year came in March, you first find: 64,000 × 24% = $15,360. Next, subtract her monthly salary: 15,360 – 3,750 = $11,610. This is the amount she made in commission, and since her commission is 10% of her sales: $11{,}610 = 0.1x$. Solve for $x$ using inverse operations to find that $x =$ $116,610.

6. **The correct answer is (D).**

In order to determine the change in the total average expenses, a new average must be calculated using an increased value for 2008.

Totaling the amount from each year, and using a value of 120 for 2008 (100 + 20) gives us 80 + 120 + 100 + 80 + 120 + 120 + 120 + 140 +100 + 120 + 160 + 140 = 1,400.

Dividing this total by the number of years will provide the new average, so 1400/12 = 116.667.

Subtracting 115 from 116.667 results in a value of 1.7, which is the increase in the average.

116.667 – 115 = 1.7

The correct answer is 2.

7. **The correct answer is (B).**

The sum collected from Alameda and Brimfield in the previous year is equivalent to 100%

The amount collected from Daytona

= 56 + 55 + 58 + 57 + 59 = 285 ≅ 100 – 5 = 95%

The sum collected from Alameda and Brimfield in the previous year =

$\frac{100}{95} \times 285$ = \$300 hundred thousand dollars

Alameda market collected (this year)

= 19 + 24 + 23 + 26 + 27 = 119 ≅ 100 + 8 = 108%

Alameda market collected (last year) =

$\frac{100}{108} \times 119$ = \$110 hundred thousand dollars

Brimfield market collected (last year)

= 300 – 110 = \$190 hundred thousand dollars

Brooklyn market collected (this year) =

24 + 26 + 25 + 24 + 25 = \$124 hundred thousand dollars

The difference is

190 – 124 = \$66 hundred thousand dollars.

The correct answer is \$6,600,000.

8. **The correct answer is (B).**

*r = Rate; t =Time; P =Principal*

Quantity A: Simple interest *I = Prt*

$= 1200 \times \frac{9.5}{100} \times 2 = \$228$

Quantity B: Simple interest *I = Prt*

$= 1000 \times \frac{11.5}{100} \times 2 = \$230$

Therefore, Quantity B is greater.

9. **The correct answers are (A) and (C).**

Simplify each expression using the properties of exponents to see if it is equivalent to $\frac{5x}{3y^2}$.

**A.** $\frac{(15x^3)(x^{-2}y^3)^2}{\left(\frac{1}{3}xy^{-4}\right)^{-2}} = \frac{15x^3x^{-4}y^6}{\frac{1}{3^{-2}}x^{-2}y^8} = \frac{15x^{-1}y^6}{9x^{-2}y^8} = \frac{5x^2}{3xy^2} = \frac{5x}{3y^2}$

**B.** $\frac{(3x^3)(3x^{-2}y^3)^2}{\left(\frac{1}{5}xy^{-4}\right)^2} = \frac{3x^3 \cdot 9x^{-4}y^6}{\frac{1}{25}x^2y^{-8}} = \frac{25 \cdot 27x^{-1}y^6}{x^2y^{-8}} = \frac{675y^{14}}{x^3}$

**C.** $\frac{(5x^2)^2(y^2)^2}{(15x^3)(y^2)^3} = \frac{25x^4y^4}{15x^3 \cdot y^6} = \frac{25x}{15y^2} = \frac{5x}{3y^2}$

**D.** $\frac{(3x^5y^2)^{-2}}{(5x^4y)^{-2}x^3} = \frac{3^{-2}x^{-10}y^{-4}}{5^{-2}x^{-8}y^{-2}x^3} = \frac{5^2x^5y^2}{3^2x^{10}y^4} = \frac{25}{9x^5y^2}$

A and C are equivalent to $\frac{5x}{3y^2}$

10. **The correct answer is 505.8**

The area of the entire figure is $\pi r^2$, and the area of the un shaded portion is $\pi(r-s)^2$. The area of the shaded area is $\pi(r^2 - (r - s)^2)$.

Therefore, $\pi(15^2 - (15 - 7)^2) = 161\pi$ which is approximately 505.8.

11. **The correct answer is (E).**

Parts of different ratios don't always refer to the same whole. In the classic ratio trap, two different ratios each share a common part that is represented by two different numbers. The two ratios do not refer to the same whole, however, so they are not in proportion to each other. To solve this type of problem, restate both ratios so that the numbers representing the common part (in this case dimes) are the same. Then all the parts will be in proportion and can be compared to each other. To find the ratio of quarters to nickels, restate both ratios so that the number of dimes is the same in both. We are given two ratios:

*quarters: dimes = 5:2 and dimes: nickels = 3:4*

The number corresponding to dimes in the first ratio is 2.

The number corresponding to dimes in the second ratio is 3.

To restate the ratios, find the least common multiple of 2 and 3.

The least common multiple of 2 and 3 is 6.

Restate the ratios with the number of dimes as 6:

*quarters : dimes = 15 : 6 and dimes: nickels = 6:8*

The ratios are still in their original proportions, but now they're in proportion to each other and they refer to the same whole.

The ratio of quarters to dimes to nickels is 15:6:8, so the ratio of quarters to nickels is 15:8, which is answer choice (E).

12. **The correct answer is (A).**

We must first determine the time it takes each vehicle to reach their destinations:

Travel time for bus = $\frac{195}{39} = 5\ hours$

Travel time for car = $\frac{195}{65} = 3\ hours$

Quantity A: Bus travel time before the car departed is

$5 - 3 = 2\ hours.$

In 2 hours, travels $39 \times 2 = 78\ miles.$

Quantity B: Time passed when car was halfway to

destination is $2\text{hrs} + \frac{3\ hrs}{2} = 3.5\ hours$

Since the bus takes 5 hours to complete the journey,

$5 - 3.5 = 1.5\ hours$ are remaining.

$39 \times 1.5 = 58.5\ miles.$

13. **The correct answer is (B).**

In our sample above, we are told that a car went from *A* to *B* at 40 *mph* and back from *B* to *A* at 60 *mph*. In other words, it went half the total distance at 40 *mph* and half the total distance at 60 *mph*.

How do you use the formula?

$$Average\ rate = \frac{Total\ Distance}{Total\ Time}$$

If you don't know the total distance?

HINT: Pick a number! Pick any number you want for the total distance.

Divide the total distance into half distances. Calculate the time needed to travel each half distance at the different rates.

HINT: Pick a number that's easy to work with.

A good number to pick here would be 240 *miles* for the total distance, because you can figure in you're the times for two 120–*mile* legs at 40 *mph* and 60 *mph*:

A to B: $\frac{120\ miles}{40\ miles} = 3\ hours$

B to A: $\frac{120\ miles}{60\ miles} = 2\ hours$

Total time= 5 *hours*

Now plug total distance=240 *miles* and total time = 5 *hours* into the general formula:

$$Average\ Rate = \frac{Total\ Distance}{Total\ Time} = \frac{240\ miles}{5\ hours} = 48\ mph$$

14. **The correct answer is (A).**

The fact that Jean takes 5 hours to complete the job implies that in one hour, $\frac{1}{5}$ of the job is done. Jean and John combined take 2 hours less, or 3 hours. In one hour, $\frac{1}{3}$ of the job is done by both together. So, the work John does per hour is $\frac{1}{3} - \frac{1}{5} = \frac{2}{15}$.

In one hour, John completes $\frac{2}{15}$ of the job, thus it takes John $\frac{1}{\frac{2}{15}} = \frac{15}{2} = 7.5$ hours to complete the job alone.

7.5 > 5 so Choice A.

15. **The correct answer is (B).**

In this problem, we are using the formula $d = rt$ and the Pythagorean Theorem to solve the problem. We need to find the distance both trains travel in Quantity A. Quantity B will be solved for in the process. If the first train left at 9:00 *am*, and we want to know the distance at 3:00 *pm*, the first train was going south for 6 *hours*. Since the second train left at 11:00 *am*, the second train was only going east for 4 *hours*, 2 *hours* less than the first train. First Train: $r = 120\ mph$, $t = 6$ hours, so the distance the first train traveled is

$D = 120\ mph \times 6\ hours = 720\ miles.$

Second Train: $r = 150mph$, $t = 4$ hours, so the distance the second train traveled is

$d = 150\ mph \times 4\ hours = 600\ miles.$

The following diagram demonstrates that we will be using the Pythagorean Theorem to solve for the shortest distance between the trains at 3:00 *pm*. The distance both trains travel will be the legs of the right triangle, while the shortest distance between them will be the hypotenuse.

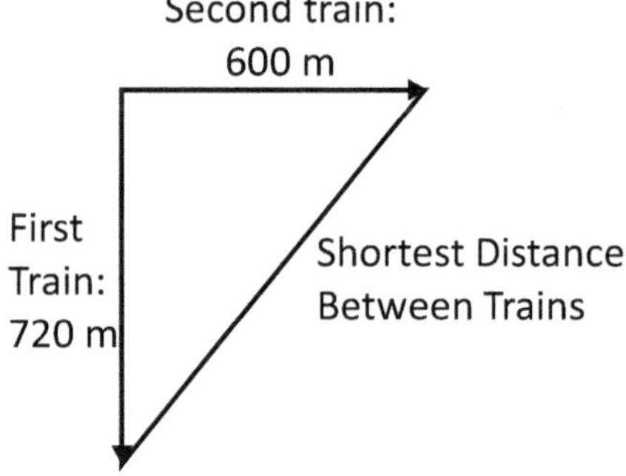


$a^2 + b^2 = c^2$

$720^2 + 600^2 = distance^2$

$518{,}400 + 360{,}000 = distance^2$

*i.e.* $distance = 937.22\ miles$

Quantity A is 937.22 miles and Quantity B is the sum of the legs of the right triangle, 600 *miles* and 720 *miles*. Quantity B will be 1,320 *miles*.

16. **The correct answer is (A).**

In these problems you must test items I, II and III for their validity. If $x$ is odd, then $x^2$ is odd. If $y$ is even then $y^2$ is even. An odd number minus an even number gives you an odd number.

Choose a number for $x$ and $y$. For instance, let $x = 3$ and $y = 4$. Then $3^2 - 4^2 = 9 - 16 = -7$, which is odd but not the square of an integer. The only correct choice is I. The following tables are useful for the solutions of problems of this type.

Addition Table for Odd and Even Integers

| + | Odd | Even |
|---|---|---|
| Odd | Even | Odd |
| Even | Odd | Even |

Multiplication Table for Odd and Even Integers

| X | Odd | Even |
|---|---|---|
| Odd | Odd | Even |
| Even | Even | Even |

Answer choice (A). Be careful when choosing values for the variables. In the above problems, if you had chosen $x = 5$ and $y=4$, then $x^2 - y^2 = 5^2 - 4^2 = 25 - 16 = 9$, which would have made I and III be correct. The problem asks which answer is ALWAYS correct. Clearly I is, but III is not.

17. **The correct answer is (E).**

(E). Percent means

$\frac{x}{100}$ so 30 percent would be $\frac{30}{100}$.

If the car originally costs y dollars, it would cost

$y + \frac{30}{100}y$ after 5 years.

Simplify: $y + \frac{30}{100}y = 1y + \frac{3}{10}y = 1.3y.$ The car's cost will increase another 30 percent over the next 5 years. Car's cost then would be:

$(1.3y) + \frac{30}{100}(1.3y) = (1.3y) + \frac{3}{10}(1.3y)$

$=1.3y+(.3)(1.3y)$

$=(1.3y)+.39y=1.69y$

If the car originally cost y dollar and after 10 year costs $1.69y$ dollars, the increase was

$69\,y$ or $\frac{69}{100}y$. This is an increase of 69 percent.

18. **The correct answer is (B).**

The key concept behind this problem is that a number $\frac{1}{x}$ smaller as X gets larger. If $2 \le y \le 3$, then the least value of $\frac{1}{y}$ would be $\frac{1}{3}$

If $4 \le z \le 5$, the least value of $\frac{1}{z}$ would be $\frac{1}{5}$. We obtain the average by using the equation

$$\text{Average} = \frac{sum\ of\ parts}{Number\ of\ parts}$$

$$\text{Average} = \frac{\frac{1}{3}+\frac{1}{5}}{2}$$

Our answer would be:

$$\frac{\frac{1}{3}+\frac{1}{5}}{\frac{2}{1}}=\frac{\frac{5+3}{15}}{\frac{2}{1}}=\frac{\frac{8}{15}}{\frac{2}{1}}=\frac{8}{15}\times\frac{2}{1}=\frac{8}{30}=\frac{4}{15}$$

Remember, dividing by 2 is the same as multiplying by $\frac{1}{2}$

19. **The correct answer is (B).**

To calculate the cost of one pencil, we divide 85 cents by 5 pencils, and we get \$0.17 per pencil. To calculate the cost of one pen, we repeat the process and divide \$1.20 by 4 and get \$0.30 per pen.

Now we calculate the cost of the quantities in A and B.

Quantity A: *2(0.17) + 3(0.30) = 0.34 + 0.90 = \$1.24*

Quantity B: *8(0.17) + 2(0.30) = 1.36 + 0.60 = \$1.96*

20. **The correct answer is (A).**

*a* is greater than *b* which is greater than *c* and *d* is less than 0 or negative. Therefore, a, b, and c are positive while d is a negative number (since it is less than 0).

We are going to use the basic properties of multiplying positive and negative numbers to determine which quantity is greater.

Quantity A:

$ab\text{-}cd=(+)(+)-(+)(-)$

$(+)-(-)=(+)+(+)=positive$

Quantity B:

$ad\text{-}cd=(+)(-)-(+)(+)$

$=(-)(+)=negative$

# Section 4 – Verbal Reasoning

1. **exemplar**

This passage is saying that while motor vehicle transportation has become safer over the past decade, "all forms of transportation aspire" to be more like airline passage. Therefore, we can infer that airline passage must be safer than other forms of transportation, and thus the ideal that they strive for. "Exemplar" means "ideal." If airline passage is what all other forms of transportation aspire to be like, then it can be safely called an "ideal." "Contrarian" means "one who rejects popular opinion." There's no indication given in the passage that airline travel is rejecting anything that has to do with popular opinion. "Subversion" means "rebellion." Again, there is no indication that airline passage is rebelling against anything. It is described as an ideal, not a "rebel." "Reprobate" means "trouble–maker." The passage doesn't indicate that the other forms of transportation would aspire to be more like a "trouble–maker." Lastly, "Scoundrel" means "villain." Again, the other forms of transportation would not aspire to be like a "villain." They would aspire to be like an "ideal."

2. **diametrically and partition**

The passage is talking about how there are many gray areas on the religious spectrum, and different classifications might have more in common with each other than they think. "Frugally" means "economically." There's nothing mentioned in the passage about economic conflict between atheism and religion. "Judiciously" means "thoughtfully." The passage does not seem to be inferring that the opposition between atheism and religion is particularly "thoughtful." "Diametrically" means "completely." This makes sense. Atheism and religion being "completely" opposed to one another would give the passage incentive to argue that they actually have much in common.

The passage goes on about a "spectrum" that runs between religion and irreligion, and how there are no "hard and fast" lines between any ideology. "Gamut" means "range." This is another way of saying spectrum. Spectrums are being proven to exist, not disproven, so this answer does not work. "Accord" means "understanding." This passage is taking about how there are more similarities between religion and atheism than many people think. It is proving, not disproving, the existence of a possible "understanding" between religion and atheism. "Partition" means "division." This passage is talking about the existence of a spectrum, so it is disproving the existence of a strict "division" between religion and atheism.

3. **The correct answer is (D).**

D is correct. The text specifically mentions fatigue, suffering and "almost useless labor" after land clearing has commenced. A is incorrect. The passage mentions that settlers have "a little money" and does not suggest that it is an insufficient amount. B is incorrect. The passage does not mention a lack of or need for cooperation. C is incorrect. The departure of the natives is not characterized as a problem. E is incorrect. The text does mention land division, but not as a negative influence on the colonists.

4. **The correct answer is (B).**

B is correct. The passage states the settlers brought "sufficient" tools and does not mention a lack of tools as a hindrance. A is incorrect. The passage indicates the settlers were divided into families. C is incorrect. The passage mentions fatigue they had not experienced before and "inconceivable suffering." D is incorrect; the passage notes colonists' complaints. E is incorrect. The passage notes a sufficiency of animals.

5. **The correct answer is (C).**

C is the one correct answer. The passage points out that the colonists have brought sufficient livestock, seeds, money, tools and food and have secured an agreement with the native population before proceeding. A is incorrect. The passage presents a hypothetical, singular group of colonists and makes no suggestion that this experience would be a typical one. B is incorrect. While one might propose this as a possible solution, the passage does not suggest that the colonists' problem is a lack of manpower or assert anything that implies that natives might be a source of assistance.

6. **catalogue and incontrovertibly**

This passage is stating how poetry doesn't use strict "genre" conventions, which would presumably make categorizing them difficult. "Inoculate" means "vaccinate." The passage makes no mention of vaccination in relation to poetry, so this answer makes no sense. "Inculcate" means "train." The passage makes no mention of poetry being difficult to train because of its lack of genre conventions.

"Catalogue" means "file." This makes sense. It would be difficult to file poems into categories if their differences are too subtle.

For the second blank, the passage is saying that poems cannot be placed in genres. "Libidinously" means "with strong sexual desire," so this answer clearly does not fit. "Debatably" means "arguably." But the subtlety of poetry would make the genres debatable, so this does not work. "Incontrovertibly" means "undeniably." This makes sense. Poetry cannot be divided into "undeniable" genres because the differences between poems, as explained in the passage, are too subtle.

7. **outstrip and mitigate**

The answer to the first blank can be found in the second sentence. The second sentence says that the size of the shadow banking industry is much larger than previously thought. "Equiponderate" means "equals." The size of the shadow banking industry is larger than previously thought, so it cannot equal previous estimations. "Endorse" means "authorize." Again, the actual size of the shadow banking industry is larger than previously estimated, so this actual size is not "endorsing" any estimates. "Outstrip" means "exceed." The actual size of the shadow banking industry is "exceeding" the previous estimations.

The second blank talks about how regulators are trying to discourage shadow bank owners from taking large financial gambles. This means that they must be trying to lessen the risk associated with these banks. "Obdurate" means "stubborn." This answer does not make any sense within the context of the question. "Conflate" means "to bring together." Nothing is being brought together with the concept of risk, so risk isn't being conflated with anything. "Mitigate" means "ease," or "lessen." This answer works. By trying to discourage shadow bank owners from taking large gambles, the regulators are trying to mitigate the risks associated with shadow banking.

8. **The correct answer is (E).**

"E" is the correct answer because it describes the main idea of the passage, which is that the definition of living organisms is more complex than what can be simply stated in one phrase. Were it that simple, a river would provide an accurate analogy, yet as the author explains, there is more to it than that.

"A" is an oversimplification of the overall argument and is therefore incomplete and incorrect.

"B" is incorrect because this passage focuses on the definition of living organisms without comparing them to those that are non-living.

"C" is also an oversimplification; though the author presents analogies to compliment the ideas in this passage, there is no mention of them being distinct from scientific data. Also, no distinction is made between analogies and scientific facts, as they work together in this passage to create a more complete explanation.

"D" is incorrect because the text in the passage cannot support the idea that a river and flame are the same; rather, the argument is made that a flame is more complex.

9. **The correct answer is (A).**

Choice A is correct because the first sentence indicates the details involved in defining a living organism beyond the 'continuity of the whole' and the second refers to the specific complexity of the flame analogy in how there is a 'change in condition' beyond simply the 'change of material.'

Choice B is incorrect because the first sentence does not talk about all living organisms in general but rather focuses on what lies beyond the general definition.

Choice C is overly simple in stating that these

sentences describe all living organisms, as neither sentence refers to such generalities but rather delves beyond general definitions.

Choice D is irrelevant; these sentences do not strive to compare organisms.

Choice E is incorrect because neither of these sentences focuses on the constant qualities of living organisms but rather describes the factors that reflect the constantly changing qualities of organisms.

10. **inconsistent and unpredictable**

The passage implies that friction should be easy to understand. It "ostensibly works just like any of the other Newtonian forces," which means that friction should follow the same rules the other Newtonian forces do. But, as the passage insinuates, it ends up going against expectations and frustrating lab students. We want words that express the contradicting of expectations. "Ironic" means satirical or insincere, which makes no sense in the context of a scientific question. "Straightforward" means direct and simple. If the application of friction was direct and simple then students would have no problem understanding it. "Deliberate" means slow or cautious. The slow and cautious application of friction would, if anything, make it easier for students to understand. "Complaisant" means obliging or agreeable. This is a personality trait and makes no sense in the context of a scientific question. This leaves us with "Inconsistent" and "Unpredictable." Both of these words mean erratic and uneven.

Notice they don't mean completely illogical, just hard to quantify reliably. Therefore, they would cause students to be confused as to their application, but could still be classified as Newtonian forces by more experienced physicists. c and f are correct.

11. **flexibility and mutability**

The sentence is saying that people flock away from science because it is too strict. Therefore, the characteristic that we want in art must be the opposite of this: fluid. "Contradictions" means inconsistencies. While contradictions definitely aren't strict that quality would not attract a person who has already left science specifically because it was "counter–intuitive." "Craftiness" means cunningness or slyness. Again, this term does break away from the rigidity of science but not in the fluid way we're looking for. "Expressivity" means eloquence. This might look like a good answer but the sciences can be expressive as well. It's fluidity we're concerned with, and this answer does not provide that. "Innovation" means novelty. Again, innovation is shared with both art and science, so a person would not leave one for the other while citing "innovation" as the reason. This leaves "Flexibility" and "Mutability." Both of these answers express a changeableness that contrasts the "rigid mechanisms" of science and are close synonyms. Therefore, B and D are correct.

12. **constituent and demarcates**

The first blank can be understood by reading the rest of the passage. The rest of the passage talks of the two topics that compose sociocultural anthropology. "Indistinct" means "unclear." The two topics are expounded on greatly, so they cannot be considered unclear. "Aggregate" means "cumulative." The two main topics of sociocultural anthropology may very well be the cumulative results of other topics, but this is not implied anywhere in the passage. "Constituent" means "component." This makes sense. If cultural anthropology and social anthropology are the two topics that make up sociocultural anthropology, then they must be its "constituent" topics.

The second blank can be understood by considering the overall theme of the passage. It is clearly trying to explain the differences between cultural and social anthropology. "Amalgamates" means "combines." This is incorrect because the passage is trying to explain what differentiates the social and cultural anthropology, not what combines them. "Denigrates" means "derides." The passage is not trying to deride the two fields of study, either. "Demarcates" means "differentiates." This makes sense. The passage is stressing what differentiates cultural and social anthropology.

13. **fortitudes and diminutive**

Reading the whole passage makes the first blank easier to complete. Upon reading it we learn that early doctors did not have the benefit of modern science and technologies, so they had to teach themselves using something else. Considering they "simply dissected corpses," this "something else" can be inferred to be great determination. "Artifice" means "deception." The doctors did not use deception to aid their learning, so this is wrong. "Precision" means "accuracy." The doctors did not have the benefit of precise, modern technology so this answer is wrong as well. "Fortitudes" means "determinations." To simply cut into a corpse and investigate would require determination. The last blank is talking about the small details that early doctors missed. Therefore, we want a word that expresses smallness. "Convoluted" means "complicated." Even though the pathogeneses of diseases may very well have been complicated, this is not what the passage is trying to express. It is clearly focusing on size. "Inconsequential" means "unimportant." Just because something is small does not mean it is unimportant, so this answer is wrong. "Diminutive" means "small" and continues the sentiment of the passage, because we are talking about "microscopic human anatomy."

14. **The correct answer is (A).**

"A" is correct in stating that the author feels certain that reality can be established if two or more people can agree on their sensory experiences of it; in the passage, it states that consistency is determined when "certain sense perceptions of different individuals correspond to each other".

"B" is incorrect because the passage does not mention lack of skill as a reason that philosophers cannot document events accurately; rather, the passage simply states that philosophers approach their analysis of events with different purposes in mind which has nothing to do with their skills or abilities.

"C" is incorrect in identifying clocks as tools, whereas the passage refers to them as an analogy but does not focus on their practical everyday use in physics aside from that.

"D" incorrectly assigns an accurate numerical value to events which the author refers to as "quite arbitrary".

"E" incorrectly states that individual senses can be objective, whereas the passage states that this individual time, or "I–time" is in fact subjective.

15. **The correct answer is (D).**

"D" is the correct answer to the question of tone in regards to the author's view of "a priori", which he refers to as "intangible", comparing it to the unreachable height of "Olympus". A sense of dissatisfaction emerges not only through the author's view of this difficult–to–grasp concept but also in the way that it is apparently misused by philosophers.

Though "A" is close to correct, it denotes too lofty an emotion to attach to a form of study, as the author sees "a priori" as intangible but not necessarily something to be revered.

"B", "C", and "E" are all similarly too dramatic, as this passage bases its information on facts that are more scientific and structured than these types of dramatic emotions would likely allow.

16. **The correct answer is (D).**

While all of these options are possible, the only one that is clearly refuted by the text in the passage is "D"; it is clear that the author was never a philosopher because he refers to philosophers as 'they' which indicates that they are a separate group to which he does not belong. Also, the author's tendency to introduce philosophers' ideas in contrast to his own further distinguishes a discord between the author and philosophy, thus eliminating this answer as a likely option.

The other options are all viable; a scientist, professor, or student could all potentially possess the type of information and passion that are presented in this passage. In discussing space and time in such scientific detail, it is clear that the author of this passage possesses the type of academic knowledge of this subject which implies some sort of academic or professional connection to science.

Choice "C" which suggests that the author might be a member of a debate team is also possible, as the passage presents an argument and supports it with evidence, which is something that a debate team participant would do in compiling research and forming an original opinion.

17. **The correct answer is (E).**

Choice E is correct because it addresses the conclusion that all people owning newspapers are more interested in the money than the cause. The fact that the new owners are hoping to increase subscribers (and therefore funds) is the most significant comment. The method of accomplishing an increase in business is based upon relevancy of the content of the paper.

Choice A is incorrect because it just illustrates an example of one reason to print a newspaper.

Choice B is incorrect because it only offers a detail. It does not address the concern of the profits of the owner.

Choice C is incorrect because, while it addresses some income benefits of printing a newspaper, it does not specifically compare profit with the cause for publishing newspapers.

Choice D is incorrect because the increased price of subscriptions could help the newspaper owner earn more income. However, the response does not address the income of the owner. It merely states a fact that the price has increased, only showing weak support for the conclusion.

18. **inessential and dispensable**

Vital organs are the essential organs of the body cavity. If certain appendages are being sacrificed by the body before the vital organs, then the appendages must be less important. Therefore, the correct answer should stress the relative lack of importance of the appendages. "Mandatory" means needed. This is the opposite sentiment that we want to express. These appendages are expendable, not needed. "Identical" means the same or matching. This doesn't complete the sentence in any logical way – why would the body go out of its way to sacrifice identical appendages? "Asymmetrical" is a word that means irregular or uneven. Whether or not your appendages were even or uneven would have no bearing on your body's tendency towards sacrificing them. "Embryological" is a word that means of or relating to the development of living organisms. Something this important would not be willingly sacrificed by the body. This leaves "Inessential" and "Dispensable." Both of these words mean expendable. The body would of course choose to sacrifice its expendable appendages before it damaged its essential viscera. b and d are the correct answers.

19. **synthesis and unity**

This sentence is saying how organic molecules have two different considerations: growing and remaining geometrically stable. Therefore, the answer should show a combination of these two ideas. "Algorithm" means process, or system. There are two systems described here: the system of growing and the system of maintaining stability. We're interested in words that show how these systems combine together. "Equation" means calculation. This answer is like "Algorithm." It describes an approach but not the necessary combination of approaches. "Deduction" means assumption or inherence. There is no assumption being made by the molecule about these two systems so this answer is wrong. "Fission" means breaking apart. This is the opposite of what we want: we want words that stress coming together. This leaves "Synthesis" and "Unity." Both of these words mean harmony or combination. And that's exactly what the molecule is doing. It is creating a combination between two different systems that govern its growth and stability.

20. **The correct answer is (D).**

"D" is correct because it explains how unreliable our senses are in determining what is real or true; this answer identifies the deeper meanings that lie below the surface of the things that we assume to be true, just as the passage mentions the 'apparent contradictions' that only become evident under 'closer scrutiny'.

"A" is incorrect because it states that there are conclusive answers in life, though this passage states that in philosophy, the quest to find answers may indeed be infinite.

"B" incorrectly states that science is more methodical and reliable than other methods of attaining information, yet the passage categorizes science in the same group as 'everyday life'.

"C" incorrectly makes the assertion that evident and unquestionable truths exist, which goes against the idea set forth in the passage that philosophy grapples with questions, not 'truth'.

"E" is incorrect in stating that philosophy can help people arrive at answers, whereas the passage explains that philosophy in fact creates more questions than it answers.

# Section 5 – Quantitative Reasoning

1. **The correct answer is (B).**

The conditions given state that $x$ is greater than 1 while $y$ is a fractional value between 0 and 1. When a number greater than 1 is raised to a power, the values get progressively larger. When a number between 0 and 1 is raised to a power, the value gets progressively smaller. To solve the problem, we must first simplify each of the exponential expressions using properties of exponents.

Quantity A: $\frac{(xy)^4}{x^3} = \frac{x^4y^4}{x^3} = xy^4$

Quantity B: $\frac{\left(\frac{x}{y}\right)^4}{x^3} = \frac{\left(\frac{x^4}{y^4}\right)}{x^3} = \frac{x^4}{y^4x^3} = \frac{x}{y^4}$

To test which quantity is greater, we can choose a number for both $x$ and $y$. Let's assume $x$=2 and $y$= $\frac{1}{2}$

Quantity A: $(2)\left(\frac{1}{2}\right)^4 = (2)\left(\frac{1}{16}\right) = \frac{2}{16} = \frac{1}{8}$

Quantity B: $\frac{(2)}{\left(\frac{1}{2}\right)^4} = \frac{2}{\left(\frac{1}{16}\right)} = 2 \div \frac{1}{16} = 32$

Based on these test values, we find that Quantity B is greater.

2. **The correct answer is (C).**

To determine which quantity is greater we need to change both values back to scientific notation.

Therefore, Quantity A can be written as $24.6 \times 10^3 = 2.46 \times 10^4$ and Quantity B cane be written as $0.246 \times 10^5 = 2.46 \times 10^4$.

Both quantities are equal.

3. **The correct answer is (D).**

The corporate sectors that decreased their support for Philanthropic causes from 2000 to 2005 are: Manufacturing, Retail, Wholesale and Others.

The total contribution by the Corporate Sectors towards Philanthropic Causes in the year 2005 was $570 million.

Amount contributed by the Manufacturing Sector in 2005 = 20% of 570 million

$= \frac{20}{100} \times 570 = \$114$ million

Amount contributed by the Retail Sector in 2005 = 8% of 570 million

$= \frac{8}{100} \times 570 = \$45.6$ million

Amount contributed by the Wholesale Sector in 2005 = 6% of 570 million

$= \frac{6}{100} \times 570 = \$34.2$ million

Amount contributed by the Other Sectors in 2005 = 18% of 570 million

$= \frac{18}{100} \times 570 = \$102.6$ million

The total amount contributed by these four sectors towards Philanthropic Causes in the year 2005 = 114 + 45.6 + 34.2 + 102.6 = $296.4 million = $300 million approximately.

4. **The correct answer is (C).**

The correct answer is (C).

Amount contributed by the Finance, Insurance and Real Estate Sector in:

Year 2000 $= \frac{5}{100} \times 680 = \$34$ million

Year 2005 $= \frac{26}{100} \times 570 = \$148.2$ million

Amount contributed by the Service Sector in:

Year 2000 $= \frac{17}{100} \times 680 = \$115.6$ million

Year 2005 $= \frac{22}{100} \times 570 = \$125.4$ million

Amount contributed by the Manufacturing Sector in:

Year 2000 $= \frac{31}{100} \times 680 = \$210.8$ million

Year 2005 $= \frac{20}{100} \times 570 = \$114$ million

Amount contributed by the Retail Sector in:

Year 2000 $= \frac{19}{100} \times 680 = \$129.2$ million

Year 2005 $= \frac{8}{100} \times 570 = \$45.6$ million

Amount contributed by the Wholesale Sector in:

Year 2000 $=\frac{8}{100}\times 680=\$54.4$ million

Year 2005 $=\frac{6}{100}\times 570=\$34.2$ million

Amount contributed by the Other Sectors in:

Year 2000 $=\frac{20}{100}\times 680=\$136$ million

Year 2005 $=\frac{18}{100}\times 570=\$102.6$ million

We see that three sectors (Service, Manufacturing and Other) contributed more than \$100 million each in total from 2000 and 2005 contributions.

Total amount contributed by the Service Sector in both years =115.6+125.4=\$241 million

Total amount contributed by the Manufacturing Sector in both years = 210.8 + 114 = \$324.8 million

Total amount contributed by the Other Sectors in both years = 136 + 102.6 = \$238.6 million

Average amount contributed by these three sectors

$=\frac{241+324.8+238.6}{3}=\$263.13$ million

5. **The correct answer is (B).**

The correct answer is (B).

Financial, Insurance and Real Estate Sector's 2005 contribution to Philanthropic Causes

$=\frac{26}{100}\times 570=\$148.2$ million

Amount given for re-building homes

$=\frac{1}{3}\times 148.2=\$49.40$ million

Amount remaining = 148.2 – 49.40 = \$98.80 million

Amount given for providing medical aid

$=\frac{1}{4}\times 98.8=\$24.7$ million

Amount spent on rebuilding homes– Amount spent on medical aid

= 49.40 – 24.70 = \$24.7 million = \$25 million approximately.

6. **The correct answer is –1**

$216^{a+2} = 6^{2-a}$ is an exponential equation.

$216^{a+2} = 6^{2-a}$ can be rewritten as:

$(6^3)^{a+2} = 6^{2-a}$

In an exponential equation, when $x^m=x^n$ then, $m=n$

Applying the concept to find the value of a:

$3(a + 2) = 2 - a$

$3a + 6 = 2 - a$

$3a + a = 2 - 6$

$4a = -4$

$a = -1$

The solution is –1.

7. **The correct answer is 16.**

Given $\frac{1}{x-3}-\frac{1}{x+5}=\frac{1}{6}$

Taking LCM in the left and side

$\frac{[1(x+5)-1(x-3)]}{(x-3)(x+5)}=\frac{[x+5-x+3]}{x^2+2x-15}=\frac{1}{6}$

$6 \times 8 = x^2 + 2x - 15$

$x^2 + 2x - 15 = 48$

$x^2 + 2x - 63 = 0$

$x^2 + 9x - 7x - 63 = 0$

$x(x + 9) - 7(x + 9) = 0$

$(x - 7)(x + 9) = 0$

$x = 7$ or $x = -9$

The absolute value of the difference = 7–(–9) = 7 + 9 = 16.

8. **The correct answer is (E).**

For lines *A*, *B* and *C* to be parallel, their slopes must be equal.

To find the slopes we need to use the slope formula

$m=\frac{y_1-y_2}{x_1-x_2}$

Slope of $A=\frac{-2-0}{0-1}=2$

Slope of $B=\frac{b-1}{1-2}=1-b$

Slope of $C=\frac{-4+2}{c+b}=\frac{-2}{c+b}$

*Slope of A = Slope of B = Slope of C*

$2=1-b=\frac{-2}{c+b}$

First we solve the first equation for b

$2 = 1 - b$

$b = -1$

Now substitute $b$ into the second equation:

$$2 = \frac{-2}{c+b}$$

$$2 = \frac{-2}{c-1}$$

$2c - 2 = -2$

$c = 0$

So $b = -1$ and $c = 0$ are the values for which the lines are parallel.

9. **The correct answer is (E).**

**A)** $4x$ is an even number regardless of $x$. This means that $4x + 3$ is always an odd number (the sum of an even number and an odd number is always an odd number)

In order for $(4x + 3) + 5y$ to be an odd integer, $5y$ must be even (the sum of two odd numbers is always an even number, so $5y$ cannot be odd)

If $5y$ is even, then y must be even

If $y$ is even, as $\frac{x^2}{y^2}$ is an integer, $x$ must be divisible by $y$.

$x$ must be even too.

If both $x$ and y are even then, $\frac{x^2}{y^2}$ could be an odd integer but it's not always necessary. Consider $x = 18$ and $y = 2$, then $\frac{x^2}{y^2} = \frac{324}{4} = 81$ which is odd. However, if $x = 36$ and $y = 2$, then $\frac{x^2}{y^2} = \frac{1296}{4} = 324$ which is even. A) is not always true.

(For reference, if $x$ and y were both odd integers, then $\frac{x^2}{y^2}$ would always be an odd integer)

**B)** $x$ must always be divisible by y in order for $\frac{x^2}{y^2}$ to be an integer, however $x$ could also be divisible by $y^2$. Consider $x = 36$ and $y = 2$, 36 is divisible by 2, but 36 is also divisible by $2^2$. B) is not always true

**C)** Consider $x = \sqrt{18}$ and $y = \sqrt{6}$ which are both irrational numbers. In this case $\frac{x^2}{y^2}$ is still a positive integer. C) is not always true

**D)** The reciprocal is $\frac{x^2}{y^2}$ . Consider again $x = 18$ and $y = 2$, then $\frac{x^2}{y^2} = \frac{4}{324}$ which is not an integer.
D) is not always true

**E)** 3 is already a multiple of 3, so in order for $xy + 3$ to be a multiple of 3, then $xy$ must be a multiple of 3. This can happen if either x or y or both are multiples of 3.

If $y$ is not a multiple of 3, then $x$ must be a multiple of 3, otherwise the product $xy$ would not be a multiple of 3.

However, if $y$ is a multiple of 3, then in order for $\frac{x^2}{y^2}$ to be an integer, $x$ also must be a multiple of 3.

In this case $x$ will always be a multiple of 3, so E) is always true.

10. **The correct answer is (B).**

Let $x$ be the number of students traveling.

Then

By the given data

$$2x + \frac{1}{2}x + \frac{1}{2}\left(\frac{1}{2}\right)x + 1 = 100$$

$$2x + \frac{1}{2}x + \frac{1}{4}x = 99$$

$$2\frac{3}{4}x = 99$$

$$\frac{11}{4}x = 99$$

$$x = 99 \times \frac{4}{11} = 36$$

$\therefore 36$ students were traveling.

11. **The correct answers are (B) and (D).**

If we are looking for an even integer as the value of $x$, the value can either be negative or positive and an even number. We must solve each equation to determine if this requirement is met.

**A)** $3x - 5 = 5x + 1$

$-6 = 2x$ or $x = -3$

**B)** $5(2x - 3) = 3x - 1$

$10x - 15 = 3x - 1$

$7x = 14$ or $x = 2$

**C)** $2x + 7 = 5x - 8$

$15 = 3x$ or $x = 5$

**D)** $7 + 3x = 7x - 9$

$16 = 4x$ or $x = 4$

**E)** $2x - 7 = 5x + 2$

$-9 = 3x$ or $x = -3$

**F)** $-10x-9 = 2x + 3$

$-12 = 12x$ or $x = -1$

B and D are the equations where $x$ is an even integer.

12. **The correct answer is 21.9 meters**

Consider the $\Delta PSR$.

The segments $PS$, $SR$ and $PR$ will be in the ratio $1:\sqrt{3}:2$ respectively, considering that the angles of the triangle are $30^\circ$, $60^\circ$ and $90^\circ$

It is given that $PR$ measures 20 *meters*.

$$\frac{SR}{PR} = \frac{\sqrt{3}}{2}$$

$$SR = \frac{\sqrt{3}}{2} \times 20 = 17.32 \ meters$$

Similarly,

$$\frac{PS}{PR} = \frac{1}{2}$$

$$PS = \frac{1}{2} \times 20 = 10 \ meters$$

Now, consider the $\Delta QSR$.

By Pythagoras theorem, $QR^2 = SR^2 + SQ^2$

$21^2 = 17.32^2 + SQ^2$

$SQ^2 = 21^2 - 17.32^2$

$= 441 - 299.98$

$= 141.02$

$\sqrt{141.02} = 11.88$ *meters*

From the figure, it can be seen that $PQ = PS + SQ$.

$PQ = 10 + 11.88 = 21.88$ *meters* or 21.9 meters

13. **The correct answer is (D).**

Set A rearranged in ascending order: *{15, 16, 16, 17, 17, 17, 18, 19}*

The mean is the average =

$$\frac{(15+16+16+17+17+18+19)}{8} = \frac{135}{8} = 16.875$$

The median is the middle number. In this case there are two middle numbers so the median is the average of the two middle numbers =

$$\frac{(17+17)}{2} = 17$$

The mode is the most frequent number in the set = 17

The range is the difference between the largest number and the smallest number =

$19 - 15 = 4$.

If a new student aged 18 is joining the class, the new mean =

$$\frac{(135+19)}{(8+1)} = \frac{154}{9} = 17$$

**A** is true. The median and the mode are the same = 17

**B** is true. The range = 4

**C** is true. As calculated, the new mean = 17

**D** is false. The mode is 17 and the mean is 16.875

**E** is true. 17 is still the most frequent number in the set, so the mode does not change

14. **The correct answer is (B).**

$\Delta ABC$ is an isosceles right triangle with hypotenuse $BC$.

$AC$ and $AB$ are perpendicular

$AB$ has a *slope* of 0 $\left( slope = \frac{(2-2)}{(b-1)} = \frac{0}{(b-1)} = 0 \right)$

$AB$ is parallel to $x$–axis.

$AC$ must be parallel to $y$–axis.

$C(c, 6) = C(1,6)$ because $c$ must be 1 to match with $A(1,2)$

$\Delta ABC$ is isosceles with hypotenuse BC

$AC = AB$

We use the coordinates of the points and the definition of the distance between the points, to rewrite the above as:

$$\sqrt{(1-c)^2 + (2-6)^2} = \sqrt{(b-1)^2 + (2-2)^2}$$

$$\sqrt{(1-1)^2 + 16} = \sqrt{(b-1)^2}$$

$b - 1 = 4$

$b = 5$

$AC = AB = 4$

Using the same the definition of the distance between the points:

$BC = \sqrt{(b-c)^2 + (2-6)^2} = \sqrt{(5-1)^2 + 16} =$

$\sqrt{2 \times 16} = 4\sqrt{2}$

$AD$ is perpendicular to $BC$. Area of $\Delta ABC$ can be calculated as $\frac{(AD \times BC)}{2}$ but because the triangle is also a right triangle the area is also equal to $\frac{(AB \times AC)}{2}$

$$AD = \frac{(AB \times AC)}{BC}$$

$$AD = \frac{(4 \times 4)}{4\sqrt{2}} = \frac{4}{\sqrt{2}} = 2\sqrt{2}$$

15. **The correct answer is (C).**

Define M as Manny' s income and F as Fran's income.

Manny's income is 72% of Fran's so M = 0.72F, or 648 = 0.72F if you plug in 648 for Manny's income. Solving for F, divide 648 by 0.72. You find that F = 900. The two quantities are equal.

16. **The correct answer is (B).**

Let $x$ be the number of minutes it takes the first worker to produce one part. Then, it takes the second worker $(x - 5)$ minutes to produce one part.

Eight hours is equal to $8 \times 60 = 480$ minutes. Within this period of time the number of parts two workers can produce are as follows:

Number of parts the first worker can make within eight hours = $\frac{480}{x}$

Number of parts the second worker can make within eight hours = $\frac{480}{x-5}$

Within eight hours also the first worker makes 16 parts less than the second workers. Therefore,

$$\frac{480}{x} + 16 = \frac{480}{x-5}$$

Multiply each side of this equation by $x(x - 5)$ to eliminate fractions.

$480(x - 5) + 16x(x - 5) = 480x$

Divide each side by 16 and then solve.

$30(x - 5) + x(x - 5) = 30x$

$30x - 150 + x^2 - 5x - 30x = 0$

$x^2 - 5x - 150 = 0$

$(x - 15)(x + 10) = 0$

This equation gives $x = 15$ and $x = -10$, which only $x = 15$ is admissible since $x$ represents the measure of time.

Thus the first worker produces $\frac{480}{15} = 32$

17. **The correct answer is (C)**

The key is to write the correct equation that reflects the data given in the question:

*(Selling price + \$351) represents 20% more than (Cost price less 3%)*

*\$1,395 + \$351 = (1+20%) × Cost price ×(1–3%)*

Cost price = $\frac{\$1746}{97\% \times 120\%} = \$1,500$

If we know the Cost price and the Selling price, we can now calculate the value of the loss incurred = *\$1,500 –\$1,395 = \$105*

*Loss percentage* = $\frac{\$105}{\$1500} = 0.07$, $0.07 \times 100 = 7\%$.

18. **The correct answer is (B).**

$m\angle BAC = 90^\circ$ So, $ABC$ is a right angle triangle

$m\angle ACB = 30^\circ$, sine of $m\angle ACB = \sin 30^\circ = \frac{1}{2}$, ,

$\frac{AB}{BC} = \frac{1}{2}$, if $BC = s$, then $AB = \frac{s}{2}$

We can apply Pythagoras' theorem in $\Delta ABC$.

$BC^2 = AB^2 + AC^2$

$$AC^2 = s^2 - \frac{s^2}{4}$$

$$AC = s\frac{\sqrt{3}}{2}$$

We can now calculate the area of each of the squares:

Area $BCGF = BC^2 = s^2$

Area $ABHI = AB^2 = \frac{s^2}{4}$

Area $ACDE = AC^2 = \frac{3s^2}{4}$

*AEJI* is a quadrilateral. We know that

$m\angle BAC = 90^\circ$ and also that

$m\angle BAI = m\angle CAE = 90^\circ$ (angles in a square)

$m\angle IAE = 90^\circ$

*HIJ* and *DEJ* are line segments and

$m\angle HIA = m\angle AED = 90^\circ$ (angles in a square)

$m\angle JIA = m\angle JEA = 90^\circ$

*AEJI* is a rectangle

Area $AEJI = AE \times AI = s\frac{\sqrt{3}}{2} \times \frac{s}{2} = s^2\frac{\sqrt{3}}{4}$

We already calculated that Area $BCGF = s^2$ and Area $ABHI = \frac{s^2}{4}$

Area *BCGF* – Area $ABHI = s^2 - \frac{s^2}{4} = \frac{3s^2}{4} =$ Area $AEJI \times \sqrt{3}$

Area $AEJI = \frac{(Area\ BCGF - Area\ ABHI)}{\sqrt{3}}$

The correct answer is B)

C is not correct because (Area *BCGF* – Area *ACDE*)=

$s^2 - \frac{3s^s}{4} = \frac{s^2}{4} = Area\ \frac{AEJI}{\sqrt{3}}$

Area *AEJI* = (Area *BCGF* – Area *ACDE*) × $\sqrt{3}$

D and E are not correct because Area ACDE $= \frac{3s^2}{4} =$

$s^2 - \frac{3s^2}{4} = \frac{s^2}{4} = Area\ \frac{AEJI}{\sqrt{3}}$

Area AEJI $= \frac{Area\ ACDE}{\sqrt{3}}$

19. **The correct answers are (A), (C) and (D).**

**A)** One hour work of P $= \frac{1}{20}$ of the tank

One hour work of Q $= \frac{1}{30}$ of the tank

One hour work both together $= \frac{1}{20} + \frac{1}{30} = \frac{5}{60} = \frac{1}{12}$ of the tank

Therefore it will take 12 minutes to get the tank filled.

Option A is correct.

**B)** From the calculation above option B is wrong.

**C)** When the pipes are opened together one minute of work $= \frac{1}{12}$ of the tank

Pipe P is closed after **10** minutes

One minute of work $= \frac{10}{12}$ of the tank $= \frac{5}{6}$ of the tank

Remaining work $= \frac{1}{6}$ of the tank

Time taken by Q alone to complete the work minutes

$= \frac{1}{6} \div \frac{1}{30} =$ **5** minutes

Hence total time taken = 10 + 5 = 15 minutes.

Option C is correct

**D)** When the pipes are opened together one minute work $= \frac{1}{12}$ of the tank

Pipe Q is closed after 7.5 minutes

7.5 minutes work $= 7.5 \times \frac{1}{12} = \frac{75}{120} = \frac{5}{8}$ of the tank

Remaining work $= \frac{3}{8}$ of the tank

Time taken by P alone to complete the work =

$= \frac{3}{8} \div \frac{1}{20} = \frac{60}{8} = 7.5$ minutes

Hence total time taken = 7.5 + 7.5 = 15 minutes.

Option D is correct

20. **The correct answers are (B), (C), (D) and (F).**

In the equation $f(x) = 2x^2 - 7x + 3$, we can determine the following without any calculation. The value of "a", the leading coefficient, is 2. Since it is positive the parabola opens up, so A is false. Find the vertex of the polynomial by calculating.

$x = -\frac{b}{2a}$

$a = 2,\ b = -7$

$x = -\frac{(-7)}{2(2)} = \frac{7}{4}$

$f\left(\frac{7}{4}\right) = 2\left(\frac{7}{4}\right)^2 - 7\left(\frac{7}{4}\right) + 3$

$= 2\left(\frac{49}{16}\right) - \frac{49}{4} + 3$

$= \frac{49}{8} - \frac{49}{4} + 3$

$= \frac{49}{8} - \frac{98}{8} + \frac{24}{8} = -\frac{25}{8}$

Therefore we know that the axis of symmetry is

$x = \frac{7}{4}$, with a minimum of $-\frac{25}{8}$. Therefore B is false but D is true.

To find the $y$–intersect of the graph we can set $x$ equal to 0, and calculate the value of $y$ or $f(x)$.

Therefore F is true.

Next we can set $f(x)$ equal to 0 and see whether the polynomial can be factored.

The factored form is $(2x-1)(x-3)$

The roots of the equation are $\frac{1}{2}$ and 3.

Therefore, the roots can be calculated using factoring but the roots are not –3 and $-\frac{1}{2}$. C is true, E is false.

This page is intentionally left blank

Chapter 7

# Practice Test 5

You are about to begin a full length Practice Test. The Test has five sections. The time allotted for each section is marked at the beginning of the section. Work on one section at a time. Use a timer to keep track of the time limits for every section.

Try to take the Practice Test under real test conditions. Find a quiet place to work, and set aside enough time to complete the test without being disturbed. At the end of the test, check your answers by referring to the Answer Key and fill in your raw score in the score card below. Also, note down the time taken by you for completing each section.

Pay particular attention to the questions that were answered incorrectly. Read the answer explanations and understand how to solve them.

## My Score Card (Raw Score)

| | Section 2 | Section 3 | Section 4 | Section 5 |
|---|---|---|---|---|
| **Out of** | 20 | 20 | 20 | 20 |
| **My Score** | ________ | ________ | ________ | ________ |
| **Time Taken** | ________ | ________ | ________ | ________ |

# Section 1 – Analytical Writing

Task 1 – Analyze an Issue | 30 mins

*People should undertake risky action only after they have carefully considered its consequences.*

*Write a response in which you discuss the extent to which you agree or disagree with the recommendation and explain your reasoning for the position you take. In developing and supporting your position, describe specific circumstances in which adopting the recommendation would or would not be advantageous and explain how these examples shape your position.*

You may start writing your response here

## Task 2 – Analyze an Argument Task | 30 mins

*The following appeared in a memorandum from the manager of WWAC radio station.*

*"To reverse a decline in listener numbers, our owners have decided that WWAC must change from its current rock-music format. The decline has occurred despite population growth in our listening area, but that growth has resulted mainly from people moving here after their retirement. We must make listeners of these new residents. We could switch to a music format tailored to their tastes, but a continuing decline in local sales of recorded music suggests limited interest in music. Instead we should change to a news and talk format, a form of radio that is increasingly popular in our area."*

*Write a response in which you discuss what specific evidence is needed to evaluate the argument and explain how the evidence would weaken or strengthen the argument.*

You may start writing your response here

# Section 2 – Verbal Reasoning

20 questions | 30 mins

---

**For Questions 1 and 2, select one entry for the blank. Fill the blank in the way that best completes the text.**

1. Music executives barely had a moment to look back over their shoulders at the _______ days of massive album sales before trudging forward and trying to carve out new revenue streams in the modern music market.

| |
|---|
| disconcerting |
| halcyon |
| intractable |
| maddening |
| recalcitrant |

2. Mastery of the business cycle has long eluded economists; every bold claim of finally conquering the volatile corporate world seems to be _______ by a subsequent collapse of stock prices.

| |
|---|
| attenuated |
| elevated |
| reinforced |
| garnished |
| subsumed |

**For each blank, select one entry from the corresponding column of choices. Fill all blanks in the way that best completes the text.**

3. The (i)_________ nature of paleontology is as exciting as it is frustrating. A team of paleontologists can spend months on one site, digging meticulously through layers of topsoil, only to come home empty–handed. And after this entire painstaking process is over, it is entirely possible that the team will be (ii)________ to discover that a rainstorm uncovered in an hour what they couldn't in an entire summer.

| Blank (i) | Blank (ii) |
|---|---|
| capricious | disillusioned |
| intractable | rapt |
| pensive | debilitated |

**Questions 4 and 5 are based on the following passage.**

In the smaller towns the itinerant players [actors] might, through a letter of recommendation from their noble patron, or through the good–will of some local dignitary, secure the use of the town–hall, of the schoolhouse, or even of the village church. In such buildings, of course, they could give their performances more advantageously, for they could place money–takers at the doors, and exact adequate payment from all who entered. In the great city of London, however, the players were necessarily forced to make use almost entirely of public inn–yards—an arrangement which, we may well believe, they found far from satisfactory. Not being masters of the inns, they were merely tolerated; they had to content themselves with hastily provided and inadequate stage facilities; and, worst of all, for their recompense they had to trust to a hat collection, at best a poor means of securing money. Often too, no doubt, they could not get the use of a given inn–yard when they most needed it, as on holidays and festive occasions; and at all times they had to leave the public in uncertainty as to where or when plays were to be seen. Their street parade, with the noise of trumpets and drums, might gather a motley crowd for the yard, but in so large a place as London it was inadequate for advertisement among the better classes. And as the troupes of the city increased in wealth and dignity, and as the playgoing public grew in size and importance, the old makeshift arrangement became more and more unsatisfactory.

**Consider each of the three choices separately and select all that apply.**

4. Which one or more of the following could be inferred about the holding of plays inside buildings rather than outside?

   [A] Inn keepers were not well prepared for plays to take place in their yard.

   [B] Actors preferred an indoor location rather than outdoors because a consistent amount of money could be collected for people's admission fee in an indoor ticket booth.

   [C] Many plays had to be cancelled or postponed on account of frequent rainstorms.

**Select only one answer choice.**

5. Writers usually have several factors of motivation in mind. What do you believe was the main reason that the author chose to write about this subject?

   (A) People needed to learn about Shakespeare, one of history's most famous playwrights.

   (B) Courtyards in that day were very unique and attractive to view. This describes one purpose for having courtyards.

   (C) Music and drama were highly esteemed in that day. It is important that an accurate history is maintained of music and drama.

   (D) The wealthy were the people who most often attended plays and concerts. This article tells about the wealthy people of the day.

   (E) This passage tells about how playhouses changed over time and the factors that came into play to promote their evolution.

**Questions 6 to 9 are based on the following passage.**

The effects of training gradually disappear. Habits wane with disuse. In the dancer, it is not possible to establish with certainty the existence of memory in the introspective psychological sense; but it is possible to measure the efficiency of the training to which the animal is subjected, and the degree of permanency of habits. The materials which constitute this chapter concern the persistence of unused habits, and the influence of previous training on the re–acquisition of a habit which has been lost or on the acquisition of a new habit. For convenience of description, I shall refer to certain of the facts which are to be discussed as facts of memory, with the clear understanding that consciousness is not necessarily implied. By memory, wherever it occurs in this book, I mean the ability of the dancer to retain the power of adaptive action which it has acquired through training.

I first discovered memory in the dancer, although there was previously no reason for doubting its existence, in connection with the ladder–climbing tests of Chapter XII. In this experiment two individuals which had perfectly learned to escape from the experiment box to the nest–box by way of the wire ladder, when tested after an interval of two weeks, during which they had remained in the nest–box without opportunity to exercise their newly acquired habit, demonstrated their memory of the method of escape by returning to the nest–box by way of the ladder as soon as they were given opportunity to do so. As it did not lend itself readily to quantitative study, no attempts were made to measure the duration of this particular habit. At best the climbing of a wire ladder is of very uncertain value as an indication of the influence of training.

Similarly, the persistence of habits has been forced upon my attention day after day in my various experiments with the mice. It is obvious, then, that the simple fact of memory is well established, and that we may turn at once to an examination of the facts revealed by special memory and re– learning experiments.

The visual discrimination method, which proved invaluable as a means of measuring the rapidity of habit formation, proved equally serviceable in the measurement of the permanency or duration of habits. Memory tests for discrimination habits were made as follows. After a dancer had been trained in the discrimination box so that it could choose the correct electric–box, white, red, blue, or green as it might be, in three successive daily series of ten tests each, it was permitted to remain for a certain length of time without training and without opportunity to exercise its habit of visual discrimination and choice. At the expiration of the rest interval, as we may designate the period during which the habit was not in use, the mouse was placed in the discrimination box under precisely the same conditions in which it had been trained and was given a series of ten memory tests with the box to be chosen alternately on the right and on the left. In order that the entire series of ten tests, and sometimes two such series given on consecutive days, might be available as indications of the duration of a habit, the mouse was permitted to enter and pass through either of the electric–boxes without receiving a shock. Had the shock been given as punishment for a wrong choice, it is obvious that only the first test of the memory series would be of value as an indication of the existence of a previously acquired habit.

**For Questions 6 to 9, select only one answer choice.**

6. Based on this passage, all of the following statements can be inferred about memory EXCEPT:

(A) Memory from rote training is much easier to identify than memories that arise spontaneously from emotional recall.

(B) Muscle memory can be measured more effectively than cerebral memory.

(C) Negative memories can increase the likelihood that habits will be repeated subconsciously.

(D) Psychological memories are difficult to track via scientific methods.

(E) It is possible to calculate how beneficial training can be within the realm of physical activities.

7. Which of the following words could be used to express the author's feelings towards mice, based on the studies of mice as inferred from the passage?

(A) critical

(B) affectionate

(C) professional

(D) hypocritical

(E) indifferent

8. Which of the following statements, if true, is textually supported by the passage?

(A) In order for this type of study to produce accurate results, the mice must have free will over their choice to select a certain box without fear of negative consequences.

(B) The action of climbing a ladder was an integral part of establishing the effect of training on habit retention in the mice.

(C) Regardless of the type of training, the results are determined more by the individual's skills than the quality of the training regimen.

(D) Memory' refers to the ability to redo a physical or mental task based on former instruction.

(E) Repeatedly using a physical skill requires conscious effort.

9. Select the sentence in the passage that most clearly indicates a transition from one main idea to another.

**For Questions 10 and 11, select the two answer choices that, when used to complete the sentence, fit the meaning of the sentence as a whole and produce completed sentences that are alike in meaning.**

10. Many advocates for prison reform point to the penal system's disproportionately harsh sentences for African–American as an example of _________ racism.

    [A] laissez–faire

    [B] institutionalized

    [C] infrequent

    [D] accidental

    [E] entrenched

    [F] progressive

11. The poet Rumi wrote volumes of ____________ poems describing the intricacies of love in thirteenth century Persia; though written hundreds of years ago, the poems described the multi-faceted nature of love with evocative, mellifluous language so enduring that they are still read and quoted throughout the world in the present day.

    [A] odoriferous

    [B] desultory

    [C] redolent

    [D] fecund

    [E] restive

    [F] nostalgic

**For Questions 12 to 14, for each blank, select one entry from the corresponding column of choices. Fill all blanks in the way that best completes the text.**

12. Until recently, nobody expected to find (i)_________ in the field of hydrology. But as population numbers keep soaring and water supplies keep drying up, the study of water distribution across planet Earth suddenly becomes essential. Countries that once (ii)__________ the notion of monitoring their water supply are now actively seeking out the top hydrologists in the field. The once obscure profession has exploded into the mainstream seemingly overnight.

| Blank (i) | Blank (ii) |
|---|---|
| prominence | recalculated |
| ignominy | denigrated |
| extravagance | co–opted |

13. His first few days on campus were exhilarating. He had come from a simple home in the country and his new, (i)_______ environment was almost overwhelming. Just seeing the wide variety of students on campus told him that the (ii)_______ opportunities of college would extend beyond the classroom. He was particularly interested in his roommate, wondering if that young man would be as enamored with this exotic milieu as he was.

| Blank (i) |
|---|
| cosmopolitan |
| bucolic |
| archaic |

| Blank (ii) |
|---|
| irksome |
| didactic |
| grievous |

14. Modern botany has an extensive history. Dating back to the ancient Greeks, the discipline has been refined for centuries. Its study is of tremendous importance for a variety of reasons. All mammalian sources of food, regardless of how (i)_________ the route, inevitably come from plants. This (ii)_________ means that botany is an applicable field of study regardless of which group of animals you might be studying.

| Blank (i) |
|---|
| malevolent |
| circuitous |
| fulminated |

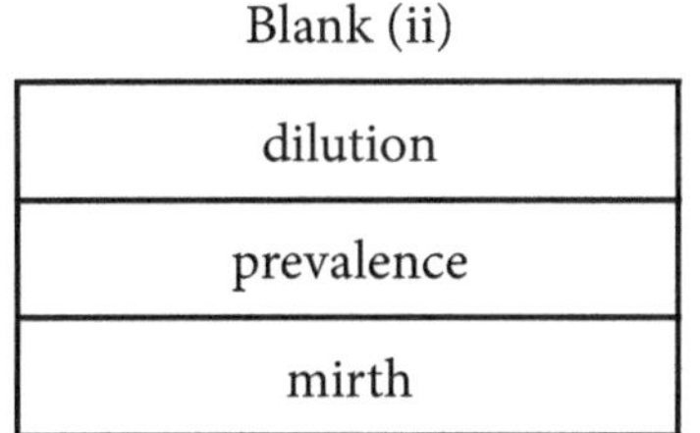

| Blank (ii) |
|---|
| dilution |
| prevalence |
| mirth |

**Question 15 is based on the following passage.**

When one becomes a father, then first one becomes a son. Standing by the crib of one's own baby, with that world–old pang of compassion and protectiveness toward this so little creature that has all its course to run, the heart flies back in yearning and gratitude to those who felt just so toward one's self. Then for the first time one understands the homely succession of sacrifices and pains by which life is transmitted and fostered down the stumbling generations of men.

**Select only one answer choice.**

15. Which of these statements describes an assumption upon which this conclusion depends?

(A) Children are very dependent upon caring adults.

(B) All parents look upon their children with heartfelt pleasure as they lay in the crib.

(C) All parents also had a parent who cared for them in much the same way.

(D) This passage only pertains to adults with children.

(E) All new parents feel rather inept upon the birth of a first child.

**For Questions 16 and 17, select the two answer choices that, when used to complete the sentence, fit the meaning of the sentence as a whole and produce completed sentences that are alike in meaning.**

16. While thematic construction and dense intellectual interpolations characterize modern art, many still find refuge in the ______ of primitive works, in some cases tracing this interest all the way back to prehistoric cave paintings.

    [A] innocence

    [B] inexperience

    [C] precision

    [D] professionalism

    [E] imperviousness

    [F] effervescence

17. He made his words as _________ and neutral as humanly possible, but he knew in the back of his mind that human nature would cause his audience to only take away from his speech what they wanted to hear.

    [A] fungible

    [B] optional

    [C] objective

    [D] subjective

    [E] figurative

    [F] impartial

**Questions 18 to 20 are based on the following passage.**

By the 1890s Social Darwinist ideas were popular and were making themselves felt, influencing social policies in the United States and elsewhere. Social Darwinism saw human society as based on a struggle for survival, in which the superior, the fittest, would triumph and the inferior would be swept to the wayside. It was more or less the ancient "predator ethic" -- the idea that might makes right, that the strong are entitled to oppress the weak - dressed up in pseudoscientific clothes. If the struggle for survival was the way of the world, then it was only natural that human society should operate in the same way. Social Darwinism also dovetailed with racist thinking: American segregationists used the idea to promote the second-class status of black folk as a positive good. In Germany, Ernst Haeckel took the idea even farther, using it as a framework to propose Aryan race-supremacy notions and German militarism.

18. Select the sentence that explains how humans justified the tenets of social Darwinism.

**Consider each of the three choices separately and select all that apply**

19. According to the passage, which of the following are examples of "predator ethic"?

[A] Cyber- bullying

[B] Involuntary commitment to a mental institution

[C] Incarcerating people based on their race

**Select only one answer choice.**

20. The use of the word "dovetailed" in the context of this passage most closely matches which of the following definitions?

(A) Coincided with

(B) Deviated from

(C) Fit together

(D) Having a series of indentations suggesting dovetails

(E) Split apart

# Section 3 – Quantitative Reasoning

20 questions | 35 mins

1. In a certain firm, the average salary of the officers is \$1510 per person and average salary of workers is \$850 per person. If the average salary of all the employees is \$960 per person and number of officers are 800 less than number of workers then the number of workers will be?

   Write your answer in the answer box.

   [ ] workers

2.

The lengths of the legs of right triangle, ΔPQR, are $x$ and $y$.
The lengths of the legs of right ΔRST are 2x and 2y.

| **Quantity A** | **Quantity B** |
|---|---|
| Twice the area of $\Delta PQR$ | The area of $\Delta RST$ |

Ⓐ Quantity A is greater.

Ⓑ Quantity B is greater

Ⓒ The two quantities are equal.

Ⓓ The relationship cannot be determined from the information given.

3.

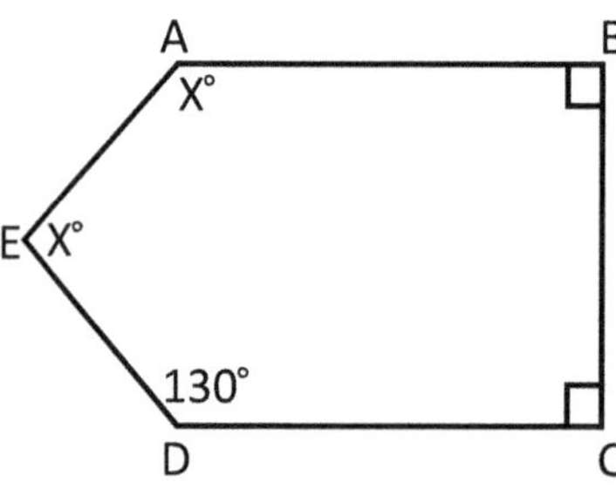


| **Quantity A** | **Quantity B** |
|---|---|
| $x$ | 130 |

Ⓐ Quantity A is greater.

Ⓑ Quantity B is greater.

Ⓒ The two quantities are equal.

Ⓓ The relationship cannot be determined from the information given.

4.

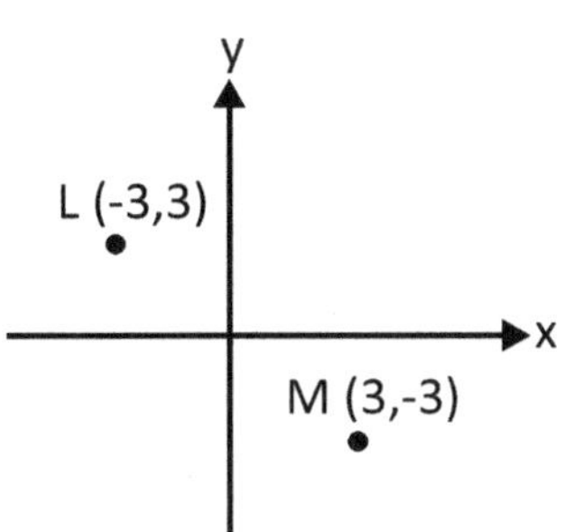


| Quantity A | Quantity B |
|---|---|
| The area of the circle with diameter *LM* | $9\pi$ |

(A) Quantity A is greater.

(B) Quantity B is greater

(C) The two quantities are equal.

(D) The relationship cannot be determined from the information given.

5.

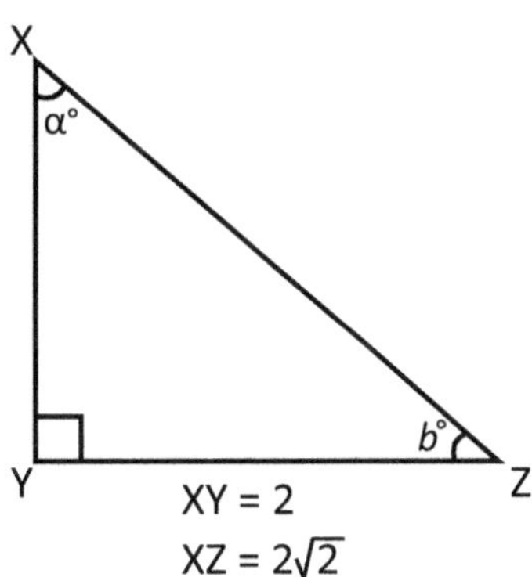


| Quantity A | Quantity B |
|---|---|
| $\alpha$ | $b$ |

(A) Quantity A is greater.

(B) Quantity B is greater.

(C) The two quantities are equal.

(D) The relationship cannot be determined from the information given.

6. The mean of the heights of the students at Mark Twain School is equal to 5 *feet* and 6 *inches*. The heights fall along a normal distribution and the standard deviation is 2 *inches*. If student Bill is 5 *feet* and 4 *inches*, he is taller than approximately what percent of Mark Twain's students?

(A) 2%

(B) 13.5%

(C) 16%

(D) 34%

(E) 47.5%

7. Charles works in a factory. For the first eight hours, he earns $20 per hour and for the next 2 hours, his salary is $30 per hour. Beyond 10 hours his salary is $40 per hour. In a single shift if he earns $340, how many hours long was the shift?

(A) 11 hours

(B) 12 hours

(C) 13 hours

(D) 14 hours

(E) 15 hours

8. If $x > 8$, $x < 17$, and $x + 5 < 19$, which of the following can be the values of $x$?

[A] 8

[B] 9

[C] 11

[D] 13

[E] 14

[F] 16

[G] 12

[H] 17

[I] 10

**Questions 9 and 10 are based on the following table:**

Five different microorganisms are placed in petri dishes A, B, C, D, and E. Then, four experiments are conducted as described below along with their results. The numbers demonstrated in the chart represent the number of microorganisms present after the phase is complete.

| Phase | Microorganism | Number of A | Number of B | Number of C | Number of D | Number of E |
|---|---|---|---|---|---|---|
| **Phase 0** | Number of Microorganisms | $7 \times 10^6$ | $7 \times 10^6$ | $7 \times 10^6$ | $7 \times 10^6$ | $7 \times 10^6$ |
| **Phase 1** | An hour later under 40° temperature and 24 grams food supply | $7 \times 10^6$ | $7 \times 10^6$ | $8 \times 10^6$ | $9.3 \times 10^6$ | $7.4 \times 10^6$ |
| **Phase 2** | Five hours later under 44° temperature and 18 grams food supply | $8 \times 10^6$ | $900 \times 10^7$ | $7 \times 10^8$ | $9.3 \times 10^6$ | $3.8 \times 10^6$ |
| **Phase 3** | An hour later under 31° temperature and 28 grams food supply | $4 \times 10^5$ | $900 \times 10^7$ | $7.7 \times 10^8$ | $9.3 \times 10^7$ | $4.8 \times 10^6$ |
| **Phase 4** | Five hours later under 40° temperature and 36 grams of food supply | $10 \times 10^5$ | $9 \times 10^{10}$ | $7.9 \times 10^8$ | $9.3 \times 10^7$ | $7.5 \times 10^6$ |

9. By what factor does the number of microorganisms increase during the highest growth from one phase to another in Population B?

- (A) $81 \times 10^7$
- (B) $81 \times 10^9$
- (C) $72 \times 10^9$
- (D) $54 \times 10^8$
- (E) $52 \times 10^8$

10. Why we cannot relate the reproduction pattern of D to any of the factors, time interval (hours), temperature, and food supply?

Ⓐ Because its population changed only once.

Ⓑ Because its population changed only after phase 0.

Ⓒ Because it reproduced more in Phase 2 than in Phase 1.

Ⓓ Because it reproduced more in Phase 2 than Phase 3

Ⓔ Because changing the measures of the three factors does not show proportional changes in its population.

11.

| Store Location | Revenue ($) | Number of customers |
|---|---|---|
| Princeton Street | 31,144 | 458 |
| St Agnes Road | 58,320 | 720 |
| Hayat Street | 34,336 | 592 |

The table above shows the revenue generated and the number of customers in three different store locations of a certain business over the last week.

What is the average of the revenues generated per customer at the three locations?

Ⓐ 55

Ⓑ 58

Ⓒ 68

Ⓓ 69

Ⓔ 81

12. Kabir is hosting a contest attended by 200 people, 80 of whom are males. The remaining contestants are females. At the end of the contest, one of the contestants will be chosen at random to win a prize. If 1/5 of male contestants and 1/6 of female contestants arrived late, what is the probability that the prize will be won by a contestant who arrived late?

Ⓐ 4/25

Ⓑ 6/35

Ⓒ 9/50

Ⓓ 9/80

Ⓔ 1/9

13. What will be the supplementary angle to Angle A if Angle A is 17 degrees?

[ ]

14.

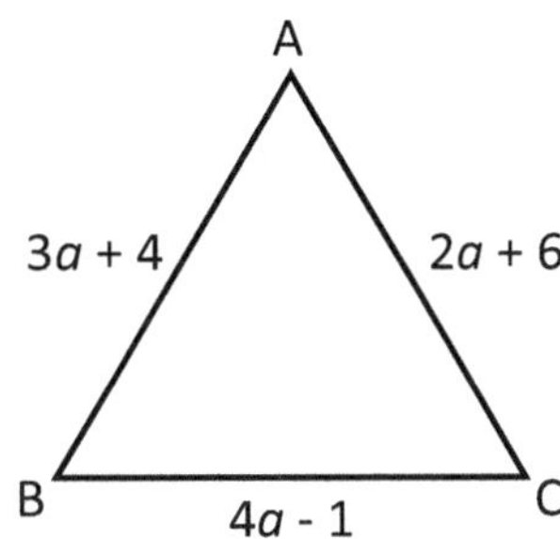


Perimeter of $\triangle ABC = 27$

| Quantity A | Quantity B |
|---|---|
| $a$ | 2 |

- (A) Quantity A is greater.
- (B) Quantity B is greater.
- (C) The two quantities are equal.
- (D) The relationship cannot be determined from the information given.

15.

| Quantity A | Quantity B |
|---|---|
| The sum of the interior angles of a convex pentagon | 500° |

- (A) Quantity A is greater.
- (B) Quantity B is greater.
- (C) The two quantities are equal.
- (D) The relationship cannot be determined from the information given

16. The center of a circle in the *xy*-plane is (5, 4). If the circle passes through (5, 14), what is the equation of the circle?

(A) $(x-5)^2+(y-4)^2=100$

(B) $(x+5)^2+(y+4)^2=100$

(C) $(x-5)^2+(y-4)^2=10$

(D) $(x+5)^2+(y+4)^2=10$

(E) $(x+5)^2+(y-4)^2=10$

17.

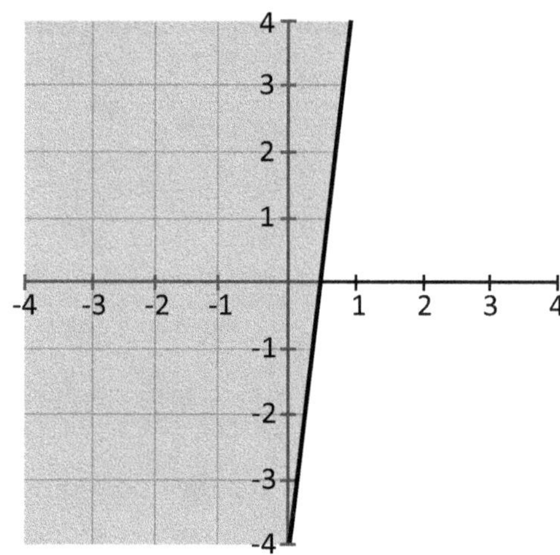


The shaded region in the graph represents which of the following inequalities?

(A) $y \geq 9x-4$

(B) $y > 9x-4$

(C) $y < 9x-4$

(D) $y \leq 9x-4$

(E) $x > 0,\ y > 0$

18. Three pipes A, B and C working together will fill a tank in 2 *hours*. On their own, pipes A and B take 8 and 6 *hours* respectively to fill the tank. If only pipes A and C are open, when does pipe C need to be turned off in order for the tank to be full after exactly 4 *hours*?

(A) 3 *hours* and 30 *minutes*

(B) 3 *hours*

(C) 2 *hours* and 48 *minutes*

(D) 2 *hours* and 24 *minutes*

(E) 2 *hours*

19.

| **Quantity A** | **Quantity B** |
|---|---|
| Area of the triangle formed by the $x$–axis, the $y$–axis, and the line $2x - 3y + 12 = 0$ | 14 |

(A) Quantity A is greater.

(B) Quantity B is greater.

(C) The two quantities are equal.

(D) The relationship cannot be determined from the information given.

20.

$$\frac{m^4}{3} = 27$$

| **Quantity A** | **Quantity B** |
|---|---|
| $m$ | 4 |

(A) Quantity A is greater.

(B) Quantity B is greater.

(C) The two quantities are equal.

(D) The relationship cannot be determined from the information given.

# Section 4 – Verbal Reasoning

20 questions | 30 mins

---

**For Questions 1 and 2, select one entry for the blank. Fill the blank in the way that best completes the text.**

1. The business of selling cutting–edge smart phones requires more guile than merely listing technical specifications; the ______ of social media, wireless connectivity, and interactivity requires corporations to present their product as lifestyles more than a new handheld device.

| reticence |
|---|
| intermittence |
| inarticulacy |
| confluence |
| obscurity |

2. Years of _________ could not sustain the surgeon's confidence – after his first malpractice lawsuit he didn't trust himself to perform even the simplest of procedures.

| laudation |
|---|
| censure |
| indictment |
| suppression |
| ingenuity |

**Question 3 is based on the following passage.**

Mankind are always happier for having been happy; so that if you make them happy now, you make them happy twenty years hence, by the memory of it. A childhood passed with a due mixture of rational indulgence, under fond and wise parents, diffuses over the whole of life a feeling of calm pleasure; and, in extreme old age, is the very last remembrance which time can erase from the mind of man. No enjoyment, however inconsiderable, is confined to the present moment. A man is the happier for life, from having made once an agreeable tour, or lived for any length of time with pleasant people, or enjoyed any considerable interval of innocent pleasure: and it is most probably the recollection of their past pleasures, which contributes to render old men so inattentive to the scenes before them; and carries them back to a world that is past, and to scenes never to be renewed again.

**Select only one answer choice.**

3. Which one of the following statements most directly contrasts with the concept proclaimed in the passage above?

   (A) My grandparents enjoy a "walk down memory lane" as we share stories at family reunions.

   (B) Kevin did not have a happy childhood, this accounts for his sour disposition today.

   (C) Julie is much happier now that she has a new house with new furniture.

   (D) The saddest people on earth are those with too many material possessions, to which they are held in bondage.

   (E) A trip to Disneyland for my family would be a waste of money, it is very expensive and there is little to show for it afterward.

**For Questions 4 and 5, select the two answer choices that, when used to complete the sentence, fit the meaning of the sentence as a whole and produce completed sentences that are alike in meaning.**

4. I have been watching this conversation grow more and more ________ and it disappoints me that such otherwise learned and productive people can sit around for an entire afternoon and waste so much time.

   [A] unreserved

   [B] vapid

   [C] insipid

   [D] insightful

   [E] sectarian

   [F] pretentious

5. The financial volatility of the massive banking institutions means that even the most innocuous of corporate action needs to be thoroughly ________ by a team of lawyers who specialize in everything from international finance to political organization.

   [A] vetted

   [B] delineated

   [C] prioritized

   [D] extemporized

   [E] assessed

   [F] rewritten

**Questions 6 to 9 are based on the following passage.**

I believe it was the old Egyptians, a very wise people, probably indeed much wiser than we know, for in the leisure of their ample centuries they had time to think out things, who declared that each individual personality is made up of six or seven different elements, although the Bible only allows us three, namely, body, soul, and spirit. The body that the man or woman wore, if I understand their theory aright which perhaps I, an ignorant person, do not, was but a kind of sack or fleshly covering containing these different principles. Or mayhap it did not contain them all, but was simply a house as it were, in which they lived from time to time and seldom all together, although one or more of them was present continually, as though to keep the place warmed and aired.

This is but a casual illustrative suggestion, for what right have I, Allan Quatermain, out of my little reading and probably erroneous deductions, to form any judgment as to the theories of the old Egyptians? S**till these, as I understand them, suffice to furnish me with the text that man is not one, but many, in which connection it may be remembered that often in Scripture he is spoken of as being the home of many demons, seven, I think.** Also, to come to another far–off example, the Zulus talk of their witch–doctors as being inhabited by "a multitude of spirits."

**For Questions 6 and 7, select only one answer choice.**

6. Which of the following statements best reflects the main purpose of the passage?

(A) Humans are simple creatures and are fairly easy to understand.

(B) Egyptians formed many theories about life despite their lack of opportunity to do so.

(C) Ancient Egyptians were, for the most part, very wise.

(D) Human personalities are multi–faceted—a theory which is supported by various cultures and texts.

(E) The Bible differs from the teachings of ancient Egyptians, especially regarding internal human characteristics.

7. How does the bold–faced sentence serve to support the author's message?

(A) It offers an explanation of evidence.

(B) It provides an alternate explanation for the author's stance.

(C) It presents a logical conclusion for the author's main argument.

(D) It explains the author's conclusion.

(E) It provides a contradictory idea to contrast the author's opinion.

**Consider each of the three choices separately and select all that apply.**

8. Which of the following words could be used to accurately depict the author's attitude towards his own knowledge in regards to the study of human personalities?

   A speculative

   B authoritative

   C dubious

9. Select the sentence from the passage that best represents the author's humility in regards to his knowledge on the subject of personality.

**For Questions 10 and 11, select the two answer choices that, when used to complete the sentence, fit the meaning of the sentence as a whole and produce completed sentences that are alike in meaning.**

10. Viscosity is the ______ between neigh boring parcels of liquid that are moving at different velocities.

    A attribute

    B resistance

    C conductivity

    D agreement

    E friction

    F altercation

11. The main property differentiating frosted window glass from regular glass is that it is ______ and blurs or softens the light that is transmitted through it.

    A translucent

    B obscured

    C crystalline

    D semi opaque

    E undiluted

    F diaphanous

**For Questions 12 and 13, select one entry for each blank. Fill the blanks in the way that best completes the text.**

12. Improvisational theater has a long history. The first attempt at improvisation in theater is believed to have been in the sixteenth century. The rules for improvisation were more stricter back then, but over time artists became comfortable (i)__________ their approach. Improvisational theater has now featured Nobel Prize-winning writers and stand-up comedians. The new-found (ii)__________ with which improvisational theater is allowed to proceed has opened up actors to attempt styles they never would have otherwise.

| Blank (i) |
|---|
| diversifying |
| conflating |
| truncating |

| Blank (ii) |
|---|
| fluidity |
| perniciousness |
| maleficence |

13. Music has been (i) __________ component of cultural life since antiquity. Choruses and instruments often accompanied Greek tragedies, and boys learned both singing and music theory from a young age. Much of the musical theory that these young Greeks learned is still (ii) __________. The theory can be seen, sometimes completely intact, in both religious and classical Western music.

| Blank (i) |
|---|
| a contested |
| an integral |
| an invidious |

| Blank (ii) |
|---|
| gamut |
| partition |
| accord |

**Questions 14 to 17 are based on the following passage.**

Much has been written upon the question as to whether an actor ought to feel the character he acts, or be dead to any sensations in this direction. Excellent artists differ in their opinions on this important point. In discussing it I must refer to some words I wrote in one of my early chapters:

"The methods by which actors arrive at great effects vary according to their own natures; this renders the teaching of the art by any strictly defined lines a difficult matter."

There has lately been a discussion on the subject, in which many have taken part, and one quite notable debate between two distinguished actors, one of the English and the other of the French stage [Henry Irving and Mons. Coquelin]. These gentlemen, though they differ entirely in their ideas, are, nevertheless, equally right. The method of one, I have no doubt, is the best he could possibly devise for himself; and the same may be said of the rules of the other as applied to himself. But they must work with their own tools; if they had to adopt each other's they would be as much confused as if compelled to exchange languages. One believes that he must feel the character he plays, even to the shedding of real tears, while the other prefers never to lose himself for an instant, and there is no doubt that they both act with more effect by adhering to their own dogmas.

For myself, I know that I act best when the heart is warm and the head is cool. In observing the works of great painters I find that they have no conventionalities except their own; hence they are masters, and each is at the head of his own school. They are original, and could not imitate even if they would.

So with acting, no master–hand can prescribe rules for the head of another school. If, then, I appear bold in putting forth my suggestions, I desire it to be clearly understood that I do not present them to original or experienced artists who have formed their school, but to the student who may have a temperament akin to my own, and who could, therefore, blend my methods with his preconceived ideas.

Many instructors in the dramatic art fall into the error of teaching too much. **The pupil should first be allowed to exhibit his quality, and so teach the teacher what to teach.** This course would answer the double purpose of first revealing how much the pupil is capable of learning, and, what is still more important, of permitting him to display his powers untrammeled. **Whereas, if the master begins by pounding his dogmas into the student, the latter becomes environed by a foreign influence which, if repugnant to his nature, may smother his ability.**

It is necessary to be cautious in studying elocution and gesticulation, lest they become our masters instead of our servants. These necessary but dangerous ingredients must be administered and taken in homeopathic doses, or the patient may die by being over–stimulated. But, even at the risk of being artificial, it is better to have studied these arbitrary rules than to enter a profession with no knowledge whatever of its mechanism. Dramatic instinct is so implanted in humanity that it sometimes misleads us, fostering the idea that because we have the natural talent within we are equally endowed with the power of bringing it out. This is the common error, the rock on which the histrionic aspirant is oftenest wrecked.

**For Questions 14 to 16, select only one answer choice.**

14. Each of the following statements is textually supported by the passage EXCEPT:

(A) It is wise for an actor to learn ways to manipulate his or her natural way of speaking and moving, yet all actors must also take care not to focus too much on these particular aspects.

(B) Acting is a much more difficult profession than it seems; although most people tend to experience a similar range of emotions in daily occurrences, expressing those emotions is a task that requires rigorous training.

(C) No matter how advanced an artist is in his or her particular craft, the advice that he or she may offer to other artists is likely to be useless.

(D) If actors attempt to exchange performance techniques, they are not likely to understand each other.

(E) Good acting requires comprehensive knowledge of a specific set of fundamental rules which actors must strictly adhere to in all performances.

15. How do the boldface sentences function in the passage?

(A) The first offers practical advice and the second sentence provides commentary on why that advice is most useful.

(B) The first makes an assertion and the second provides evidence to prove it.

(C) The first defines one method of acting preparation and the second presents a warning to those who follow other methods.

(D) The first sentence summarizes a previous statement and the second further explains the author's stance by providing more detail.

(E) The first sentence provides evidence to support the author's main point and the second provides a conclusion to that argument.

16. Based on the passage, which of the following words best describes the author's attitude towards the various methods that theatrical teachers employ?

(A) smug

(B) compassionate

(C) critical

(D) impartial

(E) fickle

**Consider each of the three choices separately and select all that apply.**

17. Which of the following are possible descriptions of the author of the passage?

[A] A journalist who has interviewed various types of artists and specializes in writing about performance arts.

[B] A retired professional actor who teaches acting at a small theatre school.

[C] An author who studies musical, visual, and performance art and learns about the intricacies of art through personal experience.

**For Questions 18 and 19, select the two answer choices that, when used to complete the sentence, fit the meaning of the sentence as a whole and produce completed sentences that are alike in meaning.**

18. The distillation process was successful. The new liquid was _______ and odorless.

    A similitude

    B homogeneity

    C unadulterated

    D impure

    E corrupted

    F homogeneous

19. If scales are not ______ properly; scientists cannot measure the amounts of chemicals and other materials with enough precision to ensure the accuracy of or replicate experiment results.

    A conjectured

    B calibrated

    C fissured

    D aligned

    E serialized

    F embroiled

**Question 20 is based on the following passage.**

The Great Economic Panic of 1893, which resulted with increased unemployment, was largely spurned by risky investments in rapid urban development and new technologies such as railroad systems that led to a series of financial institutions faltering. The potential for the economic catastrophe first became apparent when, on February 23rd, the Philadelphia and Reading Railroad company went bankrupt. Much of the overdevelopment was initiated by confidence in the growing economy experienced in the United States over the prior two decades, an era often referred to as "The Gilded Age" in America. During this time the United States was undergoing industrialization, focusing development on both growing cities and connecting communities through new technologies such as railroads. This sort of development encouraged investors to flood the market with capital, however, when these investments proved more costly than profitable, investors quickly began withdrawing their investments creating a sudden shrinkage in the economy of the United States that had far reaching consequences, such as a halting of currently underway projects and the subsequent loss of jobs. The Great Economic Panic of 1893 serves as an example of how the activities of investors can be injurious to the economic well–being of a nation.

**Select only one answer choice.**

20. In this passage the author lays out an argument concerning the causes of the great panic of 1893. If true, which statement from the list given below would undermine the argument presented in this passage?

    (A) In 1892 the value of gold had reached unprecedented highs, and since at the time money was backed by gold, this indicated that the value of investments was peaking.

    (B) The Philadelphia and Reading Railroad continued operating even after the panic of 1893, all the way up until, after many identity changes, its final dissolution in 1976.

    (C) Many new companies were funded by venture capitalist in the years following the great panic which would eventually become some of the largest in the world.

    (D) Investments in new technologies and urban development projects gradually increased throughout the Gilded Age, but the investments that were made yielded large financial returns to the investors.

    (E) Unemployment had been a long-standing concern prior to 1893 due to mounting immigration spurned by a growing economy that encouraged laborers from Europe to take work in the USA.

# Section 5 – Quantitative Reasoning

20 questions | 35 mins

1.

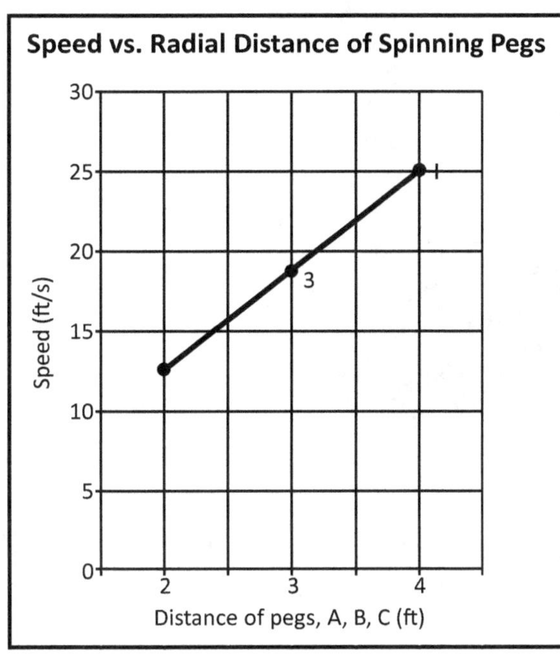


A, B, and C are three pegs on a spinning wheel. If they are placed at the distances $r_a$, $r_b$, $r_c$ from the center, then given the data below, what is the relationship of these distances to each of the pegs' linear speeds, $v$?

(A) $v = kr^3$, $k$ a constant

(B) $v = k/r$, $k$ a constant

(C) $v = r^2/k$, $k$ a constant

(D) $v = rk$, $k$ a constant

(E) $v = r^2$

2.

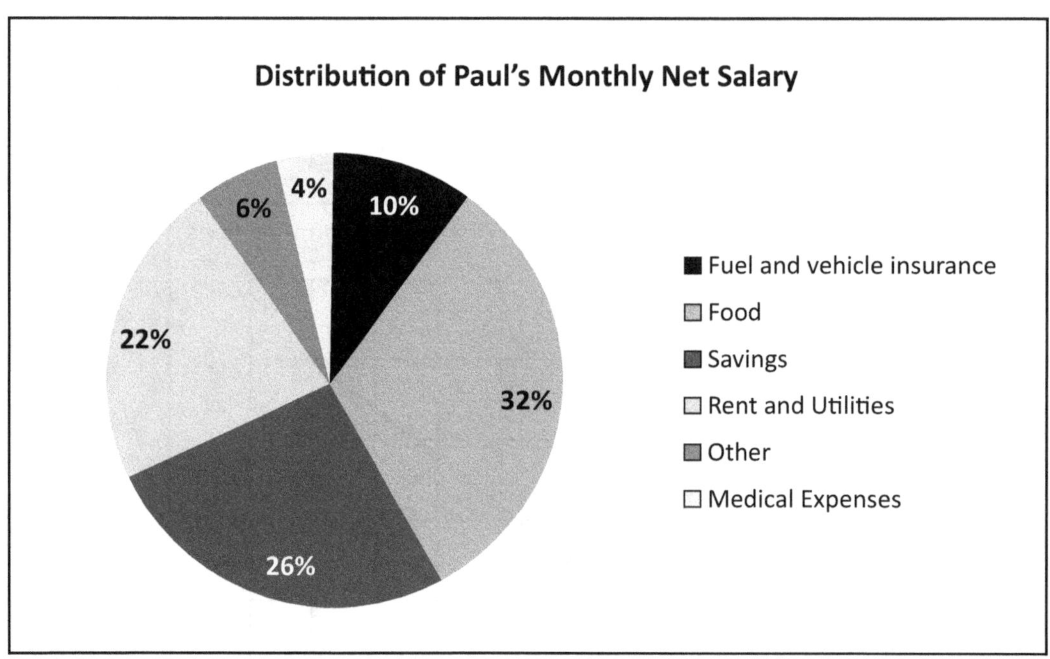


Paul's monthly salary is $3500. The distribution of his net salary in percentage is given in the above pie chart. How many categories does Paul allocate at least $850 to monthly?

(A) 0

(B) 1

(C) 2

(D) 3

(E) 4

3. Given that $2^a \times 2^b = 1024$, what will be the value of $a + b$?

4.

A two–pound box of brand A costs \$7.88.

A three pound box of brand B costs \$11.79.

| **Quantity A** | **Quantity B** |
|---|---|
| Cost per pound of Brand A | Cost per pound of Brand B |

(A) Quantity A is greater.

(B) Quantity B is greater.

(C) The two quantities are equal.

(D) The relationship cannot be determined from the information given.

5.

| **Quantity A** | **Quantity B** |
|---|---|
| The average of the degrees in all the angles in Quadrilateral | The average of the degrees in all the angles of two triangles |

(A) Quantity A is greater.

(B) Quantity B is greater.

(C) The two quantities are equal.

(D) The relationship cannot be determined from the information given.

6.

The distance from A to B is 12 miles

The distance from A to C is 10 miles.

| **Quantity A** | **Quantity B** |
|---|---|
| The distance from A to B | The distance from B to C |

(A) Quantity A is greater.

(B) Quantity B is greater.

(C) The two quantities are equal.

(D) The relationship cannot be determined from the information given.

7. Solve for $x$:

$$3^{x+2} + 3^{x-1} = \left(\frac{28}{9}\right)$$

(A) 2

(B) $\frac{1}{2}$

(C) $-2$

(D) $-\frac{1}{2}$

(E) $-1$

8. Let M and N be events such that $P(M) = \frac{1}{2}$, $P(M \text{ and } N) = \frac{1}{6}$ and $P(M \text{ or } N) = \frac{3}{4}$. Find $P(N)$.

(A) $\frac{1}{12}$

(B) $\frac{1}{4}$

(C) $\frac{5}{12}$

(D) $\frac{5}{6}$

(E) 1

9. A cyclist travels the length of a bike path that is 225 *miles* long, rounded to the nearest *mile*. If the trip took him 5 *hours*, rounded to the nearest hour, then which of the following can be his average speeds?

[A] 37

[B] 39

[C] 40

[D] 41

[E] 43

[F] 44

[G] 48

[H] 50

[I] 51

[J] 52

10. In a regular polygon with n sides, the ratio of each interior angle to each exterior angle is 3:2, the polygon is

(A) Square

(B) Pentagon

(C) Hexagon

(D) Heptagon

(E) Octagon

11. $\left(3+\sqrt{2}\right)\times\sqrt{11-3\sqrt{8}}=?$

(A) $9+\sqrt{2}-3\sqrt{8}$

(B) 7

(C) $4+6\sqrt{2}$

(D) 13

(E) $3\sqrt{11}-12$

12.

*a* is 28% of 200

15 is *b* percent of 90

| **Quantity A** | **Quantity B** |
|---|---|
| *a* | *b* |

(A) Quantity A is greater.

(B) Quantity B is greater.

(C) The two quantities are equal.

(D) The relationship cannot be determined from the information given.

13.

| **Quantity A** | **Quantity B** |
|---|---|
| Circumference of circle with radius $2r$ | Perimeter of square with side $\pi r$ |

(A) Quantity A is greater.

(B) Quantity B is greater.

(C) The two quantities are equal.

(D) The relationship cannot be determined from the information given.

14.

| Quantity A | Quantity B |
|---|---|
| 42% of 165 | The number that 80 is 20% of |

(A) Quantity A is greater.

(B) Quantity B is greater.

(C) The two quantities are equal.

(D) The relationship cannot be determined from the information given.

15. There are two boxes X and Y. Box X contains orange, white, and black balls in the ratio 2:6:11. Box Y contains orange and white balls in the ratio of 1:4. Together the boxes contain 80 white balls. How many orange balls could be in box X?

[A] 2

[B] 3

[C] 4

[D] 6

[E] 8

[F] 10

[G] 12

[H] 14

16. Alex took out a personal loan that charged 5% simple interest over 36 months. He repaid the $1,000 principal and the interest. What percent of his repayment was just interest, rounded to the nearest whole percent?

(A) 5%

(B) 10%

(C) 13%

(D) 14%

(E) 12%

17. There are 400 oranges in a bag. The average weight of these 400 oranges is 120 grams. The weights follow a normal distribution. If the standard deviation of the weights is 30 grams, how many of the oranges weigh at least 90 grams?

(A) 304

(B) 320

(C) 336

(D) 352

(E) 356

18. 36% of the total number of students in Nowhere Town go to Albert School. Bellevue School has 55% of the number of students at Albert School, while Cloudy Lane School's number of students represents 15% of Bellevue's. What is Dean School's number of students as a percentage of Nowhere Town's total students, if it can be calculated as the number of students attending Cloudy Lane School plus 35% of Bellevue School's students.

(A) 5%

(B) 7.5%

(C) 9%

(D) 9.9%

(E) 12%

19. Albert can do a job in 20 hours. Albert teams up with Benjamin and they complete the job together. Albert receives more than 60% of the wages that is fixed for the job. Which of the following could be the number of hours that Benjamin could take to complete this job on his own? (Wages refers to total payment on a hourly basis)

Indicate all such answers.

[A] 35

[B] 34

[C] 33

[D] 32

[E] 31

[F] 30

[G] 29

20. A company produces widgets at a cost of $2 labor, $5.50 materials and $1.25 overhead per widget. The company sells them to distributors with a 25% markup, unless the distributor purchases over 10,000 widgets, in which case any amount over 10,000 is marked up only 20%. The company just received an order of 14,000 widgets, and the manager would like to offer a coupon to the distributor. Also, it was recently discovered that 9,000 of the widgets incurred a labor cost of $2.50, not the $2 originally planned. What is the maximum coupon value that can be issued if the manager would like to keep the average markup at 20%?

Make sure that the widgets with the lower cost receive the higher markup.

[ ]

# Answers Key

## Section 2

1. halcyon
2. attenuated
3. capricious and disillusioned
4. A and B
5. E
6. D
7. C
8. A
9. “It is obvious, then, that the simple fact of memory is well established, and that we may turn at once to an examination of the facts revealed by special memory and re– learning experiments.
10. institutionalized and entrenched
11. redolent and dulcet
12. prominence and denigrated
13. cosmopolitan and didactic
14. circuitous and prevalence
15. C
16. innocence and inexperience
17. objective and impartial
18. "If the struggle for survival was the way of the world, then it was only natural that human society should operate in the same way."
19. A and C
20. C

## Section 3

1. 1000 workers
2. B
3. B
4. A
5. C
6. C
7. C
8. B, C, D, G and I
9. B
10. E
11. D
12. C
13. 163°
14. C
15. A
16. A
17. A
18. D
19. B
20. B

## Section 4

1. confluence
2. laudation
3. E
4. vapid and insipid
5. vetted and assessed
6. D
7. C
8. A and C
9. *This is but a casual illustrative suggestion, for what right have I, Allan Quatermain, out of my little reading and probably erroneous deductions, to form any judgment as to the theories of the old Egyptians?"*
10. resistance and friction
11. translucent and semi opaque
12. diversifying and fluidity
13. an integral and extant
14. E
15. A
16. C
17. B and C
18. unadulterated and homogeneous
19. calibrated and aligned
20. D

## Section 5

1. D
2. C
3. 10
4. A
5. A
6. D
7. E
8. C
9. D, E, F, G and H
10. B
11. B
12. A
13. C
14. B
15. A, C, D, E, F and G
16. A
17. C
18. D
19. A, B, C, D and E
20. $4,500

# Explanations

## Section 1 – Analytical Writing

### Task 1 – Analyze an Issue

**The sample essay that follows was written in response to the prompt that appeared in the question.**

Some people are born risk takers. Psychologists will tell you that it is component of one's personality, and those who take risks sometimes exhibit negative behavior while others take risks that ultimately benefit themselves and others. The names of risk takers can be found in various halls of fame as well as on Wanted Posters. Famous risk takers range from the infamous like Al Capone and Bernie Maidoff to the innovators like Bill Gates, Mark Zuckerberg, and Frank Lloyd Wright. Even though these and others knew the possible consequences of their actions, they were not deterred from reaching their goals. Those who do not take risks will not suffer the possible negative consequences, but neither will they experience the rewards.

Where would we be without those who took great risks with general disregard for the consequences? Marie and Pierre Curie literally risked their lives to experiment with radioactivity. The medical progress that resulted from their work not only earned the Curies the Noble Prize but made possible early treatment of some cancers. Other scientists followed in their footsteps, and the benefits to mankind have been enormous. Other medical pioneers include Jonas Salk who saved countless children from death or paralysis when he tested his new polio vaccine on himself, his wife and his own children. Risking his and his family's lives led to mass administration of the vaccine to school children all over America, and virtually made the iron lung obsolete.

Early explorers risked traveling to areas marked on maps with the foreboding phrase, "Here there be dragons", and expanded the known world. In efforts to find a shorter route to India, sailors like Christopher Columbus set off with his crew in three small boats and bumped into the Western Hemisphere. Charles Lindbergh flew solo across the Atlantic in a small plane in hopes of reaching the European continent. Since that time, man has used flight to reach the moon and establish space stations. If these adventurers had spent too much time thinking about the consequences, they may very well have just stayed home.

In the later years of the twentieth century pioneers in technology arose. Bill Gates, founder of Microsoft and one of the richest men in the world, dropped out of prestigious Harvard University to pursue computing. Steve Jobs, the brains behind Apple computers, also dropped out of college. These men defied the popular wisdom that one needs a college education to get anywhere in this world and created a universe of communication on a level never before seen.

Great political leaders have taken great risks for the sake of reform or revolution. Martin Luther King, Jr and Mohandas Gandhi (after whom King modeled his protests), risked everything and, ultimately, lost their lives for the sake of equality and independence. Both men certainly considered the consequences of their actions, but deemed that the potential rewards made the risks acceptable. All minorities and repressed populations in the United States lead lives of greater opportunity thanks to the leadership of Martin Luther King, Jr, and India exists as an independent country as a result of Gandhi's actions.

Just as there are consequences for taking risks, there are consequences for failing to take risks. Those who fear the unknown are doomed to live meager lives. It may be trite but nonetheless true to say that if you do what you've always done, you'll get what you've always had.

## Task 2 – Analyze an Argument

**The sample essay that follows was written in response to the prompt that appeared in the question.**

The station manager has assumed that a decline in listener numbers should lead to a change in format at WWAC. This is an executive decision based on lack of concrete evidence. He or she must find out why listeners are abandoning the station before making any drastic changes that could further alienate listeners.

The station manager contradicts the impact of the population growth in the area. On one hand, he implies that population growth should create more listeners, but, on the other hand, intimates that, because most of the new residents are retirees, he doesn't expect them to become fans of the current format anyway. Despite that, he wants to make listeners of them and feels that changing the format will do the trick. This could very well alienate the station's faithful listeners.

This manager associates the low sales of recorded music with a decline in his station's listeners. He further assumes that people have a limited interest in music overall. The popularity of MP3 players contradicts this assumption. One only has to walk down the halls of any high school or the streets of any city to observe this phenomenon. People are going about their daily routines with wires trailing from earbuds that keep them tuned in. The online music store, iTunes, is doing a brisk business, and one can preview and buy music from the comfort of home. Satellite radio has cornered a portion of the listeners, as well. New cars come equipped with satellite receivers, and satellite dishes attached to homes in every neighborhood bring every genre of music imaginable into homes across the country. Those satellite connections and cable television may deliver a number of stations devoted to news and talk shows.

Local brick–and–mortar radio stations face many challenges. They, indeed, may have to make some format adjustments, not only to attract new listeners, but to keep the ones that they have. This manager should discover the demographic of the area. Does one particular culture dominate? Does a large portion of the population speak Spanish or French? Are there a number of devotees of opera or classical music? It could be that the station doesn't offer enough variety. Switching to a talk format would still make WWAC a one–note station. If the manager is basing his decision on the popularity of talk shows already being broadcast in the area, is he moving into a market that is already saturated? It certainly won't make WWAC stand out among its competitors.

WWAC's manager may need to revisit what has worked for the station in the past. When were its listener numbers the greatest? What was the station doing at that time? Was it running a promotion? Were listeners able to call in and make requests for special songs? When did listener numbers begin to decline? Has the decline been gradual or sudden? Are other stations experiencing the same phenomenon?

At the very least, the station manager should conduct a survey of resident's in the station's broadcast range to find out their ages, interests, and tastes in music. If he tunes his listeners out, they won't tune in to WWAC.

# Section 2 – Verbal Reasoning

1. **halcyon**

This passage says that music industry executives are moving forward into an unsure time, while looking back at the days of "massive album sales." These must have been good days for them. "Disconcerting" means "worrying." The executives would not be disconcerted by massive album sales, so this answer is wrong. "Intractable" means "stubborn." If the old days were stubborn then they would not have been replaced by the new ones. "Maddening" means "infuriating." Executives would not consider the days of massive album sales to be "infuriating."

"Recalcitrant" means "disobedient." Executives would not consider the days of massive album sales to be "disobedient." "Halcyon" means "untroubled." The executives would consider the days of massive album sales to be "untroubled."

2. **attenuated**

This passage is saying that whenever economists claim to have "mastered" the business cycle stocks inevitably collapse. The collapse of the stocks is clearly weakening the claims of the economists. "Elevated" means "raised up." The collapse of stock prices would weaken the claims of economist, not raise them up. "Reinforced" means "supported." Again, falling stock prices do not support the claim of business cycle mastery. "Garnished" means "decorated." The falling of stock market prices would not decorate or dress up bold claims by economists. It would reveal them to have been false. "Subsumed" means "included." The falling of stock prices wouldn't "include" the claims of economists. It would run contrary to them. "Attenuated" means "weakened." Bold claims of having conquered the business cycle would certainly be weakened by having the price of stocks collapse.

3. **capricious and disillusioned**

The first blank is easier to solve after subsequent sentences have been read. The paragraph explains that paleontology has a hit-or-miss nature. "Intractable" means stubborn. The unknown quality of paleontology is described as being exciting as well as frustrating, and stubbornness would not excite. "Pensive" means thoughtful. This would be considered a possible answer if the subsequent paragraph had not been read. But the rest of the passage mentions the hit–or–miss nature of paleontology, so "pensive" doesn't work. "Capricious" means "given to sudden changes." Based on what we learn about paleontology from the passage, this word fits.

The second blank expresses how paleontologists feel when they learn that something was discovered by accident after they failed to discover it on purpose. "Rapt" means engrossed, but they would not be engrossed in the news of their own failure. "Debilitated" means "weak and infirm." They might be tired out, but they would not necessarily be ill. The remaining word, "disillusioned," means "rendered cynical," so it describes their mood perfectly.

4. **The correct answers are (A) and (B).**

a) The article says that Inn facilities were hastily provided, meaning little forethought or effort went into the provisions for the actors.

b) A regular facility would allow for a box office area rather than having to trust the audience to pay a fair amount through hat collection.

Incorrect responses

a) This is just one of the two correct answers. Both must be selected to be the best response.

b) Actors preferred an indoor location rather than outdoors because money was often missing from the hats that actors set out for people's admission fee.– This is just one of the two correct answers. Both must be selected to be the best response.

c) While this is likely to have been the case, the passage does not say anything about weather interruptions.

5. **The correct answer is (E).**

e) The passage describes playhouses, the difficulties of finding a suitable place, and their increased popularity. As the last sentence tells, as their popularity increased, the need for changes of venue became more evident.

Incorrect responses:

a) Little was said about Shakespeare in this passage.

b) While this is a true statement, it is not the best statement. The courtyard was not the main focus of the passage.

c) Drama could have been highly esteemed then, but that is not what this passage was trying to convey. The focus was on drama facilities.

d) The passage only mentioned wealthy people about one time, not many times.

6. **The correct answer is (D).**

"D" is the correct answer as it is the only one that cannot be supported by the passage. Though cerebral memories are briefly mentioned in the passage, the author only discusses these types of memories as distinct from the types that he discusses at length.

This answer makes a claim about these types of memories beyond what the passage discusses, as the author instead focuses on physical, not psychological, memories.

"A" and "B" both state that physical memories are easier to track and identify than those pertaining to the mind. This idea is supported by the statement in the passage that says "it is not possible to establish with certainty the existence of memory in the introspective psychological sense". In this way, the author explains that psychological memories cannot be clearly defined, and he goes on to say that "it is possible to measure the efficiency of the training to which the animal is subjected" which in this case has to do with physical training.

"C" explains that associating a punishment, or negative experience, with a certain action will affect future choices based on that experience, which is why the author explains that "had the shock been given as punishment for a wrong choice" the results of the study would have been skewed because the mouse's decision would have been based on more sensory memories than training alone.

"E" is true as it summarizes the objective of the author's studies: to track the effectiveness of physical training by finding out how long the memories of that training will last.

7. **The correct answer is (C).**

"C" is the best answer choice because the author's interaction with the mice is presented as purely professional; he studies them to further his knowledge, and does not express any emotional involvement as "B" would suggest. "A" incorrectly suggests that the author attempts to criticise the behavior of the mice, implying a desire to critique their behavior in order to improve it, whereas he is simply an observer of their actions. "D" is irrelevant, and "E" suggests a disproportionate amount of detachment.

8. **The correct answer is (A).**

"A" is correct in identifying the way in which a punishment for entering the wrong box would have skewed the results of this study; in order to accurately test memory, the mice had to make their decisions based on unbiased past experiences.

"B" is incorrect because though the climbing of a ladder is mentioned as part of the experiment, it is not, in fact, an 'integral' part of the study; the author states that "the climbing of a wire ladder is of very uncertain value".

"C" is incorrect in stating that training is as effective as the person who undergoes the training, yet the passage makes a general statement that "the effects of training gradually disappear" without determining whether individual results vary.

"D" incorrectly identifies mental tasks as part of memory; in this passage, however, the author directly defines 'memory' as the ability of the dancer to retain the power of adaptive action" without mentioning the ability to retain mental power of any kind.

"E" incorrectly discusses 'conscious effort'; the passage does not determine a discrepancy between conscious and subconscious efforts and thus does not textually support this claim.

9. **"It is obvious, then, that the simple fact of memory is well established, and that we may turn at once to an examination of the facts revealed by special memory and re- learning experiments."**

The author establishes in this sentence that, having defined 'memory', he will be moving on to take a closer look at the implications of memory in the results of his studies.

### 10. institutionalized and entrenched

This sentence is saying that something about the prison system, something on a fundamental level, causes black defendants to receive harsher charges than they deserve. "Laissez-faire" means lax or hands off. This is obviously a decidedly hands on type of racism, therefore that answer makes no sense. "Infrequent" means not happening often.

Obviously, if this issue has caused reformers to take up arms then it must be happening frequently. "Accidental" means unplanned. Again, it is unlikely that these reformers would focus on a few cases of "accidental" racism. "Progressive" means enlightened or open-minded. Progressive racism is therefore a contradiction and makes no sense. This leaves "Institutionalized" and "Entrenched." Both of these words mean happening on a fundamental level. And that's exactly what must be bothering the reformers. They are concerned that the racism of the penal system is dug firmly into it, to the point where it happens every day with no eyebrows being raised. b and e are the correct answers.

### 11. redolent and dulcet

The poems describe the nature of love using language that is "evocative," meaning they remind the reader of past experiences, and "mellifluous," which refers to something sweet, honeyed, or melodic. The correct answers therefore must reflect that the poems bring back sweet memories. Choice B, desultory, meaning without direction in life, random, or unmethodical and Choice E, restive, meaning impatient or on edge, do not fit the context. Choice A, odoriferous, refers to having of giving off a smell, especially an unpleasant or distinctive one, and Choice D, fecund, refers to being highly fruitful or productive, The poems do not have an actual smell and they do not produce anything, eliminating those answers. The correct answers are Choice C, redolent, which means serving to bring something, often memories, forth to mind, and Choice F, nostalgic, which means evocative of pleasant feelings for the past.

### 12. prominence and denigrated

The passage clearly indicates a sudden increase in stature for those who work in the field of hydrology. With this information we can complete the first blank. "Ignominy" means "humiliation." There is nothing in the passage to insinuate that hydrologists are experiencing humiliation because of their rise to prominence. "Extravagance" means "luxury," or "indulgence." While the passage notes a rise in popularity of the hydrologists, it does not claim they are suddenly leading luxurious lives. We are left with "Prominence." This fits with what we've learned in the passage. The hydrologists are being sought out by various countries for counsel. That is a definite rise in prominence.

The second blank is contained in a sentence that says countries have begun searching for hydrologists. This is contrasted with their attitude towards hydrologists prior to dwindling water supplies. Therefore, we can infer that these countries were not kind to hydrologists before. "Recalculated" means analyzed again. This answer does not make sense in the context of the sentence. "Co-opted" means to absorb or assimilate. This answer does not make sense, either.

Co-opting a notion would mean that you believe in it. But the tone of the passage doesn't indicate that countries were coming around to the idea of water monitoring before water supplies started drying up. "Denigrated" means "degraded." It makes sense in the context of the passage. It can be inferred that before the drying up of water supplies and rising of populations, the work of hydrologists was often degraded.

### 13. cosmopolitan and didactic

This passage is stating that a young man has come from a simple home to another location, one he finds "almost overwhelming." "Bucolic" means "rustic." This is the type of environment that the student just left. He would not find it new or overwhelming. "Archaic" means "old." His environment is described as being new, so it can't also be old. "Cosmopolitan" means "diverse." A simple person from the country would find a "diverse" environment to be "almost overwhelming."

For the second blank, the young man considers that he will have opportunities that will extend beyond the classroom. These can be inferred to be learning opportunities, since they are mentioned in the context of a classroom. "Irksome" means "annoying." The boy in the passage seems very interested in college, so he would not be describing it as "annoying." "Grievous" means "grave." The young man seems to be looking forward to these opportunities, so he would not consider them to be "grave." "Didactic" means "educational." Being in a new environment, the young man would consider himself to have just as many opportunities to learn outside of the classroom as inside of it.

14. **circuitous and prevalence**

The first blank is in a sentence that says how all food comes from plants. The sentence says that, regardless of a certain quality of the route the food takes, it still can be traced to plants. So we want a word that describes a convoluted route. "Malevolent" means "wicked." Obviously, the route cannot have personality traits, so this answer makes no sense. "Fulminated" means "raged." This answer does not make sense in the context of the question. We are left with "circuitous." This word means "indirect." This is the exact quality of a route that would make it difficult to trace. For the second blank, we want a word that stresses how plants provide food for all animals. "Dilution" means "weakening." The passage does not imply that the widespread appearance of plants "weakens" them in any way. "Mirth" means "happiness." This answer does not make sense in the context of the question. "Prevalence means "commonness." The fact that plants provide food for all animals would indeed make them very prevalent in the food chain.

15. **The correct answer is (C).**

c) The response of the new parent in this passage is one of generalization. He is thinking on the terms that everyone has a caring parent who responds to their child in the same way he is responding to the sight of his baby in the crib. He is enjoying this special moment. Unfortunately, not all children have parents, let alone parents who are thrilled to have children.

Incorrect responses

a) This statement is true, but not the main subject of this passage. It is not the main assumption behind the conclusion.

b) This is an attractive choice, and points to the assumption, but is not the main assumption. Whether parents like to watch their children in the crib is just a piece of the main idea.

d) This is an assumption that could be made in reading the passage, however, does not affect the validity of the conclusion.

e) This might be a true statement, but not the main focus of the passage. Like answer b, this is a sideline factor.

16. **innocence and inexperience**

This sentence is saying that people often find comfort in a certain aspect of primitive art, one that separates it from modern art. If modern art is described as being "dense" and "intellectual," we want terms that express an opposite sentiment. "Precision" means accuracy. The "thematic constructions" of modern art clearly imply tremendous planning going in. Therefore "Precision" does not separate ancient art from modern art. "Professionalism" means expertise. Again, this is a characteristic of modern art and not ancient art. We know this because modern art is described as being highly professional and ancient art is described as being an escape from it. Therefore, ancient art must not be as professional. "Imperviousness" means unyieldingness. While primitive art might be impervious (and if it has survived to the present day it's a good bet it is) but there is nothing about the description given to modern art that implies it is not impervious. Therefore, "Imperviousness" is not a good answer. "Effervescence" means vivacity. Like "Imperviousness," there is nothing specifically given in the description of modern art that would imply it cannot be effervescent even in its intellectualism. So we are left with "Innocence" and "Inexperience." These two terms both express a purity and naivete. The concept of intellectual innocence would contrast perfectly with the "dense" intellectualism of modern art and explain why people find refuge from it in ancient art.

The correct answers are a and b.

17. **objective and impartial**

This sentence is trying to say that, in spite of the speaker's best efforts, the audience will only hear what they want to hear. Therefore, we want words that establish the speaker's attempts to speak non-subjectively. "Fungible" means interchangeable. If the speaker is trying to make himself as clear and concise as possible then he would not be using "interchangeable" language. That would open his words to reinterpretation, which he would not like.

"Optional" means voluntary. This is also a bad choice. If the speaker doesn't want his words to be twisted into new meanings then he will not use “optional” language. “Subjective” mean personal, or debatable. This sentiment is the exact opposite of what we’re trying to say. The speaker is trying hard not to be subjective. He doesn’t want his words open for interpretation. “Figurative” means symbolic. Once again, this is a very poor choice. Figurative language is open to interpretation, which, once again, is not what the speaker wants. This leaves “Objective” and “Impartial.” Both of these answers mean neutral and unbiased. This is the exact sentiment we want to describe the speaker, because it shows him trying to speak in a way that cannot be deliberately misunderstood. Therefore, answers c and f are correct.

18. **"If the struggle for survival was the way of the world, then it was only natural that human society should operate in the same way."**

This sentence is an example of conditional logic. Social Darwinists assumed that if this condition exists in the animal world, then it must also exist in the human world.

19. **The correct answers are (A) and (C).**

The passage defines “predator ethic” as when a strong group or individual takes advantage of weaker ones. Choice A is correct because bullies adopt the role of predator when they select those who are weak in some way as targets of rumors or harmful insults. Choice C is also correct because it involves using power to target innocent people based on something they cannot control. Choice B is incorrect because involuntary commitment could be the result of a court proceeding that relies on expert testimony and is not necessarily a predatory action.

20. **The correct answer is (C).**

A dovetail is a type of joint used in carpentry to make pieces of wood fit together smoothly. Social Darwinism fit well with segregationists ideas that white people were superior to black people and so had the right to repress them. Coincided implies that the two ideas occurred at the same time rather than one idea's being used to justify the other. Deviated would imply that segregationists did not agree with the idea of social Darwinism. D is a definition used in heraldry, and the definition in E suggests disagreement.

# Section 3 – Quantitative Reasoning

1. **The correct answer is 1000 workers**

Let number of officers be $x$, then salary of officers = 1,510$x$

Workers will be $x + 800$, total salary of workers = $850(x + 800) = 850x + 680{,}000$

Total number of workers will be $2x + 800$, Total salary will be = $(2x + 800) \times 960 = 1920x + 768{,}000$

So, $1{,}510x + 850x + 680{,}000 = 1920x + 768{,}000$

$x = 200$

So number of workers will be 1000.

2. **The correct answer is (B).**

The area of triangle = $\frac{1}{2} \times base \times height$. In a right triangle, the legs are the base and the height. Quantity A equals twice the area of $\Delta PQR$: $2 \times (\frac{1}{2} \times x \times y) = xy$.

Quantity B equals the area of $\Delta RST$: $\frac{1}{2} \times 2x \times 2y = 2xy$. So Quantity B is greater than Quantity A.

$\Delta PQR$ and $\Delta RST$ are similarly right triangles because each leg of $\Delta RST$ is twice the length of a corresponding leg in $\Delta PQR$. However; this does not mean that the area of $\Delta RST$ is twice that of $\Delta PQR$. The ratio of the areas of two similar figures is the ratio of their lengths squared. In the case, the area of $\Delta RST$ is 4 times that of $\Delta PQR$.

3. **The correct answer is (B).**

What is the sum of the interior angles of a pentagon? Drawing two diagonals from a single vertex, we can divide a pentagon into three triangles.

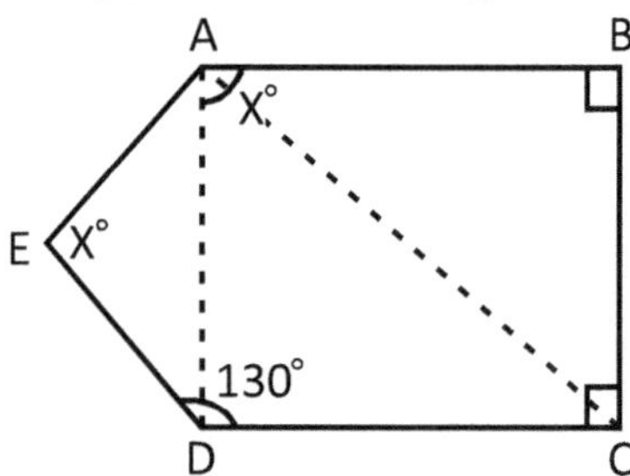


The sum of the interior angles must be three times the sum for each triangle: $3 \times 180° = 540°$

Therefore, the two angles with measure $x$ degrees, the two right angles, and the 130° angle must sum to 540°. Now we can set up an equation to solve for $x$:

$x + x + 90 + 90 + 130 = 540$

$2x + 310 = 540$

$2x = 230$

$x = 115$

4. **The correct answer is (A).**

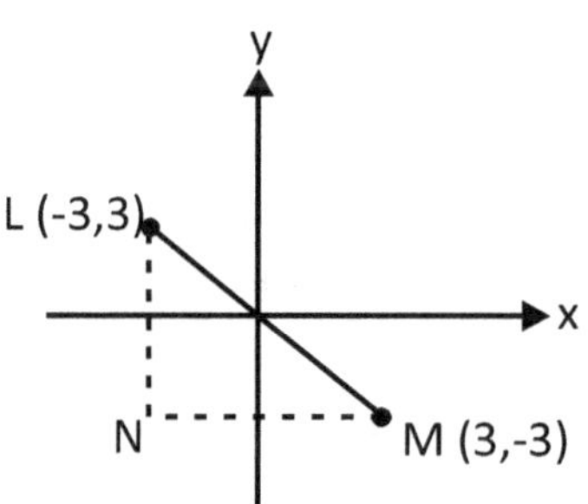


To find the area of a circle with diameter LM, we need to find the length of LM, so start by drawing in line segment LM. We can find the length of LM by treating it as the hypotenuse of a right triangle. Draw a line down from point L parallel to the y–axis and draw a line from point M parallel to the x–axis. The point where they meet –let's call it N– has coordinates (–3, –3). The length of LN = 3 – (3)= 6; the length of MN = 3 – (–3) = 6. So LMN is an isosceles right triangle, and the hypotenuse LM must equal $6\sqrt{2}$. If LM is the diameter of a circle, its radius is $3\sqrt{2}$, and its area is $\pi r^2 = \pi\left(3\sqrt{2}\right)^2 = 18\pi$, which is greater than $9\pi$ in Quantity B.

5. **The correct answer is (C).**

Use the Pythagorean Theorem.

$2^2 + YZ^2 = (2\sqrt{2})^2$

$4 + YZ^2 = 8$

$YZ^2 = 4$

$YZ = 2$

*Since XY = YZ, by the property of isosceles triangle, α° = b°.*

6. **The correct answer is (C).**

According to the standard deviation bell curve:

50% of the students are less than 5 *feet* and 6 *inches* tall (the mean) and 50% of the students are taller than 5 *feet* and 6 *inches*

Also, 34% of the students' heights should be within 1 standard deviation below the mean

34% of the students are within 5 *feet* and 4 *inches* and 5 *feet* and 6 *inches* tall

At 5 feet and 4 *inches* tall, Bill is shorter than 50% + 34% = 84% of the students

Bill is taller than 16% of the students at Mark Twain School

7. **The correct answer is (C).**

Let Charles works for $x$ hours in that shift.

For the first eight hours rate = \$20 per hour

For the next hours, rate = \$30 per hour

For the remaining hours, rate = \$40 per hour

Total earning = \$340

Hence we get

$$\text{Total earnings} = 8 \times 20 + 2 \times 30 + (x - 10) \times 40$$
$$= 160 + 60 + 40x - 400$$
$$= 40x - 180$$

By data, $40x - 180 = 340$

$$40x = 520$$

$$x = \frac{520}{40} = 13 \text{ hours}$$

8. **The correct answers are (B), (C), (D), (G) and (I).**

First solve any inequalities that need to be solved. In this example only the last inequality needs to be solved.

$x+5 < 19$ or $x < 14$

Second, simplify the inequalities so that all the inequality symbols point in the same direction, preferably to the left (less than)

$8 < x$; $x < 17$; $x < 14$

Third, line up the common variables in the inequalities.

$8 < x$; $x < 17$; $x < 14$

Finally, combine the inequalities by taking the more limiting upper and lower extremes $8 < x < 14$. So, the possible values of $x$ are 9, 10, 11, 12 and 13.

9. **The correct answer is (B).**

Increase of the population of B from phase 3 to phase 4:

$9 \times 10^{10} - 900 \times 10^{7} = 9 \times 10^{9} \times (10 - 1) = 9 \times 9 \times 10^{9}$
$= 81 \times 10^{9}$

10. **The correct answer is (E).**

The increase occurred in phase 1, which lasted through all the following phases. Even in phase 4, which was five hours no increase occurred in the population. The other two factors, temperature and food supply do not show any effective pattern in its reproduction.

11. **The correct answer is (D).**

Revenue generated per customer is given as Revenue/Number of customers

Revenue generated per customer at Princeton Street = \$31,144/458 = \$68

Revenue generated per customer at St Agnes Road = \$58,320/720 = \$81

Revenue generated per customer at Hayat Street = \$34,336/592 = \$58

Average of all three = (\$68 + \$81 + \$58)/3 = \$69

12. **The correct answer is (C).**

Number of female contestants = 200 – 80 = 120

Number of male contestants arriving late = 1/5 of 80 = 16

Number of female contestants arriving late = 1/6 of 120 = 20

Total number of contestants arriving late = 16 + 20 = 36

Probability that the prize will be won by a contestant who arrived late

= Number of people arriving late/Total number of contestants

= 36/200 that simplifies to 9/50

13. **The correct answer is 163°**

Supplementary angles are angles that sum to 180 degrees.

Supplementary angle of 17° is 163°

14. **The correct answer is (C).**

$(3a + 4) + (2a + 6) + (4a - 1) = 27$

$9a + 9 = 27$

$9a = 18;\ a = 2$

15. **The correct answer is (A).**

To find the sum of the interior angles of a convex pentagon, use the formula $180 \times (n - 2)$, where $n$ is the number of sides. Therefore, $180 \times (5 - 2) = 180 \times 3 = 540°$

$540° > 500°$

Another method would be to draw the pentagon and break it into triangles connecting verticals (lines cannot cross), as shown here.

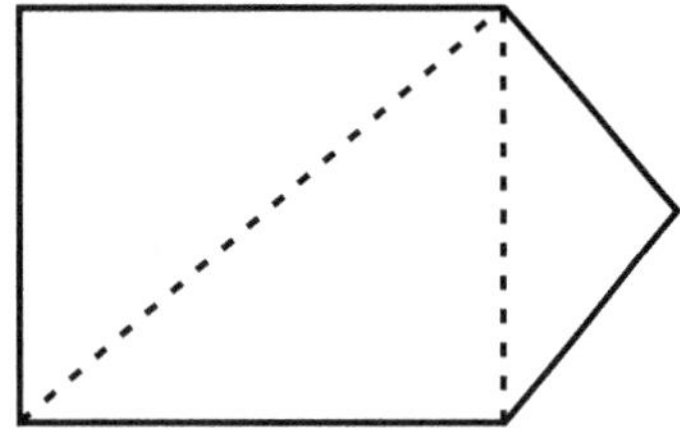

Multiplying the number of triangles (3) by 180° (degrees in a triangle) gives the same result, 540°.

16. **The correct answer is (A).**

If $(h, k)$ is the center and $r$ is the radius of the circle then the equation of the circle is

$(x - h)^2 + (y - k)^2 = r^2$.

Hence the equation of the circle is

$(x - 5)^2 + (y - 4)^2 = r^2$

Since the circle passes through (5,14) it will satisfy the equation.

Hence

$(5 - 5)^2 + (14 - 4)^2 = r^2$

$0 + 10^2 = r^2$

*hence* $100 = r^2$

Hence the equation is

$(x - 5)^2 + (y - 4)^2 = 100$

17. **The correct answer is (A).**

The continuous red line indicates the $\geq$ or $\leq$ sign. Eliminate B. C and E.

In A, substitute (0,0) .

Left-hand side =0

Right-hand side $= 9 \times 0 - 4 = -4$

$0 \geq -4$

It satisfies the inequality A.

In D, substitute (0,0)

Left-hand side = 0

Right hand side $= 9 \times 0 - 4 = -4$

0 is not less than −4

D is not satisfied by (0,0)

Therefore, the answer is Choice A.

18. **The correct answer is (D).**

Part of the tank filled by pipe A in 1 hour: $\frac{1}{8}$

Part of the tank filled by pipe B in 1 hour: $\frac{1}{6}$

Part of the tank filled by pipe C in 1 hour: $\frac{1}{c}$

Part of the tank filled by the three pipes together in 1 hour: $\frac{1}{2}$

$\frac{1}{8} + \frac{1}{6} + \frac{1}{c} = \frac{1}{2}$

Multiply entire equation by 48c

2(3c + 4c + 24) = 24c

6c+8c+48=24c

$c = \frac{24}{5}$

Time taken by pipe C on its own to fill the tank = $\frac{24}{5}$ hours or 4 hours and 48 minutes

Let C be turned off after $x$ hours. We know that:

Part of the tank filled by pipes A and C in $x$ hours + Part of the tank filled by pipe A in $(4 - x)$ hours = 1

$$x\left(\frac{1}{8}+\frac{5}{24}\right)+(4-x)\frac{1}{8}=1$$

$$\frac{x}{3}+\frac{(4-x)}{8}=1$$

$8x + 12 - 3x = 24$

$$x=\frac{12}{5}$$

Pipe C needs to be turned off after $\frac{12}{5}$ hours or 2 hours and 24 minutes

19. **The correct answer is (B).**

First finds the $x$ and $y$ intercepts of the line

$2x - 3y + 12 = 0.$

$x$ intercept: let $y = 0$, solve for x

$2x - 3(0) + 12 = 0$

$2x = -12; x = -6$

$y$ intercept: let $x = 0$, solve for $y$

$- 3y + 12 = 0, y = 4$

Area of the triangle equals $\frac{1}{2}$ (4)(6) =12

20. **The correct answer is (B).**

If you multiply both sides by 3, you find that $m^4 = 81$. Therefore, $m$ can equal 3 or –3. In either case, $m$ is less than 4.

Because $(-3)^4 = 81$ and $(3)^4 = 81$, both solutions work here.

# Section 4 – Verbal Reasoning

1. **confluence**

The passage is saying that smart phone companies need to increase the scope of the marketing strategies because the features available on modern smart phones combine to make the product more than just a phone. "Reticence" means "silence." Calling social media "silent" does not fit with the tone of the rest of the passage. "Intermittence" is the quality of stopping and restarting. Again, this does not fit with the tone of the passage. The passage focuses on how smart phone features come together, not how inconsistently they work. "Inarticulacy" means "incoherence." Again, the virtues, not the faults, of smart phone features are being listed here. "Obscurity" means "anonymity." Nothing about the passage implies that smart phone features are "anonymous." "Confluence" means "convergence." A convergence of smart phone features would make it "more than just a phone," and require companies to market the phone as such.

2. **laudation**

This sentence says that something bad (a malpractice suit) that has happened to a surgeon has undone years of something else. We can therefore infer that this "something else" must have been something good. "Censure" means "criticism." This is not something that would support a doctor's confidence. "Indictment" means "accusation." Once again, this is not something that would help a doctor's confidence. "Suppression" means "defeat." This is another thing that would hurt, not help, a doctor's confidence. "Ingenuity" means "inventiveness." There's no clear connection between inventiveness and confidence, therefore this is a flimsy answer. "Laudation" means "praise." This is what would help a surgeon's confidence, and cause it to be high before a malpractice lawsuit brought it down.

3. **The correct answer is (E).**

e) A trip to Disneyland would provide a lot of happy memories to provide pleasant feelings at a later date. The idea of happiness in the future as a result of special happy moments in the past is what this passage is all about. By calling the trip a "waste of money", that is a direct contrast with the main concept of the passage.

Incorrect responses

a) The question asks for a contrast to the concept, rather than one consistent with the concept. This statement is consistent rather than contrasting.

b) This is also consistent with the concept of the passage. Lack of happiness as a child has led to unhappiness now.

c) This statement is describing happiness in relation to material possessions rather than memories. That is slightly inconsistent, but mostly irrelevant to the main topic.

d) Being sad contrasts with happiness, but again, the discussion is not about materialism, it is about experiences and memories.

4. **vapid and insipid**

It seems like any words should be able to fit in, but look at the context clues. The people holding the conversation are described as being "otherwise learned and productive" yet still sitting around and "wast[ing] so much time." This means that the people holding the conversation must be doing something useless. Not offensive, not out-of-character – useless. "Unreserved" means frank or open. Being unreserved would not be inherently considered a waste of time (it depends on the topic) so this doesn't work. "Insightful" means perceptive. The speaker wouldn't be disappointed if the people being talked about were having an insightful conversation. "Sectarian" means religious. There's nothing inherent about religious that would make the speaker particularly happy or sad to see intelligent people talking about it. "Pretentious" means conceited or shallow. While this one works on its own there are no other words that go with it. Besides, this answer doesn't completely tie in with the "pointless" argument the speaker is making. This leaves "Vapid" and "Insipid." These two answers both mean uninspiring or pointless. It would make sense that somebody wouldn't want to see a group of people spending all day talking about pointless topics. Therefore, b and c are correct.

5. **vetted and assessed**

This sentence is saying that all actions undertaken at large banks have the potential to go awry. Moreover, because of the size of these "massive banking institutions" it can be inferred that these mistakes would carry large consequences. It can also therefore be inferred that these actions must be checked before being allowed to transpire. "Delineated' means described. This doesn't work because the bankers don't need their own actions described to them. They need them proofread. "Prioritized" means listed or arranged. Again, this doesn't shed any analysis on an action about to be taken. It is useless from an analysis standpoint. "Extemporized" means produced in an unprepared manner. This obviously makes no sense because the entire reason for having lawyers who check the material is to remain prepared. "Rewritten" means to rephrase in different writing. This is a flimsy answer because it doesn't say if any analysis has taken place before the rewriting. This leaves "Vetted" and "Assessed." These two words mean judged and calculated. This is what needs to be done to analyze any action taken at the corporate level. a and e are the correct answers.

6. **The correct answer is (D).**

"D" is the correct answer in identifying the main idea of the passage; though some of the other choices are correct, this one best represents the overall message that the author strives to impart in this text. The author repeatedly refers to the notion of personalities as having several different components and supports this claim with various sources.

"A" is in direct contrast to the idea of the passage, as it oversimplifies humans and refutes the idea that people are multi-dimensional by incorrectly calling them 'simple'.

"B" is only partially correct; the second part of this statement disagrees with the text in the passage, which states that Egyptians had ample time to reflect and theorize, whereas this choice states that they had little opportunity to do so.

"C", though correct and supported by the text, does not represent the main idea; though the author mentions that Egyptians were indeed wise, he makes only a small reference to that fact.

"E" is also correct, yet it does not uphold the main idea; this passage focuses on the nature of human personalities rather than attempting to dissect the differences between varying viewpoints on this subject.

7. **The correct answer is (C).**

"C" is the correct answer because it exemplifies the function of this sentence as a logical explanation for the author's message: that people consist of many personality components. By explaining that he has found many written works that support this notion, and that they "suffice to furnish [him] with the text that man is not one, but many", the author explains that he arrived at his conclusion based on written evidence.

"A" and "D" both incorrectly state that this sentence is more explanatory than it is; though this sentence does in fact demonstrate that the author has found textual support for his stance, it does not explicitly shed light on how this evidence upholds that opinion or provide more detail about the author's main idea.

"B" is incorrect because this sentence restates the author's opinion rather than providing an alternate explanation.

"E" is also incorrect in suggesting that this sentence presents a differing viewpoint, as the main idea of this sentence is in line with the author's findings.

8. **The correct answers are (A) and (C).**

"A" and "C" are both correct; the author approaches this subject matter with a curious, inquisitive outlook, as 'speculative' suggests. He also refers to his own lack of definitive knowledge and admits that he is not an authority on this matter, thus supporting 'dubious' as an option and refuting "B", authoritative. He does not claim certainty but rather expresses personal musings based on what he has read.

9. ***"This is but a casual illustrative suggestion, for what right have I, Allan Quatermain, out of my little reading and probably erroneous deductions, to form any judgment as to the theories of the old Egyptians?"***

This sentence openly illustrates the author's inconclusive stance on this subject. He admits that his research is limited and that his comprehension of what he has read may very well be "erroneous." Though he strives to impart his understanding of human personalities, he says that his explanation is "casual" and that he thus holds little authority on the subject.

10. **resistance and friction**

B and E. Resistance and friction are the only two possible choices in this sentence because viscosity is the rubbing together of particles, in other words, resistance or friction, found in a liquid when it is in movement.

While viscosity is an attribute of a liquid, what is being described above is what happens when a liquid is viscous, for that reason this is not the correct answer. Conductivity refers to power and its conductive properties and does not make sense in the sentence. Lastly, altercation which means disagreement would not make any logical sense when completing the sentence; nor would agreement make any sense because an agreement is an understanding between individuals.

11. **translucent and semi opaque**

A and D. While crystalline and diaphanous are synonyms of translucent, they have different meanings. Crystalline means something that is clear or has crystal like formations and diaphanous means light and delicate. The text is about frosted glass which is not usually thin or delicate; nor does it tend to be sparkly or crystal clear like something that is crystalline. It is a type of glass that is opaque that one cannot see through. Undiluted is generally used with liquids and, obscured means blocked which would not make sense when completing the sentence.

12. **diversifying and fluidity**

This passage states that improvisational theater used to have strict rules, but there is more room to experiment now. "Conflating" means "combining." Improvisational actors would not be "combing" their approach in light of less strict rules. "Truncating" means "cutting." Again, improvisational actors have less strict rules now, so they would not need to cut their approach to theater. "Diversifying" means "expanding." This makes sense. In light of less strict rules, improvisational actors would feel comfortable expanding the approach they take to their craft.

For the second blank, the passage is still talking about how fluidity has allowed actors to try new things. "Perniciousness" means "malice." Malice would not cause improvisational actors to try new things. "Maleficence" means "the doing of evil or harm." Performing harmful acts would not cause improvisational actors to try new things, either. "Fluidity" means "variability." This makes sense. A feeling of variability would cause improvisational comedians to feel comfortable in attempting new styles of comedy.

13. **an integral and extant**

The passage says that music was used frequently in Greek life. "Invidious" means "unpleasant." Music would most likely not have been used frequently in Greek life if it was unpleasant. "Contested" means "disputed." Again, if music was disputed, it would most likely have not featured so prominently in Greek life. "Integral" means "essential." This answer makes sense. If music was used so heavily in Greek life, then it can be accurately described as "integral."

For the second blank, the passage says how music theory from antiquity is still around today. "Detested" means "hated." If the music theory of the Greeks was hated, it would not still be around today. "Bellicose" means "warlike." If Greek music theory were warlike, it would most likely not be heard in religious and classical music. "Extant" means "existing." This makes sense. If the music theory of the Greeks is still heard in modern times, then it still exists.

14. **The correct answer is (E).**

"E" is incorrect as it is the only statement that is not supported by the text; though the author does state that it is a good idea for actors to study the rules of their craft, the text does not support that these rules should be followed in every performance. Instead, the advice given in this passage is to learn the rules and then create methods that work best for each individual performer, whatever they may be.

All of the other statements are supported by the following quotes from the passage:

A: "It is necessary to be cautious in studying elocution and gesticulation, lest they become our masters instead of our servants. These necessary but dangerous ingredients must be administered and taken in homeopathic doses, or the patient may die by being over–stimulated."

B: "Dramatic instinct is so implanted in humanity that it sometimes misleads us, fostering the idea that because we have the natural talent within, we are equally endowed with the power of bringing it out."

C: "So with acting, no master–hand can prescribe rules for the head of another school."

D: "But they must work with their own tools; if they had to adopt each other's they would be as much confused as if compelled to exchange languages."

15. **The correct answer is (A).**

"A" is correct; by explaining how acting teachers can actively figure out what the student needs to learn (by first allowing the student to "exhibit his quality"), the author gives practical advice. Then, by explaining the contrasting idea of allowing the teacher to instruct the student without first figuring out what must be taught, the author explains that the result of doing so (rather than following the aforementioned advice) will be that the student's ability will be 'smothered'.

"B" is incorrect because the second sentence does not provide evidence as this answer states; it simply outlines a hypothetical situation which is based on the author's opinion rather than fact.

"C" is too vague; the first sentence is not simply outlining a method of acting preparation but instead is delving into a method of teaching, and the second sentence, though it does offer a sort of warning, presents a specific method that should be avoided rather than mentioning several alternate possibilities.

"D" is incorrect in its assertion that the second sentence provides further detail to support the first; though they are related, these two sentences present contrasting ideas, rather than a vague statement that is then supported by more information.

"E" is incorrect because neither of these sentences deals with the main idea of the passage, which is the question of whether or not an actor should become fully immersed in a character; rather, this answer focuses on methods of teaching, which is more specific than the main point of the passage.

16. **The correct answer is (C).**

"C" is correct in describing the author's most likely attitude towards the subject of teaching methods; by picking apart specific approaches and offering a better way, the author explains what he thinks is wrong with common approaches to teaching.

The passage does not imply a sense of superiority in the author's tone, thus "A" is incorrect in calling the author 'smug'.

There is also nothing in the passage to support that the author is 'compassionate', as there is no mention of understanding why teachers currently follow the methods that the author criticizes, thus "B" is incorrect.

"D" is incorrect because the author clearly states his opinion and therefore does not present this information in an 'impartial' way.

"E" assumes that the author changes his viewpoint on the subject which he approaches with such fervor, and there is nothing in the text to support that he may alter his opinion, thus 'fickle' is inaccurate.

17. **The correct answers are (B) and (C).**

"B" and "C" could both be possible professions for the author of this passage; it is possible that a retired actor who moved into teaching would have enough knowledge both on stage and in the classroom to write with such authority on this topic. Also, the writer of this passage touches upon other art forms which suggests interest in various types of arts and refers to 'personal experience' by explaining his personal preferences for acting preparatory work.

"A" is incorrect as it fails to mention the author's firsthand knowledge of acting. The passage offers advice from personal performing experience when the author expresses his personal viewpoint ("I know that I act best when…") whereas a journalist who simply interviews performers would not be likely to perform as well.

18. **unadulterated and homogeneous**

C and F. Because distillation is a process that removes impurities, we can assume that the missing word refers to something that is uniform in nature. We are also looking for two words that are adjectives, for that reason unadulterated and homogeneous are the correct answers. Homogeneity is a noun and cannot be used correctly in this sentence. Similitude means similar but not necessarily uniform in its nature and corrupted and impure are both opposites of the missing word.

19. **calibrated and aligned**

As scales are precise machines, their mechanisms or systems are put in their correct positions very carefully. The correct choices are B and D, "aligned" and "calibrated," which both refer to the correct placement and tuning of parts. The other choices do not fit the context of the sentence. "Fissured" refers to when something has been cracked and has a long and narrow opening, "conjectured" means speculated, "serialized" refers to arranging in a logical or numerical order, and "embroiled" means to put in disorder or cause confusion.

20. **The correct answer is (D).**

If Choice D were true, then the point that sudden increases of investment which did not yield the expected returns would be false and the central argument that it was this which led to the economic downturn would have to be false because it presents facts contrary to those in the passage.

Choice A is actually be an additional piece of related evidence demonstrating the growth of the economy prior to the great panic.

Since Choices B and D concern events following the great panic, they do not bear any influence on the causes of the great panic, which is the focus of this passage.

Choice E is not relevant to the central argument. Unemployment is an example of a result of the economic downturn, so even if unemployment had been an issue prior to the great panic, there is no reason it could not have gotten worse following the great panic.

# Section 5– Quantitative Reasoning

1. **The correct answer is (D).**

Direct proportionality is demonstrated by a linear function, shown in the graph. Direct proportions have an exponent of 1 for the variable, and the variable will always be in the numerator.

The relationship is direct proportionality, so the answer is D.

2. **The correct answer is (C).**

Total net salary = \$3600

The total percentage given is 100%

We can see $\frac{850}{3500}$ is approximately equal to 24%.

Hence only two items are more than 24%, namely, food and savings.

Hence option C is correct

3. **The correct answer is 10.**

$2^a \times 2^b = 1024$

$2^{a+b} = 2^{10}$

Now, we can set the exponents equal to each other because the bases are both 2.

$a + b = 10$

4. **The correct answer is (A).**

\$7.88 divide by 2 equals \$3.94.

\$11.79 divided by 3 equals \$3.93.

5. **The correct answer is (A).**

There are 360 degrees and 4 angles in all quadrilaterals and 360 ÷ 4 is 90. A triangle contains 180 degrees and 3 angles. For two triangles the average would be 360 ÷ 6, or 60.

6. **The correct answer is (D).**

Since we know nothing about the placement of A, B, and C, We cannot determine anything about their distances.

7. **The correct answer is (E).**

Given $3^{x+2} + 3^{x-1} = \left(\frac{28}{9}\right)$

$\Rightarrow 3^x\left(3^2 + 3^{-1}\right) = \left(\frac{28}{9}\right)$

$\Rightarrow 3^x\left(9 + \frac{1}{3}\right) = \left(\frac{28}{9}\right)$

$\Rightarrow 3^x\left(\frac{28}{3}\right) = \left(\frac{28}{9}\right) \Rightarrow 3^x\left(\frac{28}{3}\right) = \left(\frac{28}{3}\right)\left(\frac{1}{3}\right)$

Because $\frac{28}{3}$ appears on both sides of the equation, you can cancel it out.

$\Rightarrow 3^x = \frac{1}{3}$

$\Rightarrow 3^x = 3^{-1}$

$\Rightarrow x = -1$

8. **The correct answer is (C).**

For combined events, the formula is

$P(A \text{ or } B) = P(A) + P(B) - P(A \text{ and } B)$

Substituting the given values,

$\frac{3}{4} = \frac{1}{2} + P(N) - \frac{1}{6}$

$\frac{9}{12} = \frac{6}{12} + P(N) - \frac{2}{12}$

$\frac{9}{12} = \frac{4}{12} + P(N)$

$P(N) = \frac{5}{12}$

9. **The correct answers are (D), (E), (F), (G) and (H).**

If the cyclist rode 225 *miles*, rounded to the nearest mile, and took 5 *hours*, rounded to the nearest hour, he traveled between 224.5 *miles* and 225.4 *miles*, and took between 4.5 and 5.4 *hours*. The maximum speed can be obtained by dividing the largest possible number of *miles* (225.4) by the SMALLEST (4.5) number of *hours*. Similarly, the minimum speed can be obtained by dividing the smallest number of *mile* (224.5) by the LARGEST number of *hours* (5.4):

Maximum speed =

$$\frac{225.4}{4.5} = \frac{225.4(2)}{4.5(2)} = \frac{451}{9} = 50\frac{1}{9}mph$$

Minimum speed =

$$\frac{224.5}{5.4} = \frac{224.5(2)}{5.4(2)} = \frac{449}{11} = 40\frac{9}{11}mph$$

Therefore, the cyclist speed must be between 40 and 51 *mph*. So out of all the given options 41, 43, 44, 48 and 50 are valid.

10. **The correct answer is (B).**

We know that the sum of the interior angles of an n-sided polygon is given by $(n-2)\times180^\circ$

$\therefore$ Each interior angle $= \frac{\left[(n-2)\times180^\circ\right]}{n}$

Also, we know that the sum of the exterior angles of an n-sided polygon is given by $360^\circ$, Irrespective of n.

$\therefore$ Each exterior angle $= \frac{360^\circ}{n}$

$$\therefore \frac{\frac{\left[(n-2)\times180^\circ\right]}{n}}{\frac{360^\circ}{n}} = \frac{3}{2}$$

$$\therefore \left[(n-2)\times180^\circ\right]360^\circ = \frac{3}{2}$$

$$\therefore \frac{(n-2)}{2} = \frac{3}{2}$$

$$\therefore n-2=3$$

$$\therefore n=5$$

Hence the regular polygon is a pentagon.

11. **The correct answer is (B).**

$$\left(3+\sqrt{2}\right)\times\sqrt{11-3\sqrt{8}}$$

$$=\sqrt{\left(3+\sqrt{2}\right)^2}\times\sqrt{11-3\sqrt{8}}$$

$$=\sqrt{\left(9+6\sqrt{2}+2\right)}\times\sqrt{11-3\sqrt{8}}$$

$$=\sqrt{11+6\sqrt{2}}\times\sqrt{11-3\sqrt{8}}$$

$$=\sqrt{11+3\sqrt{8}}\times\sqrt{11-3\sqrt{8}}$$

Use FOIL method.

You then get $121+33\sqrt{(8)}-33\sqrt{(8)}-72$

$$=\sqrt{\left(11+3\sqrt{8}\right)\left(11-3\sqrt{8}\right)}$$

$$=\sqrt{11^2-\left(3\sqrt{8}\right)^2}=\sqrt{121-72}$$

$$=\sqrt{49}=7$$

12. **The correct answer is (A).**

*a* is 28% of 200:

$$a=\frac{28}{100}(200)=\frac{5600}{100}=56$$

15 is *b* percent of 90:

$$15=\frac{b}{100}(90)=b\frac{90}{100}$$

$$b=\frac{100}{90}(15)=16\frac{2}{3}$$

13. **The correct answer is (C).**

Circumference of a circle is C=2*pi*r, where r = radius of the circle. Perimeter of a square is P = 4*s, where s = the length of one side.

The circumference of a circle with radius $2r$ is $2\pi(2r)$ = $4\pi r$. The perimeter of a square with side $\pi$r is $4\pi r$, so Quantity A and B are equal.

14. **The correct answer is (B).**

42% of 165 × 0.42 = 69.3. The number which 80 is 20% is N × 0.20

= 80, or N = $\frac{80}{0.20}$ = 400. Thus, Quantity B is larger than Quantity A

15. **The correct answers are (A), (C), (D), (E), (F) and (G).**

**Box X**

The ratio of orange, white and blackballs = 2:6:11

Let the balls be $2x$, $6x$, and $11x$, where $x$ is a positive integer demonstrating the scaling of the proportion to get to the total amount for each type of ball.

**Box Y**

The ratio of orange and white balls = 1:4

Let the balls be $y$ and $4y$, where $y$ is a positive integer demonstrating the scaling of the proportion to get to the total amount for each type of ball, different from $x$.

According to the problem,

$6x + 4y = 80$ represents the total white balls.

i.e. $3x + 2y = 40$ represents the total orange balls.

Both $x$ and $y$ are integers

The different possibilities of $x$ and $y$ are given by

| $x$ | $y$ |
|---|---|
| 2 | 17 |
| 4 | 14 |
| 6 | 11 |
| 8 | 8 |
| 10 | 5 |
| 12 | 2 |

So the number of orange balls could be 4, 8, 12, 16, 20, 24

16. **The correct answer is (A).**

Simple interest is found using $I = PRT$, where $I$ is *interest*, $P$ is *principal*, $R$ is *rate*, and $T$ is *time in years*.

In this scenario: $150 = $1,000 × 5% × 3 years.

His total repayment is the principal plus the interest: $1,000 + $150 = $1,150. To find the percent of his repayment that is interest, divide the interest by the total repayment: 150 / 1,150 = 0.1304... Rounded to the nearest percent that is 13%.

17. **The correct answer is (C).**

The following is the curve of a normal distribution where m is the mean and d is the standard deviation.

34% of the observations lie between $m{-}d$ and $m$. Half ( 50%) of the values lie after mean $m$. Hence 84% of the observations lie after $m{-}d$

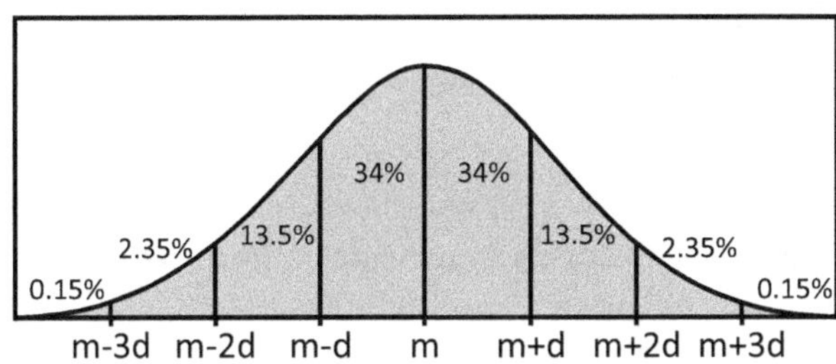


In the given problem, $m = 120$ and $d = 30$. Hence 84% of the oranges weigh at least 90 grams.

Therefore $400 \times 84\% = 400 \times \frac{84}{100} = 336$ oranges weigh at least 90 grams

18. **The correct answer is (D).**

Let $N$ = total number of students in Nowhere Town.

Number of students going to Albert School = 36% × $N$

Number of students going to Bellevue School = 55% × 36% × $N$

Number of students going to Cloudy Lane School = 15% × 55% × 36% × $N$

Number of students going to Dean School = 15% × 55% × 36% × $N$ + 35% × 55% × 36% × $N$ =

= 55% × 36% × $N$ (15% + 35%) =

= 55% × 36% × 50% × N =

= 9.9% × $N$

Number of students going to Dean School represent 9.9% of total number of students in Nowhere Town

19. **The correct answers are (A), (B), (C), (D) and (E).**

Albert receives more than 60% of the wages.

Suppose that he receives exactly 60% of the wages.

Then Benjamin will receive 40% of the wages.

Time and wages are in inverse proportions.

So for 60% of the wages it is 20 hours and 40% of the wages it will be $60 \times \left(\frac{20}{40}\right) = 30$ hours

Since Albert is getting more than 60% of the wages, Benjamin will take more than 30 hours.

So, options A, B, C, D, and E are correct.

20. **The correct answer is $4,500**

Start by determining the costs of the widgets:

The per-widget cost of those widgets with a $2 labor cost is: $2 + $5.50 + $1.25 = $8.75. Since 14,000 – 9,000 = 5000 widgets were made at the lower cost, the total cost for these widgets is 5,000 * $8.75 = $43,750.

The per-widget cost of those widgets with a $2.50 labor cost is: $2.50 + $5.50 + $1.25 = $9.25. Since 9,000 widgets were made at the higher cost, the total cost for these widgets is 9,000 * $9.25 = $83,250.

The total overall cost is $43,750 + $83,250 = $127,000

The total price is determined by applying a 25% markup to 10,000 widgets and a 20% markup to the rest. The first 10,000 widgets will be comprised of 5,000 widgets of lower cost and 5,000 widgets of higher cost:

Price for the first 10,000 widgets is (5,000 * $8.75/each + 5,000 * $9.25/each) * 1.25 = $112,500

Price for the remaining 4,000 widgets is (4,000 * $9.25 * 1.20) = $44,400

Total price is $112,500 + $44,400 = $156,900

Total markup before the coupon is $\left(\frac{\$156{,}900}{\$127{,}000}\right) - 1 =$ 0.235 = 23.5%

To find the maximum coupon, use the formula

$$\left(\frac{(\$156{,}900 - x)}{\$127{,}000}\right) - 1 = 0.20$$

156,900–$x$ = 1.20*127,000

$x$ = 4,500

The answer is $4,500

## Chapter 8

# Practice Test 6

You are about to begin a full length Practice Test. The Test has five sections. The time allotted for each section is marked at the beginning of the section. Work on one section at a time. Use a timer to keep track of the time limits for every section.

Try to take the Practice Test under real test conditions. Find a quiet place to work, and set aside enough time to complete the test without being disturbed. At the end of the test, check your answers by referring to the Answer Key and fill in your raw score in the score card below. Also, note down the time taken by you for completing each section.

Pay particular attention to the questions that were answered incorrectly. Read the answer explanations and understand how to solve them.

### My Score Card (Raw Score)

| | Section 2 | Section 3 | Section 4 | Section 5 |
|---|---|---|---|---|
| **Out of** | 20 | 20 | 20 | 20 |
| **My Score** | ______ | ______ | ______ | ______ |
| **Time Taken** | ______ | ______ | ______ | ______ |

# Section 1 – Analytical Writing

## Task 1 – Analyze an Issue | 30 mins

*The best ideas arise from a passionate interest in commonplace things.*

*Write a response in which you discuss the extent to which you agree or disagree with the statement and explain your reasoning for the position you take. In developing and supporting your position, you should consider ways in which the statement might or might not hold true and explain how these considerations shape your position.*

You may start writing your response here

## Task 2 – Analyze an Argument Task | 30 mins

*A recent sales study indicates that consumption of seafood dishes in Bay City restaurants has increased by 30 percent during the past five years. Yet there are no currently operating city restaurants whose specialty is seafood. Moreover, the majority of families in Bay City are two-income families, and a nationwide study has shown that such families eat significantly fewer home-cooked meals than they did a decade ago but at the same time express more concern about healthful eating. Therefore, the new Captain Seafood restaurant that specializes in seafood should be quite popular and profitable.*

*Write a response in which you discuss what specific evidence is needed to evaluate the argument and explain how the evidence would weaken or strengthen the argument.*

You may start writing your response here

# Section 2 – Verbal Reasoning

20 questions | 30 mins

---

**For Questions 1 and 2, select one entry for the blank. Fill the blank in the way that best completes the text.**

1. By apparently ________ their status as the eccentrics of the biological sciences, botanists have delivered functional solutions to real–world problems – their latest odd achievement is discovering a genus of mushroom that can break down oil spills.

| mystifying |
|---|
| denigrating |
| reinventing |
| abiding |
| shirking |

2. Its cross–discipline application and depth of study has caused organic chemistry to receive a level of importance in the biological sciences that is ________ to the role of physics in the physical sciences.

| subservient |
|---|
| sequestered |
| correspondent |
| variable |
| unconnected |

**Question 3 is based on the following passage.**

Certain things are true of all news stories; whether the story be the baldest recital of facts or the most sensational featuring of an imaginary thrill in a commonplace happening, certain characteristics are always present. And these characteristics can always be traced to one cause—the effort to catch and hold the reader's interest. When a busy American glances over his newspaper while he sips his breakfast coffee or while he clings to a strap on the way to his office, he reads only the stories that catch his interest—and he reads down the column in any one story only so long as his interest is maintained. Hence the ideal news story is one which will catch the reader's attention by its beginning and hold his interest to the very end. This is the principle of all newspaper writing.

**Select only one answer choice.**

3. Which statement below casts the most doubt upon a main assumption in the passage?

    (A) The reader's past experiences will heavily affect his reaction to news articles.

    (B) Only carefully written articles will interest the reader for its entirety.

    (C) Many Americans only read the front page of the newspaper.

    (D) The beginning and ending are the best remembered portions of any news article.

    (E) There are many distractions competing for one's time, that could be spent reading the newspaper.

**Questions 4 to 7 are based on the following passage.**

Amid the many styles of architecture contending for mastery in Italy, three, before the age of the Revival, bid fair to win the battle. These were the Lombard, the Tuscan Romanesque, and the Gothic. Chronologically the two former flourished nearly during the same centuries, while Gothic, coming from without, suspended their development. But chronology is of little help in the history of Italian architecture; its main features being, not uniformity of progression, but synchronous diversity and salience of local type. What remained fixed through all changes in Italy was a bias toward the forms of Roman building, which eventually in the Renaissance, becoming scientifically apprehended, determined the taste of the whole nation.

**For Questions 4 to 6, select only one answer choice.**

4. According to the author, which of the following had the strongest influence upon Italian architecture during the period discussed?

    (A) Lombard, Tuscan Romanesque and Gothic styles in equal measures

    (B) Lombard and Tuscan Romanesque styles

    (C) Roman building forms

    (D) Revival style

    (E) Renaissance tastes

5. According to the passage, which choice best characterizes the development of Italian architecture?

(A) The history of Italian architecture is one of steady progression, each new style or trend building upon the previous one.

(B) Italian architecture followed the Roman form until the Gothic style was introduced and became predominant.

(C) The history of Italian architecture can be divided into the Lombard, Tuscan Romanesque and Gothic periods.

(D) Italian architectural history is best described in terms of contemporaneously competing styles and regional variation.

(E) The arrival of the Renaissance undermined the popularity of traditional Italian architectural tastes.

6. According to the passage, which of the following best describes the relationship between the Lombard, Tuscan Romanesque and Gothic styles?

(A) Gothic style arrived in Italy after the other two had run their course.

(B) When Gothic style arrived, the Lombard and Tuscan styles became stagnant.

(C) Gothic style supplanted the other two because it was based upon traditional Roman forms.

(D) Gothic style supplanted the other two because it diverged from traditional Roman forms.

(E) The Gothic, Lombard and Tuscan Romanesque flourished until they were supplanted by a return to traditional Roman forms.

**Consider each of the three choices separately and select all that apply.**

7. According to the passage, which of the following features are important in the study of the history of Italian architecture?

[A] The existence of different styles simultaneously

[B] The sequential evolution of styles

[C] The importance of different styles to different regions

**For Questions 8 and 9, select the two answer choices that, when used to complete the sentence, fit the meaning of the sentence as a whole and produce completed sentences that are alike in meaning.**

8. The _______ of using quantum physics to discover new universes is not yet known.

   A transfusion

   B broadcast

   C ramifications

   D ratifications

   E strident

   F consequences

9. The objective of earthquake engineering is to_______ the impact of earthquakes on buildings and to minimize the risk of damage.

   A prognosticate

   B presage

   C augment

   D stave off

   E forewarn

   F aggrandize

**For Questions 10 and 11, select one entry for the blank. Fill the blank in the way that best completes the text.**

10. Astronomers can estimate the distance between earth and another planet through a procedure that is ________ to a bat's sonar – bouncing radio waves off of a distant object and measuring the amount of time it takes to return.

| superior |
|---|
| indebted |
| abhorrent |
| deleterious |
| debased |

11. The wide variety of complicated physical phenomena in the observable universe can, ironically, be explained in terms of four _________forces and their interactions: the gravitational force, electromagnetic force, strong nuclear force, and weak nuclear force.

| fundamental |
|---|
| superfluous |
| regressive |
| excessive |
| intricate |

**Questions 12 to 14 are based on the following passage.**

Itis an unfortunate fact that very few people are able to be idle successfully. I think it is not so much because we misuse idleness as because we misinterpret it that the long days become increasingly demoralizing. I would ask no one to accept a forced idleness without objection or regret. Such an acceptance would imply a lack of spirit, to say the least. But idleness and rest are not incompatible; neither are idleness and service, nor idleness and contentment. If we can look upon rest as a preparation for service, if we can make it serve us in the opportunity it gives for quiet growth and legitimate enjoyment, then it is fully justified and it may offer advantages and opportunity of the best.

The chief trouble with idleness is that it so often means introspection, worry, and impatience, especially to those conscientious souls who would fain be about their business.

I have for a long time been accustomed to combat the worry and fret of necessary idleness—not by forbidding it, not by advising struggle and fight against it, but by insisting that the best way to get rid of it is to leave it alone, to accept it. When we do this there may come a kind of fallow time in which the mind enriches and refreshes itself beyond our conception.

I would rather my patient who must rest for a long time would give up all thought of method, would give up all idea of making his mind follow any particular line of thought or absence of thought. I know that the mind which has been under conscious control a good deal of the time is apt to rebel at this freedom and to indulge in all kinds of alarming extravagances. I am sure, however, that the best way to meet these demands for conscious control is to be careless of them, to be willing to experience these extravagances and inconsistencies without fear, in the belief that finally will come a quiet and peace which will be all that we can ask. **The peace of mind that is unguided, in the conscious and literal sense, is a thing which too few of us know.**

Mr. Arnold Bennett, in his little book, "How to Live on Twenty–four Hours a Day," teaches that we should leave no time unused in our lives; that we should accomplish a great deal more and be infinitely more effective and progressive if we devoted our minds to the definite working–out of necessary problems whenever those times occur in which we are apt to be desultory. I wish here to make a plea for desultoriness and for an idleness which goes even beyond the idleness of the man who reads the newspaper and forgets what he has read. It seems to me better, whether we are sick or well, to allow long periods in our lives when we think only casually. To the good old adage, "Work while you work and play while you play," we might well add, "Rest while you rest," lest in the end you should be unable successfully either to work or play.

**For Questions 12 and 13, select only one answer choice.**

12. According to the passage, which of the following is a result that is NOT produced by idleness?

(A) corruption

(B) restlessness

(C) memory loss

(D) laziness

(E) contemplation

13. What is the main purpose of the boldface sentence?

(A) Present an argument which concludes several of the previously stated opinions.

(B) Provides evidence to support the author's stance on mind control.

(C) Introduces the ideas set forth in Bennett's book.

(D) Summarize the main idea of the whole passage.

(E) Explain the benefits of relinquishing mental control.

14. Select the sentence that presents a paradox in regards to how a person can effectively govern his or her own thoughts.

**Questions 15 and 16 are based on the following passage.**

When Donato di Niccolo di Betto Bardi, called Donatello because men loved his sweet and cheerful temper, died in 1466 at the age of eighty, the brightest light of Italian sculpture in its most promising period was extinguished. Donatello's influence, felt far and wide through Italy, was of inestimable value in correcting the false direction toward pictorial sculpture which Ghiberti, had he flourished alone at Florence, might have given to the art. His style was always eminently masculine. However tastes may differ about the positive merits of his several works, there can be no doubt that the principles of sincerity, truth to nature, and technical accuracy they illustrate, were all–important in an age that lent itself too readily to the caprices of the fancy and the puerilities of florid taste. To regret that Donatello lacked Ghiberti's exquisite sense of beauty, is tantamount to wishing that two of the greatest artists of the world had made one man between them.

**For Questions 15 and 16, select only one answer choice.**

15. Which of the following best summarizes this passage?

(A) The author presents several arguments supporting his assertion that Donatello and Ghiberti were the greatest sculptors of their era.

(B) The author describes the positive influence that Donatello's work had upon Ghiberti's style.

(C) The author describes the negative influence that Ghiberti's work had upon Donatello's style.

(D) The author argues that Donatello's style had a favorable influence upon the art of sculpture.

(E) The author argues that the styles of Donatello and Ghiberti actually complemented one another.

16. Which of the following best describes the author's assessment of Ghiberti?

(A) Ghiberti's work tended toward the masculine while Donatello's had a more graceful form.

(B) Ghiberti's work, while often beautiful, tended to be too fanciful and overwrought.

(C) Ghiberti's work heavily influenced Florentine sculpture until Donatello came along.

(D) Ghiberti's work is significantly overrated.

(E) Ghiberti's work is significantly underrated.

**For Questions 17 and 18, select the two answer choices that, when used to complete the sentence, fit the meaning of the sentence as a whole and produce completed sentences that are alike in meaning.**

17. The newly patented polymer attracts other chemicals in the water, including dissolved metals, and _______ them for easy removal.

[A] rainfall

[B] accelerates

[C] consolidates

[D] precipitation

[E] impels

[F] precipitates

18. Scientists were able to create a vaccine for the ______ flu strain that had caused the death of thirteen people in the area.

- [A] innocuous
- [B] deadly
- [C] malevolent
- [D] acrimonious
- [E] harmless
- [F] virulent

**For Questions 19 and 20, select one entry for the blank. Fill the blank in the way that best completes the text.**

19. Because human _________ of light is wavelength–dependent and short wavelength blue light is the most widely scattered in the atmosphere, the sky appears blue to human eyes.

| |
|---|
| perception |
| acumen |
| perspicacity |
| awareness |
| conception |

20. The music industry saw tremendous innovations in both technology and artistry during the 20th century. The invention of the radio (i)_________ many of the stylistic changes. Because of the radio, music was no longer (ii)_________ to concert houses and clubs. As a result, it became possible for all citizens to hear music and contribute to its development. This explains the massive (iii)_________ of musical genres in the 20th century. From psychedelic to rockabilly, popular music no longer followed the strict rules of the previous centuries.

| Blank (i) | Blank (ii) | Blank (iii) |
|---|---|---|
| circumvented | sardonic | guileless |
| facilitated | schematized | portly |
| barred | quiescent | tumultuous |

# Section 3 – Quantitative Reasoning

20 questions | 35 mins

1.

| Number of children in the family | Relative frequency |
|---|---|
| 0 | 11% |
| 1 | 22% |
| 2 | 40% |
| 3 | 20% |
| 4 and above | 7% |
| Total | 100% |

Relative frequency distribution of the number of children in a family of 60 families in a locality is shown above in the table

In the above distribution, which of the following could be the number of children per family for which the probability is > 0.3?

[A] P( 0 or 1)

[B] P(2)

[C] P(3 or more)

[D] P(1 or 4)

[E] P(1 or 3)

[F] P(3)

[G] P(4 or more)

2. Number *abc*, where *a*, *b*, and *c* are distinct digits, is an even positive integer that is a multiple of 33. Number abc is a three digit number with a,b, and c being positive one-digit integers and *abc* being less than 300. If *abc* was one unit more, it would be a prime number. Which of the following satisfy the the requirements for *a*, *b*, and *c*?

(A) $a = 1, b = 3, c = 2$

(B) $a = 1, b = 5, c = 4$

(C) $a = 1, b = 7, c = 6$

(D) $a = 2, b = 6, c = 4$

(E) $a = 1, b = 9, c = 8$

3.

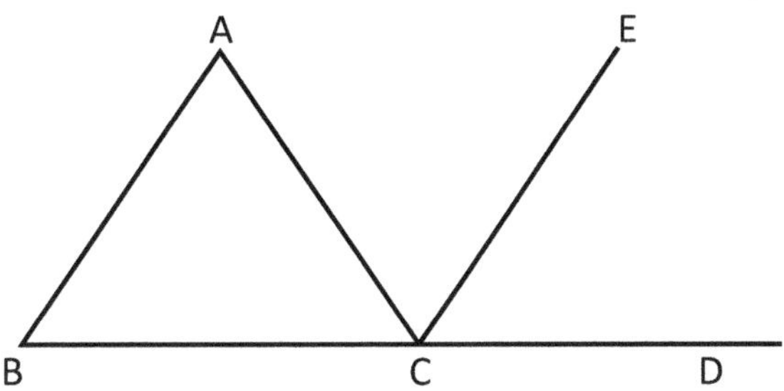


In the above figure AB is parallel to EC. CE is the bisector of external $\angle ACD$ and $\angle ACD = 140°$

What is the value of $\angle$ BAC (Omit the degree symbol)

[ ]

4. A cube has an edge length of 6 *inches*. The areas of the top and the bottom of a right cylinder each equal 25 *square inches* and its height is 7 *inches*. A rectangular prism has a length, width and height equal to 6, 3 and 4 *inches* respectively. All three are filled with water and then emptied into a canister with the capacity of 6 *gallons*. Roughly how much of the capacity of the canister remains unfilled? (1 *gallon* = 231 *cubic inches*)

(A) 1 *gallon*

(B) 2 *gallon*

(C) 3 *gallon*

(D) 4 *gallon*

(E) 5 *gallon*

5.

Charles takes 40 minutes to cycle to his office.

| **Quantity A** | **Quantity B** |
|---|---|
| Additional time taken by Charles to reach his office when his speed is 80% of his usual speed | 10 minutes |

(A) Quantity A is greater.

(B) Quantity B is greater.

(C) The two quantities are equal.

(D) The relationship cannot be determined from the information given.

6. David rented a luxury car for an excursion with his family. The rental rate is \$60 per day plus \$0.75 per mile. In all, he spent 4 days and paid \$525 as rent. How many miles did David drive?

(A) 360

(B) 380

(C) 390

(D) 400

(E) 420

7.

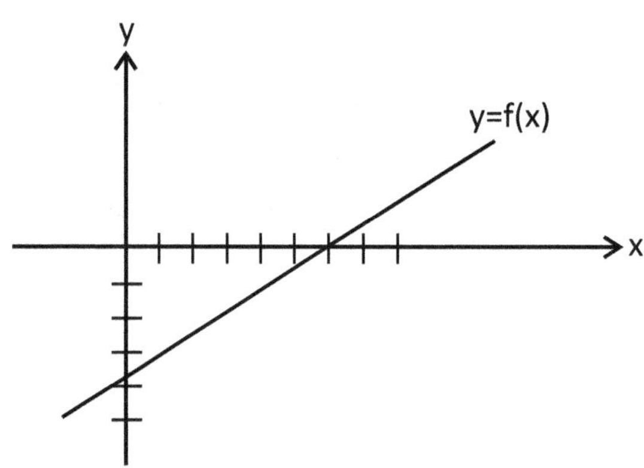


The figure shows the graph of function *f(x)* with *y* intercept *–4* and *x* intercept *6*.

| **Quantity A** | **Quantity B** |
|---|---|
| The slope of *f*(*x*) | The sum of the slopes of the following linear functions<br>*g(x)* = *3/4x* – *2*, *h(x)* = *4* and *i(x)* = *x* – *2* |

(A) Quantity A is greater.

(B) Quantity B is greater.

(C) The two quantities are equal.

(D) The relationship cannot be determined from the information given.

8. Which of the following equations is for the line that is perpendicular to $y = 1 - 2x$ and passes through the point $(0,3)$?

(A) $y = \frac{x}{2} + 3$

(B) $y = 2x + 8$

(C) $y = 4x + 1$

(D) $y = 3x - \frac{1}{2}$

(E) $y = 4x - 4$

9. A and B are two different numbers selected from the numbers 1 through 10, both inclusive. What is the difference between the largest and smallest positive values of $\frac{(A \times B)}{(A - B)}$ ?

[ ]

10.

A positive integer of the form 39*ab*, where *a* and *b* are digits, is divisible by 4, 5 and 9.

| Quantity A | Quantity B |
|---|---|
| The sum of the largest and the smallest prime factors of 39*ab* | The largest prime factor of *abba* |

(A) Quantity A is greater.

(B) Quantity B is greater.

(C) The two quantities are equal.

(D) The relationship cannot be determined from the information given.

11. When $x \neq 1$, what is the sum of the roots of the equation?

$$x + 5 = \frac{-4x - 17}{x + 1} - \frac{-x - 2}{x + 1}$$

(A) 7

(B) –7

(C) 9

(D) -9

(E) 11

12.

The mean of a group of 10 numbers is 83. A different group of 20 numbers has a mean of 65. When k is added to the first 10 numbers, the new mean is 82.

| **Quantity A** | **Quantity B** |
|---|---|
| The mean of the 30 numbers | $k$ |

(A) Quantity A is greater.

(B) Quantity B is greater.

(C) The two quantities are equal.

(D) The relationship cannot be determined from the information given.

13.

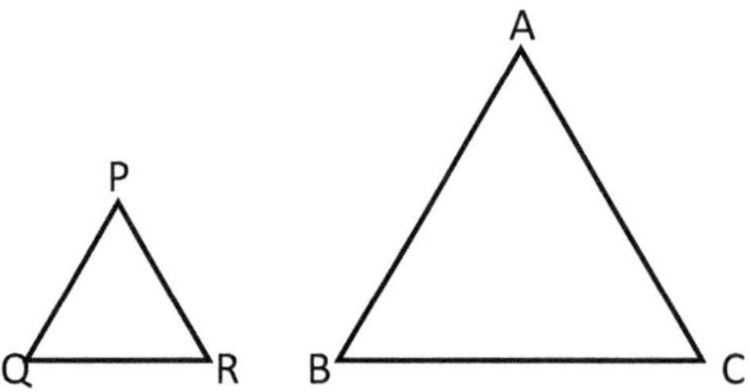


Triangle PQR and triangle ABC are similar (ΔPQR ~ ΔABC). PQ=2 cm and AB = 5 cm and area of triangle ABC =100 $cm^2$

| **Quantity A** | **Quantity B** |
|---|---|
| The area of triangle PQR | 25 cm2 |

(A) Quantity A is greater.

(B) Quantity B is greater.

(C) The two quantities are equal.

(D) The relationship cannot be determined from the information given.

14. Matthew is on a tour of The Grand Canyon. He has $300 for his daily expenses. If he extends the tour for additional 5 days, he has to cut down his daily expenses by $5. What is the original duration of the tour?

(A) 5 days

(B) 10 days

(C) 15 days

(D) 20 days

(E) 25 days

15. A set consists of consecutive positive integers starting from 2 to n. For what values of n would the sum of the numbers in the set lie between 120 and 200, both inclusive?

Indicate all such numbers.

[A] 14

[B] 15

[C] 16

[D] 17

[E] 18

[F] 19

[G] 20

16. If $f(x) = \pi x^2 + 5x$, $g(x) = 3x + 2$ and $h(x) = x^3$, what is the value of $f\left(g(h(-1))\right)$?

(A) $\pi - 7$

(B) $\pi - 5$

(C) $\pi - 3$

(D) $\pi - 1$

(E) $\pi + 1$

17. A manufacturing company produces radios at different rates depending on the total order size. The company charges $7 per radio for the first 70 radios, and then $5 for each additional radio. If *x* represents radios and y represents total costs, select all the following true statements:

[A] The equation that represents this situation if there are 70 or more radios produced is $y = 7(70) + 5(x - 70)$

[B] The equation that represents this situation if there are 70 or more radios produced is $y = 7x + 5x$

[C] If there are 140 radios produced the total cost is $840.

[D] If there are 70 or less radios produced, the equation that represents this situation is $y = 7x$

[E] If there are 70 or less radios produced, the equation that represents this situation is $y = 5x$

**Questions 18 and 19 are based on the following dada:**

Refer to the following table, which shows the amount of rain that fell during a 30- day period in 1998.

| **Rainfall** | |
|---|---|
| **Rainfall (in inches)** | **Number of Days** |
| 0 | 17 |
| 1 | 5 |
| 2 | 3 |
| 3 | 3 |
| 4 | 2 |

18. What is the mode of the amount of rainfall, in inches, over these 30 days?

(A) 0

(B) 1

(C) 2

(D) 3

(E) 4

19. If 200 inches of rainfall were expected to fall during all of 1998, what percent of the expected yearly rainfall was reached during this 30-day period?

(A) 56%

(B) 42%

(C) 28%

(D) 14%

(E) 7%

20.

One root of the equation $2x^2-(3-k)x+17(x-2) - 20 = 0$ is the other root squared.

| Quantity A | Quantity B |
|---|---|
| The smallest root of the equation | $k$ |

(A) Quantity A is greater.

(B) Quantity B is greater.

(C) The two quantities are equal.

(D) The relationship cannot be determined from the information given.

# Section 4 – Verbal Reasoning

20 questions | 30 mins

---

**For Questions 1 and 2, select one entry for the blank. Fill the blank in the way that best completes the text.**

1. Particle physicists continue to wrestle with the _________problem of why the universe is made of matter and not antimatter, as logic would prescribe.

| wayward |
|---|
| intractable |
| resolute |
| perverse |
| pliant |

2. The unit of time known as a second is a scientific measurement of the time it takes for a cesium atom to _________9,192,631,770 times between two radiation states.

| persist |
|---|
| forge |
| feign |
| fluctuate |
| oscillate |

**Questions 3 and 4 are based on the following passage.**

[Thomas] Jefferson nurtured a bold visionof America's future, one that was predicated on territorial expansion. Only thirty–three years old in 1776, he penned America's Declaration of Independence, proclaiming the inalienable rights of "life, liberty, and the pursuit of happiness." As Jefferson matured, he came to envision an increasingly populous and prosperous nation governed by virtuous republican leaders.

Jefferson thought that societies progressed in stages, from unruly barbarism to law–abiding communities of farmers, market townships, and representative governments.

He contended that a large, civilized, and wealthy United States would command respect, wield influence, and enjoy independence on the world stage. However, not all forms of progress were desirable. Jefferson deplored England's industrialization and urbanization, both of which he considered socially corrosive. England's vision of progress was to be avoided. The survival of America's good, corruption–free government, he argued, depended on the practices and rewards of farming and rural living.

**For Questions 3 and 4, select only one answer choice.**

3. According to the author, which of the following is true of Jefferson's vision of the United States?

   (A) He predicted that it would remain largely agrarian and rural, in contrast to England.

   (B) He believed the United States would gain influence as it accrued more material wealth.

   (C) He believed the United States would not follow the historical pattern of progressing in stages.

   (D) He believed good government would develop as population and prosperity increased.

   (E) He predicted that the republican government outlined in the Declaration of Independence would become corrupted when the country became urbanized and industrial.

4. Based on the passage, Jefferson would probably agree with which statement below?

   (A) As a market township grows in population, its government grows in strength and influence, thus strengthening the United States as a whole.

   (B) The United States should follow England's example, except in matters of urbanization and industrialization.

   (C) It is more important to maintain the United States' rural and agrarian nature than to seek respect on the world stage.

   (D) The United States needs to acquire more land if it is to prosper.

   (E) Urbanization and industrialization will negatively impact a country's prosperity and influence.

**Question 5 is based on the following passage.**

Although frequently concerned with news, a special feature article is more than a mere news story. It aims to supplement the bare facts of the news report by giving more detailed information regarding the persons, places, and circumstances that appear in the news columns. News must be published as fast as it develops, with only enough explanatory material to make it intelligible. The special article, written with the perspective afforded by an interval of a few days or weeks, fills in the bare outlines of the hurried news sketch with the life and color that make the picture complete.

**Select only one answer choice.**

5. Which sentence below weakens the conclusion presented in this paragraph?

   (A) Mike's mother rewrote her editorial ten times before she submitted it to be published.

   (B) John's news sketches are rather boring to read as they lack detail.

   (C) Jane is such a talented writer that she can spin an interesting masterpiece almost faster than she can write it down on paper.

   (D) Bob only writes human interest stories because he writes so slowly.

   (E) Julie's assignment develops as the day progresses, not knowing ahead of time what emergency might occur.

**For Questions 6 to 10, select the two answer choices that, when used to complete the sentence, fit the meaning of the sentence as a whole and produce completed sentences that are alike in meaning.**

6. The new _______ of the skin cell left cancer researchers perplexed as it did not appear to be like any other cell that had been radiated.

A structure

B edifice

C department

D morphology

E genus

F tabulation

7. That tree blooms at the end of summer, when many others are becoming ______ and no longer producing fruit.

A stagnant

B quiescent

C inertia

D indolence

E dormant

F sloth

8. Some metals such as gold are ________. They can be shaped and easily molded into different forms.

A salubrious

B unyielding

C intractable

D malleable

E ductile

F valuable

9. Mt. Everest is one of the most challenging peaks to ascend for even the most experienced climbers, who say that among all the valleys and _________, the most difficult is one dubbed the Khumbu Icefall due to the ever-present chance of an avalanche.

A precipices

B escarpment

C declivities

D eradication

E rifts

F declensions

10. Solar distillation is a means of converting ______ water, such as water collected from the ocean or estuaries, into potable water.

A pollution

B brackish

C alkaline

D saliferous

E putrid

F stationery

**Questions 11 to 13 are based on the following passage.**

In 1990 there came a nationwide crackdown on illicit computer hackers, with arrests, criminal charges, one dramatic show–trial, several guilty pleas, and huge confiscations of data and equipment all over the USA. The Hacker Crackdown of 1990 was larger, better organized, more deliberate, and more resolute than any previous effort in the brave new world of computer crime. The U.S. Secret Service, private telephone security, and state and local law enforcement groups across the country all joined forces in a determined attempt to break the back of America's electronic underground. It was a fascinating effort, with very mixed results. The Hacker Crackdown had another unprecedented effect; it spurred the creation, within "the computer community," of the Electronic Frontier Foundation, a new and very odd interest group, fiercely dedicated to the establishment and preservation of electronic civil liberties. The crackdown, remarkable in itself, has created a melee of debate over electronic crime, punishment, freedom of the press, and issues of search and seizure. Politics has entered cyberspace.

**For Questions 11 and 12, select only one answer choice.**

11. Which of the following aspects of computer crime is NOT mentioned in the passage?

    Ⓐ Seizure of computer equipment by law–enforcement authorities

    Ⓑ Public discourse about computer crime

    Ⓒ Criminal prosecution of computer crime

    Ⓓ Anti–computer crime legislation

    Ⓔ The goals of the Electronic Frontier Foundation

12. According to the passage, what was true about the 1990 crackdown?

    Ⓐ The crackdown was spear–headed by the federal government.

    Ⓑ The crackdown was considered a success by law–enforcement authorities.

    Ⓒ The crackdown spurred new debate about the prosecution of computer crime.

    Ⓓ The Electronic Frontier Foundation tried to stop the 1990 crackdown.

    Ⓔ The crackdown spurred calls for new laws against computer crime.

**Consider each of the three choices separately and select all that apply.**

13. According to the passage, which of the following were results of the 1990 crackdown?

    [A] The creation of the Electronic Frontier Foundation

    [B] A new focus on political issues within the computer community

    [C] A temporary decrease in computer–related crime

**Questions 14 to 17 are based on the following passage.**

What study is more sublime, inspiring and profitable, in the highest sense, than the "language of the stars"—those silent monitors of the midnight sky, who reveal His will as secondary causes in the administration of universal law? The science of the stars is the Divine parent of all science.

The more earnest our study, the more recondite our research and thorough our investigation of the "Science of the Stars," the more fully shall we realize the truth of the teacher's words: "Astrology is the key that opens the door to all occult knowledge."It is the key that unlocks the mysteries of man's being; his why, whence, whither. Within the temple of Urania lies concealed the mystery of life. The indices are there, written by the finger of the Infinite in the heavens above.

It is our privilege to make this language our own, and it should be the earnest work of every true student of Nature to acquire a right understanding and correct interpretation of these Divine symbols. **And, as thorough students of any language seek out the derivation of words and expressions, search for the root, or stem word, and its origin, so should the student of astrology, by sincere desire and earnest study, seek to know the origin and root of these**

**starry words and complex expressions of the "language of the stars."**

The Sun, Moon and five [known] planets of our solar system are to us symbols of the reflected and refracted rays of the triune attributes of the great Central, Spiritual Sun: Life, Light and Love, analogous to the three primary colors in Nature, which become still further refracted into four secondary or complementary colors, rays or attributes, the seven constituting the active principles of Nature, the seven rays of the solar spectrum, the seven notes of a perfect musical scale, there being throughout a perfect correspondence, and all are but different modes of vibration or activities of the Supreme Intelligence.

And, as we know, the seven rays of color reflect an almost infinite variety of tints, that, octave upon octave, are built upon the seven natural tones in music, so, also, are these seven active principles divided and subdivided into innumerable forms, qualities and manifestations of the first trinity—Life, Light, Love, life being the manifestation of the second two, love and wisdom, which in turn are the dual expressions of the "One."

Upon the knowledge of these Divine truths Pythagoras built the theory of the "music of the spheres." Let us pause and listen to this celestial music.

Suns and their systems of planets sound forth the deep bass tones and rich tenor, while angelic races take the silvery treble of the Divine melody, octave upon octave, by more and ever more ethereal system upon system, to the very throne of Deity—the Infinite, Eternal source of Light, Life and Love.

[*] Uranus and Neptune belonging to a higher octave.

**For Questions 14 to 16, select only one answer choice.**

14. Based on information found in the passage, which of the following qualities would most likely be symbolically represented by 'darkness'?

(A) evil

(B) hatred

(C) ignorance

(D) anger

(E) turmoil

15. Which choice describes the function of the boldface sentence function in the author's main argument?

(A) It confirms the author's conclusion.

(B) It presents an explanation of evidence.

(C) It provides factual support for the author's argument.

(D) It reiterates the author's point.

(E) It introduces an opinion.

16. Which of the following combinations of literary devices does the author employ in comparing astrology to colors and music?

(A) Metonymy and onomatopoeia

(B) Analogy, hyperbole, and allegory

(C) Metaphor, simile, and analogy

(D) Personification and metaphor

(E) Allegory and synecdoche

**Consider each of the three choices separately and select all that apply.**

17. Based on the passage, what subjects aside from astrology would the author most likely pursue?

[A] Religion and Theology

[B] Quantum Physics

[C] Performance Arts

**For Question 18, select one entry for the blank. Fill the blank in the way that best completes the text.**

18. By carefully comparing the sounds of musical scales performed by an opera singer and several violinists playing Stradivarius violins, researcher Joseph Nagyvary has shown that the Italian master–violin makers, including Antonio Stradavari, were able to _______the vowel and consonant sounds of speech into their instruments.

| disclose |
| --- |
| yield |
| impart |
| output |
| relinquish |

**For each blank, select one entry from the corresponding column of choices. Fill all blanks in the way that best completes the text.**

19. There are several key (i)______ that are made by linguists. The most prominent is that spoken language is more (ii)______ to the human psyche than written language. Most linguists feel justified in making this postulation for a variety of reasons: all cultures have spoken communication, but not all have written communication; vocal communication (iii) written communication; developing humans learn to speak before they learn to write.

| Blank (i) |
|---|
| gaffes |
| concessions |
| presuppositions |

| Blank (ii) |
|---|
| superfluous |
| fundamental |
| distressing |

| Blank (iii) |
|---|
| antecedes |
| succeeds |
| ignores |

20. Johannes Kepler, a fifteenth century astronomer, (i)______information gathered from hundreds of hours of meticulous observations of planetary movement to develop three laws used to calculate the motion of planets. Kepler's first law identifies the path of a planet as an ellipse. The Sun serves as the (ii)______of the ellipses, meaning it is within the ellipses and the point on which the planets depend. The second law establishes a relationship between the speed of a planet's rotation to its distance from the Sun. The third law provides guidance for calculating the period of a planet's orbit.

| Blank (i) |
|---|
| synthesized |
| unified |
| amalgamated |

Blank (ii)

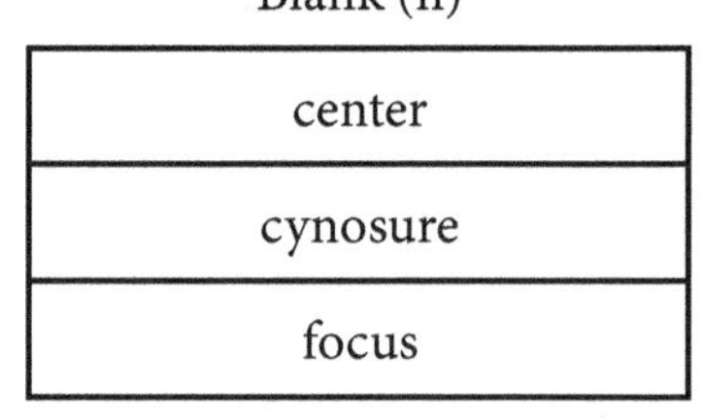

| |
|---|
| center |
| cynosure |
| focus |

# Section 5 – Quantitative Reasoning

20 questions | 35 mins

1.

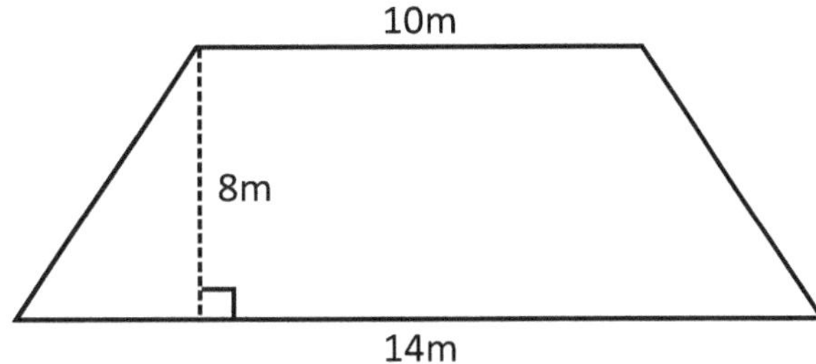


The sandpit in a park is in the shape of a trapezoid. The parallel sides of the section measure 10 m and 14 m. The distance between the parallel sides is 8 m.

The section was remodeled to have an area that was *96 square* meters more than the original area. What change in the dimensions of the trapezoid was made to create the remodeled section?

(A) The length of the parallel sides and the height were doubled.

(B) The height was doubled.

(C) The length of the parallel sides and the height were multiplied by four.

(D) The height was multiplied by four.

(E) The lengths of the parallel sides were increased by *5 m*.

2. Which of the following operations will result in a negative integer less than or equal to –8?

[A] $(-4)(-2)-(3)$

[B] $(4)(-2)-(-3)$

[C] $(-6)(2)-(10)(-2)$

[D] $\frac{(-8)}{2}+(-1)(4)$

[E] $(-5+3)(-2+7)-(-4)$

[F] $(2)[(4)(-5)-(-4)]-(-7)(2)$

3.

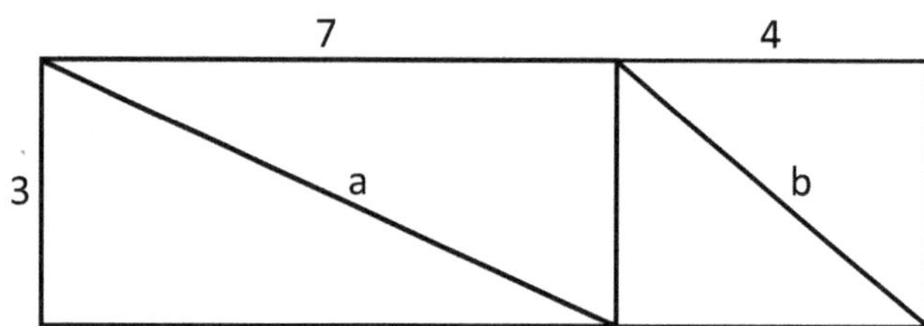


In the diagram above, the sum a + b is equal to:

(A) $5+\sqrt{58}$

(B) $16+\sqrt{2}$

(C) 14

(D) $\frac{25}{3}$

(E) $17+3\sqrt{6}$

4. *B* dozen oranges cost a total of *C* cents. At this rate, how many oranges can be brought for *E* cents?

(A) BC/E

(B) EC/B

(C) 12BE/C

(D) BE/C

(E) BEC

5.

A machine depreciates 50% in the first year, 40% in the second year 25% in the third year, and 20% in the fourth year. The depreciated value of the machine at the end of four years is $18 million

| Quantity A | Quantity B |
|---|---|
| The initial value of the machine | $100,000,000 |

(A) Quantity A is greater.

(B) Quantity B is greater.

(C) The two quantities are equal.

(D) The relationship cannot be determined from the information given.

6. An army had provisions for certain number of days during a war. After fighting for 10 days the enemy was under control of the army, therefore it was decided that 1/5th of the army men go back to their base. It was found that the food provision will now last just as long as before with unchanged ration amounts. How many days would that be?

[ ] days

7. A parallelogram has a base of 15m and a height that is $\frac{3}{5}$ the base. What is the area of the parallelogram?

Ⓐ $9m^2$

Ⓑ $25m^2$

Ⓒ $135m^2$

Ⓓ $375m^2$

Ⓔ $48m^2$

8.

$$2187^x = 9$$

| Quantity A | Quantity B |
|---|---|
| $x$ | $\frac{3}{7}$ |

Ⓐ Quantity A is greater.

Ⓑ Quantity B is greater.

Ⓒ The two quantities are equal.

Ⓓ The relationship cannot be determined from the information given.

9.

| Quantity A | Quantity B |
|---|---|
| The number of right angles that is equivalent to the sum of the interior angles of a heptagon | The greatest number of inner right angles that a hexagon (concave) can have |

Ⓐ Quantity A is greater.

Ⓑ Quantity B is greater.

Ⓒ The two quantities are equal.

Ⓓ The relationship cannot be determined from the information given.

10. What will be a single discount equivalent to a discount series of 30%, 20% and 10%? Express your answer in percent.

[ ] %

**Questions 11 to 14 are based on the following table:**

A group of college students took GRE every year during their college tenure.

The following table shows percent changes of the statistical measures of their scores.

| GRE Scaled Scores | | | |
|---|---|---|---|
| | **Percent Change from Freshman to Sophomore** | **Percent Change from Sophomore to Junior** | **Percent Change from Junior to Senior** |
| **Mean** | 3 | -5 | 3 |
| **Median** | 5 | 4 | 6 |
| **Mode** | 6 | 5 | -6 |

11. In which year(s) was the mode the highest?

- (A) Freshman and senior years
- (B) Sophomore and senior years
- (C) Freshman year
- (D) Junior year
- (E) Senior year

12. Which statistical measure was constantly growing from one year to another year?

- (A) Mean and mode values of the total scores
- (B) Median and mode values of the total scores
- (C) Mean value of the total scores
- (D) Mode value of the total scores
- (E) Median value of the total scores

13. What is the percent change from the freshman year to the senior year in the means of the scores?

[ ]

14. In which year was the median highest?

(A) Freshman and sophomore years

(B) Sophomore and senior years

(C) Freshman year

(D) Sophomore year

(E) Senior year

15.

There are 84 girls in Happy Town's school and they represent 48% of the total number of school's students. The neighboring Sunny City's school has 8% fewer students than Happy Town's. The ratio girls in Happy Town's school : girls in Sunny City's school is 12:9.

| **Quantity A** | **Quantity B** |
|---|---|
| The number of boy students that need to stop going to Sunny City's school, in order for the ratio boys : girls in Sunny City's school to become *13:9* | The number of girl students that need to stop going to Happy Town's school, in order for the ratio boys : girls in Happy Town's school to become *13:11* |

(A) Quantity A is greater.

(B) Quantity B is greater.

(C) The two quantities are equal.

(D) The relationship cannot be determined from the information given.

16.

An airplane flew 400 km from point P due east to point Q, then 400 km due north to point R, then 100 km due west to the point S, and finally straight back to P from S. The average speed from R to P is 50% more than the average speed form P to R.

| **Quantity A** | **Quantity B** |
|---|---|
| The ratio of time taken to fly from point P to R to the time taken to return to point P | 2:1 |

(A) Quantity A is greater.

(B) Quantity B is greater.

(C) The two quantities are equal.

(D) The relationship cannot be determined from the information given.

17. There are three cubes with volumes of 27 cubic feet, 1 cubic foot, and 1/27 cubic foot respectively. The second cube is placed on the first cube and the third cube is placed on the second cube. What is the height in inches of the stacked cubes?

Ⓐ 44

Ⓑ 48

Ⓒ 52

Ⓓ 56

Ⓔ 60

18.

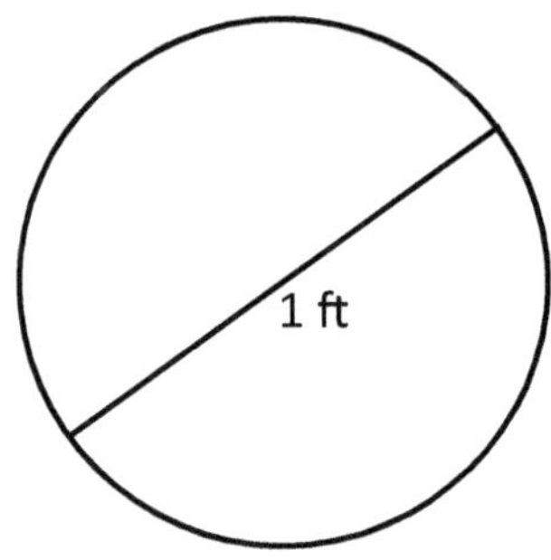


Your car wheels are as above, and you drive for one hour, making sure to maintain 20 rpm. How far does your car move?

Ⓐ 1 *mile*

Ⓑ 300 ft

Ⓒ $800\pi$ ft

Ⓓ 1000 ft

Ⓔ $1200\pi$ ft

19.

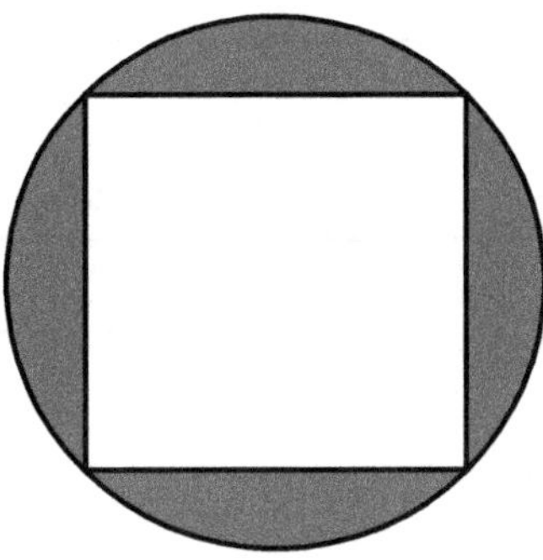

The square inscribed in the circle above has side length s. What is the area of the shaded portion?

(A) $\pi s^2$

(B) $\frac{\pi s - \pi}{2}$

(C) $\left(\frac{\pi}{2}\right)s^2 - s^2$

(D) $\pi^2 s$

(E) $\frac{s^2}{\pi}$

20.

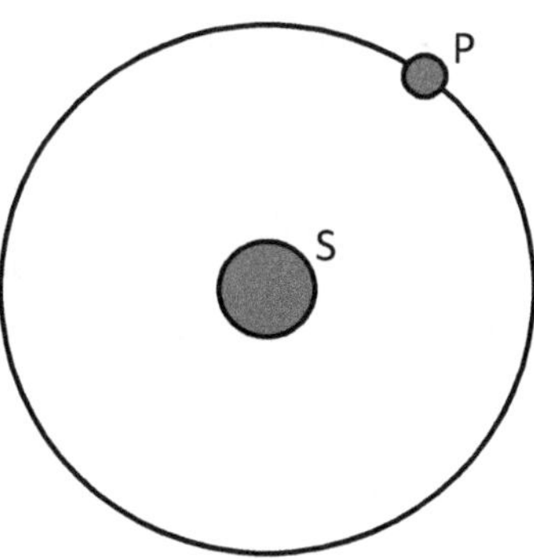


If planet P orbits star S at a constant distance of $4 \times 10^7$, and orbits one full rotation in 30 days, then what arc length does it cover in 6 days.

(A) $5 \times 10^7$

(B) $5pi \times 10^9$

(C) $\left(\frac{8}{5}\right)\pi \times 10^7$

(D) $1.2 \times 10^5$

(E) $1.5 \times 10^9$

# Answers Key

## Section 2

1. C
2. D
3. abiding
4. correspondent
5. A
6. B
7. A and C
8. ramifications and consequences
9. prognosticate and presage
10. indebted
11. fundamental
12. D
13. A
14. *"I am sure, however, that the best way to meet these demands for conscious control is to be careless of them, to be willing to experience these extravagances and inconsistencies without fear, in the belief that finally will come a quiet and peace which will be all that we can ask."*
15. D
16. B
17. consolidates and precipitates
18. deadly and virulent
19. A
20. facilitated, shackled, and proliferation

## Section 3

1. A, B and E
2. E
3. 70°
4. D
5. C
6. B
7. B
8. A
9. $\frac{800}{9}$
10. C
11. D
12. B
13. B
14. C
15. C, D, E and F
16. B
17. A, C and D
18. A
19. D
20. A

## Section 4

1. B
2. D
3. C
4. B
5. E
6. structure and morphology
7. quiescent and dormant
8. malleable and ductile
9. precipices and escarpments
10. brackish and saliferous
11. D
12. C
13. A and B
14. C
15. D
16. C
17. A and C
18. C
19. presuppositions, fundamental, and antecedents
20. synthesized and focus

## Section 5

1. B
2. D and F
3. A
4. $\frac{12BE}{C}$
5. C
6. 50 days
7. C
8. B
9. A
10. 49.6%
11. D
12. E
13. 0.79%
14. E
15. C
16. C
17. C
18. E
19. C
20. C

# Explanations

## Section 1 – Analytical Writing

### Task 1 – Analyze an Issue

**The sample essay that follows was written in response to the prompt that appeared in the question.**

One tends to think of visionaries as those men and women who can see things that the minds of mere mortals cannot even imagine. Modern conveniences like the telephone and the television seem like miracles. How can a camera take a moving picture on the other side of the world and send it to the television in my little corner of the world? How is it possible that my voice can travel into space and be retrieved by my friend on her phone in the middle of the country? These inventions are, indeed, beyond the ken of the common man who probably can't even fathom where the ideas came from. Other wonders of the modern world, however, do have their roots in objects that we observe every day.

Man has always envied birds. The desire to fly has given rise to myths as old as the ability of man to speak. The most familiar of these myths is populated by the master craftsman, Daedalus and his son, Icarus. Icarus' desire to fly led his father to craft wings made of feather and wax. Daedalus' copied what he could observe of the wings of birds. His only warning to his son was not to fly too close to the sun lest the wax melt and cause the wings to be destroyed. Icarus, enthralled by the freedom of flight, ignored his father's warning and soared higher and higher until he did, indeed, fly too close to the sun. The wax melted, the wings fell apart, and Icarus' plummeted to his death in the sea. In the fifteenth century, Leonardo da Vinci drew plans for a flying device that became the inspiration for the modern helicopter. Some of the earliest planes attempted to imitate the motion of birds' wings. Now that man can actually fly not only around the world but out of it, one must wonder, "Do the birds envy man."

As the birds move in the sky above us, so do the sun, the stars, and the moon. For much of the history of man, the stars and planets were sources of myth and inspired poets, artists and musicians. The earliest ideas about the sun and the stars made the Earth the center of the universe. Later astronomers created the heliocentric theory of our solar system. The first practical use of the stars was for navigation. The longer the scientists observed the heavenly bodies, the greater the desire grew to reach them. When it became possible to measure the distances to the sun, the moon, and other planets, the idea of reaching them became a possibility. Now man has been to the moon, and has set his sights on Mars. The Hubble telescope continues to send back crystal–clear pictures of deep space, and man's fascination continues to grow.

When man looks up, he cannot avoid seeing the birds and the heavenly bodies. They are ubiquitous, and man's envy, fascination, and eventual understanding of them has made incredible journeys possible. The best ideas of the future are likely to come from man's continued passion for commonplace things.

### Task 2 – Analyze an Argument

**The sample essay that follows was written in response to the prompt that appeared in the question.**

The strength of the writer's argument depends on some dubious statistics and assumptions. Any business would be wise to delve deeper into the spurious evidence offered in this passage before accepting the writer's argument.

The writer offers the reader some statistics that presume to prove a significant increase in the popularity of seafood dishes in Bay City's restaurants despite the fact that none of those eateries specialize in seafood. Some might mistakenly understand that seafood entrees comprise 30 percent of restaurant sales, and that would be impressive. In actuality, the sale of such dishes has increased by 30 percent, or roughly 1/3, over the past five years. If we know that restaurant A sold

6 seafood dishes each day five years ago, then we can calculate that the same restaurant sells 8 per day now. An increase of two dishes per day is not cause for celebration. Should we discover, however, that restaurant A sold 30 seafood dishes every day five years ago, a 30 percent increase would now be 40 dishes per day. Depending on the restaurant's overall volume, an additional 10 seafood dishes might be meaningful.

Another statistic employed by the writer relates to the domestic habits of the two–income families that comprise the majority of Bay City's population. Nationwide studies show that families in this demographic eat significantly fewer home–cooked meals than they did a decade ago. Significant is a subjective term. What is significant for one family may be trifling for another. The reader would be wise to apply the logic from the previous paragraph to this fact. In addition, the fact that they eat fewer home–cooked meals does not lead inevitably to the conclusion that they are not eating at home. These families may very well be purchasing prepared or frozen meals at the local supermarket. Counting on their patronage to ensure the popularity and profitability of a new restaurant would be a mistake without further evidence about their dining habits. The same study cited in the previous paragraph reveals that two–income families express more concern about healthy eating. Expressing concern and taking some action are two widely different concepts. Many people are concerned about heart disease but continue to smoke. In the context of this passage, the writer would lead the reader to assume that seafood entrees are more healthful than other dishes. A fillet of haddock smothered in buttered bread crumbs or served with a cream sauce is no healthier for a diner than a lean piece of beef cooked on the grill. The writer should examine the menus at the restaurants to determine the ingredients and cooking methods used for the seafood dishes. If the entrees are baked, steamed, or poached and served with lemon and fresh vegetables, they could be considered more healthful than dishes that naturally have more animal fat and cholesterol.

Finally, the writer claims that the current lack of a restaurant specializing in seafood in Bay City is certain to insure the success of the new Captain Seafood restaurant. Was there a seafood restaurant in Bay City at one time? If so, why did it close? If a seafood restaurant closed in the city, which could account, at least in part, for the increase in seafood entrees' popularity in the other eateries. A closer examination of some of the facts and assumptions in the passage reveals that the popularity and profitability of Captain Seafood is not a foregone conclusion. It relies on evidence that easily could be obtained to support the writer's claim.

# Section 2 – Verbal Reasoning

1. **The correct answer is (C).**

The correct answer is C. The passage states that Roman Style did not change as the others did and had great influence. A is incorrect. The passage does state that the three styles competed for predominance, but also notes their transient nature compared to Roman forms. B is incorrect. The passage groups the two together chronologically, but also notes that the advent of Gothic stopped their development. D is incorrect. The passage does not discuss "The Revival" as an influence upon architecture, but rather as a marker of time. E is incorrect. The Renaissance is also discussed as a time period—one whose tastes were influenced by Roman forms.

2. **The correct answer is (D).**

Choice D is the correct answer. The passage specifically notes that Italian architecture should be understood in terms of simultaneous styles and local variation. Choice A is incorrect because the sentence states that chronological progression is not a useful way to understand Italian architecture. Choice B is incorrect because the passage notes the Roman form remained fixed throughout Italian history. Choice C is incorrect. The three styles are discussed as near contemporaneous styles, not as chronological periods. Choice E is incorrect. According to the passage, the Renaissance actually helped solidify the traditional Roman influence through scientific codification.

3. **abiding**

This sentence states that botanists made a choice in regards to their reputation as "eccentrics" and then went out and accomplished something "odd." If they acted in a way they are perceived to behave, then they must be accepting this perception. "Mystifying" means "confusing." If the botanists are living up to their eccentric status, then they are not "confusing" it. "Denigrating" means "belittling." If the botanists are living up to their eccentric status, then they are not belittling it. They are accepting it. "Reinventing" means "changing." Once again, the botanists are clearly accepting their status, not changing it. "Shirking" means "throwing off." Again, the botanists are not throwing off their status, they are accepting it. "Abiding" means "enduring." If the botanists are acting the way everybody thinks they act then they are enduring their stereotype.

4. **correspondent**

This sentence is setting up a simple comparison. Therefore, we want a word that facilitates the comparison of biological sciences to physical sciences. "Subservient" means "deferential to." The two sciences are described as being very important. There is no implication that biological sciences are "subservient" to physical sciences. "Sequestered" means "seized." This answer does not make sense in the context of the question. "Variable" means "flexible." If the sentence is implying a similar level of importance between the two sciences then a "variable" level of importance for the biological sciences does not make any sense. "Unconnected" means "distinct." This is the opposite of what we want. We want a word that shows the two as being similar, not "distinct." "Correspondent" means "similar." This completes the comparison that is being set up in the sentence.

5. **The correct answer is (A).**

a) This response describes influences external to the newspaper itself that have much bearing on the amount of interest a person has in reading an article. The writer is attributing the ability to influence strictly to the responsibility writer of the article, not on the side of the reader. Therefore a shift to the reader's responsibility will negate the writer's assumption.

Incorrect responses

b) Special techniques used in writing do influence interest. This question instructs one to find the negation of the assumption, therefore this response is incorrect. This response is in support of the assumption.

c) This comment is supportive of the assumption

rather than a negation of the assumption. The fact that Americans read the front page only goes along with the interest factor the writer was describing.

d) This tendency applies to many situations. However, it more closely relates to the assumption, the interest factor, than the negation of the assumption.

e) This comment may explain the reason why American's are in such a hurry when they read, thus limiting what they read. However, this does not illustrate the main point of the article or negate it either.

6. **The correct answer is (B).**

B is the correct answer. The passage states that the Lombard and Tuscan styles existed simultaneously and that their development was halted by the arrival of Gothic style. A is incorrect because the passage indicates that the arrival of Gothic caused the stagnation, not that they had already stagnated. C is incorrect. The passage does not indicate that Gothic was based on Roman forms. D is incorrect.

The passage does not suggest exactly why Gothic supplanted the other two. E is incorrect. The passage indicates that the Roman influence remained fixed through all the styles. This is also another reason why D is incorrect.

7. **The correct answers are (A) and (C).**

A and C are correct. The passage notes that steady chronological progression is not a key factor in the history of Italian architecture, but rather that the history may be understood in terms of separate styles existing at the same time and different localities preferring different styles.

8. **ramifications and consequences**

C and F. In the sentence, we are using quantum physics to discover something that means we are looking for a result. The only two words that are synonyms of the word result are ramifications and consequences. The word broadcast means to emit, strident means loud and transfusion which is the act of transfusing make no logical sense in the sentence and, to ratify something as in ratifications means to approve something formally.

9. **prognosticate and presage**

A and B. In this sentence, we cannot actually stave off or stop the impact of an earthquake; nor can we forewarn of the impact that a certain earthquake might have on a building, hence stave off and forewarn are not the correct choices. You would obviously not want to aggrandize or augment, which also means maximize, the impact of an earthquake. As a result, the only word options left available are prognosticate and presage which both mean to foresee or predict.

10. **indebted**

This sentence is explaining how an astronomical technique has been taken from bats – the use of radio waves to detect how far away an object is. Therefore, we want words that explain that this technique originally came from bats. "Superior" means better than. This doesn't make any sense because the idea is directly lifted from bats. It can't be better if it's the same thing. "Abhorrent" means "repulsive." There is no reason to believe that the procedure would be "repulsive" to a bat's sonar as the idea is directly lifted from bats. "Deleterious" means harmful.

Astronomers adopting a technique would not harm the technique. "Debased" means "cheapened." There's no information in the passage that implies the astronomer version of a radio wave is "cheapened" to a bat's version – a radio wave is a radio wave. The correct answer is "Indebted." The bat clearly came before the study of astronomy. So astronomy is "indebted" to the bat for introducing it to the concept of sonar.

11. **fundamental**

This passage says that there are lots of "complicated physical phenomena" in the universe, but they can be explained by only four forces. These forces must be the foundation on which everything else is built. "Superfluous" means unnecessary. Since these four forces are the building blocks of all physical phenomena, they can't be unnecessary. "Regressive" means relapsing, or backsliding. If these four forces work together to make all other physical phenomena, they clearly aren't "backsliding."

They're creating. "Excessive" means unnecessary

as well. Once again, these forces are the building blocks of the universe. They can't be unnecessary. "Intricate" means convoluted or elaborate. The physical phenomena that the four forces create are described as "complicated," and it's noted that this is "ironic." Therefore, the forces must be different from the phenomena. So they can't be "intricate" because that is too close to complicated. The answer is "Fundamental." This word means central. If these four forces are the building blocks of higher levels of interaction then they are certainly central.

12. **The correct answer is (D).**

"D" is the correct answer because it identifies the only quality that is not discussed in the passage as a possible side effect of being 'idle'.

"A" is referred to as "demoralization", "B" as "impatience", and "E" as "introspection".

"C" is also mentioned with the example of "the man who reads the newspaper and forgets what he has read" thus demonstrating that the type of idleness that dulls awareness can cause a person to become so distracted that he or she cannot retain information beyond the present moment.

13. **The correct answer is (A).**

"A" correctly identifies the function of the boldface sentence in the passage, stating that this sentence sums up many of the ideas that were presented in the passage thus far. By saying that more people should experience this type of peace of mind when control is relinquished, the author further suggests that in order to have better mind control, a person must first learn to accept all thoughts that enter the mind without 'guiding' them.

"B" is incorrect as this sentence presents an opinion, not a fact which could be considered evidence.

"C" incorrectly draws a connection between the idea of an unguided mind and Bennett's book, which discusses how to use time more efficiently, not methods for how to control thoughts more effectively.

"D" is incorrect in stating that this sentence brings together the main idea of the passage, which focuses more on the state of being idle, which is distinguished from the type of inactivity that comes from a relaxed mind.

"E" is almost correct; though this sentence discusses the topic of having a relaxed mind and states that it is beneficial, there is no listing of specific benefits that may occur.

14. ***"I am sure, however, that the best way to meet these demands for conscious control is to be careless of them, to be willing to experience these extravagances and inconsistencies without fear, in the belief that finally will come a quiet and peace which will be all that we can ask."***

This sentence presents a paradox by explaining that the best way to gain mental control is to let go of control; in other words, by letting go of the very thing that a person is trying to have more of, they will gain that control that they seek.

15. **The correct answer is (D).**

D is the correct answer. Besides lauding Donatello as "the brightest light," the passage specifically states that his style acted as a corrective to Ghiberti's influence and that Donatello's proclivity for natural realism and accurate detail helped steer sculptural trends away from more fanciful and less–tasteful styles. A is incorrect. The author clearly states that Donatello was the greatest of his time and admits that Ghiberti was a great artist of the world, but does not clearly place Ghiberti on the same level aesthetically, to the exclusion of other artists. B is incorrect. The passage describes Donatello's positive effect on Renaissance sculpture in general, not on Ghiberti. C is incorrect for much the same reason. The negative influence discussed applies to the art world in general, not Donatello. E is incorrect. The author admits that Ghiberti was a great artist and superior to Donatello in one specific aspect, but does not suggest that their styles complemented one another.

16. **The correct answer is (B).**

The correct answer is B. The author characterizes Ghiberti's work as exemplary of the overly florid style criticized in the passage. He does admit, however, that the artist was great and had an exquisite sense of beauty. A is incorrect because the "masculine" work referred to is Donatello's. C is incorrect because the author only states that Ghiberti "might" have been influential had Donatello not been there. D and E are incorrect because the author does not imply that the artist's work is either under or overrated. He both criticizes and compliments the artist, but does not suggest that popular opinion has placed Ghiberti higher or lower than where he ought to be.

17. **consolidates and precipitates**

C and F. In the sentence, two of the key words are attracting and removal. These words imply that the substance attracts the metals particles so that they can be easily removed from the water. We are looking for a word that means bring something together. The words consolidates and precipitates are the only two options that have this meaning. The words rainfall and precipitation are synonyms and would not complete the sentence properly. The word accelerates means to hurry and the word impels means to prompt or compel, both words do not complete the sentence in a logical manner.

18. **deadly and virulent**

B and F. In the sentence, we can see that the flu strain has caused people to die. Therefore, the missing word is probably something that means dangerous or lethal. The best word options from above are deadly and virulent. Innocuous and harmless both have the same meaning – something that causes no harm. Malevolent means evil and acrimonious means hateful, both of which would not complete the sentence logically.

19. **The correct answer is (A).**

Perception is specifically the ability to see, hear, or otherwise perceive a state. Acumen refers to one's ability to make judgments or decisions. Perspicacity is shrewdness in making a decision in a business situation. Awareness is knowledge of existence. Conception is the understanding of a situation or state. Since this sentence refers specifically to what humans are able to see, perception is the correct term.

20. **facilitated, shackled, and proliferation**

The passage states how radio allowed many developments to happen in the world of music. "Circumvented" means "avoided." The passage doesn't say that radio avoided changes, it says that radio helped them come about. "Barred" means "prevented." The passage argues that radio allowed changes to happen, not that it prevented them. "Facilitated" means "helped." If developments in music happened "because of the radio," then radio helped the process.

For the second blank, the passage states how radio helped music expand beyond its typical venues. "Defiant" means "disobedient." Music was confined to concert houses before radio, not "disobedient" to them. "Dastardly" means "reprehensible." This answer doesn't make any sense in the context of the question. "Shackled" means "bound." This makes sense. Before the advent of radio, music was bound to concert houses and clubs, and most citizens could not hear it on a regular basis.

For the last blank, the passage is talking about how there was a massive expansion of musical genres in the 20th century. "Expiry" means "end." Obviously, musical genres were not ending at this time. "Condescension" means "arrogance." The passage makes no reference to any arrogance of musical genres in the 20th century. We are left with "Proliferation." This word means "multiplication." This makes sense. The increased number of musical genres in the 20th century clearly means that musical genres were multiplying.

# Section 3 – Quantitative Reasoning

1. **The correct answers are (A), (B) and (E).**

(A) Probability of children 0 or 1 = 11% + 22% = 33% = 0.33 > 0.3

(B) Probability of children 2 = 40% = 0.4 > 0.3

(C) Probability of children 3 and above = 20% + 7% = 27% = 0.27 < 0.3

(D) Probability of children 1 or 4 = 22% + 7% = 29% = 0.29 < 0.3

(E) Probability of children 1 or 3 = 22% + 20% = 42% = 0.44 > 0.3

(F) Probability of children 3 = 20% = 0.2 < 0.3

(G) Probability of children 4 and above = 7% = 0.07 < .3

2. **The correct answer is (E).**

If *abc* is even, *abc* is also a multiple of 2

abc is multiple of 33 × 2 = 66

The only multiples of 66 that are made up of three digits and are less than 300 are:

66 × 2 = 132,

66 × 3 = 198,

66 × 4 = 264

132 + 1 = 133; the factors of 133 are 7 and 19

133 is not a prime number

198 + 1 = 199 which does not have any factors

199 is a prime number

264 + 1 = 265; the factors of 265 are 5 and 53

265 is not a prime number

198 is the number we are looking for

$a = 1, b = 9$ and $c = 8$

3. **The correct answer is 70°.**

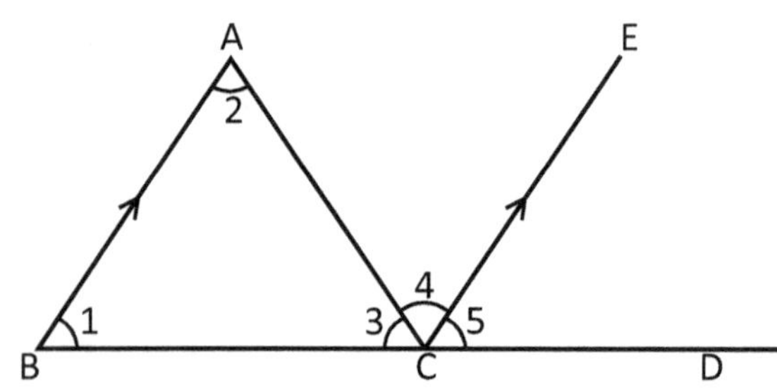


Name the angles, 1,2,3,4, and 5 as in the figure.

CE is the bisector

$\angle 4 = \angle 5 = 70^\circ$

AB||CE (Given)

BCD is a transversal

$\angle 1 = \angle 5$ (Corresponding angles)

AC is a transversal

$\angle 2 = \angle 4$ (Alternate interior angles)

$\therefore \angle 1 = \angle 2 = \angle 4 = \angle 5 = 70^\circ$

$\angle BAC = 70^\circ$

4. **The correct answer is (D).**

The volume of a cube is the edge cubed

Volume = $6^3$ = 216 *cubicinches*

The volume of a right cylinder is the area of the top (or bottom) multiplied with the height

Volume = 25 × 7 = 175 *cubicinches*

The volume of the rectangular prism is equal to *length* × *width* × *height* = 6 × 3 × 4 = 72 *cubic inches*

The volume of water in all three shapes = 216 + 175 + 72 = 463 *cubicinches*

There are 231 *cubicinches* in 1 *gallon*

463 *cubicinches* is roughly 2 *gallons*

Part of the canister that remains unfilled = 6 *gallons* – 2 *gallons* = 4 *gallons*

5. **The correct answer is (C).**

Usual Time =40 *minutes*

When his speed is 80% of his usual speed, new speed= .80% of Usula Speed = $\frac{4}{5}$ of Usual Speed

Since the distance is the same, new time = $\frac{5}{4}$ of Usual Time= $\frac{5}{4}$ of 40 minutes=50 minutes

Additional time=50-40= 10 minutes

6. **The correct answer is (B).**

Let d be the number of days and $m$ be the distance in *miles*

$\therefore\ d \times 60 + m \times 0.75 = 525$

*i.e.* $4 \times 60 + m \times 0.75 = 525$

i.e.$240 + 0.75m = 525$

*i.e.* $0.75m = 525 - 240$

*i.e* $0.75\ m = 285$

i.e $m = \dfrac{285}{0.75} = 380\ miles$

7. **The correct answer is (B).**

To find the slopes we need to use the formula

$m = \dfrac{x_1 - y_2}{x_1 - x_2}$ so we will need two points from each line.

We know two points on $f(x)$, as we were told the $y$ and $x$ intercepts – the points are (0, – 4) and (6,0)

The slope of $f$ is $\dfrac{-4-0}{0-6} = \dfrac{2}{3}$

For $h(x) = 4$ we can easily established that this is a horizontal line and all horizontal lines have a slope of 0. No need to calculate.

Pick two $x$'s and solve for each the corresponding y to find the slope of g(x).

If $x = 0$, $y = -2$ and if $x = 4$, $y = 1$

The slope of $g$ is $\dfrac{-2-1}{0-4} = \dfrac{3}{4}$

Similarly for $i(x)$, if $x = 0$, $y = -2$ and if $x = 2$, $y = 0$,

the slope of $i$ is $\dfrac{-2-0}{0-2} = 1$

$i(x)$ has the greatest slope out of $g(x)$, $h(x)$ and $i(x)$ (i.e.1) which is greater than the slope of $f(x)$ which is $\dfrac{2}{3}$

The right column is greater than the left column.

8. **The correct answer is (A).**

The equation of the first line can be rewritten as $y = -2x + 1$. Therefore, the first line's slope is –2. Use the rule that perpendicular lines have opposite reciprocal slopes and just flip –2 and change the sign to get $\dfrac{1}{2}$.

Use slope intercept form from here. Now we know the slope of the perpendicular line, which is $\dfrac{1}{2}$.

Because it passes through (0.3), we also know the $y$ intercept. Using $y = mx + b$ and plugging in $\dfrac{1}{2}$ for m and 3 for $b$, we obtain $y = \dfrac{1}{2}x + 3$.

9. **The correct answer is** $\dfrac{800}{9}$

The largest value of $\dfrac{A \times B}{A - B}$ occurs when the value of the denominator is minimum and value of the numerator is maximum.

Numerator is maximum when $A$ and $B$ are the two largest numbers.

Denominator can be positive only when $A$ is the larger of the two numbers.

$A$ and $B$ are, therefore, 10 and 9 respectively.

Hence largest value of $\dfrac{A \times B}{A - B} = \dfrac{10 \times 9}{10 - 9} = 90$

The smallest value of $\dfrac{A \times B}{A - B}$ occurs when the denominator is maximum.

Denominator is maximum only when A is 10 and B is 1.

Hence smallest value of $\dfrac{A \times B}{A - B} = \dfrac{10 + 1}{10 - 1} = \dfrac{10}{9}$

The difference between the largest and smallest values is $90 - \dfrac{10}{9} = \dfrac{810 - 10}{9} = \dfrac{800}{9}$

10. **The correct answer is (C).**

For an integer to be divisible by 5, the last digit of the number must be either 0 or 5. As we are told that 39ab is also divisible by 4 (i.e. even), $b = 0$

For an integer to be divisible by 4, the number formed by its last two digits must be divisible by 4.

We already established that $b = 0$. So, $ab$ must be 20, 40, 60 or 80

For an integer to be divisible by 9, the sum of all its digits must be divisible by 9.

The sum of $3 + 9 + a + b = 3 + 9 + a + 0 = 12 + a$. $a$ must be 6

*39ab* is *3960*

Prime factorization of 3960 = $2^3 \times 3^2 \times 5 \times 11$

Now that we know $a = 6$ and $b = 0$, we can write *abba* as 6006

Prime factorization of 6006 = $2 \times 3 \times 7 \times 11 \times 13$

The sum of the largest and the smallest prime factors of 3960 = 2 + 11 = 13

(don't forget that 1 is not a prime factor)

The largest prime factor of 6006 = 13

The right column is equal to the left column (both = 13).

11. **The correct answer is (D).**

$$x+5=\frac{-4x-17}{x+1}-\frac{-x-2}{x+1}$$

$$\therefore (x+5)(x+1)=\left[\frac{-4x-17}{x+1}-\frac{-x-2}{x+1}\right](x+1)$$

$\therefore$ $x^2 + 6x + 5 = (-4x - 17) - (-x - 2)$

$\therefore$ $x^2 + 6x + 5 = -3x - 15$

$\therefore$ $x^2 + 9x + 20 = 0$

$\therefore$ $x^2 + 5x + 4x + 20 = 0$

$\therefore$ $x(x + 5) + 4(x + 5) = 0$

$\therefore$ $(x + 4)(x + 5) = 0$

$\therefore$ $(x + 4) = 0$ or $(x + 5) = 0$

$\therefore$ $x = -4$ or $x = -5$

$\therefore$ Sum of the roots = –5 – 4 = –9

12. **The correct answer is (B).**

The sum of n numbers is their mean multiplied by *n*

The sum of the first 10 numbers = 10 × 83 = 830

The sum of the second group of 20 numbers = 20 × 65 = 1300

The mean of the 30 numbers is =

$$\frac{(830+1300)}{(10+20)}=\frac{2130}{30}=71$$

When *k* is added to the 10 numbers, the new mean is 82 and we have 11 numbers

The sum of the 10 numbers + *k* = 11 × 82 = 902

*k* = 902 – 830 = 72

72 is greater than 71. Hence the right column is greater than the left column.

13. **The correct answer is (B).**

In similar triangles, if the sides are in the ratio a:b then the areas will be in the ratio $a^2 : b^2$

Hence areas will be in the ratio $2^2:5^2=4:25$

Since the area of triangle ABC= 100 Cm2

If A is the area of triangle PQR then

A:100=4:25

$$A=100\times\frac{4}{25}=16\text{ cm}^2$$

14. **The correct answer is (C).**

If we take the original duration of Matthew's tour as *x* days, then he has $300 to spend in x days.

Matthew's expenditure per day during original tour = $\$\frac{300}{x}$

If Matthew extends his tour by 5 days, then the duration of the tour = $x + 5$ days.

Matthew's expenditure per day for the extended tour = $\$\frac{300}{x+5}$

If he extends the tour then the daily expenses are cut down by $5.

$$\$\frac{300}{x}-\$\frac{300}{x+5}=\$5$$

$$\frac{300}{x}-\frac{300}{x+5}=5$$

$$\frac{300(x+5)-300(x)}{x(x+5)}=5$$

$$\frac{300x+1500-300x}{x^2+5x}=5$$

Cross multiplying:

$1500 = 5x^2 + 25x$

$5x^2 + 25x - 1500 = 0$

$x^2 + 5x - 300 = 0$

Factoring the quadratic equation:

$x^2 + 20x - 15x - 300 = 0$

$x(x + 20) - 15(x + 20) = 0$

$(x + 20)(x - 15) = 0$

$(x + 20) = 0 \quad (x - 15) = 0$

$x = -20 = 15$

$x$ is the number of days of the original tour and the number of days cannot be negative.

So, the original duration of the tour = 15 days.

15. **The correct answers are (C), (D), (E) and (F).**

We know that the sum of n consecutive integers from 1 to $n$ is $\frac{n(n+1)}{2}$. And hence the sum of n consecutive integers from 2 to $n$ is $\frac{n(n+1)}{2}-1$

The sum lies between 120 and 200

$$120 \leq \frac{n(n+1)}{2} - 1 \leq 200$$

$$121 \leq \frac{n(n+1)}{2} \leq 201$$

$$242 \leq n(n+1) \leq 402$$

We will check the numbers one by one.

When $n$ = 14, $n(n + 1)$ = 210, Not satisfied

When $n$ = 15, $n$(n + 1) = 240, Not satisfied

When $n$ = 16, $n(n + 1)$ = 272, Satisfied

When $n$ = 17, $n(n + 1)$ = 306, Satisfied

When $n$ = 18, $n(n + 1)$ = 342 Satisfied

When $n$ = 19, $n(n + 1)$ = 380, Satisfied

When $n$ = 20, $n(n + 1)$ = 420, Not satisfied

16. **The correct answer is (B).**

$$f(x) = \pi x^2 + 5x,\ g(x) = 3x + 2\ and\ h(x) = x^3$$

$$h(-1) = (-1)^3 = -1$$

$$g\left(h(-1)\right) = g(-1) = 3(-1) + 2 = -3 + 2 = -1$$

$$f\left(g(h(-1))\right) = f(-1) = \pi(-1)^2 + 5(-1) = \pi - 5$$

17. **The correct answers are (A), (C) and (D).**

Choice A: If there are 70 or more radios and x represents the total number of radios, then 7(70) represents the cost of the first 70 radios. The additional radios are represented by $x$ – 70, and this value is multiplied by 5 to get the total cost of the additional radios. The sum of 7(70) + 5($x$ – 70) will give the total cost for the radios, $y$. Choice A is correct.

Choice B: If there are 70 or more radios, it costs \$5 for each additional radio, so we would need ($x$ –70) as in option A. Choice B is not correct.

Choice C: If there are 140 radios produced, the total cost will be 7 × 70 + 5 × 70, which is 490 + 350, which is \$840. Choice C is correct.

Choice D: If there are less than 70 radios produced, the \$5 per additional radio does not apply, so it will be \$7 per radio, $y = 7x$. Choice D is correct.

Choice E: If there are less than 70 radios, it will be \$7 per radio rather than \$5 per radio, so the equation will be $y = 7x$. Choice E is incorrect.

18. **The correct answer is (A).**

Remember that the mode is the number that appears the most often in a list. The number that appears most often (17 times) in the rainfall chart is 0.

19. **The correct answer is (D).**

If we add up the amount of rainfall accounted for in the chart, this makes:

5 days of 1 inch = 5 total inches of rain

3 days of 2 inches = 6 total inches of rain

3 days of 3 inches = 9 total inches of rain

3 days of 4 inches = 8 total inches of rain for a grand total of 28 inches.

If we expect 200 inches in a year, what percent of 200 is 28 inches?

Translate this into algebra as

$\frac{x}{100} \times 200 = 28$, and we get $x$=14 %

20. **The correct answer is (A).**

$2x^2 - (3 - k)x + 17(x - 2) - 20 = 0$ is a quadratic equation, and any quadratic equation can be written as:

$x^2 - Sx + P = 0$ where $S$ is the sum of the roots and $P$ is the product of the roots. We need to bring it to this form.

$2x^2 - (3 - k)x + 17(x - 2) - 20$

$= 2x^2 - 3x + kx + 17x - 34 - 20$

$= 2x^2 + (14 + k)x - 54 = 0$

If we divide by 2, $x^2 + \frac{(14+k)x}{2} - 27 = 0$

We know that one root of the equation is the other root squared, we can express the roots as y and $y^2$

The product of the roots is –27

$y \times y^2 = -27$

$y^3 = -27$

$y = -3$

The roots of the equation are –3 and 9. The smallest root is –3.

The sum of the roots is $\frac{(14+k)}{2}$

$\frac{(14+k)}{2} = -(-3+9) = -6$

$14 + k = -12$

$k = -26$

–3 is greater than –26, hence Quantity A is greater.

# Section 4 – Verbal Reasoning

1. **The correct answer is (B).**

B is the correct answer. The passage clearly states that Jefferson envisioned a prosperous nation and that he felt a wealthy nation would command respect. A is incorrect. Jefferson thought the country should remain agrarian and rural in contrast to England but he did not predict it would remain so. C is incorrect. The passage presents the theory of progression as a general principle and does not suggest that Jefferson thought the U.S. was an exception. D is incorrect. The passage suggests that good government is a desirable virtue, alongside growth and prosperity, but not that it follows or grows from them. E is incorrect. Jefferson believed that urbanization and industrialization would corrupt the government if they occurred but he did not predict that this process would definitely take place.

2. **The correct answer is (D).**

D is correct. The passage notes Jefferson's focus on territorial expansion. The passage also states that Jefferson wanted a more populous nation but disdained urban concentration. This, along with Jefferson's preference for an economy based on farming rather than industry, implies the eventual need for more land to accommodate a growing population of farmers. A is incorrect. The passage specifically notes Jefferson's disdain for urbanization and implies that the population growth he envisioned would be widely distributed. B is incorrect. The passage does not state or imply that Jefferson recommended emulating England in any way. C is incorrect. The passage does not state or imply the comparative value of the two goals. It does imply, to some extent, that the former would ultimately support the latter. E is incorrect. The passage states that Jefferson thought that the trends were "socially corrosive" and a threat to good government, but does not state or imply that they would diminish either prosperity or influence. It does imply that Jefferson saw them as forms of progress, albeit undesirable ones.

3. **The correct answer is (C).**

Choice C is correct. This sentence addresses both writing an article that is interesting, and the speed of doing so. In the passage the author indicates that one cannot write an interesting article quickly. Those articles require days and weeks of time. However, some people are able to write both interestingly and quickly.

Choice A is incorrect because it is an account of a large amount of time spent on a special article. This would not negate the author's claim.

Choice B is incorrect because it is in line with the author's belief that the news sketches lack life and color since they are hurried.

Choice D is incorrect. The author claims hurried writing lacks life and color, while human interest stories are usually fun to read. However, Bob writes slowly, consistent with the author's claim.

Choice E is unrelated to the article's argument about speed in writing, so can be eliminated.

4. **The correct answer is (B).**

The verb "wrestle" is the key clue to the correct word choice in this sentence. Something pliant, or flexible, would not need to be wrestled. If not for the verb, "perverse "might apply, as it refers to something out of the ordinary. Resolute means purposeful, and while it is close in meaning to intractable, it does not provide the precise definition of being hard to control or manage.

5. **The correct answer is (E).**

To oscillate is to move between two points as a pendulum would. The atom moves back and forth between states which is a repetitive motion, so the best answer is E. To fluctuate is to change the state or level from one to another. For example, when the temperature in a room rises or falls, it fluctuates, as the state of the air is changed. Fluctuate does not include the idea of repetitive motion present in oscillate, so it cannot be accurate. To persist is to remain constant. The sentence clearly suggests that the atom moves between two points, so option A is incorrect. To forge is to move forward on a defined course against resistance. Again, the atoms move back and forth between the two states, so B is incorrect. To feign is to pretend an action, that is to present the appearance of an action or state, but not actually perform the action or be in the state noted. The movement of the atom actually occurs, so C is not the correct answer.

6. **structure and morphology**

A and D. The main key word in this sentence is appeared. It means that the missing word describes what the cell looks like, as in its structure or morphology. Tabulation refers to the systematic recording or counting of something, edifice is another word for building, genus refers to a specific species or category and, the word department does not complete the sentence logically.

7. **quiescent and dormant**

B and E. Logically, at the end of summer, trees stop producing fruit and/or new leaves. The trees become dormant, inactive or quiescent until spring. Stagnant is incorrect because it refers to decay or motionlessness. Inertia is mainly used with movement or things in motion. Indolence means to be lazy or to procrastinate which doesn't make any logical sense and, the word sloth means laziness.

8. **malleable and ductile**

D and E. The correct answers are ductile and malleable because gold is a soft material and can be easily shaped. Unyielding and intractable are used to describe something that is difficult or hard to break. Salubrious refers to health, and while gold is valuable, it has nothing to do with the fact that it can be easily shaped or molded.

9. **precipices and escarpments**

Choices A and B. are the best answer. The sentence compares the dangerous valleys of Mt. Everest and something else. Since "precipices" and "escarpments" are steep slopes, they fit the context of rugged terrain. Choice C, "declivities," could fit the context because it refers to a downward slope, but there is no synonym among the answer choices. Choice D, "eradications," refers to completely eliminating something, so does not fit the context. Choice E, "rifts," is a steep gash or cut, but it acts as a synonym of "valleys" and is redundant in the sentence; there is also no matching answer choice. Choice F, "declensions," refers to moral degeneration rather than a physical location.

10. **brackish and saliferous**

Choices B and D are the correct answers. The missing word is an adjective that describes the type of water being distilled; the examples given are sources of salt water. "Pollution" refers to the thing which is causing the contamination rather than the liquid it is in, so does not fit the context. "Putrid" refers to something rotting or decaying; it can also mean "offensive." While this choice loosely fits the context, it does not have a synonym among the answer choices, and ocean water is not always repulsive. "Alkaline" refers to having a high pH, and "stationery" refers to items for writing letters, like pens and paper. The correct answers are "brackish" and "saliferous," which both accurately describe ocean and estuary water because they mean "salty."

11. **The correct answer is (D).**

D is correct. The passage does discuss law–enforcement and judicial process but does not discuss the creation or nature of laws against computer crime. A is incorrect. The passage notes equipment confiscations. B is incorrect. The passage describes public debate on the topic. C is incorrect. The passage mentions various levels of criminal prosecution. E is incorrect. The passage does state the group's goals.

12. **The correct answer is (C).**

C is correct. The author asserts that the crackdown has resulted in such debate. A is incorrect. The article mentions the involvement of the Secret Service, but only that it worked with other law enforcement agencies, not that it headed the efforts. B is incorrect. The passage notes that the crackdown had "mixed results" and does not mention the authorities' opinion of the results. D is incorrect. The passage notes that the Foundation's creation was "spurred" by the crackdown. Therefore, it originated after the crackdown occurred. E is incorrect. The passage does not mention any such calls or legislation.

13. **The correct answers are (A) and (B).**

A and B are correct. The passage specifically states that the crackdown resulted in the creation of the EFF. It also concludes that politics entered the computer world as a result of the crackdown. C is incorrect. The passage makes no statement about a decrease in crime.

14. **The correct answer is (C).**

This question asks the reader to use deductive reasoning to figure out what qualities would be associated with darkness based on what the passage says about 'light' as its opposite. The correct answer is "C" because ignorance is in contrast to 'wisdom', which the passage says equates to 'light' as demonstrated in the following sentence: "Life, Light, Love, life being the manifestation of the second two, love and wisdom." By replacing, in the second part of the sentence, "light" with "wisdom", the author draws a direct connection between the two. Thus, it is possible to conclude that if the opposite of 'lightness' is 'darkness', then the opposite of 'wisdom' could thus be equated with 'darkness' as well. "Ignorance" is one possible antonym for "wisdom" and is the only one of the options that can be considered so. All of the incorrect options are also too extreme or emotional to be supported by this scientific text.

15. **The correct answer is (D).**

"D" is the correct answer; this sentence restates the author's main point that astrology is a science worth studying in detail by providing a comparison to the study of language.

"A", "B", and "C" are all incorrect in suggesting that this sentence provides support for the author's main point; though it presents a different view of why astrology is important, it does not confirm the author's message with any extra facts or evidence.

"E" is incorrect because this sentence is not introducing a new opinion; rather, it is simply restating an opinion that has already been presented previously in the passage.

16. **The correct answer is (C).**

The author employs each of the literary devices listed in the correct answer choice, "C". An example of metaphoric use can be found in the passage where the author says that "suns and their systems of planets sound forth the deep bass tones and rich tenor, while angelic races take the silvery treble of the Divine melody." The author uses an analogy by directly stating that "Life, Light and Love, [are] analogous to the three primary colors in Nature". The use of simile is employed when the author draws a symbolic comparison between the solar system and the spiritual characteristics of the sun, saying that "The Sun, Moon and five planets[*] of our solar system are to us symbols of the reflected and refracted rays of the triune attributes of the great Central, Spiritual Sun".

All other options are incorrect because they each have one or more answers that are not found in the text. There is no metonymy, as all literal names are used for the objects and concepts that are discussed, and there is no mention of sounds being made that could possibly resemble the spelling of those sounds, thus choice "A" is incorrect.

"B" is incorrect because there are no stories in the text that would resemble a use of allegory, and there is also no instance of extreme exaggeration, which the term "hyperbole" suggests. Though this answer correctly identifies "analogy" as seen in the text, it is only partially correct and thus the answer is incorrect in its entirety.

"D" is incorrect in identifying "personification" as one of the literary devices used. Though the metaphor of the solar system as a musical symphony seems to come close to personification, it does not in fact personify the planets; rather than displaying human-like qualities by playing musical instruments, the planets are in fact the instruments themselves and thus represent inanimate objects rather than people.

"E" also incorrectly mentions allegory, and there is no example of synecdoche (exemplified by something representing a part of a larger whole) in this text either.

17. **The correct answers are (A) and (C).**

It is possible that the author of this passage would take an interest in the subjects mentioned in both choices "A" and "C". The text mentions a Deity several times, suggesting the author's belief in God, which implies a connection to religious and theological studies. The author may also enjoy performance arts, which is suggested by his mention of music as a metaphor for astrology. However, the passage does not refer to other sciences aside from astrology and thus fails to imply the author's connection to any other sciences such as quantum physics, as choice "B" suggests. Thus, choice "B" is incorrect.

18. **The correct answer is (C).**

To impart is to bestow or give a gift, talent, or skill. This sentence describes something that is put into the violins, which is similar to giving. The best answer, then, is C. The verb to yield means to produce or put out. To disclose is to make known or reveal. Since not all violins have the inherent quality of producing the sounds of speech, this is not a situation where the maker has exposed an existing characteristic. Output is similar to yield. Again, the violin makers added something to the construction of the violin to make it capable of outputting speech–like sounds. To relinquish is to surrender or give up with resistance. Since the sentence clearly states that the violin makers added the capacity for speech sounds into their instruments, any words referring to output are inaccurate.

19. **presuppositions, fundamental, and antecedents**

The first blank can be better understood by reading subsequent sentences. The first sentence talks of a key "something" that is made by linguists. The rest of the passage talks about a "postulation" that is made. We can infer that this is the general idea being alluded towards in the first sentence. "Gaffes" means "mistakes." The rest of the passage does not talk about mistakes; it talks about suppositions, so this is wrong. "Concessions" means admitting defeat on a particular point. The rest of the passage does not talk about linguists "conceding" anything, so this answer is wrong. We are left with "Presuppositions." This word means "conjectures." This makes sense. The list of evidences provided at the end of the passage make good justifications for making a "presupposition."

The second blank deals with the relationship between spoken and written language. The subsequent sentence lists all of the ways in which spoken language appears more readily than written language.

Therefore, we can infer that this relationship is that spoken language is more central to the human psyche than written language. "Superfluous" means "unnecessary." This is wrong; the passage clearly states how spoken language appears more often than written, so it cannot be "unnecessary." "Distressing" means "worrisome." There is no evidence provided in the passage to assert that the prevalence of spoken language makes it "worrisome." "Fundamental" means "important," or "central." This makes sense. If spoken language is more prevalent than written language then it must be more "fundamental."

The last blank comes in the middle of a list that shows the various ways in which spoken language predates written language. "Succeeds" means "comes after." This is the opposite of what we want. The passage clearly indicates that spoken language comes before written. "Ignores" means "disregards." There is no mention of the relationship between spoken and written language besides how often they appear relative to one another. Therefore, this answer is wrong. "Antecedents" means "comes before." This completes the sentiment of the list and is the correct answer.

20. **synthesized and focus**

To synthesize is to combine diverse elements to create a whole, using deductive reasoning. Kepler combined information from hundreds of hours of observations to develop his three laws. Synthesized is the best choice. To unify is to make several elements into a single whole. Unify does not include the idea of diversity, or the necessity of reasoning to develop the whole. Amalgamate is similar to unify as it refers to combining many elements into a whole. Again, there is no indication of reasoning. Hence, unified and amalgamated are incorrect.

The focus is the central point, around which other entities revolve. Center is not accurate because the focus of an orbit may not be the exact center of that orbit. The cynosure is the most important part, but does not communicate the notion of a hub.

# Section 5 – Quantitative Reasoning

1. **The correct answer is (B).**

Area of a trapezium is calculated using the formula $\frac{1}{2}\times h\times(a+b)$, where $h$ is the height and $a$ and $b$ are the dimensions of the sides.

Area of the original trapezium

$=\frac{1}{2}\times 8\times(10+14)=96$ *square units.*

Area of the remodeled toddler section = 96 + 96 = 192 *square units*

The change represents a scaling by a factor of 2. Therefore, we want to look for an answer choice that doubles just one dimension.

Option B: The height was doubled.

Height after remodeling = 2 × 8 = 16 *units*

Area after remodeling

$\frac{1}{2}\times 16\times(10+14)=192$ *square units*

2. **The correct answers are (D) and (F).**

Simplify each expression using the following properties:

- Multiplying/Dividing, (+)(+) = (+), (−)(−) = (+), (+)(−) = (−)
- Double negatives turn into a positive.
- Adding/Subtracting Integers
- If two numbers have the same sign, add the numbers and keep the sign.
- If two numbers have different signs, subtract the numbers and keep the sign of the bigger number.

Now simplify each expression to see if the resulting value is less than or equal to −8.

**A.** (−4)(−2) − (3) = 8 − 3 = 5

**B.** (4)(−2) − (−3)= −8 + 3 = −5

**C.** (−6)(2) − (10)(−2) = −12 + 20 + 8

**D.** $\frac{(-8)}{(2)}$ + (−1)(4) = −4 − 4 = −8

**E.** (−5 + 3)(−2 + 7) − (−4) = (−2)(5) + 4= −10 + 4 = −6

**F.** (2)[(4)(−5)−4) − (7)(2) = −2[−20 + 4] + 14 = −2[−16] + 14 = −32 + 14 = −18.

The only answers that are less than or equal to −8 are D and F.

3. **The correct answer is (A).**

Because we have right triangles, we are able to use the Pythagorean Theorem, where $a^2+b^2=c^2$. We are able to plug in the legs of the triangle for a and b, and find the hypotenuse by solving for c

Answer: $b^2= 4^2 + 3^2 = 25$ so $b = 5$.

$a^2= 3^2 + 7^2 = \sqrt{58}$ .

The answer is $5 + \sqrt{58}$

4. **The correct answer is** $\frac{12BE}{C}$

We first calculate the cost of each orange. If $B$ dozen oranges costs $C$ cents, then each orange would cost $\frac{C}{12B}$ cents.(Remember, you must multiply $B$ by 12 to get the total number of oranges). Next, divide $E$ cents by $\frac{C}{12B}$ to bet the number of oranges you could buy with $E$ cents if each orange costs $\frac{C}{12B}$ cents.

$$\frac{E}{\frac{C}{12B}}=E\frac{12B}{C}$$

$$=\frac{12BE}{C}$$

5. **The correct answer is (C).**

Let the initial value be $x$;

There was a 50% depreciation in the first year.

$\therefore$ Value after one year=50% of $x=\frac{50}{100}x=\frac{1}{2}x$

There was a 40% depreciation in the second year.

The value will be 60% of the first year.

$\therefore$ Value after two years $=\frac{60}{100}\times\frac{1}{2}x=\frac{60}{200}x=\frac{3}{10}x$

There was a 25% depreciation in the third year.

The value will be 75% of the second year

$\therefore$ Value after two years $=\frac{75}{100}\times\frac{3}{10}x=\frac{9}{40}x$

There was a 20% depreciation in the fourth year.

The value will be 80% of the third year.

$\therefore$ Value after four years $=\frac{80}{100}\times\frac{9}{40}x=\frac{9}{50}x$

$\therefore\frac{9}{50}x=18$

$x$ = $100 million

6. **The correct answer is 50 days**

Initially let there be $x$ army men having food for $y$ days.

After 10 days, $x$ army men had food for $(y-10)$ days.

Now only 80% of the soldiers remain with food provision equal to that before the war,

Therefore, $\frac{4x}{5}$ men have food for $y$ days

Equating both conditions gives,

$x(y-10)=\left(\frac{4x}{5}\right)y$

$xy-50x=0$

Or $x(y-50)=0$. So, $y=50$ (since $x\neq0$)

7. **The correct answer is (C).**

The formula for the area of a parallelogram is:

$A = base \times height$

$A=15\times\frac{3}{5}(15)=15\times9=135$

8. **The correct answer is (B).**

$2187^{x}=9$

Note that 9 raised any whole number will not result in 2187

So write 2187 as a power of 3.

$\therefore\left(3^{7}\right)^{x}=9=3^{2}$

When bases are the same powers will be the same

$\therefore7x=2$

$\therefore x=\frac{2}{7}$

Now $\frac{2}{7}<\frac{3}{7}$

9. **The correct answer is (A).**

The sum of the interior angles of a heptagon is always 900°

This is equivalent to the sum of ten right angles (If you do not remember this, an easy way to arrive at the sum is starting with the smallest polygon – the triangle – for which the sum of the interior angles is 180° and remember that for each additional number of sides in a polygon the sum of the interior angles increases by 180° i.e.the sum of the interior angles of the quadrilateral is 360°, for the pentagon it is 540° and so on) The greatest number of inner right angles that a hexagon (convex or concave) can have is five. Six right angles are not possible because 6 x 90° = 540° which is less than the sum of the interior angles of a hexagon (i.e. 720°)

Ten is greater than five, hence the correct answer is A)

10. **The correct answer is 49.6%**

Let the price before the discount be \$100. A discount of 30% implies new price of $(1-0.3)\times\$100=\$70$.A further discount of 20% implies a newer price of $(1-0.2)\times\$70=\$56$. Yet another discount of 10% implies final price equal to $(1-0.1)\times\$56=\$50.40$. This final price is equivalent to a single discount of $(100-50.4)=49.6\%$

11. **The correct answer is (D).**

Denote the modes for freshman up to senior years by $a$, $b$, $c$, and $d$, respectively. Then

$\frac{b-a}{a}=0.06$, $b=1.06a$

$\frac{c-b}{b}=0.05$, $c=1.05b$

$\frac{d-c}{c}=-0.06$, $d=0.94c$

Comparing the values above indicates that $c$ has the greatest value; that is, the mode was highest during junior year.

This is because, $c$=1.05$b$, which is larger than $a$. And 0.94$c$=$d$. Therefore, a,b,and d are all smaller than $c$. C represents junior year, so our solution is therefore junior year!

12. **The correct answer is (E).**

The percentage changes of median for all years are positive. So, the median was constantly increasing.

13. **The correct answer is 0.79%.**

Denote the mean scores from freshman to senior year by $u$, $v$, $x$, and $y$, respectively. Then,

$\frac{v-u}{u}=0.03, \quad v = 1.03u$

$\frac{x-v}{v}=-0.05, \quad x = 0.95v$

$\frac{y-x}{x}=0.03, \quad y = 1.03x$

$y = 1.03x = (1.03)(0.95v) = (1.03)(0.95)(1.03u) = 1.0079u$

$y = 1.0079u$

$y - u = 0.0079u$

$\frac{y-u}{u}=0.0079$

$= 0.79\%$

14. **The correct answer is (E).**

Denote the medians from freshman year to the senior year by m, n, p, and q, respectively. Then,

$\frac{n-m}{m}=0.05 \ldots n = 1.05m$

$\frac{p-n}{n}=0.04 \; p = 1.04n$

$\frac{q-p}{p}=0.006; \; q = 1.06p$

Comparing the values above verifies that in senior year the median was highest.

15. **The correct answer is (C).**

First you need to calculate how many students are in Happy Town's school. If 84 students represent 48% of the total

Total number of students $=\frac{84}{48\%}=175$

Boys in Happy Town's school = 175 – 84 = 91

The number of girl students that need to stop going to Happy Town's school, in order for the ratio boys to girls in Happy Town's school to become 13:11 = 84 – 11 × 91/13 = 7

The total number of students in Sunny City's school = (100% – 8%) × 175 = 161

The girls in Happy Town to girls in Sunny City ratio is 12:9

Girls in Sunny City = 9 × 84/12 = 63

Boys in Sunny City's school = 161 – 63 = 98

The number of boy students that need to stop going to Sunny City's school, in order for the ratio boys to girls in Sunny City's school to become 13:9 = 98 – 13 × 63/9 = 98 – 91 = 7

The right column is equal to the left column (= 7).

16. **The correct answer is (C).**

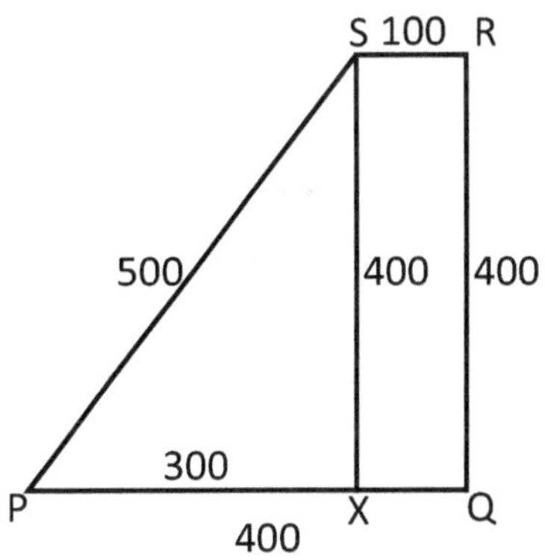


Let s be the speed from point P to point R. The distance is 800 km.

$\therefore$ Time taken from P to R $=\frac{800}{s}$

Draw SX ||RQ.

By Pythagorean triplets, SP =500km.

$\therefore$ The distance from R to P is 600 km.

The speed is 1.5s

Time taken from R to P $=\frac{600}{1.5s}$

$\therefore$ The required ratio $=\frac{800}{s}:\frac{600}{1.5s}=800:\frac{600}{1.5}=$

$800:400=2:1$

17. **The correct answer is (C).**

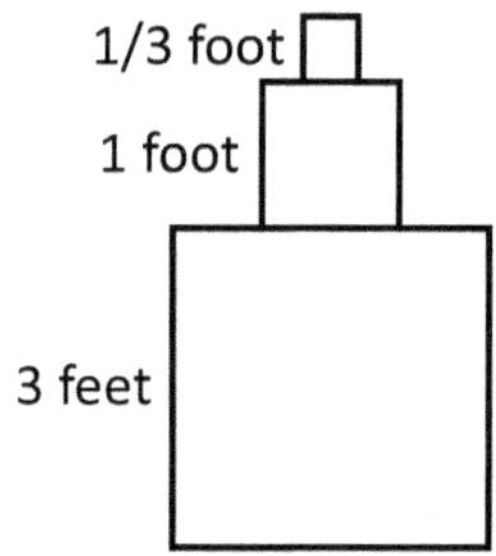


The volume of the first cube = 27 cubic feet

∴ Height of the first cube = 3 feet

The volume of the second cube = 1 cubic foot

∴ Height of the second cube = 1 feet

The volume of the third cube $\frac{1}{27}$ cubic foot

∴ Height of the third cube = $\frac{1}{3}$ feet

∴ Total height of the stack = 3 + 1 + $\frac{1}{3}$ feet = $4\frac{1}{3}$ feet = 52 inches

18. **The correct answer is (E).**

The circumference of the wheel is C = π ft. In 60 minutes, the wheel rotates 60 × 20 = 1,200 times. Therefore, the wheel and the car move 1,200πft in linear distance.

19. **The correct answer is (C).**

By using the diameter as the hypotenuse of the square, you can apply the Pythagorean Theorem. The Pythagorean Theorem will have the two sides as the legs and the diameter as the hypotenuse. This is plugged in as follows; $s^2 + s^2 = D^2$. Combine the $s^2$ terms to get $2s^2 = D^2$.

Call the diameter of the circle D. $D^2 = 2s^2$ by the Pythagorean theorem, and so $r = \left(\frac{s}{2}\right)\sqrt{2}$ . The area of the circle is $\pi r^2 = \left(\frac{\pi}{2}\right)s^2$ . The area of the unshaded square is $s^2$, and so the area of the shaded portion is $\left(\frac{\pi}{2}\right)s^2 - s^2$.

20. **The correct answer is (C).**

In 6 days, the planet travels $\frac{6}{30} = \frac{1}{5}$ of the total distance. The radius of the circle is $r = 4\times10^7$ miles, so its circumference is $2\pi r = 8\pi\times10^7$ . And the 6–day arc is $\left(\frac{8}{5}\right)\pi\times10^7$.

www.ingramcontent.com/pod-product-compliance
Lightning Source LLC
LaVergne TN
LVHW081250100826
845148LV00009B/1180
*9781636510903*